Deciding
to
Leave

SUNY series in American Constitutionalism

Robert J. Spitzer, editor

Deciding
to
Leave

The Politics of Retirement
from the
United States Supreme Court

Artemus Ward

State University of New York Press

Cover Photo: The Justices' Conference Room (1993).
Franz Jantzen, Collection of the Supreme Court of the United States.

Published by
State University of New York Press, Albany

© 2003 State University of New York

All rights reserved

Printed in the United States of America

For information, address State University of New York Press,
90 State Street, Suite 700, Albany, NY 12207

Production by Michael Haggett
Marketing by Jennifer Giovani

Library of Congress Cataloging-in-Publication Data

Ward, Artemus, 1971–
    Deciding to leave : the politics of retirement from the United States Supreme Court /
Artemus Ward.
        p. cm. — (SUNY series in American constitutionalism)
    Includes bibliographical references and index.
    ISBN 0-7914-5651-X (hbk. : alk. paper) — ISBN 0-7914-5652-8 (pbk. : alk. paper)
    1. United States. Supreme Court—Officials and employees—Retirement. 2.
Judges—Retirement—United States. I. Title. II. Series.

KF8742 .W368 2003
347.73'2634—dc21
                                                                        2002030977

10 9 8 7 6 5 4 3 2 1

Contents

List of Illustrations and Tables

FIGURES

TABLES

Preface:

Resisting the Irresistible

_____

It is not surprising that justices are reluctant to discuss the topic of retirement with anyone other than close friends and family. I found this out at the inception of this project when I wrote the current and former members of the Court. After explaining the project and why I thought it was important, I asked each justice if they would grant me a brief interview. While every justice declined, their responses varied considerably. The letters were generally of three types. I thought it was interesting how different the responses were and decided to include examples to give the reader a sense of how the current members of the Court respond not only to interview requests, but also to inquiries about their retirement decisions.

The first group were written by a secretary or administrative assistant and demonstrate the gatekeeping function provided by a justice's staff. For example, this letter from the chambers of Justice Ruth Bader Ginsburg is typical:

> Justice Ginsburg is sorry she cannot say yes to your proposal, but she has been overwhelmed with interview requests. To avoid commitments that might intrude on time needed for the Court's heavy work, she must follow the wise counsel of Justice Brandeis and resist even the irresistible.
>
> Sincerely,
> Cathy J. Vaughn
> Secretary to Justice Ginsburg

The second group of letters appear to be written by the justices themselves, passing through the crucial outer barrier of the staff. For example:

> My summer break has kept me from replying sooner to your letter . . .
> I'm sorry that I will not be able to be of help to you. I have a general

rule against judicial interviews, and in any case, would not wish to give any opinion on the subject.

Yours sincerely,
David Souter

Though the final group of justices have declined the interview like the all the rest, they wrote more personally and provided encouragement for the project. For example:

You have selected an interesting and important topic. I hope that it is published in time to provide me with some guidance in making the retirement decision. In the meantime, I shall welcome any advice that you offer me, but prefer to keep my thoughts about that subject to myself.

Sincerely,
John Paul Stevens

The fact that every justice declined is significant. Members of the Court have previously spoken to authors about other judicial decisions such as granting or denying certiorari. The very personal decision of stepping down from a lifetime post is undoubtedly a sensitive matter. Since the justices would not submit to interviews, I necessarily had to rely on their private papers, contemporary published sources, and secondary accounts to try to piece together departure decisions. While the justices would not speak to me about their departure decisions, many justices throughout the Court's history have spoken to family, friends, colleagues, and even reporters about their thinking. As a result, in the following chapters you will often hear from the justices themselves as they struggled, and sometimes schemed, over their decisions to leave the bench.

Some of the data and arguments presented in this book were previously presented at the annual meetings of the Midwest Political Science Association, Western Political Science Association, and New York State Political Science Association. I am grateful to the discussants, fellow panelists, and audieance members who offered suggestions for improvement. The section of the book on the retirement of William O. Douglas was awarded the 1999 *Hughes-Gossett Prize* by the Supreme Court Historical Society and appeared in the *Journal of Supreme Court History*. Also, the section on Lyndon Johnson and the fall of the Warren Court appeared in *White House Studies*.

What follows, of course, is solely my responsibility. Still, a project of this sort does not get off the ground without the support and encouragement of friends and colleagues. I would like to thank my adviser, Marie Provine, for her comments, criticisms, and helpfulness from this project's inception. You certainly cannot ask for a better adviser than one who tries to help you gather data: "I went to a reception tonight . . . and had a nice chat with Justice Ginsburg," Marie wrote, "Tell Art that she looks awfully skinny . . . but I don't think she's likely to retire any time soon." I would also like to thank Steve Macedo for his friendship and encouragement. I always value Steve's counsel. He once wrote me, "Always follow my advice to the letter and you will do well!" I am also grateful to Steve Wasby who spent countless hours reading and rereading drafts and continually pushing me to challenge some of my earliest assumptions about this project. Rogan Kersh also deserves much thanks for his support and very helpful comments on earlier drafts of this manuscript. Henry J. Abraham, David Atkinson, Sue Behuniak, Daan Braveman, Cornell Clayton, Norman Dorsen, Lee Epstein, David Garrow, Howard Gillman, H. W. Perry, Robert Stanley, and William Wiecek were also helpful for their comments and suggestions at various stages of this project. I would also like to thank Alyssa Del Rubio and Sue Cardinal at the H. Barclay Law Library of Syracuse Univeristy who put up with me year in and year out while I practically moved in doing research for this book. Many thanks to the Roscoe Martin grant committee at the Maxwell School of Citizenship for funding my travel to the Library of Congress to do research for this book. Last, I would like to thank my family and friends who helped make it all possible.

1

The Politics of Departure
in the U.S. Supreme Court

This is terrible.
> —Justice Sandra Day O'Connor after learning
> on election night 2000 that Democrat
> Al Gore had won the key state of Florida

Don't try to apply the rules of the political world to this institution; they do not apply.
> —Justice Clarence Thomas the day after
> the Court's decision in *Bush v. Gore*

On election night, November 7, 2000, just before 8 P.M. EST, CBS anchor Dan Rather announced that Democrat Al Gore had won the important battleground state of Florida and its twenty-five electoral votes. Surrounded by friends and acquaintances at an election night party, Justice Sandra Day O'Connor was visibly upset and remarked, "This is terrible," when Rather made the announcement. She explained to a partygoer that essentially the election was "over" as Gore had already won the two other key swing states of Michigan and Illinois. Her husband John went on to say that they were planning on retiring to Arizona but that a Gore presidency meant they would have to wait another four years since she did not want a Democrat to name her successor.[1]

Later that night, Rather and his colleagues at the other networks were forced to recant and an extraordinary set of events unfolded ultimately leading to O'Connor casting a crucial deciding vote in the unprecedented Supreme Court case of *Bush v. Gore*.[2] The decision effectively ended Al Gore's chance at the presidency and he quickly conceded. The day following the Court's judgment, Justice Clarence Thomas was asked by a group of high school students how political party affiliation affected the Court's decision making. "Zero," he answered. "I've been here nine years. I haven't seen it. I plead with you that, whatever you do, don't try to apply the rules of the political world to this institution; they do not apply. The last political act we engage in is confirmation." When Chief Justice Rehnquist was asked by reporters later that day whether he agreed with Thomas's statement in light of *Bush v. Gore*, the Chief responded, "Absolutely . . . absolutely."[3]

Still, some commentators suggested that O'Connor and Rehnquist wanted to retire and sided with Bush, at least in part, to ensure that a Republican president could name their successors. With George W. Bush now in office, are O'Connor and Rehnquist, the Court's two most senior conservatives, more inclined to step down? Are John Paul Stevens and Ruth Bader Ginsburg, two of the Court's more liberal justices, more inclined to stay?

In the following chapters, I set about trying to answer the question of what influences the departure decisions of the justices and whether the justices ought to have the power to make those decisions. My analysis carefully examines the retirements, resignations, and deaths of each justice who has been a member of and ultimately left the Supreme Court (see Table 1.1). Over the more than 200-year-history of the process, dramatic transformations have occurred changing the way justices have thought about leaving. Currently, the process is pervaded with partisanship as justices enjoy generous retirement benefits and have lengthy windows with which to time their departures and influence the choice of their successors.[4] Also, justices are staying on the bench longer than ever before and incidences of mental decrepitude have increased.

On announcing his retirement, Justice Sherman Minton remarked, "There will be more interest in who will succeed me than in my passing. I'm an echo."[5] Why is the process of departure from the Supreme Court given so little attention in comparison to appointments?[6] After all, there cannot be an appointment before there is a vacancy. And although vacancies can be created by adding seats to the Court, nearly every appointment in the Court's history has been preceded by the retirement, resignation, or death of a sitting justice with the remainder either the original appointees or those appointed to an expansion position on the Court. Of the 108 justices who have served on the Supreme Court, all but twelve (89%) were appointed following the resignation, retirement, or death of a sitting justice. Six justices were originally appointed in 1789—John Jay, John Rutledge, James Wilson, John Blair, William Cushing, and Robert Harrison, who declined and was succeeded by James Iredell. Congress added a seventh seat in 1807 and Thomas Todd was appointed. In 1837 Congress added two more seats and John Catron and John McKinley joined the Court. A tenth seat was added in 1863 and Stephen J. Field was appointed.

TABLE 1.1
Departures from the U.S. Supreme Court: 1789–Present

Departing Justice	Departure Date	Departing President	Age	Departure Mode
Justices Departing between 1789 and 1800				
Robert Harrison	Jan. 21, 1790	Washington	45	Resignation
John Rutledge	Mar. 5, 1791	Washington	51	Resignation
Thomas Johnson	Jan. 16, 1793	Washington	60	Resignation
John Jay	June 29, 1795	Washington	49	Resignation
John Rutledge	Dec. 15, 1795	Washington	56	Rejection
John Blair	Oct. 25, 1795	Washington	64	Resignation
James Wilson	Aug. 21, 1798	Adams	55	Death
James Iredell	Oct. 20, 1799	Adams	48	Death
Oliver Ellsworth	Dec. 15, 1800	Adams	55	Resignation
Justices Departing between 1801 and 1868				
Alfred Moore	Jan. 26, 1804	Jefferson	48	Resignation
William Patterson	Sept. 9, 1806	Jefferson	60	Death
William Cushing	Sept. 13, 1810	Madison	78	Death
Samuel Chase	June 19, 1811	Madison	70	Death
Brockholst Livingston	Mar. 18, 1823	Monroe	65	Death
Thomas Todd	Feb. 7, 1826	J. Q. Adams	61	Death
Robert Trimble	Aug. 25, 1828	Jackson	51	Death
Bushrod Washington	Nov. 26, 1829	Jackson	67	Death
William Johnson	Aug. 4, 1834	Jackson	62	Death
Gabriel Duvall	Jan. 14, 1835	Jackson	82	Resignation
John Marshall	July 6, 1835	Jackson	79	Death
Philip Barbour	Feb. 25, 1841	Van Buren	57	Death
Smith Thompson	Dec. 18, 1843	Tyler	75	Death
Henry Baldwin	Apr. 21, 1844	Tyler[a]	64	Death
Joseph Story	Sept. 10, 1845	Polk	65	Death
Levi Woodbury	Sept. 4, 1851	Fillmore	61	Death
John McKinley	July 19, 1852	Fillmore[b]	72	Death
Benjamin R. Curtis	Sept. 30, 1857	Buchanan	47	Resignation
Peter V. Daniel	May 31, 1860	Buchanan[c]	76	Death

a. Whig President Andrew Tyler was in office at the time of the vacancy, and tried to make an appointment, but Democrat James K. Polk ended up filling the seat.
b. President Millard Fillmore was in office at the time of the vacancy but President Franklin Pierce actually filled the seat.
c. President James Buchanan was in office at the time of the vacancy but President Abraham Lincoln actually filled the seat.

(continued on next page)

TABLE 1.1 *(continued)*

Departing Justice	Departure Date	Departing President	Age	Departure Mode
Justices Departing between 1801 and 1868 (cont'd.)				
John McLean	Apr. 4, 1861	Lincoln	76	Death
John A. Campbell	Apr. 30, 1861	Lincoln	49	Resignation
Roger B. Taney	Oct. 12, 1864	Lincoln	87	Death
John Catron[d]	May 30, 1865	Johnson	79	Death
James M. Wayne[e]	July 5, 1867	Johnson	77	Death
Justices Departing between 1869 and 1936				
Robert C. Grier	Jan. 31, 1870	Grant	75	Retirement
Samuel Nelson	Nov. 28, 1872	Grant	80	Retirement
Salmon P. Chase	May 7, 1873	Grant	65	Death
David Davis	Mar. 4, 1877	Grant[f]	61	Resignation
William Strong	Dec. 14, 1880	Hayes	72	Retirement
Noah H. Swayne	Jan. 24, 1881	Hayes[g]	76	Retirement
Nathan Clifford	July 25, 1881	Garfield[h]	77	Death
Ward Hunt	Jan. 27, 1882	Arthur	71	Retirement
William B. Woods	May 14, 1887	Cleveland	62	Death
Morrison R. Waite	Mar. 23, 1888	Cleveland	71	Death
Stanley Matthews	Mar. 22, 1889	Harrison	64	Death
Samuel F. Miller	Oct. 13, 1890	Harrison	74	Death
Joseph P. Bradley	Jan. 22, 1892	Harrison	78	Death
Lucius Q. C. Lamar	Jan. 23, 1893	Harrison	67	Death
Samuel Blatchford	July 7, 1893	Cleveland	73	Death
Howell E. Jackson	Aug. 8, 1895	Cleveland	63	Death
Stephen J. Field	Dec. 1, 1897	McKinley	81	Retirement
Horace Gray	Sept. 15, 1902	Roosevelt	74	Death
George Shiras, Jr.	Feb. 23, 1903	Roosevelt	71	Retirement
Henry B. Brown	May 28, 1906	Roosevelt	70	Retirement

d. Catron's seat was abolished by an act of Congress, July 23, 1866.

e. Wayne's seat was abolished by an act of Congress, July 23, 1866.

f. President Ulysses Grant had only days left in office when this vacancy occurred. President Rutherford B. Hayes filled the seat.

g. Hayes was in office at the time of this resignation, but President James Garfield filled the seat.

h. Though Garfield was in office at the time of this vacancy, he was fighting for his life after being shot. His successor President Chester A. Arthur filled the seat.

(continued on next page)

TABLE 1.1 *(continued)*

Departing Justice	Departure Date	Departing President	Age	Departure Mode
Justices Departing between 1869 and 1936 (cont'd.)				
Rufus W. Peckham	Oct. 24, 1909	Taft	70	Death
David J. Brewer	Mar. 28, 1910	Taft	72	Death
Melville W. Fuller	July 4, 1910	Taft	77	Death
William H. Moody	Nov. 20, 1910	Taft	56	Retirement
John Marshall Harlan	Oct. 14, 1911	Taft	78	Death
Horace H. Lurton	July 12, 1914	Wilson	70	Death
Joseph R. Lamar	Jan. 2, 1916	Wilson	58	Death
Charles Evans Hughes	June 10, 1916	Wilson	54	Resignation
Edward D. White	May 19, 1921	Harding	75	Death
John H. Clarke	Sept. 18, 1922	Harding	65	Resignation
William R. Day	Nov. 13, 1922	Harding	73	Retirement
Mahlon Pitney	Dec. 31, 1922	Harding	64	Retirement
Joseph McKenna	Jan. 5, 1925	Coolidge	81	Retirement
William Howard Taft	Feb. 3, 1930	Hoover	72	Retirement
Edward T. Sanford	Mar. 8, 1930	Hoover	64	Death
Oliver Wendell Holmes, Jr.	Jan. 12, 1932	Hoover	90	Retirement
Justices Departing Between 1937 and 1954				
Willis Van Devanter	June 2, 1937	Roosevelt	78	Retirement
George Sutherland	Jan. 17, 1938	Roosevelt	75	Retirement
Benjamin N. Cardozo	July 9, 1938	Roosevelt	68	Death
Louis D. Brandeis	Feb. 13, 1939	Roosevelt	82	Retirement
Pierce Butler	Nov. 16, 1939	Roosevelt	73	Death
James Clark McReynolds	Feb. 1, 1941	Roosevelt	78	Retirement
Charles Evans Hughes	July 1, 1941	Roosevelt	79	Retirement
James F. Byrnes	Oct. 3, 1942	Roosevelt	63	Resignation
Owen J. Roberts	July 31, 1945	Truman	70	Resignation
Harlan Fiske Stone	Apr. 22, 1946	Truman	73	Death
Frank Murphy	July 19, 1949	Truman	59	Death
Wiley B. Rutledge	Sept. 10, 1949	Truman	55	Death
Fred M. Vinson	Sept. 8, 1953	Eisenhower	63	Death
Robert H. Jackson	Oct. 9, 1954	Eisenhower	62	Death
Justices Departing between 1954 to Present				
Sherman Minton	Oct. 15, 1956	Eisenhower	65	Retirement
Stanley F. Reed	Feb. 25, 1957	Eisenhower	72	Retirement

(continued on next page)

TABLE 1.1 *(continued)*

Departing Justice	Departure Date	Departing President	Age	Departure Mode
Justices Departing between 1954 to Present (cont'd.)				
Harold H. Burton	Oct. 13, 1958	Eisenhower	70	Retirement
Charles Evans Whittaker	Apr. 1, 1962	Kennedy	61	Retirement
Felix Frankfurter	Aug. 28, 1962	Kennedy	79	Retirement
Arthur Goldberg	July 25, 1965	Johnson	56	Resignation
Thomas C. Clark	June 12, 1967	Johnson	67	Retirement
Abe Fortas	May 14, 1969	Nixon	58	Resignation
Earl Warren	June 23, 1969	Nixon	78	Retirement
Hugo L. Black	Sept. 17, 1971	Nixon	85	Retirement
John Marshall Harlan II	Sept. 23, 1971	Nixon	72	Retirement
William O. Douglas	Nov. 12, 1975	Ford	77	Retirement
Potter Stewart	July 3, 1981	Reagan	66	Retirement
Warren E. Burger	Sept. 26, 1986	Reagan	79	Retirement
Lewis F. Powell, Jr.	June 26, 1987	Reagan	79	Retirement
William J. Brennan, Jr.	July 20, 1990	Bush	84	Retirement
Thurgood Marshall	June 27, 1991	Bush	82	Retirement
Byron R. White	June 28, 1993	Clinton	75	Retirement
Harry A. Blackmun	Aug. 3, 1994	Clinton	85	Retirement
William H. Rehnquist				
Sandra Day O'Connor				
John Paul Stevens				
Ruth Bader Ginsburg				

The Court's membership was reduced to seven and subsequently increased to nine in 1869 and William Strong and Joseph Bradley were appointed.

Judicial departure poses an interesting puzzle for those who study and follow the Court. The issue also has broad implications for American constitutional development. What is significant about departure is the power of the justices themselves to influence who their successor will be by the timing of that departure.[7] Their decisions, therefore, help shape the future direction of the Court. This power is a direct result of justices having life tenure, and the resultant prerogative of being able to leave whenever they wish. Cognizant of their own policy preferences in relation to those of the current president, justices have been in a unique position to be strategic and engage in succession politics simply by choosing when to leave the Court.

The relatively small literature that focused on departure has been largely of two types.[8] The first treatments were chronological, descriptive accounts with little or no analytical framework. The second group of studies were ahistorical quantitative analyses that sought to explain the key factors in the departure decision. The sole book-length treatment of the subject is David N. Atkinson's *Leaving the Bench: Supreme Court Justices at the End*. Rather than concentrate on the politics of departure decisions, Atkinson focused on the aging and infirmities of the justices. He concluded that justices in recent times have not overstayed their usefulness and burdened the Court as past justices did.[9] As a result, Atkinson argued that the constitutional system of life tenure be left unchanged but some statutory reforms adopted such as pooling law clerks and instating an FDR-like Court-packing plan for aged justices. While rich in the details of justices' illnesses, declines, deaths, and final resting places, what Atkinson's research fails to address is how institutional arrangements have led to pervasive partisanship in the current departure system as well as the continuing problem of failing justices remaining on the bench past their usefulness.

Why did previous research miss these crucial developments? While these works furthered our understanding of the politics of departure by adding pieces to the puzzle, a comprehensive analysis that is centered on contextual factors is needed to complete the picture. By employing an historical institutional approach, a complete contextual analysis is possible. The approach is particularly useful for revealing the multiple transformations that institutions experience over time and how those transformations organize behavior. It is only by examining the departure process by the transformations that it has undergone, that we are able to see the relatively recent partisanship and increased mental decrepitude that now characterize it.

The purpose of this research is twofold. First, I want to explain how and why Supreme Court justices have left the Court. What factors have contributed to their decisions to step down? Certainly age and infirmity are part of the story, but to what extent have justices been motivated by strategic, partisan, personal, and institutional concerns? Second, I will normatively assess the arguments for and against the current constitutional arrangement that justices have life tenure to examine whether current retirement provisions are satisfactory and whether there should be a mandatory retirement age.

On the first, empirical, questions, it is often thought that justices are strategic policy-maximizers and make their departure decisions based on which party occupies the White House. Indeed, when posed this question, Chief Justice Rehnquist recently responded, "That's not one hundred percent true, but it certainly is true in more cases than not, I would think."[10] The following analysis shows, however, that historically, partisan departures have been the exception rather than the rule. Institutional factors, such as not being a burden to their colleagues, and personal concerns, like the enjoyment of their work and the fear of death have played a much more significant role. This does not mean, however, that partisanship is absent from the decision-making process. Indeed, as I will discuss later, when examined over time partisan concerns have recently begun to play a much more significant role in the thought processes of the justices. Still, over time the main factor in the departure decision of Supreme Court justices has been formal provision for their retirement. As retirement benefits have been established and expanded, the number of justices voluntarily departing from the Court has increased substantially (see Figure 1.1).

The politics surrounding the provision for and extent of retirement benefits can be conceptualized as an ongoing historical dialogue between Congress and the Court. The founders' initial attempts to set the tenure of the justices, and Congress's decision to have the justices ride circuit, set the tone for the Court's behavior. The early justices responded by resigning their seats rather than repeatedly face their arduous circuit duties. When Congress responded by diluting the circuit-riding requirement, the justices no longer had this major reason to resign. As a result, they remained in their places until death. When a number of aging justices hampered the Court's ability to function, Congress responded with the first retirement provision. Though it was initially successful, it soon became apparent that the provision was ultimately ineffective in getting justices to step down. Once again, Congress responded with much more generous retirement laws that ultimately met with success,

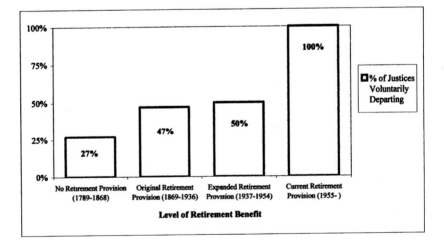

FIGURE 1.1
Retirement Benefits and Voluntary Departure in the U.S. Supreme Court

by inducing voluntary departures. One byproduct of the increased provisions, however, has been a dramatic rise in the number of justices engaging in succession politics by trying to time their departures to coincide with a compatible president. The most recent departures have been partisan, some more blatantly than others, and have bolstered arguments to reform the process. A second byproduct has been an increase in justices staying on the Court past their ability to adequately contribute.

Though partisanship has only recently become the chief organizing factor for departing justices, changes in the emergent structures of the departure process were caused, in part, by the partisan politics that were rampant in the years 1801, 1869, 1937, and 1954—years in which Congress was dominated by new policy-making regimes. The Jeffersonian Congress of 1801 sought to remake politics, as did the radical Republican Congress of 1869, the New Deal Democrat Congress of 1937, and the post–World War II Republican Congress of 1954. In each case, the Supreme Court was composed of a number of aged, declining justices left over from an old regime, now repudiated at the ballot box.[11] As Table 1.2 shows, after each act's passage, opposition justices did indeed step down, just as Congress had hoped.

This analysis also shows a lack of partisanship on the part of the departing justices. With partisan Congresses passing legislation affecting opposition Supreme Court justices, one might expect that opposition justices would fight fire with fire and refuse to step down. Just the opposite occurred, however.

Before the Federalists gave up the reins of power in Congress in 1801, they passed a law to abolish circuit riding. When the Jeffersonian Republicans took office, they quickly tried to reinstate the practice, fearing that otherwise the aged justices would remain on the bench forever, but the new Congress made circuit riding optional. The result was the same that the Federalists' abolition of the practice would have had. It is difficult to know whether Federalist justices like William Cushing and Samuel Chase would have voluntarily departed, had circuit riding been required as it had in the past. Given the behavior of their colleagues under mandatory circuit riding, and the actions of future justices faced with similar decisions, I would argue that Cushing and Chase would have eventually resigned rather than ride their circuits and burden their colleagues. With circuit riding optional, and no formal retirement provision in place, however, Cushing and Chase remained in their seats.

Many in the radical Republican Congress of 1869 were eager to see Democratic justices Robert Grier and Samuel Nelson leave the Court. And with the passage of the first formal retirement provision, both opposition justices stepped down. If Grier and Nelson were primarily concerned with thwarting their opponents, they would have remained in their seats until death. Because they were more concerned with personal factors, they quickly

TABLE 1.2

The Effect of Partisan Politics in the Executive and Legislative Branch
on Departure in the U.S. Supreme Court

	President's Party	House Majority Party	Senate Majority Party	Retirement Eligible Departing Justices		
Judiciary Act of 1801	R	R	R	Alfred Moore (F)	Resignation	1804
Retirement Act of 1869	R	R	R	Robert C. Grier (D)	Retirement	1870
				Samuel Nelson (D)	Retirement	1872
Retirement Act of 1937	D	D	D	Willis Van Devanter (R)	Retirement	1937
				George Sutherland (R)	Retirement	1938
				Louis Brandeis (R)	Retirement	1939
				Pierce Butler (R)	Death	1939
				James McReynolds (D)	Retirement	1941
				Charles E. Hughes (R)	Retirement	1941
Retirement Act of 1954	R	R	R	Sherman Minton (D)	Retirement	1956
				Stanley F. Reed (D)	Retirement	1957
				Harold H. Burton (R)	Retirement	1958

took advantage of the new law. Grier retired immediately and Nelson also retired after his successor was confirmed.

While this shows that Congress may have been acting in a partisan fashion in 1869, it also shows that key opposition justices were not. Some opposition justices have viewed new regimes as unbearable and left at least partially because they knew they could no longer influence the Court's jurisprudence. In deciding against remaining in their seats until a favorable president, Senate, or both took power, they relinquished their influence, abandoning any chance of influencing the Court's future direction. If justices were primarily concerned with departing under a like-minded President, Senate, or both, these opposition justices would have died on the bench in the effort rather than give in to the partisan scheming of their political opponents in Congress. Indeed, that is precisely what Pierce Butler did after 1937. Rather than follow the example of his colleagues Willis Van Devanter and George Sutherland, who retired immediately following the act's passage and were at least partially resigned to the new regime's ascendance, Butler remained in his seat until his death in 1939 at age seventy-three. But his decision not to take advantage of the expanded retirement act was unique.

1954 marked the first time since before the Great Depression that the Republicans controlled both houses of Congress and the presidency.[12] Seeking to remake the federal judiciary, including the Supreme Court, by purging aging New Deal Democrats appointed by Franklin Roosevelt and Harry Truman, the Republicans dramatically expanded the parameters of the original 1869 Act. Now justices could retire at age sixty-five with fifteen years of service on the federal bench. They succeeded in prompting the departures of three High Court Roosevelt/Truman appointees: Sherman Minton, Stanley Reed, and Harold Burton. Added to the two vacancies caused by the deaths of Fred Vinson and Robert Jackson, Eisenhower was able to appoint five new justices during his two terms as president.

Interestingly, each time Congress enacted retirement legislation, it was also considering a constitutional amendment for compulsory retirement at a set age such as seventy or seventy-five. But for reasons I explain later, including the fact that constitutional changes are much more difficult to enact than statutory reforms, Congress chose each time to make retirement more attractive by guaranteeing salaries and judicial status. As such, we can view the passage of retirement legislation as continually undercutting constitutional reform.

Accounting for both the success and failure of retirement provisions over time are the recurring institutional and personal concerns of the justices. The following analysis shows that in the beginning, justices nearing the close of their tenure were primarily concerned with institutional and personal factors. Over time, however, as benefits were instated and expanded, partisan and strategic concerns, involving the timing and choice of a successor, played an increasingly larger role in the decision-making process. When partisanship and strategy is at work, institutional and personal factors are also considered.

Determining departure considerations is crucial for assessing normative claims about life tenure for members of the Court.

Is judicial independence a desirable end? While scholars differ on this issue, the purpose of this book is not so much to take sides in this debate but instead to provide an explanation and analysis of the departure process. While debates about the merits of granting life tenure to judges go back to the time of the framers, there is no shortage of contemporary proposals for reforming the process. Calls for term limits, mandatory retirement ages, and judicial elections are often supported by a view of the judiciary as partisan. The assumption is that because judges behave in a partisan fashion, they ought to be accountable like other partisan actors. Indeed, there is considerable evidence suggesting that not unlike congressional or executive decision making, judicial decision making is based on policy-preferences or attitudes.[13]

Perhaps the key argument in favor of having life tenure for judges is the goal of preserving a "politically independent" judiciary. In general this means that judges will act on the basis of their own sincerely held preferences, regardless of the preferences of other relevant political actors, and be free from reprisals by the public or other governmental actors, institutions, or both.[14]

If justices are making their departure decisions based on who the president is and who controls the Senate, then it can be argued that unelected and unaccountable justices ought not to have this power. Furthermore, if justices are remaining in their seats past their ability to effectively discharge the duties of their office, then arguments for reforming the life tenure system are further bolstered. It is in this context that I examine the merits of proposals to change the existing arrangement.

Ultimately, I argue that generous retirement benefits coupled with a decreasing workload have reduced the departure process to partisan maneuvering. If the only goal is to decrease partisanship, I suggest that calls for term limits and mandatory retirement ages may not be necessary. Such reforms are not only difficult to obtain (requiring a constitutional amendment), but more easily achievable policies could remedy much of the problem. Specifically, strengthening internal Court norms regarding departure, increasing the Court's workload, and reforming the existing retirement laws by making retirement more difficult to obtain, will likely go a long way toward reducing partisanship. Still, when coupled with the recent increase in mental decrepitude, it is hard to argue against compulsory retirement.

DEPARTURE IN COMPARATIVE PERSPECTIVE

Nowhere does the United States Constitution specifically address when or under what circumstances justices ought to depart from the Court. Article I requires members of Congress to vacate their seats after two years in the House and six years in the Senate, unless they win reelection. Article II requires the president to depart after four years, unless he or she is reelected, in which case he or she is limited to a single additional term, as specified in the Twenty-second Amendment.[15] Article III, Section 1 states that the justices "shall hold their Offices during good Behaviour." This phrase, in effect, grants the justices life tenure, meaning they can remain on the Court for as long as they desire, absent removal from office by impeachment and conviction. Retirement provisions like those enacted in 1869, 1937, and 1954 can only encourage, not require, departure. By way of contrast, within the United States, thirty-six states (72%) have mandatory retirement provisions.[16]

I will not attempt to be exhaustive in this brief comparative section but want to provide some comparative context to departure in the United States. In their article on comparative judicial selection systems, Lee Epstein, Jack Knight, and Olga Schvetsova reported that of the twenty-seven European nations in their sample nearly half (n = 12) had a compulsory retirement age for judges, with a mean of sixty-nine years for those who had it.[17] They also found that twenty-one of twenty-seven (78%) nations had either renewable or nonrenewable terms ranging from six to twelve, with a mean term length of nine years regardless of renewability. Of the twenty-one nations with limited terms, only eight (38%) had a mandatory retirement age. Of the twenty-seven, only six had security of tenure—tenure beyond limited terms. For example, after World War II, the Allies reinstated the provision of German judges serving for life.[18] After the fall of the Soviet Union, Russian judges were granted life tenure.[19] Still, of these six, two-thirds (n = 4) had a mandatory retirement provision. In Austria, for example, judges must retire on a pension at age sixty-five.[20] What is plain from this prevalence of limited terms, compulsory retirement ages, or both found in Europe is the uniqueness of the American case.

In the United States, Congress is ultimately responsible for the administration of the federal courts. This arrangement comes from the common-law tradition of England. A very different culture, however, governs the administration of both French and Italian courts. Rooted in the civil-law tradition, judges in both France and Italy are subject to oversight by administrative bodies and not by a coordinate branch of government as in the United States. This has generally meant that French and Italian judges have been much more removable than American judges.[21] The differing common-law and civil-law traditions are only exemplified by the four cases mentioned below.[22]

The idea of judges having life tenure was first established by Louis XI in 1467 through the principle of "irremovability." The law prevented the king from removing any judge, including those he himself had nominated, for any reason. This gave judges lifetime terms and total independence from the king.[23] France has undergone numerous transformations since then, including popularly elected judges, with current judges acting more as bureaucrats than as professionals and subject to a ministry for continuance in office.[24] Removals are possible, but only for official misconduct.[25]

Italian judges generally enjoy life tenure, but are subject to review by a regionally elected disciplinary committee. The committee is part of a system of "self-government" through the National Council of Magistrates, which is established by the constitution and composed mostly of judges.[26] Judges can be prosecuted and admonished, censured, lose seniority, and be temporarily and permanently removed from office for failing to uphold the duties of their office, damaging the public image of the profession, or compromising the prestige of the judiciary.[27] While this process is used to remove disabled judges, it is generally reserved for criminal and unethical conduct. From 1957 to 1974, only seven judges were removed for mental or physical infirmity.[28] This is quite different from the United States, where no Supreme Court justice has ever been removed for disability.

In Britain, the monarch historically had the power to remove judges. In 1376, Parliament established the impeachment process as a political device to remove judges and other officials beholden to the crown. British judges were not granted life tenure until 1761 under King George III, who remarked:

> I look upon the independence and uprightness of the Judges of the land as essential to the impartial administration of justice, as one of the best securities to the rights and liberties of my loving subjects and as most conducive to the honor of the crown; and I come now to recommend . . . that such farther provision may be made, for securing the Judges in the enjoyment of their office during good behavior, not withstanding any such demise, as shall be most expedient.[29]

Life tenure brought an end to Parliamentary impeachment. Judges could still be removed, however, by the monarch on the recommendation, or "address," of both the Commons and the Lords with the sole exception, the Lord Chancellor, who can only be removed by the Prime Minister. For High Court Judges, address is the only means of removal.[30] As of 1993, the mandatory retirement age for judges has been seventy, with an extension to age seventy-five if granted by the Lord Chancellor.[31]

Disability poses a delicate problem for judicial systems. There have been a number of British judges over the years who were forced to resign due to disability. One striking example occurred in the 1950s when a High Court judge refused to retire when it was clear that he could no longer discharge the duties of his office due to mental incapacity. To induce his departure and ensure that he did not cause harm to the institution, no cases were assigned to him. He soon acquiesced and retired from his seat.[32] This internal solution has also occurred in the U.S. Supreme Court. Following his stroke, Justice William O. Douglas was not assigned any opinions and ultimately stripped of his power before he finally retired.

The relatively recent reforms of mandatory retirement laws in Britain and generous retirement provisions in the United States suggests that High Court judges in common-law systems have become increasingly removable, much like their counterparts in nations with a civil-law tradition. Though none have passed, calls for mandatory retirement laws in the United States have been prevalent since the founding.

DEPARTURE POLITICS IN HISTORICAL CONTEXT: EMERGENT AND RECURRENT STRUCTURES

Out of historical institutional work by Karren Orren and Stephen Skowronek we can usefully borrow the notion of "regimes."[33] Comprised of intellectual, political, and educational components, regimes are often defined as stable partisan governing coalitions in American national politics.[34] Orren and Skowronek suggest that regimes often come about by "elite engineering . . . rearranging institutional relationships to stabilize and routinize governmental operations around a new set of political assumption."[35] In the present study, what is being examined are "departure regimes" that constitute a single although complex process. One departure regime is replaced by another and the politics of departure decision making are transformed from one regime to the next.

Regimes are in a constant state of transformation. Regimes are comprised of multiple orders where elements of the old regime are present and somewhat influential in the new regime.[36] For example, the old order of circuit riding which was the dominant force in departure decisions during the first departure regime (1789–1800) was still influential, though no longer decisive, during the next regime. Circuit riding became optional in 1801 and the justices continued to attend circuit courts, though not as frequently and not when they were in ill health. Continued circuit riding took its toll on some justices in the new regime, and was therefore a factor. It was no longer decisive, however, in the departure decision, as personal financial concerns became dominant.

In the chapters that follow, I focus on the institutional history of departure in the U.S. Supreme Court. I argue that the politics of departure has been transformed on four occasions, each time creating a new regime. These transformations occurred when old departure eras, consisting of unpopular, outdated and ineffective policies, were largely replaced by new eras and different ideas. For example, the first transformation occurred in 1801 when new legislation was passed making optional the old requirement that justices ride circuit. Though it is often thought that justices have always been partisan in their departure decisions, the subsequent analysis demonstrates that historically such motivations have been the exception. Personal and institutional factors have instead been predominant. It has only been in the latter half of the twentieth century that partisanship has been widespread.

The politics of departure in the U.S. Supreme Court has historically been driven by *emergent patterns* of structural and statutory forces. For example, circuit riding was the first important structural factor affecting the departure decisions of the justices, while the passage of retirement legislation would become crucial in later years. Changing circuit duties and formal retirement benefits make up the four emergent patterns, throughout Supreme Court history. Though justices ultimately consider a range of factors when making their decision, the primary impetus and basis for all the considerations that follow are the departure mechanisms that emerge at important points in time (see Table 1.3). The emergent structures organized the justices' departure decisions.

The first emergent structure in the departure process was the requirement that the justices attend circuit courts throughout the country. Traveling was arduous and many justices, particularly those in ill health, resigned rather than face the difficult journeys. Table 1.3 shows that 71 percent (5 of 7) of the justices facing such circumstances resigned. When the circuit riding burden was made optional in 1801, the departure process was transformed. Under the relaxed provision, justices had no reason to depart, especially when their health was deteriorating. Aged and infirm justices, who otherwise would have difficulty drawing an income, could not afford to resign their seats and lose their salaries.[37] As a result, they simply chose not to attend their circuit courts, and many times the meetings of the Supreme Court, and instead concentrated on recovering from their maladies. As Table 1.3 shows, from 1801 to 1867 only 17 percent (4 of 24) of the departures came by way of resignation, with nearly every justice staying in office until death.

Another major transformation of the departure process occurred with the passage of the Judiciary Act of 1869 and the emergence of the first retirement provision (see Table 1.4). Until its passage, justices wishing to leave the Court had to resign their seats, severing all ties with the federal judiciary. Following the 1869 Act, justices could "retire" at age seventy after ten years on the bench and continue to draw their full salary. As Table 1.3 shows, 31 percent (11 of 36) of justices departing between 1869 and 1936 took advantage of the new provision, but more than half (53%) were still dying while in office, often because they did not meet the seventy/ten requirement of the 1869 Act and also because they would relinquish their status and position as federal judges. Some justices (17%) still used resignation as a means to depart from the Court, however. Resigning is generally done when a justice intends to leave

TABLE 1.3

The Effect of Emergent Patterns on Resignation and Retirement in the U.S. Supreme Court

Years	Emergent Structures: Departure Mechanism	Total Number of Departing Justices	Number of Resigning Justices	Percentage of Resigning Justices	Number of Retiring Justices	Percentage of Retiring Justices
1791–1800	Circuit Riding Required	7	5	71%	—	—
1801–1867	Circuit Riding Optional	24	4	17%	—	—
1868–1936	Original Retirement Provision	36	6	17%	11	31%
1937–1954	Expanded Retirement Provision	14	2	14%	5	36%
1955–	Current Retirement Provision	19	2	11%	17	89%

Note: Technically justices could not "retire" until 1937, however the 1869 Act was the first time benefits were given for resigning. Hence, beginning in 1869 the term *retire* was conventionally used to denote departure with benefits and the term *resign* meant departure without benefits.

TABLE 1.4
Significant Retirement and Pension Provisions: 1869–1954

Year	Provisions
1869	All federal judges, including Supreme Court justices, may retire at age seventy with at least ten years of service as a federal judge and continue to receive the salary of their office after their resignation.
1937	Justices having reached the age of seventy with at least ten years of service as a federal judge are allowed to retire in senior status rather than to resign. Senior justices retain the authority to perform judicial duties in any circuit when called on by the Chief Justice. Senior justices receive the same pension benefits as resigned justices. (Lower court judges were given the "senior status" option in 1919.)
1954	All federal judges, including Supreme Court justices, may retire at age seventy with at least ten years of service as a federal judge OR at age sixty-five with fifteen years of service as a federal judge and receive the salary of their office at the time of their retirement for life. These provisions also apply to retiring in senior status.

Adapted from: Lee Epstein et al., *The Supreme Court Compendium* (Washington, D.C.: Congressional Quarterly Press, 1994), 36–37 and 28 U.S.C 371–372.

the federal judiciary for another position, either in the private or public sector. Justices have resigned and gone on to serve in the U.S. Senate, and run for president of the United States, among other things.

In 1937 another important development occurred in departure politics. Congress made retirement more attractive to the justices by not only granting them full salary, but also allowing them to take "senior status" and continue to work as federal judges on lower courts.[38] Justices who resigned, however, were no longer federal judges and could not sit on the appeals courts. This added benefit resulted in increased retirements as 36 percent (5 of 14) of the justices availed themselves of the expanded provisions between 1937 and 1954. Congress provided further incentive to leave in 1954 by expanding the parameters of retirement beyond the original 1869 Act to include full pay after age sixty-five and fifteen years of service. This provision became the "Rule of Eighty," where after reaching age sixty-five, retirement eligibility was determined by any combination of years and service totaling eighty. The Rule of Eighty is the current statute governing retirement for all federal judges, including justices of the U.S. Supreme Court. Since 1955, these developments have resulted in 100 percent (19 of 19) of the justices voluntarily departing and all justices since Abe Fortas choosing to retire.

The importance of the effect of more generous retirement provisions on departure is plain. The emergent patterns of the various departure mechanisms provide the foundation on which decisions are based. Interwoven with the emergent patterns are several recurring factors that the justices consider in making their departure decision. The *recurrent patterns* are present across the emergent patterns and are influenced by them (see Table 1.5). Financial, personal, and institutional concerns become more or less important to the justices depending on the emergent structure in ascendance. Justices departing in the Court's early years were particularly concerned with financial and personal health issues because of the circuit-riding requirement. Justices in later eras minimized these concerns as circuit riding was gutted and finally abolished. As retirement benefits were established and increased, justices could focus more on institutional and personal factors. Ultimately, partisanship became the dominant recurrent factor in the departure process. The analysis that follows explores the recurring patterns in light of the emergent structures for each departure era.

Interestingly, partisanship has only recently become a dominant factor in the departure decision-making process. How do we know when a justice is being partisan? For the purposes of departure, justices behave in a partisan way by seeking to have a broad influence on the selection of their successor. Partisan justices base their departure decisions on their perceived agreement with the policy positions of the president, the Senate, or both. While some cases are clearer than others, evidence of parisanship is often mixed. Partisanship usually manifests itself in two ways: either the justice departs under a like-minded president or the justice remains in his place in order to keep the vacancy away from an opposition president. For example, as I discuss in chapter 7, Thurgood Marshall disagreed with the policies of the Reagan and Bush

TABLE 1.5

Emergent and Recurrent Patterns of Departure in the U.S. Supreme Court

Years	Dominant Emergent Structure	Dominant Recurrent Structure	Dominant Departure Mode
1791–1800	Circuit-Riding Required	Health	Resignation
1801–1868	Circuit-Riding Optional	Financial	Death
1869–1936	Original Retirement Provision	Personal	Death & Retirement
1937–1954	Expanded Retirement Provision	Institutional	Death & Retirement
1955–	Current Retirement Provision	Partisan	Retirement

administrations and stayed in his place for partisan reasons. Unable and unwilling to hang on any longer, Marshall bowed to the inevitable and ultimately retired. Though he did not depart under a like-minded president, his decision not to depart still reflects partisan concerns. It also reflects a major weakness of the life-tenure system: justices can remain on the Court past their ability to effectively participate in the work of the Court in order to hold out for a favorable president, senate, or both. In the following chapters I show that early on in the Court's history, partisan concerns were subordinated to institutional and personal factors but eventually structural changes in the process allowed partisan concerns, like those exhibited by Marshall, to control departure decisions.

Still, partisanship is always tempered by institutional constraints. As Table 1.6 shows, there are three factors that almost always trump all others in making departure decisions. The first check on a justice is the regular cycle of the Court Term. Nearly every justice who has retired since 1954 has done so when the Court is in recess. This decision gives the Court the best chance to operate with a full contingent of nine members, provided the new Justice is confirmed and sworn in before the new Term begins. This constraint was present from the Court's beginnings when John Blair wrote George Washington, "I hope that I have not procrastinated my resignation, so as not to allow you

TABLE 1.6

Institutional Constraints on Partisan Departures in the U.S. Supreme Court

Court Term	Justices retire when the Court is in recess. Often at the close of a Term in late June or early July, on the last day when opinions are read from the bench, the Chief Justice announces the retirement of the justice. For example, Justice Scalia told me on the last day of the 2001–02 term, "If there was going to be an announcement, it would have been today." This allows the Court to have a full contingent of members during the Term and, ideally, a new justice to be appointed before the new Term begins the following October.
Presidential Campaign	Justices do not retire in presidential election years. Because the appointment process can be highly controversial, justices do not want to add controversy by making a specific nomination a campaign issue.
"Rule of Eight"	Two or more justices never retire at the same time. This allows the Court to have the largest number of active justices, currently eight, in case an appointment is not made before a new Term begins.

sufficient time to make up your mind, as to a person proper to supply the vacancy, & to give such early notice of the appointment, as to have my successor ready to take his seat in February at the next Supreme Court."[39]

A second constraint on partisanship is the presidential election cycle. With the exception of Sherman Minton who was in failing health, no justice in the modern era has retired during a presidential campaign. As I discuss in chapter 6, Earl Warren's attempt and ultimate failure to depart during the 1968 campaign demonstrates the near impossibility of such a decision. Any vacancy would be a campaign issue ripe for increased political controversy.

A third limitation on partisan departures is the "Rule of Eight." There are many advantages, from workload to divided Courts, to having a full contingent of nine members. As a result, two justices rarely depart at the same time. Still, this may happen occasionally due to illness as with the near simultaneous retirements of Hugo Black and John Harlan II in September 1971. While these constraints temper partisan retirement decisions, they have been easily navigated by recent justices.

OVERVIEW

In the chapters that follow, I discuss the interaction between the emergent and recurrent structures of departure politics in the U.S. Supreme Court and ultimately make a judgment about the adequacy of current provisions governing the departure process. The chapters are organized around the five departure eras or regimes, with an additional chapter for the current justices. Each chapter begins with a discussion of the statutory provision (the emergent structure) that shaped the departure politics of that era. The factors considered by the justices in making their departure decisions (the recurrent structures) are then discussed in terms of the context in which they take place. The departures of each justice are then analyzed in light of the emergent and recurrent structures in that era.

Chapter 2 begins with a discussion of the original requirement that the justices attend circuit courts throughout the country. The recurrent factors that influence the departure decisions of the justices are then analyzed for each justice departing in that era. In the period from 1789 to 1800, justices were primarily concerned with the effects of circuit riding on their health. When they became ill, or felt that making the arduous journey to attend their circuit courts would be too difficult to endure or even fatal, they resigned. Though the justices in this and subsequent chapters are for the most part analyzed chronologically, the factors that are important in their departure decisions are remarkably clustered. Groups of successive departing justices often show important similarities in their behavior. This chronological, yet clustered, pattern allows the focus to be on the recurrent factors and their interaction with the emergent structure for that era but also shows, to a lesser extent, the impact of individual idiosyncratic factors. Ultimately, the behavior of the justices illustrates the complexity of the interplay between emergent and recurrent structures and how their interaction organizes departure politics.

Because circuit riding became optional in 1801, I discuss in chapter 3 how the lack of an incentive to leave the Court caused most of the justices to remain on the bench until their deaths. This resulted in the Court as an institution being crippled by aged and incapacitated justices who could not shoulder their fair share of the burden. Following the Civil War, calls to remove the aging justices grew louder as the old men of the hobbled Court became the talk of Washington.

In chapter 4, I discuss the passage of the first formal retirement provision. Though the Retirement Act of 1869 proved successful initially, it soon became clear that the requirements, age seventy with ten years of service on the Supreme Court, were difficult to attain for many justices. Furthermore, there was no provision for disabled justices who had not yet met the retirement threshold. Many justices enjoyed their work and the prestige of their office and were reluctant to step down. Also, the creation of the Courts of Appeal and dramatic changes in the Supreme Court's docket had an impact on departure decisions. The Court's direct involvement in resolving the disputed Hayes/Tilden election of 1876 spurred a brief wave of partisan departures. Still, overall, partisanship was the exception rather than the rule.

I continue discussing the era precipitated by the 1869 Retirement Act in chapter 5. The superannuation effect caused by the decline of Justice Stephen J. Field immediately influenced the retirement choices of his colleagues. But as the period progressed, and the effects of the 1876 election and Field's mental decline waned, it became increasingly evident that something further needed to be done to make it easier for justices to retire. When Democrat Franklin D. Roosevelt took office in 1932 and the Republican-dominated Supreme Court began striking down his New Deal proposals, the issue of judicial departure was once again on the agenda.

Chapter 6 begins with a discussion of the events surrounding FDR's court-packing plan. Amid the rancorous debate surrounding increasing the Court's size, the 1937 Retirement Act supplemented the original provisions by allowing justices to retire in "senior status" keeping their salaries and offices and being allowed to continue judging on lower federal courts. Its effect was immediate, with two of the anti-Roosevelt "four horsemen" retiring under its provisions. When it became clear, however, that justices were having difficulty reaching the age seventy plateau for retirement, there were calls for further reforms.

Chapter 7 analyzes the politics surrounding the 1954 Retirement Act passed by the first GOP administration and Congress since before the Great Depression. In general, I discuss how the new legislation expanded the original 1869 provisions, allowing for retirement at a younger age. Coupled with earlier reforms, the 1954 Act had an immediate effect, prompting three democratic-appointed justices to voluntarily step down.

In chapter 8 I continue to show how these reforms so dominated the modern era that every justice since 1955 has voluntarily departed. The major development of this era was a byproduct of the expanded retirement provisions: increased partisanship in the departure decisions of the justices. Though there are a few exception, I discuss how most of the justices engaged in partisan maneuvering when deciding to depart and how this partisanship continues to this day. Another byproduct, however was an increase in the mental decline of a number of the Court's active members.

In chapter 9 I discuss the current justices in light of the extraordinary events of the 2000 election. Indeed, the parallel between the disputed election of 1876 between Democrat Samuel Tilden and Republican Rutherford B. Hayes and the 2000 election between Democrat Al Gore and Republican George W. Bush is instructive. The Tilden/Hayes dispute directly involved five members of the Court who were appointed to the electoral commission to decide the outcome.[40] Justice Joseph Bradley cast the deciding vote, giving Florida's electors to Hayes. Similarly, the Bush/Gore dispute was decided by a 5–4 vote in the U.S. Supreme Court, again with one justice casting the deciding vote, effectively giving Florida's electors to the Republican candidate. The 1876 election had an important effect on the departures of at least three and possibly four justices. David Davis, Nathan Clifford, Noah Swayne, and possibly William Strong based their departure decisions on whether they favored Hayes. Partisanship waned after this event, however, largely due to the ineffective initial retirement provision. But in the wake of the contentious events of the Bush/Gore election, and with the current justices enjoying expanded retirement benefit, I suggest that at least the next three or four departures, and possibly more, will likely be characterized by partisan maneuvering. Indeed, Justice O'Connor has already tipped her hand.

Given the increasing popularity of term limits and judicial elections on the state level, in chapter 10 I discuss a number of proposals for reforming the Supreme Court's succession process. Because my analysis shows that justices come to politicize the departure process, and mental decrepitude is on the rise, I suggest that reform is needed. Specifically, I demonstrate why the retirement age should be increased and calls to further liberalize retirement benefits must be rejected out of hand. Workload could be increased. I also suggest that the justices themselves must remain vigilant against their own failings and take proper precautions against burdening the Court as an institution. As such, I propose a list of steps that should be taken by the Court if one of its members has stayed too long and is noticeably failing. But ultimately, it is a constitutional amendment for a mandatory retirement age that goes the farthest in combating patisanship, mental decrepitude, and preserving judicial independence.

The goal of the succession process should be stability. The Court should have a perpetual full contingent of able members. Justices ought to step down at the close of a Term and their successors ought to be confirmed before the new Term begins. Justices ought to base their departure decisions on the effective functioning of the institution together with their own personal satisfaction. Though the departure process is not a perfect one, I argue that these goals can be achieved with reform. While the people of the United States will be served well by modest internal and statutory reforms, they will be better served by changes in current constitutional arrangements.

2

1789–1800

Traveling Postboys

There is nothing I more ardently wish for than retirement and
leisure . . .

— Chief Justice John Jay

To lead a life of perpetual traveling, and almost continual absence
from home, is a very severe lot to be doomed to in the decline
of life . . .

— Justice James Iredell

The Court's earliest years were dominated by discussions of the dreaded
requirement of circuit riding.[1] Because the justices were required to attend circuit courts throughout the country, the earliest departures came by way of resignation. Rather than face hazardous, life-threatening journeys, the first
Supreme Court justices chose to resign their seats and preserve their health.
When the lame-duck Federalists tried to abolish the practice as part of a comprehensive reorganization of the federal judiciary, the Jeffersonian Republicans
cried foul and reinstated it when they took power. Though this first period in
the Court's departure history ended in partisan struggle, the departures of the
earliest justices were precipitated by personal health and financial concerns.

The potential harmful effects that a departure decision could have on the
legitimacy of the Supreme Court was anticipated from the institution's inception. In reply to Justice Thomas Johnson's resignation from the Court in 1793,
President George Washington said "the resignation of persons holding that
high office [justice of the Supreme Court] conveys to the public mind a want
of stability in that Department, where perhaps it is more essential than in any

other."[2] Though the justices of the early Supreme Court were no doubt aware of the link between stability and legitimacy, their departure decisions did not take this consideration into account. Instead, personal concerns dominated their decision making.

Departure from the Court in its very early years came by way of resignation. The earliest justices regularly weighed the pros and cons of leaving the Court for greener pastures. Distaste for the rigors of circuit riding, coupled with health concerns and the availability of governmental positions of comparable pay and prestige, made it easy for the earliest justices to step down. Of the seven justices to depart in the Court's early years, all but two resigned after serving a relatively short time (see Table 2.1). For the five who resigned, the average Court tenure was three years, ten months. The two justices who chose not to resign, James Wilson and James Iredell, died while in office at the relatively young ages of fifty-five and forty-eight, respectively. Both served for approximately nine years. Though there was no formal policy to induce resignations, the requirement of attending circuit courts acted as an informal departure mechanism during the Court's earliest years.

TABLE 2.1
Length of Service: Justices Departing between 1789–1800

Justice	Length of Tenure	Mode of Departure
Robert Harrison	4 months	Resignation
John Rutledge	1 year, 5 months	Resignation
Thomas Johnson	1 year, 2 months	Resignation
John Jay	5 years, 9 months	Resignation
John Blair	6 years, 4 months	Resignation
James Wilson	8 years, 10 months	Death
James Iredell	9 years, 8 months	Death
Oliver Ellsworth	4 years, 6 months	Resignation
John Rutledge	5 months	Rejection
Average Tenure of Justices who Resigned	1 year, 8 months	
Average Tenure of Justices who Died	9 years, 3 months	

Note: Length of tenure measured from the date of confirmation to the date of departure, plus any time served under a recess appointment. Data are presented to the nearest completed month. Ties are broken by the number of days served beyond the last completed month. Excluding Robert Harrison, the average length of tenure for justices who resigned is 3 years, 7 months.

Source: Elder Witt, Congressional Quarterly's Guide to the U.S. Supreme Court, 2d ed. (Washington, D.C.: Congressional Quarterly, 1990).

INDISPOSITION AND THE
EARLY SUPREME COURT

Illness was common in late-eighteenth and nineteenth century America and the justices of the Supreme Court were often stricken. It was not unusual to read in the early volumes of the U.S. Reports, "Mr. Justice . . . was absent the whole of this term, from indisposition."[3] As Table 2.2 shows, the average white male could only expect to live to age forty-six at the end of the nineteenth century. Such was the state of medicine and general public health conditions that one never knew whether recovery or death was in store.

As a result, discussion of the health of colleagues and friends was commonplace in the correspondence of the day. In February 1792, twenty-seven years before his death, Justice Thomas Johnson fell ill and was unable to join his colleagues for the Court's term in Philadelphia. President Washington remarked to a friend: "That Mr. Johnson's health did not permit him to come to this City as he proposed and was expected is a matter of exceeding great regret . . . but as there is no contending against acts of Providence, we must submit as it becomes us so to do."[4] Justice Bushrod Washington remarked on the absence of one of his colleagues from the Court's August 1799 term, "Judge Cushing was seized upon the road by an indisposition, so severe as to prevent his proceeding."[5] Cushing remained on the Court for eleven more years. Justice Samuel Chase, like the rest of his colleagues, was also frequently in ill health. At age fifty-eight, twelve years before his death, Justice Chase wrote:

> For five weeks after you left Me I was confined to my Bed-Chamber, and three to my Bed. For some Days I was very ill. I was

TABLE 2.2
Average Life Expectancy of White Males: 1900–2000

Year	Average Life Expectancy
1900	46.6
1920	54.4
1940	62.1
1960	67.4
1980	70.7
1990	72.7
2000	74.2

Source: National Vital Statistics Report, Center for Disease Control.

so very weak, that I could not walk across my Room without assistance. It is 14 Days, this Day, since I came below Stairs, and I have been only able, this last Week, to go in a close Carriage into the City for Exercise. I have not the least Hope of being able to travel in time to attend the Circuit Court at New York, on the 1ˢᵗ day of next Month. A Relapse would be fatal. My Cough is still bad and the Spitting continues. My Lungs are so very weak, that I cannot bear any but very gentle Exercise.[6]

While riding circuit in the South, five years before his death, Chief Justice Rutledge fell ill. The *Charleston Gazette* reported:

By a gentleman who left Camden on Wednesday last, we are informed that the Chief justice of the United States left that place on the Saturday preceding, on his way to hold the circuit Court in North Carolina; that on the evening of that day he reached Evans' tavern, on Lynch's creek, which he left the next morning. A few hour after, he was taken so unwell, that he was obliged to return to Mr. Evans'. When the account came away, he was so much indisposed as to make it doubtful whether he would be able to proceed in time to hold the Court in North Carolina.[7]

In 1793, 1794, and 1797, the brief August terms of the Supreme Court in Philadelphia was canceled because of yellow fever outbreaks. There was often little way to tell whether a justice would pull through or succumb to an illness. As a result, those stricken often reasonably expected to recover, given time. Life expectancy was difficult to predict. For the justices of the Supreme Court, circuit duties exacerbated the situation. Because of the relative unimportance of the early Court, it was not damaged or burdened by infirm justices remaining in their seats. There were no public outcries to remove incapacitated justices and even though healthy justices did have to fill in for their ailing colleagues on circuit, their complaints were largely ignored by Congress.

DISAGREEABLE TOURS

RIDING CIRCUIT

Foremost in the mind of every justice in the Court's early period was the arduous task of riding circuit. In addition to their duties on the Supreme Court, which met for two sessions each year, justices were required to hold circuit courts twice a year throughout the country. In 1791, Congress established a district court and a judgeship for every state. Each district court was placed in one of three circuits—the Eastern, Middle, and Southern. Circuit courts convened in either one or two specified cities of each district, with the district judge and two justices of the Supreme Court presiding.[8] After 1793, only one justice was required to join the district court judge.[9] Because the circuit courts were the principal trial courts of general jurisdiction, many important cases, such as those involving federal crimes, came up while the justices rode circuit.[10]

Having the justices travel throughout the country and attend circuit courts was attractive to Congress for a number of reasons. Already having to contend with the president on a regular basis, Congress simply wanted the justices out of town, far removed from the daily politics of the nation's capitol. Also, by not having a separate group of federal circuit judges, Congress could save money. A Georgia district court judge remarked that "money matters have so strong a hold on the thoughts and personal feelings of men, that everything else seems little in comparison."[11] The justices could "mingle in the strife of jury trials,"[12] said a proponent of circuit riding in 1864, expressing the sentiment that justices needed to be directly exposed to the state laws they were interpreting as well as the varying legal practices from around the country. Also, circuit riding was seen as a way of promoting the new national government. The justices, for example, always delivered a lengthy speech to the grand jury on reaching their circuits. Attorney General Edmund Randolph said it would "impress the citizens of the United States favorably toward the general government, should the most distinguished judges visit every state."[13]

Congress's ideal of using the members of the Court in an educative, nationalizing function was plainly at odds with the harsh reality of the daily lives of the justices. While each justice felt it his duty to attend the courts in his circuit, the arduousness of the journeys resulted in the justices' physical and mental decline. Because Congress was unwilling to change the policy, the justices ultimately resigned rather than further risking their heath. This disconnect between Congress's idealized notion and the realities of the Court would continue throughout history.[14] Though the issue of circuit riding was their initial obstacle, the absence and subsequent inadequacy of a formal retirement provision became the chief stumbling block for future Courts and Congresses.

The mode of travel in the Court's early years, riding horseback or in horse-drawn carriages over dirt roads and streams, gave rise to the phrase "riding circuit." The justices were often forced to use other forms of transportation, such as boats and sleighs. Justice Cushing complained to President Washington in February 1792 about his journey, "The travelling is difficult this Season: —I left Boston, the 13th of Jan in a Phaeton, in which I made out to reach Middleton as the Snow of the 18th began, which fell so deep there as to oblige me to take a Slay, & now again wheels seem necessary."[15] Just how to go about traversing the Southern circuit was on Justice Samuel Chase's mind in 1797 when he wrote Justice Iredell:

> I intend to embark from this city (Baltimore), about the first of next Month for Savanah *[sic]*, which will allow 20 days for the Passage; will this be time enough, or will less be sufficient? I have been advised to come from Savannah to Charles Town, by Water. What is your Opinion? I take a Carriage with Me to Savannah, and, as at present advised, I propose to bring it with Me, by Water, to Charles Town; if I come by land I must purchase Horses at Savannah, which would (you) advise? . . . I fear the Journey; and am anxious for information.[16]

Chase had every reason to be afraid of the rigorous trek. Often far from their homes and families, justices were forced at their own expense to endure slow, fatiguing, and many times dangerous journeys through unfamiliar territory. The Southern circuit, for example, required a justice to travel over 1,800 miles in the poorest conditions. Iredell wrote in 1791, "I will venture to say no Judge can conscientiously undertake to ride the Southern circuit constantly, and perform the other parts of his duty . . . I rode upon the last circuit 1,900 miles."[17] Chase described Iredell's daunting Middle circuit in 1798:

> He holds the circuit court for New Jersey at Trenton, on 1st of April; and, at Philadelphia, on the 11th of the same month; he then passes through the State of Delaware (by Annapolis) to hold the Court, on 22nd of May, at Richmond, in Virginia (267 miles.); from thence he must return, the same distance to hold circuit Court on the 27th June, at New Castle in Delaware . . . A permanent system should not impose such a hardship on any officer of Government.[18]

From its inception, circuit riding was lamented by the justices. They immediately sought to abolish the practice, even offering to take a cut in pay. Chief Justice Jay wrote a letter, signed by Associate Justices Blair, Cushing, Iredell, Johnson, and Wilson, criticizing circuit riding because "some of the present judges do not enjoy health and straight of body sufficient to enable them to undergo the toilsome journeys through different climates and seasons."[19] He added that no group of judges, "however robust" could endure the rigors of such frequent travel. Justice Iredell sarcastically remarked that the justices saw themselves as "traveling postboys."[20] In 1802, a Senate ally, Gouverneur Morris, added that the justices doubted "that riding rapidly from one end of this country to another is the best way to study law."[21]

ROBERT HARRISON

One of the original six justices nominated by Washington and confirmed by the Senate, Robert Harrison is generally overlooked by those who study the Court. While Harrison never rode circuit or attended a session of the Court, his intention but ultimate inability to serve demonstrates the significance of health issues and the dangers of travel in the nation's early history. Confirmed on September 26, 1789, Harrison received a letter from Washington two days later urging him to accept.[22] After thinking the matter over for a month, Harrison declined and wrote back that family considerations, including caring for his brother's children, were paramount. Harrison recognized the physical and mental demands the job would entail when he explained to the president: "In the most favourable view of the Subject it appeared, that the duties required from a Judge of the Supreme Court would be extremely difficult & burthensome, even to a Man of the most active comprehenseive mind; and vigorous frame."[23]

But Harrison hedged and told a friend, James McHenry, that he wished to consider the matter further. When McHenry informed Washington, both the president as well as Alexander Hamilton wrote Harrison in hopes of gaining his acceptance. They assured him that the judiciary would be reorganized to give the justices more time at home with their families.[24] Harrison was convinced and set out from his home in Annapolis, Maryland, for New York where the Court was to meet. But Harrison became ill along the way and could not continue. From Bladensburg, Maryland he wrote Washington:

> I left Home on the 14th Inst with a view of making a Journey to New York, and after being several days detained at Alexandria by indisposition came thus far on the way. I now unhappily find myself in such a situation, as not to be able to proceed further. From this unfortunate event and the apprehension that my indisposition may continue, I pray you to consider that I cannot accept the Appointment.[25]

Less than three months later, Harrison died, on April 2, 1790 at the age of 45.

THOMAS JOHNSON

The notorious reputation of circuit riding did not escape Thomas Johnson who was asked by President Washington to fill the vacancy left by Justice Rutledge's resignation in 1791. Johnson was reluctant to serve because of the circuit court requirement. He wrote Washington, "[If] the next Southern Circuit would fall to me . . . my weak Frame and the Interest of my Family have in me forbid my engaging in it."[26] The president replied:

> The Judges of the Supreme Court were with me on an invitation to dinner. I took this opportunity of laying your letter before the Chief Justice in order that it might be communicated to the other judges. After a few minutes' consultation together, the Chief Justice informed me that the arrangement had been, or would be, agreed upon, that you might be wholly exempted from performing this tour of duty at that time. And I take the present occasion to observe that an opinion prevails pretty generally among the judges, as well as others, who have turned their minds to the subject, against the expediency of continuing the circuits of the Associate Judges, and that it is expected some alterations in the Judicial System will be brought forward at the next session of Congress, among which this may be one. Upon considering the arrangements of the Judges with respect to the ensuing circuit, and the probability of future relief from these disagreeable tours, I thought it best to direct your Commission to be made out and transmitted to you, which has accordingly been done; and I have no doubt that the public will be benefited, and the wishes of your friends gratified, by you acceptance.[27]

After accepting the post, Johnson was almost at once called on to sit at an important circuit case. Johnson dutifully rode circuit, while still protesting to the chief justice. Jay was sympathetic and replied that he too hoped Congress would free the justices from the task. In his late fifties, Johnson longed to retire from public life and spend time with his family. He wrote Justice James Wilson, "I have a discouraging prospect as to Health. If it does not mend I shall not be able to discharge the Duties of the Office and must withdraw. I some times repent having engaged in it. I am too old for Circuits."[28]

Less than two years after being appointed by President Washington, he resigned, citing failing health resulting from his arduous circuit Court travels. In his resignation letter to Washington he wrote, "I cannot resolve to spend six Months in the Year of the few I may have left from my Family on Roads at Taverns chiefly and often in Situations where the most moderate Desires are disapointed: My Time of Life Temper and other Circumstances forbid it."[29] The President replied: "I cannot but express the regret with which I received the resignation of your office, and sincerely lament the causes that produced it. It is unnecessary for me to say how much I should have been pleased had your health permitted you to continue in office."[30] After Johnson left the Court, Washington again urged him to serve the public, this time as Secretary of State. Content with home life, Johnson respectfully declined.

JOHN JAY

Chief Justice John Jay longed to free himself from the burdens of the Court and public life in general. While still chief justice, he accepted President Washington's assignment as special envoy to London in the Spring of 1794. In his response to the President, he added:

> There is nothing I more ardently wish for than retirement and leisure to attend to my books and papers; but parental duties not permitting it, I must acquiesce and thank God for the many blessings I enjoy. If the judiciary was on its proper footing, there is not a public station that I should prefer to the one in which you have placed me. It accords with my turn of mind, my education, and my habits.[31]

Critics charged that Jay was being less than impartial in accepting the assignment while still chief justice. Calling the step "unconstitutional" and "dangerous," many thought Jay had degraded his office.[32] Jay was unhappy on the Court, not only because of the circuit riding requirement, but because he felt it had not yet become the important institution he hoped it would. Still, he felt it his duty to help stabilize and legitimize the fledgling institution and tried to juggle the Chief Justiceship and the administration's foreign policy concerns—all while battling the illness and fatigue brought about by his circuit duties. He wrote Justice Cushing:

> I am prepared and purpose to set out for Pha Tomorrow if the weather should prove fair. For although I have regained more Health thatn I had Reason to expect to have done so soon; yet I find it delicate, and not sufficiently confirmed to admit of my traveling in bad weather . . . It is my wish as well as my Duty to attend the court, and every Exertion that prudence may permit, shall be made for that purpose. I hope the Benevolence of Congress will induce them to fix the Terms at more convenient Seasons, especially as the public good does not require that we should be subjected to the Cold of Feby, or the Heat of August.[33]

Jay decided to leave the Court and its circuit demands to accept the Governorship of New York, relieved that he was leaving "an office . . . which takes me from my Family half the Year, and obliges me to pass too considerable a part of my Time on the Road, in Lodging Houses, & Inns."[34] Justice William Cushing wrote Jay:

> I cannot so heartily relish the gubernatorial office, which is presented to you, and with so much advantage in the choice. It will

doubtless be for the good of New York, as well of the public in general; and what is of some consequence, more for your ease and comfort, than rambling in the Carolina woods in June. If you accept, as the newspapers seem to announce, I must, though reluctantly, acquiesce.[35]

JOHN RUTLEDGE

Aside from Robert Harrison, who never officially participated in the work of the Court, John Rutledge is often listed as the first justice to resign his seat. One of the original six justices, Rutledge never sat with the Court but did participate in circuit court proceedings for nearly a year and a half before resigning his seat. Rutledge returned to his home state of South Carolina to become Chief Justice of the Court of Common Pleas. But when John Jay was elected Governor of New York, Rutledge informed Washington that he was willing to return to the Court as Chief Justice. Washington agreed and gave Rutledge a recess appointment, which meant that the Senate would still have to confirm the nomination once they returned from their break. In the meantime, Rutledge made a speech attacking the Jay Treaty and was the target of much criticism. Not only were critics outraged at Rutlege's opposition to the treaty, they charged that he had become mentally unstable. But mental decline may have been mistaken for depression. Ralph Izard, wrote of Rutledge:

> After the death of his Wife, his mind was frequently so much deranged, as to be in a great measure deprived of his senses; & I am persuaded he was in that situation when the Treaty was under consideration. I have frequently been in company with him since his return, & find him totally altered. I am of the opinion that no Man in the United States would execute the Office of Chief Justice with more ability, & integrity than he would.[36]

Washington refused to recind the commission, but the full Senate formally rejected the nomination five months later by a vote of fourteen to ten on December 15, 1795.

While the charge of mental instability is debatable, the historical record shows Rutledge most certainly suffered from ill health, indebtedness, and severe depression.[37] A little over a week after he was rejected by the Senate, Rutledge attempted suicide—at least twice. On the morning of either December 26 or 27, 1795, he tried drowning himself in the river near his home. Forcibly "rescued" by some locals, Rutledge protested that he had nothing to live for, cared nothing for his children, and had the right to take his own life.[38] It is unclear whether he knew of his Senate rejection as he wrote Washington on December 28, to resign his commission, explaining, "after having made a fair Experiment of the Strength of my Constitution, I find it totally unequal to the discharge of the duties of the Office, & therefore consider it as incumbent on me, to quit, the Station."[39] Though Rutledge's official nomination was rejected by the senate, his "temporary commission" as issued by Washington, lasted "until the end of the next Session of the senate of the United States and no longer."[40] This is likely why Rutledge resigned despite the senate rejection.

JOHN BLAIR

Justice John Blair was in increasingly ill health for most of his tenure on the Court. In 1791 he wrote to Samuel Meredith, treasurer of the United States, concerning payment of his salary, "I expected to have settled with you in Philadelphia; but sickness has detained me til too late to go on."[41] In a letter to Willaim Cushing, Blair alluded to his chronic health problems and, in an extraordinary admission, how they were affecting his work and the disposition of cases:

> I ought to inform you, that a malady which I have had for some years, in a smaller degree, has since I had the pleasure of seeing you increased so greatly as to disqualify me totally for business—It is a rattling, distracting noise in my head—I had much of it at Savannah; besides almost continual cholic. I would fain have declined the decision of several Admiralty cases there, if I had not been told that delay would be greatly injurious, on account of the prize-goods being stored at a very great daily expense. This circumstance prompted me to go thro that business, although in a condition not fit for any; & I have some reason to fear that in doing so I have effected nothing but work for the Supreme court, to undo what I have done. It is, however, a consolation to me, that there is yet a court where my errors may be corrected. When I came to Columbia, I found much business of the same sort; but as in those cases bond & security had been given, & the goods not stored, although I heard an argument on two of them, I thought it advisable (my disorder still increasing) to decline making any decree & adjourn the court. The same cause induced me to decline holding the court at Raleigh, but make the best of my way home, having first done every thing I could to prevent the fruitless attendance of others; & from every thing I have experienced since my being at home, I have little encouragement to

think that I shall be able to attend court in August; I fear I never shall; & if I find no speedy amendment, so as to justify an expectation that I may be again qualified to execute the duties of my office, I shall certainly resign it.[42]

Blair's candid admission of his struggles to decide when and if to participate in deciding cases—and even an admission that he decided cases when he should not have—demonstrate the very real problem of incapacity and mental decline on the Court. It is plain that Blair is torn between what he sees as his duty: the necessity of deciding important issues, and the knowledge that he may be incapable of faithfully executing his office. Blair ultimately decided to resign because of his increasingly poor health, impending circuit duties, and because he could allow Washington sufficient time to name a successor. He wrote to Justice Iredell:

My trip up the country has not brought me any relief from the strange disorder, which for a considerable time past has afflicted my head, and renders me incapable of business, which I have been obliged to neglect, in a degree very painful to me. Sensible of the advantages of my official character, I have not been in haste to resign. I have been willing to take every chance for a removal of the complaint, consistent with a resolution I have taken, in case an unexpected recovery should not prevent it, to resign so long before the Court in February next, as to give the President sufficient time to supply the vacancy against that Court. The time I had limited for that purpose will shortly expire, and then I shall not think of any further experiment . . . My infirmity will, I fear, deprive me of the pleasure of ever seeing you again. God bless you.[43]

Iredell offered to ride circuit for his colleague and urged Blair not to resign, in hopes of raising the spirits and combating the illness of the ailing justice. Blair was not persuaded, however, and replied:

I feel much gratitude for the concern which you and Mrs. Iredell take at my loss of health, for your anxiety that I should not resign, and for your obliging readiness to assume for my accommodation still further fatigue of duty than is properly your own. You may, probably, be right also in the confidence you express, that in this the rest of the Judges would willingly concur with you; but this appears to me so unreasonable an imposition that I cannot think of it.[44]

In his resignation letter to Washington, Blair wrote, "A strange disorder of my head, which has lately compel'd me to neglect my official duties . . . has for some time past made me contemplate the resignation of my office, as an event highly probable . . . I return you now the commission by which I have been so highly honoured."[45]

JAMES WILSON

Unlike his predecessors, Justice James Wilson did not resign upon becoming gravely ill. This is due, however, to Wilson's peculiar financial situation. Justice Wilson had accumulated a great many debts due to speculative business ventures and poor business practices. He desperately needed the salary he earned as an associate justice to pay the rent, the tailor, and his more substantial debts. In 1796, while riding circuit in the south, his creditors had him arrested and he was jailed in Burlington, New Jersey. He wrote his son to bail him out. "Bring with you shirts and stockings—I want them exceedingly—also money, as much as possible, without which I cannot leave this place."[46] Released because of his status as a Supreme Court justice, he hid in the home of his colleague Justice James Iredell in Edenton, North Carolina. Again discovered, this time by Pierce Butler, a former Senator from South Carolina to whom Wilson owed $197,000, he was again put in jail. His health deteriorating, he was released and spent his final days in a cheap boardinghouse in Edenton. On July 28, 1798, North Carolina Governor Samuel Johnston wrote Justice Iredell:

> I feel very much for Judge Wilson. I hear that he has been ill. What upon earth will become of him . . . ? He discovers no disposition to resign his office. Surely, if his feelings are not rendered altogether callous by his misfortunes, he will not suffer himself to be disgraced by a conviction on an impeachment.[47]

For over a year, the Court had been without Justice Wilson. The justices knew that their institution was relatively vulnerable and could be seriously damaged by impeachment proceedings. But before any action was taken, Wilson contracted malaria and subsequently had a stroke. He died on August 21, 1798, only a few hours after Justice Iredell had returned from Philadelphia to be by his bedside.

JAMES IREDELL

Like his friend Wilson, James Iredell did not resign his seat after becoming gravely ill. The arduous duties of riding the Southern circuit year after year were catching up with Justice James Iredell. In 1796 he wrote his wife:

It is impossible I can lead this life much longer, and I see no prospect of any material change. To lead a life of perpetual traveling, and almost continual absence from home, is a very severe lot to be doomed to in the decline of life, after incessant attention to business the preceding part of it.[48]

Nearing the end of the Court's term on May 11, 1799, Justice Iredell remarked: "The extraordinary fatigue I underwent made my head ache a little yesterday, though it did not prevent my attending the Court."[49] A month later, his friend Governor Samuel Johnston of North Carolina wrote: "Let me entreat you, carefully, and in defiance of every consequence, to avoid, by every means in your power, the most distant probability of taking the infection of that fatal fever."[50] Justice Bushrod Washington wrote: "I heard from Judge Chase, with great concern, that you were too much indisposed to attend the Supreme Court. The fatigue to which you had been exposed during the circuit was well calculated to produce this consequence, and you would have acted imprudently, I think, to venture upon so long a journey in your then state of health. It will afford me very sincere pleasure to hear of your recovery."[51] Justice Iredell did not recover, succumbing to his illness on October 20, 1799. Though he felt his circuit riding duties were "a very severe lot," he hung on until his death. Iredell was unique in his commitment to his office and in choosing not to resign.

OLIVER ELLSWORTH AND THE 1800 PRESIDENTIAL ELECTION

Oliver Ellsworth's departure was part of a series of events that led to a fundamental transformation in the departure process. Not only did Ellsworth's departure reflect the dominant concern of arduous travel and poor health, he was also probably the first justice to resign, at least in part, for partisan reasons. The timing of Ellsworth's resignation demonstrates the importance of the presidential election cycle for departure decision making as John Adams and Thomas Jefferson vied for the presidency.

Like his predecessor Jay, Oliver Ellsworth also held the simultaneous posts of Chief Justice and special envoy. Having been appointed to the chief justiceship in 1796 by President Washington, Ellsworth later accepted an appointment as envoy to France by President Adams in early 1799. Like his colleagues, Ellsworth was often ill and unable to attend Court sessions. In 1797 James Iredell wrote, "The Chief Justice has been sick the whole Court, and tho' better is still unable to attend."[52] Frederick Wolcott noted, "He is considerably unwell, & I understand quite hypocondriac."[53] Ellsworth regretted his absence, writing to William Cushing, "Want of health . . . requires that my movements should be gentle & cautious . . . You will be so good as to make my apology with my respects to our brethren."[54]

Still Chief Justice, he became ill while in France, his pains "constant" and "excruciating."[55] On October 16, 1800, he sent his letter of resignation to President Adams, "Constantly afflicted with the gravel, and the gout in my kidnies, the unfortunate fruit of sufferings at sea, and by a winters journey through Spain, I am not in a condition to undertake a voyage to America at this late season of the year; nor if I were there, would I be able to discharge my official duties."[56] President Adams, imploring John Jay to once again accept the office of chief justice, described Ellsworth's situation: "Mr. Ellsworth afflicted with the gravel and the gout, and intending to pass the winter in the south of France, after a few weeks in England, has resigned his office of chief justice."[57]

There was some suggestion at the time that Ellsworth had declined mentally, though the charge was most likely the result of political opposition. Theodore Sedgwick wrote Alexander Hamilton about his displeasure with the results of Ellsworth's negotiations with France, "After this information it will be needless to add that the mind as well as body of Mr. Ellsworth are rendered feeble by disease."[58]

A different criticism of Ellsworth's decision to step down came from presidential candidate Thomas Jefferson who speculated that Ellsworth's decision was a partisan attempt to keep the chief justiceship in the hands of the Federalists. Having lost the presidential election, Adams moved quickly to name Ellsworth's successor. Adams knew that John Jay was nearing the end of his governorship, and fearing Thomas Jefferson and the new regime, the lame-duck president wrote Jay, "I have nominated you to your old station. In the future administration of our country, the firmest security we can have against the effects of visionary schemes or fluctuating theories, will be in a solid judiciary.[59] Jefferson wrote James Madison, "Ellsworth remains in France for his health. He has resigned his office of C.J. putting these two things together we cannot misconstrue his views. He must have had great confidence in Mr. A's continuance to risk such a certainty as he held. Jay was yesterday nominated Chief Justice. We were afraid of something worse."[60]

Although Adams and the Federalists lost the election, they endeavored to win the war. Because both Republican candidates, Jefferson and Aaron Burr, had an equal number of electoral votes, there was no president-elect. Jefferson, and others, speculated that the now lame-duck Federalists, who still controlled Congress, were maneuvering to name the next president. Jefferson wrote Madison, "All the votes are now come in except Vermont & Kentucky, and there is no doubt that the result is a perfect parity between the two republican characters. The Feds appear determined to prevent an election, & to pass a bill giving the government to Mr. Jay, appointed Chief Justice, or to Marshall as Sec of state."[61]

Despite his confirmation by the Senate, Jay was intent on retiring to a quiet family life. Indeed he had already decided not to seek or accept a third term as Governor. He declined Adams' offer, citing the hazards of circuit riding, health reasons, and the Court's lack of legitimacy:

> The efforts repeatedly made to place the judicial department on a proper footing have proved fruitless. I left the bench perfectly convinced that under a system so defective it would not obtain the energy, weight, and dignity which are essential to its affording due support to the national government, nor acquire the public confidence and respect which, as the last resort of the justice of the nation, it should possess . . . Altho' I wish and am prepared to be and remain in retirement, yet I have carefully considered what is my duty, and ought to be my conduct, on this unexpected and interesting occasion. I find that, independent of other considerations, the state of my health removes every doubt, it being clearly and decidedly incompetent to the fatigues incident to the office.[62]

Adams's failed attempt to reinstall Jay led to one of the most significant political accidents in American history—the appointment of John Marshall as chief justice. Though neither Jay nor Marshall nor any other Federalist became president, Adams and his now lame-duck Federalist colleagues were able to install Marshall as chief justice and revamp the entire federal judiciary, creating six new circuit courts to be staffed by newly appointed circuit judges. The Judiciary Act of 1801 also abolished circuit riding for Supreme Court justices, though this was not the driving force behind what became known as the "Midnight Judges" bill. Indeed, President Adams was signing commissions on his last day in office. Though the Jeffersonian Republicans promptly overturned the Act on taking office, the circuit riding requirement for Supreme Court justices was made optional. As a result, in the new era, the departure mechanism of circuit riding would slowly disappear, leaving little or no incentive for the justices to resign. In time, new proposals were offered to prod the justices to leave the bench.

CONCLUSION

What emerges from this account of the Court's early period is the primacy of circuit riding. In the absence of any formal retirement provision, circuit riding became an informal mechanism for departure. Circuit riding assured that justices who were in ill health would eventually have little choice but to resign or force their colleagues to ride circuit in their place. The departures of the first justices demonstrate the fragility of health, the problem of debt, and the difficulty of travel in the nation's early years. Mental decline was also an issue at least in the cases of John Blair and John Rutledge and possibly with others. The timing of Oliver Ellsworth's resignation shows how partisanship is a very real part of the succession process.

The following chapters chronicle the struggle between Congress and the Court over the enactment and expansion of a formal retirement provision and its effects on the departure decisions of the justices. Though partisanship played a role for some departing justices during the new era of "crippled courts," the lingering effects of circuit riding, institutional, and personal concerns were still decisive for most of the justices nearing the end of their tenures on the bench.

3

1801–1868

Crippled Courts

No one seems heartily to exert himself to save the present judges
from starving in splendid poverty.

—Justice Joseph Story

I have devoted six of the best years of my life to the public service,
at great pecuniary loss.

—Justice Benjamin R. Curtis

As in the Court's earliest years, departure in the U.S. Supreme Court during
the first half of the nineteenth century was dominated by the absence of a formal retirement provision. Starting in 1801 circuit riding became optional and
for the next seven decades justices chose to remain in their seats. Financial
considerations coupled with the growing prestige of the Court kept justices in
office. Since resigning meant giving up their salary, most ignored partisan and
institutional concerns and died on the bench. As I will argue, only seven of the
twenty-three justices who departed during this period had partisan concerns.
The Court's workload increased due to population growth, territorial expansion, and increased federal regulation, and each justice became more integral
to the Court's daily activities (see Figure 3.1).[1] As a result, infirm justices like
William Cushing and Henry Baldwin placed a new burden on the institution.
Following the Civil War, the Radical Republican Congress turned its attention to the Court and set out to reform the departure process. The fact that
the infirm justices who were hanging on to their seats were Democrats provided the impetus for change.

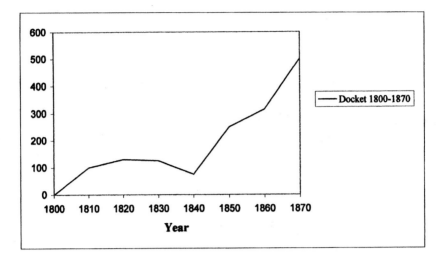

FIGURE 3.1
U.S. Supreme Court Caseload: 1800–1870

ARMY OF JUDGES

THE JUDICIARY ACTS OF 1801 AND 1802

The Judiciary Act of 1801 was the result of many years of attempts to stream-line the federal judiciary. While the Federalists' defeat in the elections of 1800 hastened its passage, the bill was not, as is often thought, a solely partisan attempt to keep themselves in a federal government that would soon be dominated by their opponents.[2] The Republican response to its passage, however, branded it as nothing more than pure partisan maneuvering. President Adams, having been turned down by former Chief Justice John Jay, appointed his Federalist colleague John Marshall to the Chief Justiceship and he was confirmed just as the Judiciary Act of 1801 was passed. As President of the Senate, Thomas Jefferson bitterly signed the legislation and charged that his political opponents "have retired into the judiciary as a stronghold. There the remains of federalism are to be preserved and fed from the treasury, and from that battery all the works of republicanism are to be beaten down and erased."[3] Jefferson, however, narrowly won the presidency and ushered in a new era of Republican politics, even with the Federalists dominating the judicial branch.

The bill established permanent circuit Court judgeships and thereby abolished the practice of circuit riding for Supreme Court justices.[4] The Act also provided for new justices of the peace for the District of Columbia. When the Jeffersonians took office, they quickly set out to undo what they saw as a lame-duck attempt to pack the judiciary with a Federalist "army of judges."[5] The commissions of the D.C. justices of the peace, for example, went undelivered. In December 1801, four of these Federalist appointees sought a writ of mandamus from the Supreme Court to order Secretary of State James Madison to deliver their commissions. The Jeffersonian Congress responded by repealing the Judiciary Act of 1801[6] and delaying the start of the Supreme Court term as part of the Judiciary Act of 1802. As a result, the case against Madison was not heard until February 1803.

Following on the heels of the Repeal Act, the new Judiciary Act of 1802 established six circuits and returned the justices to their circuit riding duties.[7] Many thought the new law unconstitutional, including the new Chief Justice, John Marshall. Marshall argued that justices should not have to preside over circuit courts unless they were commissioned as circuit court judges. He wrote the other justices, "I am not of opinion that we can under our present appointments hold circuit courts, but I presume a contrary opinion is held by the Court and, if so, I shall conform to it. I am endeavoring to collect the opinion of the judges and will, when I shall have done so, communicate the result."[8] Justice Samuel Chase agreed with Marshall, but the other justices did not.

The Federalists wasted no time in publicly responding to the flurry of Republican legislation. Their primary complaint was that the abolition of the courts created under the 1801 Act constituted an unconstitutional attack on the independence of the federal judiciary. Gouverneur Morris said that the Act "renders the judicial system manifestly defective and hazards the existence of the Constitution."[9] Federalists argued that judges were appointed for life and therefore could not be constitutionally removed by a repeal act. Ultimately, the Supreme Court decided the divisive issues in two cases handed down within one week of each other.

In *Marbury v. Madison,*[10] John Marshall held for a unanimous Court that Madison had wrongfully withheld the commissions from Marbury and his district court colleagues. Marshall further held that the section of the Judiciary Act of 1789, which authorized Congress to issue mandamus writs, conflicted with Article III of the Constitution. The Court established its power of judicial review with the invalidation of the mandamus section of the 1789 Act.[11]

The Repeal Act was formally challenged in the Supreme Court in the case of *Stuart v. Laird.*[12] With John Marshall not participating, William Paterson held for a unanimous Court that Congress did have the authority under the Constitution both to establish and abolish lower federal courts. The Court appeased all sides, both federalists with the Marbury ruling, and Republicans by the holding in *Laird.* The Court's skillful judicial diplomacy during this tense, partisan confrontation was not without criticism, however, and as I will discuss below, it was not long before the Republicans attacked the Federalist Court directly with formal impeachment proceedings.

CIRCUIT RIDING REFORMS

It is often reported that, in the midst of this partisan struggle, the desirable reform of alleviating the justices from their arduous circuit duties was seemingly lost.[13] Important reforms, however, were made. The justices' travel load was lightened by the elimination of the Supreme Court's summer sessions in Washington, and the new requirement that the justice assigned to a particular circuit only had to hold one session in each district within the circuit per year. But most important, a quorum of only one federal judge was sufficient to hear a circuit case, often allowing the district judge to convene a circuit court. This flexibility proved crucial to the demise of circuit riding. By the 1840s, the justices had all but stopped holding circuit courts. Communications had improved and the justices became increasingly preoccupied with business in Washington. No longer would the burdens of circuit riding influence the departure decisions of justices.

With circuit riding considerably more manageable, justices no longer had so great a reason to resign their seats when they became ill. If a justice was too ill to travel through his circuit, he did not have to ask one of his fellow justices to make the journey in his place, as had regularly been done in the past. Now a justice could rely on the district court judge to convene the circuit court, as the single judge quorum provision of the Judiciary Act of 1802 allowed. Resignation was seldom necessary and justices held on to their seats until death; only four out of twenty-four justices resigned during this period (see Table 3.1). The twenty justices who chose to remain on the Court until their deaths had an average tenure twice as long as the resigning justices (twenty-two years v. ten years, four months). The average tenure of departing justices in the previous era, on the other hand, was only four years, seven months.

Table 3.1 also demonstrates the high number of justices who had exceptionally lengthy tenures. Eleven justices served for twenty years or longer while eight were close to or surpassed the thirty-year mark. With extended terms common during this era, and aged and infirm justices remaining in their seats until death, calls to reform the departure process became increasingly prevalent and ultimately resulted in the passage of the first formal retirement provision in 1869.

Departing justices in the second era considered a range of factors in deciding whether or not to remain on the bench. While personal health concerns, institutional factors, and partisanship played important roles, the key

TABLE 3.1
Length of Service: Justices Departing Between 1801 and 1868

Justice	*Length of Tenure*	*Mode of Departure*
Alfred Moore	4 years, 1 month	Resignation
William Paterson	13 years, 6 months	Death
William Cushing	20 years, 11 months	Death
Samuel Chase	15 years, 4 months	Death
Brockholst Livingston	16 years, 3 months	Death
Thomas Todd	18 years, 11 months	Death
Robert Trimble	2 years, 3 months	Death
Bushrod Washington	30 years, 11 months	Death
William Johnson	30 years, 4 months	Death
Gabriel Duvall	23 years, 1 month	Resignation
John Marshall	34 years, 5 months	Death
Philip B. Barbour	4 years, 11 months	Death
Smith Thompson	19 years, 11 months	Death
Henry Baldwin	14 years, 3 months	Death
Joseph Story	33 years, 9 months	Death
Levi Woodbury	5 years, 8 months	Death
John McKinley	14 years, 9 months	Death
Benjamin R. Curtis	5 years, 11 months	Resignation
Peter V. Daniel	19 years, 2 months	Death
John McLean	32 years, 2 months	Death
John A. Campbell	8 years, 1 month	Resignation
Roger B. Taney	28 years, 6 months	Death
John Catron	28 years, 2 months	Death
James M. Wayne	32 years, 5 months	Death

Average Tenure of Justices who Resigned	10 years, 4 months
Average Tenure of Justices who Died	22 years, 0 months

Note: Length of tenure measured from the date of confirmation to the date of departure, plus any time served under a recess appointment. Data are presented to the nearest completed month. Ties are broken by the number of days served beyond the last completed month.

Source: Elder Witt, Congressional Quarterly's Guide to the U.S. Supreme Court, 2d ed. (Washington, D.C.: Congressional Quarterly, 1990).

factor for a justice nearing the end of his tenure on the bench was his financial situation. Due to the lack of a pension plan, justices who might otherwise have stepped down remained in their seats, continued to draw salaries, and eventually died while members of the Court. With circuit riding optional, and no retirement provision in place, infirm justices did not resign. The result was a crippled Court. Still, circuit riding continued to take its toll on the Court's dutiful members. Though it was now optional, justices who were able continued to attend the courts in their circuits. Consequently, they continued to complain about it throughout the second era.

IMMINENT DANGER OF SUDDEN DEATH

In December 1816, President James Madison implored Congress to act: "The time seems to have arrived, which claims for members of the Supreme Court a relief from itinerary fatigues, incompatible as well with the age which a portion of them will always have attained as with the researches and preparations which are due to their stations and to the juridical reputation of their country."[14] Madison's plea fell on deaf ears. Congress was still reluctant to abolish circuit riding entirely. In a speech to his colleagues on January 12, 1819, Senator Abner Lacock of Pennsylvania argued that if circuit duties ended, the justices would become "completely cloistered within the City of Washington, and their decisions, instead of emanating from enlarged and liberalized minds, would assume a severe and local character." The justices might also become "another appendage of the Executive authority" being influenced by the "dazzling splendors of the palace and the drawing room" and the "flattery and soothing attention of a designing Executive."[15]

ALFRED MOORE AND WILLIAM PATERSON

The earliest departures in the second era still bore the scars of circuit riding. Justice Alfred Moore was assigned the exhausting southern circuit on his appointment to the Court. After only five years of service and with only one opinion to his name, Moore resigned on January 26, 1804, citing ill health—the burdens of his circuit being too great. The grind of the southern circuit had also taken a toll on Justice Paterson. In 1798, he wrote his wife: "I am fast declining into the veil of life. Every new year warns me of my decay, and that time to me will soon be no more."[16] On October 26, 1803, Justice Paterson's carriage went off a poorly constructed road and plunged down a steep embankment. While his son and wife were not seriously hurt, Paterson suffered injuries to his right side and shoulder that kept him confined to his house. He wrote to Justice Chase that "it was several weeks before I could change my position in bed and rise out of my chair without help."[17] Paterson attended the Court's next session in Washington and continued to ride circuit, despite persistent pain from the accident. He soon fell ill with what he described as an "inflammatory fever" and finally missed a circuit Court, leaving the district judge to preside. He explained to his wife "that a few turns in my room bring on lassitude." He added that his "naturally delicate and slender" constitution appeared "to be almost worn out."[18] Paterson dutifully attended one more circuit Court. His health was deteriorating, however, and he was unable to finish the session. Again, taking advantage of the 1801 Act, he left the district judge to preside. The end nearing, Paterson sought to put his affairs in order. He did not choose to resign from the Court, however. Three months before his death, he wrote a friend, "a wise man ought to endeavor to arrange all his concerns, both for time and eternity, in such a manner, that, when his last hour approaches, he may have nothing to do but die."[19]

SAMUEL CHASE

After considering him for the chief justiceship, President Washington nominated Samuel Chase to the Court as an Associate Justice. Though he originally opposed the Constitution, Chase became a strong Federalist and was publicly critical of Thomas Jefferson and the Republicans. For his public criticisms of Jefferson, who had since been elected President, the House of Representatives voted seventy-five to thirty-two to impeach Justice Chase in March 1804. The following year, he was tried and acquitted in the Senate, as his detractors fell four votes short of the necessary two-thirds. During the trial, he became afflicted with a severe case of gout.

Chase had escaped death before. Still recovering from a respiratory infection, in January 1800, he traveled on horseback with his son, Sammy, to attend the Supreme Court in Philadelphia. At one point in the journey, the ailing, overweight Justice broke through the ice and nearly drowned while attempting to cross the Susquehanna River. He recounted the event to his wife:

> I asked Capt Barney, who said the Ice had been tried, & there was no Danger. Two Negroes went before Me with the Baggage on a sleigh. I followed directly on the Track. Sammy went about ten feet on my right Hand. The other Passengers followed. Myself and Son carried a long Boat-Hook. About 150 Yards from the shore, (in about fifteen feet Water) one of my feet broke in, I stepped forward with the other foot, and both broke in. I sent the Boat-Hook, & across, which prevented my sinking. Sammy immediately ran up, and

caught hold of my Cloaths, and fell in. He got out and lay on the Side of the Hole, and held Me and broke in twice afterwards. I was heavily cloathed. My Fur Coat was very heavy when it got wet.[20]

After five minutes in the freezing water, the Justice was finally placed on the baggage sledge, drawn ashore, and rushed to a nearby house where he stayed for two days recovering from his spills. Justice Chase attributed his rescue to God, whom he said "it has pleased once more to spare me from the most imminent Danger of sudden Death."[21] The gout, however, stayed with him and he was absent from the entire Supreme Court terms of 1806 and 1810. Joseph Story wrote in 1807 that Chase "yet possesses considerable vigor and vivacity; but flashes are irregular and sometimes ill directed."[22] As his health deteriorated, Chase attended circuit Courts less frequently. George Read attributed his absences to "rancorous hostility to the (Jefferson) administration."[23] Chase had also gone bankrupt and used his salary to speculate in real estate. His debts large and finances constantly low, Chase most certainly remained on the Court, in part for monetary reasons. The Court did not meet in 1811, and Chase finally succumbed to his illness that year.

Thomas Todd, Robert Trimble, and Bushrod Washington

Though Justice Thomas Todd was a Jeffersonian, he sided with the majority and Chief Justice Marshall during his tenure on the Court. Todd felt it his duty to ride the 2,600 mile circuit between Ohio, Kentucky, Tennessee, and Washington D.C. Though it rendered him physically exhausted, he did his best to make the trip when his health permitted it. Todd's grueling circuit and numerous illnesses forced him to miss five Supreme Court terms during his nineteen years as a justice. Justice Story wrote, "For some years before his death, he was sensible that his health was declining, and that he might soon leave the Bench."[24] But, like nearly every justice of the second era, Todd had little reason to leave the Court. Health concerns were not decisive because he was not required to ride his lengthy circuit and could even miss meetings of the Supreme Court. In 1823, Story wrote to wish Justice Todd well, describing the indispositions of his colleagues:

> We have all missed you exceedingly during this term, and particularly in the Kentucky Causes, many or which have been continued, solely on account of your absence. God grant that your health may be restored, and that you may join us next year.
> Poor Livingston has been very ill of a peripneumony, and is still very ill; whether he will ever recover is doubtful. I rather think not.

At one time he was supposed to be dying; but he has since been better, and now again has had a relapse. There is great reason to believe that he will never, even if he recovers, be a healthy man again. He is attended by his wife daughter, and two physicians.

Judge Washington has also been quite sick, and was absent for a fortnight. He is now recovered. The Chief Justice has been somewhat indisposed; so that we have been a crippled Court.[25]

Todd remained on the bench until his death in February 1826. Justices Trimble and Washington followed in succession, both choosing to remain on the Court until their deaths. Washington, the nephew of the former president, had dutifully attended every circuit Court up until the year of his death.[26]

JOHN MCKINLEY

Justice John McKinley complained to Congress for years about the difficulty of riding circuit. He never did attend circuit court in Arkansas, stating in an 1838 report to Congress, "I have never yet been at Little Rock, the place of holding the court in Arkansas; but from the best information I can obtain, it could not be conveniently approached in the spring of the year except by water, and by that route the distance would be greatly increased."[27] McKinley's last years on the bench were unproductive due to his ill health. He died after fifteen years as a justice on July 19, 1852. The Attorney General recalled that "for many of the last years of his life he was enfeebled and afflicted by disease, and his active usefulness interrupted and impaired; but his devotion to his official duties remained unabated, and his death was probably hastened by his last ineffectual attempt at their performance by attending the last term of the Court."[28]

NEEDY AND HALF-PAID MEN

In additional to circuit riding, financial considerations were paramount for many justices in the Court's early years. For example, Henry Baldwin was mentally decrepit after only two years into his tenure on the Court.[29] Yet, he hung on to his seat for fourteen years until death in order to continue drawing his salary; and money still had to be raised to pay for his funeral. Though most if not all of the justices could have earned more in private law practice, the growing influence and prestige of occupying a seat on the nation's high Court nearly always won out. Furthermore, aged justices were understandably reluctant to start new occupations so late in life. A resignation meant that a justice would not only lose a prestigious position, but would also stop drawing a salary. The lack of a pension plan made it particularly difficult for justices to consider other factors, such as partisan or institutional concerns, in their departure decisions.

JUDICIAL SALARIES: SPLENDID POVERTY

At the Court's inception, Associate Justices made $3,500 a year, while the Chief Justice received $4,000, split into four quarterly payments.[30] Over the next thirty years, other government positions received increases, while the justices did not. In 1816, Justice Joseph Story and his colleagues asked Congress to increase their salaries above the $3,500 they had always earned. Story informed Congress, in a manuscript written for delivery on the House floor by his friend Charles Pinkney, that "the necessaries and comforts of life, the manner of living and the habits of ordinary expenses, in the same rank of society, have, between 1789 and 1815, increased in price from 100 to 200 percent. The business of the judges of the Supreme Court, both at the Law Term in February and on the circuits, has during the same period increased in more than a quadruple ratio and is increasing annually."[31] When Congress refused, Story had an offer to take over Pinckney's law practice in Baltimore. Story declined the offer and the guaranteed annual income of at least $10,000. Two years later he remarked: "Unfortunately, no one seems heartily to exert himself to save the present judges from starving in splendid poverty."[32]

In 1819, the justices finally received an increase, of $1,000 each (see Table 3.2). Even with the increases, the justices were still paid considerably less than their colleagues in private practice and elsewhere. Justice James Moore Wayne remarked, "What are we in social life without adequate means to live up to our positions and to give to our children the chance of doing so too, with the aid of something to begin life!"[33] North Carolina Senator George Badger sympathetically called the justices "needy and half paid men" adding that they were "hampered in their private relations, with all the inconvenience and embarrassments of a deficient support."[34] Many justices did other things to supplement their relatively modest income. Land speculation, for example, was a common practice from James Wilson to John Marshall. Those justices who found themselves in financial difficulty nearly always chose to remain on the Court, bowing to public duty and prestige, rather than depart for a higher paying job. This is probably the result of self-selection. Public servants may be less likely to be concerned with amassing material fortunes. Benjamin R. Curtis was the lone exception, choosing to leave the bench for higher wages.

TABLE 3.2
Supreme Court Salaries

Years	Associate Justice	Chief Justice
1789–1818	$3,500	$4,000
1819–1854	$4,500	$5,000
1855–1870	$6,000	$6,500
1871–1872	$8,000	$8,500
1873–1902	$10,000	$10,500
1903–1910	$12,500	$13,000
1911–1925	$14,500	$15,000
1926–1945	$20,000	$20,500
1946–1954	$25,000	$25,500
1955–1963	$35,000	$35,500
1964–1968	$39,500	$40,000
1969–1974	$60,000	$62,500
1975	$63,000	$65,625
1980	$88,700	$92,400
1985	$104,100	$108,400
1990	$118,000	$124,000
1996	$171,500	$164,100
2001	$178,300	$186,300

Note: In 1975, Congress passed a law providing for cost-of-living increases for the federal judiciary, ensuring that salaries would not stagnate.

Adapted from: Lee Epstein et al., *The Supreme Court Compendium* (Washington, D.C.: Congressional Quarterly Press, 1992), 35.

BENJAMIN R. CURTIS

A Whig and adherent to the judicial philosophy of John Marshall and Joseph Story, Justice Curtis resigned, after only six years on the Court, at the age of forty-seven. Curtis dissented in the *Dred Scott*[35] case and was upset with what he saw as a politically expedient majority decision by Chief Justice Taney. Curtis stepped down, citing financial considerations as the main reason, with the slavery question also playing a role. He explained his reasoning in a letter to a friend:

> Before (September) I shall have to come to a decision upon a matter of great moment to myself,—whether to continue to hold my present office. The expenses of living have so largely increased, that I do not find it practicable to live on my salary, even now; and, as my younger

children will soon call for much increased expenses of education, I shall soon find it difficult to meet expenses by my entire income. Indeed I do not think I can do so without changing, in important particulars, my mode of life. Added to this, I cannot have a house in Washington, and I must either live apart from my family for four to six months every year while I go there, or subject them to a kind of migrant life in boardinghouses, neither congenial or useful. I had hoped it would prove otherwise, and looked forward to being able to have a house there for six months in a year. But what with the increase of luxury and the greatly enhanced prices there, I have now no hope of being able to do this. I can add something to my means by making books, but at the expense of all my vacations, when perhaps I ought not to labor hard. The constant labor of the summer has told on my health during the last two years. Such is the actual state of the case as respects my duty to my family. Then as regards the Courts and the public, I say to you in confidence, that I can not feel that confidence in the Court, and that willingness to cooperate with them, which are essential to the satisfactory discharge of my duties as member of that body; and I do not expect its condition to be improved. On the other hand, I suppose there is a pretty large number of conservative people in the Northern, and some of the Southern States, who would esteem my retirement a public loss, and who would think that I had disappointed reasonable expectations in ceasing to hold the office; and particularly in my own circuit I believe my retirement would be felt to be a loss which would not presently be fully supplied. But I do not myself think it of great public importance that I should remain where I believe I can exercise little beneficial influence and I think all might abstain from blaming me when they remember that I have devoted six of the best years of my life to the public service, at great pecuniary loss, which the interest of my family will not permit me longer to incur. I have no right to blame the public for not being willing to pay a larger salary; but they have no right to blame me for declining it on account of its inadequacy.[36]

While Curtis was obviously concerned with the relatively low salary of his post, he also cites the rigors of attending circuit court every summer. His letter also indicates that he was unwilling to continue opposing Chief Justice Taney and remain in the Court's minority. Justice Campbell wrote to Curtis after learning of his resignation:

I deeply regret the decision you have made to resign your place on the bench of the Supreme Court. Had I been aware that such a measure was in contemplation, I should have placed before you an earnest remonstrance on the subject. There are public considerations which, in my judgment, render your resignation a misfortune to the country.[37]

ABRIDGMENT OF TENURE, FACILITY OF REMOVAL, OR SOME OTHER MODIFICATION

Following the diminished circuit riding requirement in the Judiciary Act of 1801, the political opponents of the Federalist-dominated courts looked for a new departure mechanism. There is no evidence that the Republicans considered passing a generous retirement provision in order to induce departure. If they had, it is likely that a number of the Federalist justices would have voluntarily departed, rather than stay until their deaths. The Republicans instead opted to test the constitutional provision of removal.

IMPEACHMENT

The Republican crusade against Federalist Justice Samuel Chase was the first attempt to remove a member of the Court. Chase was an outspoken political opponent of the Jeffersonian regime and was, in the eyes of many, the test case for a Republican plan to remove a number of entrenched Federalist Supreme Court justices for partisan reasons. Senator William Plumer, a staunch Federalist from New Hampshire was resigned to the Republican plan, knowing that they had the votes to carry it out.[38] He remarked that given the raw political power possessed by the Republicans, "the Judges of the Supreme Court must fall. They are denounced by the Executive as well as the House."[39] John Stephenson considered the proceedings against Chase "the entering wedge to the complete anhilation [sic] of our wise and independent judiciary."[40] Jefferson himself was reported to have said, "Now we have caught the whale, let us have an eye to the boat."[41] After being impeached by the House, Chase was acquitted in the Senate. Defeated, Jefferson dubbed the removal mechanism of impeachment and conviction "(a)n impracticable thing—a mere scarecrow" and Republicans were forced to look elsewhere for a way to induce departures.

Campaigning for elected office did not prompt departures in the Court's early periods. Though some justices did run for elected office, none considered resigning their seats in order to campaign. John Jay had been elected governor of New York while still chief justice in 1795. Justice Smith Thompson was nominated for governor of New York in 1828, but was a reluctant candidate.

He would have declined the nomination "had it not been, that it would have thrown the party into confusion, and put at hazard some of the Presidential electors. It is a circumstance, I most sincerely regret particularly if I should be so unfortunate as to be elected."[42] Thompson lost to Martin Van Buren, however.[43] In keeping with Court tradition, Thompson did not resign from the Court in order to campaign. Like Jay and Thompson, Justice John McLean also ran unsuccessfully, numerous times, for elected office while sitting on the Court. In analyzing McLean's 1831 candidacy for president, Daniel Webster noted the dangers of sitting justices running for office:

> It appears to me there is one view of the [nomination of McLean for president], which has not yet been presented to the public in its proper strength; that is, the impropriety of setting up a member of the Supreme Court as a Candidate for the Presidency. In my opinion, it is very objectionable for various reasons. It inflames popular prejudice against the Court, in the first place; &, in the next, it more or less weakens confidence in the Tribunal. A judge, looking over popularity, is not likely to inspire the highest degree of confidence & regard. A late writer in the N.Y. Journal of Commerce, in a pretty well written & sensible piece, has brought forward the name of Chief Justice Marshall for the Presidency . . . Much prejudice [is] already against the judges. The present party in power are willing enough to increase those prejudices; & nothing, I think, would aid their views more, than to have an opportunity to tell the People that hereafter our Presidents are to be taken from the Bench. I am quite sure, that such are Ch. Jus Marshall's notions, on this subject, that nothing in the world would induce him to be a Candidate.[44]

SERIATIM OPINIONS AS A DEPARTURE MECHANISM

With impeachment thus-far ineffective, political campaigns being conducted from the bench, and circuit riding optional, the Republicans needed other ways to induce Court vacancies. Republican Justice William Johnson, along with his nominating President Thomas Jefferson, were the key players in attempting to increase judicial accountability and fill the departure void by resurrecting the common-law practice of seriatim opinion-writing.

Johnson became known as the first great dissenter, often disagreeing with Marshall and the Federalist cadre that dominated the Court in the early nineteenth century. He died on the bench under rather bizarre circumstances. His health deteriorating rapidly, probably due to cancer of the jaw, he underwent risky surgery without anesthetics (unknown at the time). A half hour after the operation, he died of exhaustion.[45] But Justice Johnson's significance for departure was not due to his grisly death, but instead owes to his frequent opposition to Chief Justice Marshall's jurisprudence and his handling of Court opinions. Fifteen years after his appointment, Johnson wrote to former President Jefferson, describing the transformation of the opinion process that had occurred and that Johnson himself had largely instigated:

> While I was on our state-bench I was accustomed to delivering seriatim opinions in our appellate Court, and was not a little surprised to find our Chief Justice in the Supreme Court delivering all the opinions in cases in which he sat, even in some instances when contrary to his own judgment and vote. But I remonstrated in vain; the answer was his willing to take the trouble and it is a mark of respect to him. I soon however found out the real cause. Cushing was incompetent. Chase could not be got to think or write—Paterson was a slow man and willingly declined the trouble, and the other two judges [Washington and Marshall] you know are commonly estimated as one judge. Some case soon occurred in which I differed from my brethren, and I thought it a thing of course to deliver my opinion. But, during the rest of the session I heard nothing but lectures on the indecency of judges cutting at each other, and the loss of reputation which the Virginia appellate Court had sustained by pursuing such a course. At length I found that I must either submit to circumstances or become such a cypher in our consultations as to effect no good at all. I therefore bent to the current, and persevered until I got them to adopt the course they now pursue, which is to appoint someone to deliver the opinion of the majority, but leave it to the discretion of the rest of the judges to record their opinions or not ad libitum.[46]

Though Johnson introduced an added measure of accountability to the Court, he was unsure of the effect that seriatim opinions would have on departure. He speculated that they would not force the incompetent justices to leave the bench, because "others would write their opinions merely to command their votes."[47] He did think that reducing the number of justices from seven to four would make it easier for his preference of seriatim opinions to be realized. Jefferson concurred in Johnson's sentiments, but disagreed on the effect that seriatim opinions might have on departure. The former president wrote to the justice:

> I must comfort myself with the hope that the judges will see the importance and the duty of giving their country the only evidence

they can give of fidelity to its constitution and integrity in the administration of its laws; that is to say, by every one's giving his opinion seriatim and publicly on the cases he decides. Let him prove by his reasoning that he has read the papers, that he has considered the case, that in the application of the law to it, he uses his own judgment, independently and unbiased by party views and personal favor or disfavor. Throw himself in every case on God and his country; both will excuse him for error and value him for his honesty. The very idea of cooking up opinions in conclave, begets suspicions that something passes which fears the public ear, and this, spreading by degrees, must produce at some time abridgment of tenure, facility of removal, or some other modification which may promise a remedy.[48]

Jefferson's closing sentence is telling. He suggests that seriatim opinions may provide a means to remove ineffective justices. Public pressure could mount against a justice if he is unable to issue competent opinions in the cases handed down. This in turn could force the issue, with the justice either resigning or Congress initiating an impeachment proceeding. It may also highlight the need for more dramatic change and a move to fixed terms, an idea Jefferson favored.[49] Jefferson wrote to James Madison with hopes of persuading Justices Todd and Duval to go along with Johnson in issuing seriatim opinions, "If Johnson could be backed by them in the practice the other would be obliged to follow suit."[50] Madison agreed with the idea of issuing separate opinions, but was uneasy about approaching the justices, calling it a "delicate experiment." Nevertheless, he did tell Jefferson that he would speak to Justice Todd and through him, reach his "intimates."[51]

Though a formal policy of issuing seriatim opinions never came about, occasionally the other justices followed Johnson's lead and each wrote separate opinions, especially when the chief was absent. Eventually, Marshall relinquished the opinion privilege, occasionally allowing others to speak for the Court. Of course we will never know whether Johnson's prediction of ghostwriting or Jefferson's suggestion of mounting public pressure and removal would have resulted from a policy of seriatim opinion writing. What is clear though, is that both Johnson and Jefferson were acutely aware that there were ineffective justices remaining in their seats past their usefulness.

The failure of impeachment and seriatim opinions as a way to induce departure meant that only death provided a vacancy. As a result, there was intense public scrutiny on the health of the justices in the second era. As the 1833 Supreme Court term was about to begin, Daniel Webster wrote a friend:

You may probably have heard of the breaking out of judge [Henry] Baldwin's insanity. When I was in Philadelphia, he was under medical treatment, & had become somewhat calm. It was feared, however, that any new excitement would occasion the return of his malady, & on that account, his professional advisers will protest agt. his coming to Washington. He had, however, already begun to talk about packing up his books; & whether he will be here, or not, is quite uncertain.

Judge [William] Johnson, as far as I can learn, is on the mending hand, & I suppose we shall have the pleasure of seeing him in his place. He is said to have pretty much abandoned South Carolina, & to be residing in N. Carolina. The fires of nullification I suppose, he found to be hotter even than his own warm temperament. judge [Gabriel] Duval is said to be hearty, tho his ability to hear causes is not so good as formerly, however unimpaired may be his capacity for deciding them.

Chief Justice [Marshall] is understood to be in exceedingly good health, both in the inner & outer man. judge [Smith] Thompson is already here, & as well as usual.[52]

IF MR. CLAY HAD BEEN ELECTED

Partisan motivations for departure are by no means a new phenomenon. As the subsequent analysis shows, nineteenth-century justices were very much aware of the implications the Court's succession process has on constitutional development. The key question, however, is whether the justices based their departure decisions on partisan concerns. The answer, I suggest, is that the lack of a formal retirement provision caused justices nearing the end of their tenures to remain on the Court in order to continue drawing salary. Other considerations, including partisan concerns, were subordinated. Partisanship played a role in only seven of the twenty-three departures during the era of crippled Courts. Though Thomas Jefferson's administration aroused the partisan ire of Federalist justices, it was Andrew Jackson's contentious tenure as president that ignited the strongest partisan feelings among the members of the Court.

WILLIAM CUSHING

After the Senate's rejection of John Rutledge for Chief Justice, Washington's second choice, Justice Cushing, was confirmed as the new Chief. Federalist William Plumer, pronounced Cushing as someone "I love and esteem . . . but Time, the enemy of man, has much impaired his mental faculties."[53] At sixty-four years of age, Cushing declined the promotion, citing age, health, and the "additional burdens" of the position. Though there were increasing claims that Cushing's mental faculties were in serious decline, he did not resign from the Court, which became sharply divided toward the end of his tenure. Thomas Jefferson had appointed three Republican justices to the seven-member body. There was some speculation at the time that Cushing's failure to resign was politically motivated. He did prepare a resignation letter but never submitted it. Two months after Cushing's death, David Howell of Rhode Island wrote to James Madison that the Federalists had persuaded Cushing "to retain his office, for several years under the failure of his powers, lest a Republican should succeed him."[54] Financial concerns also played a role as his friends urged him to remain in his place despite his mental decline.[55]

GABRIEL DUVAL

Though a loyal Jeffersonian before joining the Court, Gabriel Duval nearly always sided with Federalists Chief Justice Marshall and Justice Story on constitutional questions. Following more than twenty-three years on the Court, and authoring only nineteen opinions, Justice Duval resigned almost totally deaf at age eighty-two. He had delayed his resignation for almost a decade, fearing the choice of an undesirable successor.[56] When he learned from the Court's clerk, Thomas William Carroll, that President Jackson was considering Roger B. Taney, Duval, generally approving of Taney, resigned.[57] Jackson officially nominated Taney and Chief Justice Marshall lobbied behind the scenes for Taney's confirmation. Marshall wrote to Senator Benjamin Watkins Leigh of Virginia, "If you have not made up your mind on the nomination of Mr. Taney, I have received some information in his favor which I would wish to communicate."[58] President Jackson's opportunity to make the appointment was nearly thwarted when the Senate voted to do away with the vacant seat. The motion failed in the House and Jackson eventually filled the seat, though not with Taney, whose nomination was "indefinitely postponed."[59]

JOHN MARSHALL

For many years before his death, Chief Justice Marshall had thought about resigning. In 1829 he told Justice Story that he planned "to read nothing but novels and poetry" after leaving the Court. He postponed any decision until after the next election, hoping Andrew Jackson would be defeated. He wrote to Story, "You know how much importance I attach to the character of the person who is to succeed me, and calculate the influence which probabilities on that subject would have on my continuance in office."[60] Though he became ill in 1831 and had surgery on his bladder, Marshall made a full recovery. Andrew Jackson won reelection and Marshall's restored health caused him to further postpone any decision on leaving the bench. He wrote a friend, "Could I find the mill which would grind old men, and restore youth, I might indulge the hope of recovering my former vigor and taste for the enjoyment of life. But as that is impossible, I must be content with patching myself up and dragging on as well as I can."[61] He began making plans for life away from the Court. He chose to live with his son James and construction began on an addition to the house. There was talk that Marshall would resign if Jackson would nominate Daniel Webster as the new Chief. Jackson was willing, but Webster would not make a firm commitment.[62] As the years progressed, Marshall's colleagues noted his declining health. Justice Story was weary of speaking to the chief on the subject:

> I have not written to the Chief Justice on the subject of his health. I know and have long known all his complaints, their nature and character; I have therefore the deepest solicitude when I hear that he is more indisposed than usual. Yet I fear to appear to him too solicitous on the subject, lest it should give him uneasiness, and perhaps precipitate his quitting the Bench. His health is visibly declining, but his mind remains perfect. I pray God that he may long live to bless his country; but I confess that I have many fears whether he can be long with us.[63]

Following the close of the Court's 1835 term, the seventy-nine-year-old Marshall injured his spine in a stagecoach accident. In early June 1835, he collapsed from exhaustion during his weekly mile-and-one-half walk from his house to visit his wife's grave. He was carried home by two men who saw the collapse. He also suffered from a diseased liver which eventually caused his death on July 6, 1835.

JOSEPH STORY

Upon the death of Chief Justice Marshall and subsequent appointment of Roger B. Taney, Justice Story contemplated resigning. He wrote:

> So impressed was I last winter, that the Court was changed—aye & that a sad change had come over us,—that I took it into most serious consideration, what my true duty was; whether I ought not immediately to resign, not from resentment, but from a consciousness, that I

could do no good in future, & whether I might not, by remaining, put
at hazard the little reputation, which I had previously endeavoured to
earn—The result of my own reflections was, that I ought to resign, &
seek some other employment for my remaining years of life—To that
same opinion a few confidential friends, with whom I conferred,
inclined; & I immediately set about to ascertain what other business
I ought to engage in to secure an addition to my private income sufficient to give me a reasonable maintenance. My private fortune is
moderate—but I owe nothing; & therefore a moderate additional
Income was all I wanted. Upon my return home some of my friends
were making arrangements entirely satisfactory to me on this head.
But upon further consideration my confidential friends (&, among
others, Mr. Jeremiah Mason & Mr. William Prescott) were all decid-
edly of opinion, that I ought not to resign—they thought that the
Business of my circuit was too important to be put at hazard under
existing circumstances; & that important public interests required
me—yet for a while—to remain on the Bench.—I yielded; & am still
a judge, but with no hopes for the future . . . While I continue on the
Bench I shall on important occasions come out with my own opinions, for which alone I shall consider myself responsible. But I shall
naturally be silent on many occasions from an anxious desire not to
appear contentious, or dissatisfied, or desirous of weakening the
[word cut off] influence of the Court.[64]

Story's candid letter is important for two reasons. First, he recognizes the
Court as an important policy-maker. Second, and most important, Story is
very aware that his opinions could damage the institutional legitimacy of the
Court. But as the years progressed, Story found it increasingly difficult to
remain in the minority. He again contemplated resigning and wrote a friend:

Ever since the close of the last Presidential election, I have determined to resign my office as a judge of the Supreme Court, thinking
that I could no longer, in the actual state of the country, be of any far-
ther use there. The time of my resignation I had not positively fixed
on, and meant it to be before the close of the present year, and probably much earlier. In case of my resignation I intended to devote my
whole future life to my Law Professorship, and in contemplation of
this, the Corporation have held out to me as an inducement, a great
increase of my salary.[65]

Story wanted to depart under a president of his liking. He would have
resigned while William Henry Harrison was in office, but the president's

death elevated Zachary Taylor to the post. Taylor had been an outspoken opponent of Story. The justice hoped that the next election would bring a more favorable chief executive. Story was hoping Henry Clay would be elected, but instead James K. Polk prevailed. Story wrote to a friend:

> If Mr. Clay had been elected, I had determined to resign my office as a judge, and to give him the appointment of my successor. How sadly I was disappointed by the results of the late election I need not say. It compelled me to consider whether I ought to resign under Mr. Polk's administration, or to await events. After much reflection I came to the conclusion that I ought to resign at some time before the close of his administration; and I left the precise time for future consideration. Many reasons induced me to this conclusion, but a single one only need be mentioned. Although my personal position and intercourse with my brethren on the Bench has always been pleasant, yet I have been long convinced that the doctrines and opinions of the "old Court" were daily losing ground, and especially those on great constitutional questions. New men and new opinions have succeeded. The doctrines of the Constitution, so vital to the country, which in former times received the support of the whole Court, no longer maintain their ascendancy. I am the last member now living, of the old Court, and I cannot consent to remain where I can no longer hope to see those doctrines recognized and enforced. For the future I must be in a dead minority of the Court, with the painful alternative of either expressing an open dissent from the opinions of the Court, or, by my silence, seeming to acquiesce in them. The former course would lead the public, as well as my brethren, to believe that I was determined, as far as I might, to diminish the just influence of the Court, and might subject me to the imputation of being, from motives of mortified ambition, or political hostility, earnest to excite popular prejudices against the Court. The latter course would subject me to the opposite imputation, of having either abandoned my old principles, or of having, in sluggish indolence, ceased to care what doctrines prevailed. Either alternative is equally disagreeable to me, and utterly repugnant to my past habits of life, and to my present feelings. I am persuaded that by remaining on the Bench I could accomplish no good, either for myself or for my country.
>
> I meditate, therefore, to fall back on my Law Professorship, and to devote the residue of my life to its duties, hoping thereby to sustain its influence and its character. I believe the University will be ready to allow me any reasonable compensation I desire.[66]

Story's analysis of the predicament faced by an old-era justice in the dawn of a burgeoning new era is crucial. While partisanship was a driving force in his departure decision, institutional and personal concerns weighed heavily, and ultimately proved decisive. Story did not want to depart under the Democrat Polk, but conceded that the institutional damage of four more years of dissents or the personal costs of acquiescing to the new regime's will was too much to bear. If partisanship was decisive for Story, he would have endeavored to stay until the next election. Story labored intensively to finish all the cases left in his circuit before his resignation. The work left him exhausted and his condition soon worsened. He died on September 10, 1845, before he had a chance to send his resignation to the president.[67] Story's case is instructive for his candid discussion of the key factors in the departure decision.

PETER V. DANIEL, JOHN McLEAN, AND JOHN ARCHIBALD CAMPBELL

Like Story, toward the close of his tenure on the Court, Justice Peter V. Daniel found himself on the side of minority doctrines and outdated philosophies. Unlike Story however, Daniel did not feel that the institutional and personal concerns of remaining on the Court in such a position warranted his resignation. An ardent supporter of states' rights and a reliable vote for his close friend Chief Justice Taney, Daniel's last three years on the bench were spent in vigorous dissent. Rather than acquiesce to majority views, he said, "I am bound to reassert all of which I have endeavored earnestly, however feebly, to maintain, and which I still believe."[68] Though he was assigned to the grueling western circuit, in his last few years he chose not to make the journey. After more than nineteen years on the Court, Justice Daniel died on May 31, 1860, giving President Buchanan, who had decided not to run for another term, his second nomination. Following the election of Lincoln, embittered Democrats had just enough votes to defeat Buchanan's lame-duck nominee and Daniel's seat was eventually filled by President Lincoln.

A year after Justice Daniel's death, Justice John McLean died of pneumonia. He had been in ill health near the end of his tenure on the Court, prompting Justice Campbell to say later in a letter to Justice Bradley that McLean was "wholly incapable of business" at the December 1859 term, even though he was in attendance.[69] McLean tried to leave the Court in the most self-aggrandizing way possible and the best way to assure a preferred successor. He ran unsuccessfully for president four times while an active Supreme Court Justice. Justice McLean died in 1861 after thirty-two years on the Court.

Justice John Archibald Campbell was a steadfast believer in states' rights, and though personally opposed to secession and the war, he felt it his duty to

resign from the Court and join his home state of Alabama in the Confederate cause. Stating his hope for peace and explaining why he did not immediately resign on Alabama's secession, he wrote:

> After the adjournment of the term of the Court there was judicial
> business of importance, but of subordinate importance, to be dis-
> posed of; there were objections to my resignation, on principle, from
> the character and counsel merited respect and deference—statesman
> from Virginia, Kentucky, Maryland, Tennessee, and North Carolina.
> And there was every reason to suppose that my holding the office
> might enable me to contribute something toward securing the great
> blessing of peace and averting from the country the direst of evils—
> civil war.[70]

Following his resignation on April 30, 1861, he accepted the post of assistant secretary of war for the Confederate States of America—an administrative position with no control over military operations or organizations. He
agreed to the post only because of his belief that it might help him to further
promote peace.

ROGER BROOKE TANEY

As the era progressed, the public became increasingly aware of the infirmity
that was often prevalent in the Court. Serious debate began on the need for a
retirement provision, as many of the justices were visibly deteriorating. While
it was often easy to spot a physical decline in many of the justices, it was more
difficult to assess the amount, if any, of mental decay. Chief Justice Taney is
exemplary of this point, as his physical decline did not correspond to his excellent mental health.

The chief justice who took over for John Marshall spent his last few years
on the Court embittered, angry, and frustrated due to the contentious *Dred
Scott* opinion he had authored and the growing rancor between the North and
South. Though Taney's physical health had deteriorated, his mental faculties
never faltered. Despite his infirmities and the changing times, he never considered resigning his seat:

> I have been sick, very sick . . . and have recovered slowly. But I am
> again in my office, and feel as well as usual, but not so strong, and am
> obliged to confine myself to my house . . . my walking days are over;
> and I feel that I am sick enough for a hospital, and that hospital must
> be my own house. Yet I hope to linger along to the next term of the

Supreme Court. Very different, however, that Court will now be from the Court as I have heretofore known it. Nor do I see any ground for hope that it will ever again be restored to the authority and rank which the Constitution intended to confer upon it. The supremacy of the military power over the civil seems to be established; and the public mind has acquiesced in it and sanctioned it. We can pray for better times.[71]

Just before his death, Taney wrote:

I have not only outlived the friends and companions of my early life, but I fear I have outlived the Government of which they were so justly proud, and which has conferred so many blessings upon us. The times are dark with evil omens, and seem to grow darker every day. At my time of life, I cannot expect to live long enough to see these evil days pass away."[72]

Following Taney's death on October 12, 1864, Justice Benjamin R. Curtis spoke of the Chief Justice as he appeared when Curtis came to the Court a decade earlier:

He was then seventy-three years old,—a period of life when . . . it is best for most men to seek that repose which belongs to old age. But it was not best for him . . . During all those years there had never been a time when his death might not reasonably have been anticipated within the next six months. Such was the impression produced on me when I first knew him. His tall, thin form, not much bent with the weight of years, but exhibiting in his carriage and motions great muscular weakness, the apparent feebleness of his vital powers, the constant and rigid care necessary to guard what little health he had, strongly impressed casual observers with the belief that the remainder of his days must be short. But a more intimate acquaintance soon produced the conviction that his was no ordinary case . . .

In respect to his mental powers, there was not then, not at any time while I knew him intimately, any infirmity or failure whatever . . . His memory was and continued to be as alert and true as that of any man I ever knew. In consultation with his brethren he could, and habitually did, state the facts of a voluminous and complicated case, with every important detail of names and dates, with extraordinary accuracy, and I may add with extraordinary clearness and skill. And his recollection of principles of law and of the decisions of the Court over which he presided was as ready as his memory of facts . . .

His physical infirmities disqualified him from making those learned researches, the results of which other great judges have illustrated and strengthened their written opinions; but it can truly be said of him that he rarely felt the need of them. The same cause prevented him from writing so large a proportion of the opinions of the Court as his eminent predecessor; and it has seemed to me probable that for this reason his real importance in the Court may not have been fully appreciated, even by the Bar of his own time. For it is certainly true . . . that the surpassing ability of the Chief Justice, and all his great qualities of character and mind, were more fully and constantly exhibited in the consultation-room, while presiding over and assisting the deliberations of his brethren, than the public knew, or can ever justly appreciate.[73]

CONCLUSION

The second era began with the circuit riding requirement gutted and the health risks faced by the justices were not as acute. Minimal salaries and the lack of a retirement plan kept justices who were nearing the end of their tenures from voluntarily departing. Partisanship played a role in only seven of the twenty-three departures in the second era. Of these seven, only Cushing, Duval, Marshall, and Daniel remained partisan until the end. Story relented and had planned to resign before his death, McLean's partisanship manifested itself in bids for the White House, and Campbell's motivation was allegiance to his home state in the War. Financial concerns often muffled partisan and other influences for the other sixteen justices. Because they could not afford to resign, they were not swayed by otherwise politically advantageous situations.

The failure of impeachment and seriatim opinions, coupled with Courts composed of aged and infirm justices unwilling to relinquish their seats, invited a new level of scrutiny and institutional criticism. Chief Justice Taney's final years intensified matters and magnified the need for reform. Like Taney, a number of the other justices were showing visible signs of infirmity as the era drew to a close. In 1864, Attorney General Edward Bates noted in his diary, "Taney, Wayne, Catron and Grier, are evidently failing, being obviously, less active in mind and body, than at the last term" and added that none could resign unless Congress enacted a pension. He noted that while Justice Nelson seemed physically able, "I do not see that his mind stands more erect than theirs, or moves onward with a steadier gait."[74] Such observations fueled debate on whether a retirement provision for the justices should be enacted. The deaths of Justices Catron and Wayne in the two and a half years after Taney's, did nothing to quell the movement for a formal retirement policy.

4

1869–1896

Old Imbeciles on the Bench

My health is good—the failure is only in my understanding &
powers of locomotion.
> —Associate Justice Robert C. Grier

There ought to be some provision for the compulsory retirement
of superannuated judges.
> —The American Law Review

The 1869 Retirement Act was initially effective in prompting the departures
of infirm justices. With financial concerns taken care of, personal factors such
as the personal enjoyment of the job, the fear of mental decline and death, and
the loss of prestige and social position in Washington, became key for most
justices. As the national government grew, the prominence and prestige of the
Court increased, making the position of justice difficult to give up. The rise of
a national press focused attention on individual justices and the Court's internal functions, placing new pressures on aged and infirm justices. When justices neared retirement age or showed hints of decline, newspapers gossiped
about a possible vacancy.

While the Retirement Act was the most important emergent structure in
this era, as Table 4.1 shows, other factors surfaced and also had an impact on
the decision making of the justices. The controversial election of 1876, where
five members of the Court sat on a special electoral commission with ten
members of Congress, gave rise to an anomalous but highly significant group
of partisan departures. Justices who served on the Court during the dispute

TABLE 4.1
1869–1936 Departure Era: Subregimes

Subregime Years	Emergent Structure	Departing Justices	Departure Mode
1869–1875	1869 Retirement Act	Robert C. Grier	Retirement
		Samuel Nelson	Retirement
		Salmon P. Chase	Death
1876–1890	Disputed Hayes/Tilden Election of 1876	David Davis	Resignation
		William Strong	Retirement
		Noah H. Swayne	Retirement
		Nathan Clifford	Death
		Ward Hunt	Retirement
		William B. Woods	Death
		Morrison R. Waite	Death
		Stanley Matthews	Death
		Samuel F. Miller	Death
1891–1896	Evarts Act	Joseph P. Bradley	Death
		Lucius Q. C. Lamar	Death
		Samuel Blatchford	Death
		Howell E. Jackson	Death
1897–1908	The Field Superannuation Effect	Stephen J. Field	Retirement
		Horace Gray	Death
		George Shiras Jr.	Retirement
		Henry B. Brown	Retirement
1909–1921	Evarts Act Redux	Rufus W. Peckham	Death
		David J. Brewer	Death
		Melville W. Fuller	Death
		William H. Moody	Retirement
		John Marshall Harlan I	Death
		Horace H. Lurton	Death
		Joseph R. Lamar	Death
		Charles Evans Hughes	Resignation
		Edward D. White	Death
1922–1936	Increased Caseloads	John H. Clarke	Resignation
		William R. Day	Retirement
		Mahlon Pitney	Retirement
		Joseph McKenna	Retirement
		William Howard Taft	Retirement
		Edward T. Sanford	Death
		Oliver Wendell Holmes, Jr.	Retirement

saw the occupant of the White House as legitimate or illegitimate depending on their partisan stance. Many based their departure decisions on this as they neared the close of their tenures. Interestingly, this partisan behavior did not last in a period dominated by personal and institutional factors.

Institutional concerns were also present. The workload of active members increased when one or more of their colleagues declined or became infirm. This problem became increasingly acute as the Court's overall workload dramatically increased with the Civil War and Reconstruction. Business growth, increased jurisdiction, and expanding congressional legislation and regulation also swelled the Court's dockets during this period (see Figure 4.1).[1] Congress passed two bills to help ease the burden. The Court of Appeals (Evarts) Act of 1891 created new appellate courts and, for the first time, gave the Supreme Court the power of discretionary review. As Figure 4.1 shows, it had a dramatic effect. The Judiciary Act of 1925 (Judges' Bill) gave the justices further control over their docket though it had less of an effect due to further increases in population, economic changes, and cases concerning World War I. By the end of the era, these factors served to counter the effect of the Evarts Act.

As the era progressed, other factors emerged. Justice Stephen J. Field's choice to remain in his place past his usefulness directly affected three of the justices who served with him. Their plans to retire, rather than burden and embarrass the Court as Field did provided a break in the long-running effect of the Evarts Act that continued to be significant. As the era drew to a close, increasing caseloads ended the influence of the Evarts Act and justices once

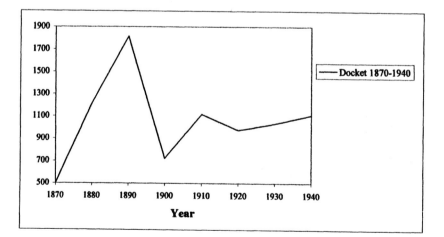

FIGURE 4.1
U.S. Supreme Court Caseload: 1870–1940

again began taking advantage of the retirement provision, just as they had when the era began. In this chapter, I will discuss the first part of the new departure era (1869–1896). I will deal with the second-half of this period (1897–1936) and its emergent structures in chapter five.

DANGEROUS IN ITS OPERATION

The period of Reconstruction following the Civil War was not only a time of conflict between the north and south, but also between Congress and the Court. To keep President Andrew Johnson from appointing justices who were sympathetic to his view that the Reconstruction Acts were unconstitutional, Congress passed legislation in 1866 decreasing the Court's membership from ten to seven; the number would be reduced by attrition.[2] Interestingly, Chief Justice Salmon P. Chase supported the bill in an unsuccessful attempt to persuade Congress to increase the salary of the remaining justices.[3] Although the Court's membership was reduced to eight by 1867, those justices who remained opposed Congress on a number of Reconstruction measures. From 1865 to 1873, the Court voided ten congressional acts, compared with only three during the previous seventy-six years.[4] In *Ex Parte Milligan,* the Court ruled against military trials for civilians.[5] Many thought the ruling a precursor to invalidating the military governments set up in the southern states under the Reconstruction legislation. Thaddeus Stevens said the decision, "although in terms perhaps not as infamous as the *Dred Scott* decision, is yet far more dangerous in its operation."[6]

Before the Court could rule on the question of military government in *Ex Parte McCardle,*[7] the House of Representatives passed a bill that required two thirds of the justices to declare acts of Congress unconstitutional.[8] But, the 1868 bill did not come to a vote in the Senate and the proposal died. Congress did, however, pass a bill withdrawing Supreme Court jurisdiction over circuit court rulings in habeas corpus cases, thereby preventing the Court from ruling on the merits of *McCardle* and the military governments. Though the justices ultimately upheld the congressional act withdrawing their jurisdiction, congressional Republicans did not want to take any further risks with the Court. In 1869, Republican Ulysses S. Grant was elected president and the Radical Republican Congress set out to remake the generally overburdened federal courts, long in need of reorganizing and streamlining, and at the same time, gain some political leverage over the entrenched Democrats in the judiciary.

The Senate passed a bill redrawing circuit boundaries and creating circuit court judgeships to alleviate the burden of the growing federal caseload. The membership of the Supreme Court was increased to nine. The House Judiciary Committee added a measure hoping to further ease the workload of the Supreme Court and dislodge one or two ineffective Democrat justices. The committee proposed a retirement provision for those justices who were age seventy and had served ten years on the Court. It was known throughout Washington that the Court was not operating at full strength, as two of its members, Justices Robert C. Grier and Samuel Nelson, were no longer adequately maintaining their share of the Court's workload. After much debate, the Judiciary Act of 1869 was passed and signed into law, with the retirement provision intact.[9]

As Congress had hoped, this first retirement act had an immediate effect on those justices nearing retirement eligibility. In the twelve years following the Act's passage, four of the Court's aged and infirm justices were induced to retire, including Grier and Nelson. Coupled with President Grant's appointments to fill the new seat created by the Act, Congress had resoundingly succeeded. Congress's initial success, however, soon gave way to failure. The next five justices who became eligible to retire chose instead to remain in their seats and ultimately died in office. Overall, voluntary retirement was more rare than not in the period from 1869–1936. Though twenty-three justices were eligible to retire under the Act, only eleven did so (see Table 4.2). The remaining twelve who were eligible chose not to retire and died while in office. Of the thirteen justices who never made it to retirement eligibility, ten died or were disabled while three resigned their seats to pursue other positions in government.

Congress's ultimate failure to induce aged justices to step down is the result of one simple fact: the justices themselves were not ready to leave. Though Congress felt that seventy was the appropriate age for retirement, nearly every justice who reached age seventy remained on the Court. Table 4.2 shows the length of tenure beyond retirement eligibility. Only four justices retired in the year they became eligible (Grier, Strong, Shiras, and Brown), while the rest remained on for at least two more years. The average length of tenure beyond retirement eligibility amounts to nearly five and a half years for the period under study. Indeed, a number of justices remained in their places well beyond the five-and-a-half-year average. Stephen J. Field and Joseph McKenna served for over a decade beyond their retirement eligibilities and Oliver Wendell Holmes, Jr., chose to remain in his seat for over two decades after reaching retirement age.

What the events surrounding the *McCardle* case and 1869 Judiciary Act show, is that Congress has enormous power to control the Court through its jurisdiction and personnel. It is often thought that the 1869 Act was solely a Republican assault on the federal judiciary. Evidence suggests, however, that Congress was just as interested in taking action to unburden the federal judiciary and responded to the explosion of cases that had occurred in the aftermath

TABLE 4.2
Retirement Eligible Justices: 1869–1936

Justices	Tenure Beyond Retirement Eligibility	Departure Mode
Robert C. Grier	2 months	Retirement
Samuel Nelson	2 years, 11 months, 27 days	Retirement
William Strong	9 months, 25 days	Retirement
Noah H. Swayne	6 years, 1 month, 17 days	Retirement
Nathan Clifford	7 years, 11 months, 7 days	Death
Morrison R. Waite	1 year, 3 months, 24 days	Death
Samuel F. Miller	4 years, 6 months, 8 days	Death
Joseph P. Bradley	8 years, 10 months, 8 days	Death
Samuel Blatchford	1 year, 3 months, 10 days	Death
Stephen J. Field	11 years, 27 days	Retirement
Horace Gray	4 years, 5 months, 22 days	Death
George Shiras, Jr.	6 months, 28 days	Retirement
Henry B. Brown	2 months, 26 days	Retirement
Rufus W. Peckham	11 months, 16 days	Death
David J. Brewer	2 years, 9 months, 8 days	Death
Melville W. Fuller	7 years, 4 months, 23 days	Death
John Marshall Harlan	8 years, 4 months, 13 days	Death
Horace H. Lurton	4 months, 16 days	Death
Edward D. White	5 years, 6 months, 16 days	Death
William R. Day	3 years, 6 months, 27 days	Retirement
Joseph McKenna	11 years, 4 months, 26 days	Retirement
William Howard Taft	2 years, 4 months, 19 days	Retirement
Oliver Wendell Holmes, Jr.	20 years, 1 month, 8 days	Retirement

Average = 5.41 years.

of the Civil War.[10] Just as Congress was not solely motivated by partisanship in passing the retirement bill, most of the justices themselves were also free from political concerns in making their retirement decisions. Of the thirty-six justices departing between 1869 and 1936, only seven could be described in any way as partisan, or politically motivated. Even among these seven, the evidence pointing to partisan motivations is circumstantial at best.

Partisanship was clearly the exception, and not the rule, in the first era under a retirement provision. Nearly all that were partisan in some fashion were on the bench during the Hayes/Tilden election struggle of 1876. Evidence suggests that David Davis was motivated, at least in part, by who would name his successor. Nathan Clifford may have remained on the bench for partisan reasons. Noah Swayne left after assurances that his favored successor would be nominated. Ward Hunt was disabled but would not step down until a change in administration. He finally left after a special retirement bill was passed for him. Rumors circulated that Joseph Bradley and Stephen J. Field remained in their seats for partisan reasons. Chief Justice Edward White plotted with President Woodrow Wilson to have Charles Evans Hughes elevated to the chief justiceship on White's departure. Former President William Howard Taft was clearly partisan in his departure decision, not wanting the liberals to gain his seat and strengthen their presence on the Court. While these cases suggest that justices can be motivated by partisan concerns, the analysis which follows suggests that such cases were rare. Most of the time, justices did not consider such factors. Of course it is possible that they may have been motivated by partisanship, and simply kept it to themselves. What is plain, however, is that the number of justices departing for partisan reasons was on the rise, largely due to the retirement benefit.

What becomes clear from the subsequent analysis is that institutional concerns played a large role in departure decisions. As the Court's workload increased, justices did not want to be a burden to their colleagues and often looked for cues that might suggest they were declining. They were acutely aware of the Court's caseload and concerned about doing a relatively equal share of the opinion writing. They wondered whether the Chief was assigning them fewer and easier cases. Friends and family wrote to them about their health and ability to contribute to the Court. These sources indicate that personal concerns also played a large and somewhat counterbalancing role. The justices enjoyed their work and worried that there would be little or nothing for them to do off the Court. Also, some feared that leaving the bench would hasten their deaths, as they would no longer have the challenge and import of being an active justice. Even family members, who did not want to lose their status in Washington social circles, pressed "their" justice to remain in his place. As the subsequent analysis demonstrates, the retirement provision ultimately did not have its intended effect because the "old fools" had "young spirits."

1869 RETIREMENT ACT

FIRST RETIREMENT PROVISION

Justice Robert C. Grier's mental and physical health had been deteriorating throughout the 1860s. His sense of duty to attend his circuit courts contributed to his decline. In 1862, however, he completely stopped riding circuit.[11] Senator Scott remarked years later: "It was well known that in consequence of Judge Grier's physical inability to travel and sit upon the bench during any long period he was not to be expected at the circuit courts."[12]

In 1866, Justice Grier informed Chief Justice Chase that he needed a study in the basement of the Capitol as he could hardly walk. Still, he insisted that he needed "the exercise both of mind and body—which sitting in court would aford me."[13] The next year, Grier wrote a shaky note to the Chief Justice: "My health is good—the failure is only in my understanding & powers of locomotion."[14] In 1867, Justice Miller noted that "Brother Grier who delivered the opinion[15] . . . is getting a little muddy and may not have conveyed the idea clearly."[16] The infirmities of Justices Grier and Nelson were widely known throughout Washington, leading to more general fears of an "aging Court," a subject Congress debated in 1869.

The retirement act Congress adopted was part of the larger judiciary act that set about to make the federal court system more efficient and tackle its increasing docket.[17] Representative John A. Bingham, chair of the House Judiciary Committee, remarked during the debate on the retirement provision:

> It is well known that at least two of the present justices of the Supreme Court of the United States [Grier and Nelson], although they may live for years, will not long be able, by reason of the infirmities of age, to take their places upon the Supreme bench. It is well known that one of the most eminent members of that bench [Grier] is not able today to reach the bench without being borne to it by the hands of others. It is but fit and proper that such a man should be given the opportunity to retire upon his salary, carrying with him his honors of office and holding his commission until the day of his death. I do not say that he will retire. But this . . . will give him the authority to retire.[18]

Passed in part due to the incapacities of Grier and Nelson, the retirement provision of the Judiciary Act of April 10, 1869, provided "that any judge of any court of the United States, who, having held his commission as such at least ten years, shall, after having attained the age of seventy years, resign his office, shall thereafter, during the residue of his natural life, receive the same salary which was by law payable to him at the time of his resignation."[19] The ten-year requirement was added to ensure the appointments were not made out of patronage to sixty-eight- and sixty-nine-year-old political allies.[20]

Congressional debates display considerable confusion surrounding the retirement proposal. Some worried that retired justices might still participate in the work of the Court. Bingham remarked, "It is clear . . . that the retired judges remain members of the court, although they are not acting judges."[21] Senator Lyman Trumbull responded that the proposed legislation "would continue the persons upon the bench as judges still although they were retired. There would be nothing to prevent their coming back in an emergency and sitting on the bench, and we might have twenty judges of the Supreme Court."[22]

There were a number of proposals and additions that ultimately did not pass. Some wanted to raise the minimum age to seventy-five or even eighty. One of the more controversial proposals would have allowed a disabled justice who reached the age seventy and had satisfied the ten-year service requirement, to retire with full salary if one of his fellow justices was persuaded of the disability and filed the retirement letter with the president. A similarly controversial suggestion provided that if a disabled justice failed to submit his retirement letter to the president within one year of reaching eligibility, the president, with the advice and consent of the Senate, could appoint a supplementary judge to take up the disabled justice's share of the workload. And, on the departure of the disabled justice, the supplementary judge would be elevated to the outgoing justice's seat. The editors of the *American Law Review* argued in favor of this idea:

> There ought to be some provision for the compulsory retirement of superannuated judges, as there is of superannuated officers of the army, or else for the appointment of supplementary judges when existing judges become superannuated, after the example of coadjutant bishops in the Catholic church—leaving the superannuated judge to jog along and do what work he may choose, and give the courts the benefit of his learning and experience, without being under the obligation of burdening himself with labor.[23]

A major shortcoming of the final bill was the omission of a provision for justices who become disabled before qualifying for retirement. As a result, Congress was directly involved in the departures of a number of third-era disabled justices who did not qualify for retirement. Attorney General Edward Bates recognized the bill's inadequacies:

> The principle is right, but the details all wrong. 70 years is no proper time; for a Judge may be much younger than that, yet, mentally or physically incapable of his duties, and still too poor to give up his salary. There ought to be no retired list of Judges; but worn out Judges ought to be respectably provided for, by allowing them to resign, upon a competent pension.[24]

Justice Samuel F. Miller suggested a constitutional amendment might be adopted that precisely stated the causes for removing a judge beyond the already existing language of "high crimes and misdemeanors" included in

Article III of the Constitution. In an address to the New York State Bar Association, he proposed that a jury or similar tribunal be convened to determine whether a judge was disabled and ought to be removed:

> There are many matters which ought to be causes of removal that are neither treason, bribery, nor high crimes or misdemeanors. Physical infirmities for which a man is not to blame, but which may wholly unfit him for judicial duty, are of this class. Deafness, loss of sight, the decay of the faculties by reason of age, insanity, prostration by disease from which there is no hope of recovery—these should all be reasons for removal, rather than that the administration of justice should be obstructed or indefinitely postponed.[25]

The 1869 Act is most often noted for its establishment of a separate circuit court judiciary. As a result of this provision, circuit riding duties for the justices were further diminished. Though up until this period attending circuit courts remained optional, the justices still felt a sense of duty to attend when they could. Under the 1869 Act, however, the justices were now encouraged to attend circuit courts only once every two years, instead of annually.

ROBERT C. GRIER

By 1869, Justice Grier had not attended circuit court in seven years. Prominent Philadelphia lawyer George Harding wrote his friend, soon-to-be Justice Joseph P. Bradley, about Justice Grier's situation:

> Grier . . . is reported to be in good health. He cannot resign so as to obtain the benefit of the late Act before December next. The other Judges would like him & Nelson to take advantage of it & resign immediately thereafter & they will bring all their influence to bear to that end.
>   A kind of pledge was made that he w(ould) resign if the bill was passed in its present form. On the other hand the human nature in Grier my tempt him to hold on. It is conceded that his mind is perfectly strong but that the infirmity in his limbs is increasing.[26]

A few months later, Harding went to see Justice Grier and again wrote Bradley:

> Called on Judge Grier saw [his daughter] & him for an hour. They are moving on to Capitol Hill. He feels his oats & doesnt talk of resigning. I sounded him but he wouldnt respond to my touch. I saw

Swayne, Nelson & Davis. They are greatly exercised at his not resigning. They declared they were going to crowd him about Dec. 1 '69. He sleeps on the bench, drops his head down & looks very badly. Congress will also crowd him if he dont resign . . .

It is supposed that [his daughters] support Grier in his wish to remain on the bench with a view to maintain their social status another winter in Washington. The Court are provoked at this—much of their time being spent in canvassing the subject.[27]

On November 27, Grier's mind and votes began to wander in conference while discussing the *Legal Tender Cases*.[28] With the Court split four to four, the confused Justice voted one way, made remarks supporting the opposite position, and subsequently changed his vote. Justice Miller later remarked, "In a week from that day every Judge on the bench authorized a committee of their number to say to [him], that it was their unanimous opinion that he ought to resign."[29]

After the retirement act had taken effect, Chief Justice Salmon P. Chase, along with Justices Nelson and possibly Stephen J. Field, were sent as a delegation on behalf of the Court to urge Grier to step down.[30] Grier's daughter wrote to Harding about the meeting:

The Chief & Judge Nelson waited on Pa this mor'g to ask him to resign saying that the politicians are determined to oust him, & if he don't, they will repeal the law giving the retiring salaries.

Pa told them if they wished him to resign he would do so—to take effect the 1st of Feb.[31]

Grier did indeed retire as promised. Justice Nelson also took advantage of the new provision and retired on November 28, 1872, due to his declining health. There is no evidence that either of their actions were influenced by partisan concerns. Still, Grier's vote in the *Legal Tender Cases* provided Chase with a five-justice majority and the decision was announced after Grier had retired. Though the case was reversed a year later, Chase's behavior in using the obviously confused Grier to gain a majority, exemplifies a major shortcoming of life tenure: not only that mentally decrepit justices are unable to contribute to the work of the Court, but they may be used by their colleagues to gain majorities on closely divided cases.

Salmon P. Chase

In August 1870, Chief Justice Chase suffered an "unusually moderate" stroke of paralysis.[32] Explaining his situation to a friend:

On the 17th of August, I was attacked, without warning . . . by paralysis, until, when I reached New York, my right side, from the toe to the scalp, was sensibly affected, so that I could scarcely speak intelligibly . . . How soon I shall get well, I can not say. At present, I do not expect to be able to take my place in court at the adjourned term; and I doubt very much whether I shall be able to take it at the regular term, though it is quite possible that I may.[33]

Chase had always been politically ambitious. He had been a prominent member of President Abraham Lincoln's cabinet, serving as Secretary of the Treasury, and was often mentioned as a possible candidate for the presidency. Justice Miller wrote to a friend, analyzing the chief's political prospects in light of his infirmity:

The more recent indications are that the Chief will recover. Whether he will be able to serve efficiently may remain doubtful. But I do not think he will resign unless his is provided with something else. This is not now probable. The paralytic stroke places him out of the list of probable candidates for the Presidency, and thereby removes any inducement for Grant to propitiate him or send him to Europe which is the only alternative to his remaining a figure head to the court. His daughters . . . will never consent to his retiring to private life.[34]

The chief was absent from the Court for a year. He recovered enough to return to the Court and presided over the following two terms, even hoping to secure a presidential nomination in 1872. He wrote his supporters in customary modest fashion: "If those who agree with me in principles think that my nomination will promote the interests of the country, I shall not refuse the use of my name."[35] At age sixty-five he was well short of the minimum age requirement of seventy needed to take advantage of the new retirement provision. The following letter reveals that Chase was not only thinking about retirement when he became ill, but hoped Congress would pass a bill admitting disabled justices to the retirement provision:

Nearly two years ago, when suffering from severe and protracted illness, [I] desired the passage of a bill . . . authorizing the President to accept the resignations of United States Judges, by reason of disability . . . but, having so far regained [my] health as to resume [my] seat upon the bench last October, and attend daily, during laborious and protracted terms, performing a reasonable share of judicial duty, not only without loss, but with steady improvement of [my] health, [I] ha[ve] ceased to take any personal interest in such legislation.[36]

At the close of the 1872–1873 term, Chase's condition had worsened. With little hope of recovery, he wrote to a friend:

> Since the adjournment, which came none too soon, I have made my way to New York . . . It seems odd to be so entirely out of the world in the midst of this great Babylon; but I am too much of an invalid to be more than a cipher. Sometimes I feel as if I were dead, though alive. I am on my way to Boston, where I am to try a treatment, from which great results are promised; but I expect little. The lapse of sixty-five years is hard to cure.[37]

Chase never made it to Boston. After eight and a half years as Chief Justice, he died on May 7, 1873, after suffering a second stroke. Though Chase had been involved in partisan politics before ascending the bench, his departure from the Court was not political.

THE DISPUTED ELECTION OF 1876

In the aftermath of the Civil War, the disputed election of 1876 between Democratic New York Governor Samuel Tilden and Republican Rutherford B. Hayes of Ohio set off a series of events that drew increased attention to the Court. Its parallels to the disputed election of 2000 are many and will be discussed in detail in subsequent chapters. Tilden won the popular vote and it appeared he had won the electoral vote as well. But with Southern states still under military occupation, electoral boards in Florida, Louisiana, and South Carolina disqualified Democratic ballots in an attempt to shift the Electoral College majority to Hayes. Both candidates sent legal staff headed by prominent lawyers into the disputed state of Florida.

Electoral votes were in dispute and because Congress was divided with the Republicans controlling the Senate and the Democrats the House, a fifteen-member electoral commission was appointed. Seven Democrats and seven Republicans were chosen, but controversy swirled around the choice of the final member. There was talk of Justice David Davis being named as the final person to serve on the Electoral Commission that would decide the outcome. Though Davis was a Republican and former trusted adviser to President Lincoln, it was no secret that he disliked the Grant administration. At the same time, the state legislature of Illinois needed to fill a U.S. Senate vacancy and the majority Democrats chose Justice Davis to fill the position hoping that he, in turn, might cast the deciding vote in favor of Tilden should he serve on the Commission. Davis accepted the Senate seat, but refused to sit on the Commission. Justice Bradley was instead chosen and cast the deciding vote in favor of Hayes.

By an eight to seven party-line vote, the commission gave the disputed Florida votes to Hayes. Though Tilden asked his supporters not to riot outside the Capitol, some Democrats threatened to obstruct the upcoming official electoral-vote count in Congress. To help ensure Hayes's legitimacy as president, the Compromise of 1877 was struck, which ended Reconstruction by removing federal troops and effectively turning Southern state capitals back over to the ex-Confederates. Three days prior to his inauguration, the Electoral College made Hayes president by a single vote.

The parallels with the 2000 election are startling.[38] The Democratic candidate won the popular vote but eventually lost disputed electoral votes. The state of Florida was crucial and both campaigns sent counsel to the state to represent their interests. Congress was divided on partisan lines with one party controlling one body and the opposition controlling the other.[39] The Supreme Court was called upon to effectively resolve the election in a direct way and the vote on a single justice determined the outcome.

The partisanship within the Court between Hayes supporters and Tilden supporters carried over into their departure decisions. Justices Davis, Clifford, Swayne, and possibly Strong based their decisions to stay or leave the bench based on whether or not they supported the president. The partisanship among these justices is particularly interesting given the initial success of the new retirement provision.

DAVID DAVIS

David Davis had been President Lincoln's campaign manager and close adviser before serving on the Court. Once on the bench, he lamented the Court's increased workload since the end of the Civil War and dreaded the longer terms which had previously gone from December through March, and now lasted from October until May: "To be on a strain fr 2nd Monday of October till the 1st of May is wearing to both body & mind . . . I get so worn every Spring that I think I will never go back . . . I ought to quit & stay at home with my wife."[40] Disgusted with the corruption of the Grant administration and frequently courted as a potential Democratic nominee for the presidency, Justice Davis endeavored to leave the Court, but was persuaded by his friends to stay until Grant's term ended.[41]

After accepting the Illinois Senate seat, but declining to cast the deciding vote on the 1876 electoral commission, Davis resigned from the Court on March 5, 1877, the day that Hayes, was inaugurated as president of the United States.[42] Though Davis was unhappy on the Court, politics played a role in his departure. Had his name not been mentioned for the commission, Illinois Democrats probably would not have offered him the Senate seat.

There was speculation that the sixty-five-year-old John Archbald Campbell, who left the Court in 1861, might be nominated by Hayes to fill the Davis vacancy. Justice Miller was constantly preoccupied with the inner workings of the Court and commented on the effect such an appointment would have on the aging institution:

> There is no man on the bench of the Supreme Court more inter-
> ested in the character and efficiency of its personnel than I am. If I
> live so long, it will still be nine years before I can retire with the
> salary. I have already been there longer than any man but two, both
> of whom are over seventy.
>
> Within five years from this time three other of the present
> Judges will be over seventy. Strong is now in his sixty ninth, Hunt in
> his sixty eighth and broken down with gout, and Bradley in feeble
> health and in his sixty sixth year.
>
> In the name of God what do I and Waite and Field, all men in
> our sixty first year, want of another old, old man on the bench.
> Paschal[']s *Constitution* [43] makes Campbell seventy-five some time
> this year, and Judge Clifford thinks that when they served together
> they were about the same age and he is near seventy-four. Campbell
> looks five years older. I have told the Attorney General that if an old
> man was appointed we should have within five years a majority of old
> imbeciles on the bench, for in the work we have to do no man ought
> to be there after he is seventy. But they will not resign. Neither
> Swayne nor Clifford whose mental failure is obvious to all the court,
> who have come to do nothing but write garrulous opinions and
> clamor for more of that work, have any thought of resigning. [44]

Campbell was not called back into service, but the aging and infirm Justices Swayne, Clifford, William Strong, and Ward Hunt would provide for much controversy and a flurry of departures in a period of a little over a year.

NATHAN CLIFFORD

After nineteen productive years on the Court, Justice Clifford began to men-tally decline in 1877 at the age of seventy-three. His decision-making ability was affected. In the case of *United States v. Morrison* (1878), [45] he voted with the majority in conference but when he was assigned the opinion by Waite, Clifford told the Chief, "I think I did not vote for the judgement." [46] Two years later, Justice Clifford suffered a stroke but still made an attempt to continue his duties on the Court. It was clear to those around him, however, that he was unable to do so. In November 1880, New York Senator Roscoe Conkling wrote of Clifford's condition:

> Judge Clifford reached Washington on the 8th of October . . . I saw him within three hours after his arrival, and he did not know me or any thing, and though his tongue framed words there was no sense in them.
>
> An effort was made . . . to call it paralysis because he was taken suddenly between Boston and Washington, but there was no paralysis in the case. He remains yet about in the same condition. His general health good as usual. Able to ride out and walk about the house, but his mind is a wreck and no one believes that he will ever try another case, though the one idea which he seems to have is a desire to get to his seat in the capitol. I have seen him twice and the other judges have also. It is doubtful if he knew any of us. His wife thought I could do more to persuade him to return home than any one else and sent for me. But when I saw him I saw also that it was no use to try for he introduced me to his wife twice in ten minutes, though I have known her for eighteen years quite intimately. His work is ended though he may live for several years.[47]

Clifford had been eligible to retire with salary since 1871, but still bitter over President Hayes's disputed election, he may have endeavored to remain on the Court until a Democratic president could name his successor.[48] Justice Miller wrote of the Court's precarious situation in November, 1880:

> In this condition of affairs Judges Swayne and Strong both announced to their brethren a short time since their purpose of resigning. They had agreed it seems to resign simultaneously but with Clifford and Hunt disabled, they would leave us without a quorum. And as the Senate might not confirm other nominations these gentlemen have hesitated. Swayne has never wished to resign, but I think that influences have been brought to bear which have induced him to agree to let Hayes have an opportunity to appoint Stanley Matthews. But as the old fox don't want to go he readily seizes on the objection that the business of the court might be suspended to delay action.
>
> Things were in this condition when Judge Strong with whom I have always been on terms of great friendship and confidence told me yesterday at conference, that without reference to Swayne's action he should send in his resignation during the second week of the approaching session of Congress. Thus far what I have said is based on satisfactory evidence. I now enter the region of conjecture.

It is said that the President is anxious to secure Matthews' confirmation at the hands of the Senate, by filling Strong's place with a Southern man. As Bradley really belongs to Strong's circuit, and wants to have it when Strong resigns it is thought to be a good occasion to appoint a Judge from the South. Whether Swayne will resign at once, or will await until some one fills Strong's place no one can tell for he is both selfish and unreliable. But that Strong will resign I have no doubt and that there is serious thought of nominating his successor from Bradley's circuit is I think very probable.

I have been told that the President favors [Circuit Judge] Woods [of Alabama], and that Swayne who is for some reason fond of Woods is trying to make his own resignation (desired for the President for Matthews' sake) dependent on the nomination of Woods. This is a nice little plan but complex and may fail of carrying out.[49]

Chief Justice Waite concurred in Miller's assessment of the weakened Court, "Both Judges Clifford and Hunt are I fear permanently disabled. Rumor says we are to lose another justice . . . this week."[50]

WILLIAM STRONG

Justice Strong stepped down on December 14, 1880, at the age of seventy-two. He said that it was better to leave while people ask "Why does he?" rather than wait too long and have people exclaim "Why doesn't he?"[51] Justice Bradley remarked that "he resigned . . . in full vigor of his powers, and much to the regret of his brethren on the bench."[52] Justice Miller added, "The loss of Judge Strong is a heavy one to the court, while the men occupying the other places could well be spared."[53] Strong had served on the Electoral Commission in 1877 and voted to seat Hayes. There is no direct evidence, however, that Strong left in order to have Hayes name his successor. The evidence that does exist is at best mixed. Strong's plan to depart with Justice Swayne was prompted at least in part by his desire to relieve the Court from its then embarrassing membership, which consisted of the disabled Justices Clifford and Hunt.

NOAH SWAYNE

A little over a month later on January 24, 1881, Justice Swayne also retired. His mental abilities began to fail him about two years earlier and he contemplated departure.[54] On his last vacation before stepping down, Swayne wrote to Justice Bradley:

I have no doubt you will resign at the close of your seventieth year or
very soon afterwards & I think you ought to. You need have no
apprehension that you will not find enough to do—constantly and
agreeably to employ you—nor that a moment of your time will necessarily be attended with a sense of tedium or ennui. You will be
brighter & happier than you have been for the last five years or will
be in the future while you remain on the bench.[55]

Swayne's departure came less than two months before lame-duck President Hayes left office. Hayes had pressured Swayne to step down, and it was
only after the assurance that a close friend, Stanley Matthews, would be
Swayne's successor, that the justice finally agreed to leave the bench.[56] Hayes's
nomination was not acted on by the Senate because of Matthews's question-
able financial background, but President Garfield resubmitted Matthews's
name and won confirmation.

Swayne's interaction with and assurance from Hayes shows a clear political element in his departure decision. The Constitution states that appointments to the Court will be made by the president with the advice and consent
of the Senate. It does not say with the advice and consent of the Senate and
the outgoing justice. As such, Swayne's actions clearly fall outside the necessarily political process envisioned by the founders. When justices act as
Swayne did, seeking an audience with the president, they enter the appointment process in a directly political way. Though Swayne's departure provides
an interesting case of political maneuvering, it is rare for justices to act in such
a manner.

Six months after Swayne's departure, Justice Clifford died. He had not sat
on the bench in over a year since his stroke and, though eligible, he chose not
to retire for partisan reasons. Instead, he hoped to recover with rest, and for a
short time he looked to be improving.[57] His infirmities caught up with him,
however, and he died on July 25, 1881, right after President Garfield had been
shot. Clifford's seat was filled by Garfield's successor, President Arthur.

WARD HUNT

Justice Hunt had been in ill health and missed a number of sessions in 1877.
By December 1878, he was no longer able to participate in any work at the
Court. In January of 1879 he suffered a disabling stroke of paralysis and lost
his ability to speak. Justice Miller discussed Hunt's situation:

Judge Hunt came to Washington ten days ago with no improvement
in his condition and it is quite certain now that he will never go on

the bench again. He will not resign while Hayes is President because [Senator Roscoe] Conklin[g] does not want Hayes to appoint his successor. It was well ascertained last winter that if Hunt had resigned [Republican Senator] Edmunds [of Vermont] whose state is in the circuit would have been nominated and confirmed, and Conklin[g] kept Hunt from resigning after he had made up his mind to do so.[58]

Retirement was not an option for Hunt, as he had not reached the ten-year minimum service requirement. Chief Justice Waite was particularly concerned at the Court's backlog of cases that had resulted from the disabilities of Hunt and Clifford, and the frequent absences of Field and Miller, resulting from their distant circuit duties. As early as 1879, Waite attempted to persuade Hunt to step down for the good of the Court. Hunt's son informed the Chief Justice that his father would not leave the Court until a pension law was passed by Congress on his behalf. The Chief Justice wrote back that the "docket is enormous" and "we have considered more than one thousand cases," adding:

I have been led to the conclusion that if your father should resign at the commencement of the session of Congress his place would probably be filled, and that a law could be got through granting him his pension quite as easily after his resignation as before, if not better. However, that is a matter we can talk about when you come here. I want your father to act firmly on his own judgments.[59]

Senator David Davis, who had left the Court in 1877, introduced a general retirement bill that would extend the provisions of the 1869 act to justices who became disabled before the age seventy, ten-year minimum. The Senate Judiciary Committee never acted on the proposal. A year later, Davis proposed a special retirement bill for Justice Hunt specifically, that would enable him to leave the Court with full benefits. The special act had numerous opponents. For example, one House member proposed that the Judiciary Committee could "in its wisdom recommend a plan by which Judge Swayne, who is still able, still in the full vigor of his glorious intellect, could be restored to the court, to take the position which would be assigned to the new judge. That would be better than establishing any precedent like that proposed in this bill."[60] Despite the criticism, the special retirement bill passed,[61] and Justice Hunt resigned that day. Even though Hunt wished to hold out for a change in administration and see his friend Roscoe Conkling fill the vacancy, the special retirement provision trumped his political concerns and plainly triggered his departure. Conkling was nominated by President Arthur to take Hunt's place, but following confirmation by the Senate, Conkling declined the post.

BRIEF STABILITY

After Hunt's departure, and the appointments of Justices William B. Woods, Stanley Matthews, Horace Gray, and Samuel Blatchford in a little over a year, the Court's membership remained stable for the next five years. Justice Miller noted:

> I believe that the Court is as strong mentally and physically as it ever was and is as capable of usefulness as it has ever been . . .
>
> The reporter and some of the Judges say that more important and well written opinions have been delivered at this term than at any previous one. I doubt this as affirming both propositions. But I think it is true that it has been a successful term and many questions of importance have been decided.[62]

With the four new justices making the Court stronger than it had been in a long time, the 1869 Retirement Act seemed to have served its purpose. Of the five justices who became eligible for retirement since its enactment, only Justice Clifford did not take advantage of the new provision. Interestingly, when coupled with the events surrounding the 1876 election, the retirement provision had the unintended effect of making it easier for justices to engage in succession politics as evidenced by the behavior of Justices Davis, Clifford, Swayne, and possibly Strong. The bill's success at inducing aged and infirm justices to step down, however, was short-lived.

After the special retirement bill was passed for Justice Hunt in 1882, fifteen years went by and eight justices died on the bench before the retirement provision was used again, and then only reluctantly. The 1869 Retirement Act did not provide the inducement that Congress had originally hoped for. Though there were individual cases of early retirement, no institutional norm developed. Personal concerns began to play a more prominent role. While justices in retirement continued to draw salary, there were other benefits that they did not have. Not only did retired justices no longer have the prestige of being federal judges, their social status declined. The justices and their families felt that with the relinquishing of power that came with retirement, Washington's social circle would no longer seek to cultivate relationships with them. Retirement often meant leaving Washington and returning home. Wives and sisters were especially important in this factor, often urging their husband or father to remain on the bench.

Another influential factor for many justices was the fear of serious mental decline on retirement. Without the mental rigor of the cases to keep them sharp, justices feared that retirement would bring on mental disability, insanity, and even death. The 1937 and 1939 Retirement Acts would address all these issues, but through 1936, the personal concerns of loss of prestige, fear of mental decline and death, and loss of social status played an important role in keeping a number of retirement-eligible justices from stepping down. The most important factor, however, was a key piece of legislation passed in 1891.

THE EVARTS ACT

The Circuit Court of Appeals Act of 1891, popularly known as the "Evarts Act" after the Chair of the Senate Judiciary Committee, William Evarts of New York, created the Courts of Appeal and made District Courts the primary trial courts at the Federal level.[63] Also the old Circuit Courts remained in place out of tradition, but stripped of their appellate jurisdiction, they were relegated to conducting Federal trials, along with the District Courts. Another important change was that it had the practical effect of finally ending the practice of circuit riding for the justices. Though circuit riding was made discretionary in 1801 when justices no longer had to be present to constitute circuit courts, they endeavored to attend out of a sense of duty. Though it was effectively optional, circuit riding was still practiced by some of the justices through the 1880s. Still, many had been neglecting their circuits, especially when they felt the journeys would damage their heath. Justices were never taken to task by Congress for failing to attend. The Evarts Act officially made attendance "optional" and the justices interpreted this as congressional approval to stop the practice. Congress did not officially abolish the circuit courts, and with them the formal practice of circuit riding, until 1911.[64] Effectively ending the practice, however, served to lessen the attractiveness of retirement.

The more important effect of the Evarts Act, however, was its dramatic influence on the Court's docket. The justices' caseload steadily shrunk from a high of 1,750 cases prior to the Act's passage to low of 500 cases ten years later (see Figure 4.1). For the first time, the Court had the power of discretionary review. The considerably lightened workload and the luxury of largely picking and choosing their own cases made the job much more enjoyable. No longer burdened with their circuits, and enjoying newfound discretion, justices found the option of retirement less appealing.

Of the eight justices who died successively in the fifteen years after Hunt's departure, William B. Woods, Stanley Matthews, Lucious Q. C. Lamar, and Howell Jackson were ineligible to retire, not having reached age seventy. While Woods and Matthews died suddenly, Lamar and Jackson had relatively lengthy illnesses that may have led to their retirements, had they been eligible.[65] Instead, their illnesses caused the Court to function at less than full strength. Conversely, Chief Justice Morrison R. Waite and Justices Miller,

Bradley, and Blatchford chose to stay on the bench well after reaching retirement eligibility. For these four justices, partisan concerns were not an issue. The personal satisfaction that each received from his work on the Court made retirement a nonoption. The cantankerous Stephen J. Field also did not see retirement as an option, but finally agreed to leave after securing a number of special considerations.

MORRISON R. WAITE

Chief Justice Waite was a notorious workaholic. He worked long hours, weekends, and even took his work with him on vacations. Even during his first term as Chief, his son had begged him to slow down.[66] Years later, Waite explained to his wife:

> You know better than I, that I must have just such work as I do have, or I cannot exist. More than fifty years of life, which has never known a minute that could be devoted to idleness, must be hard worked or it will go off on a switch. I do work all the time, but I am not overworked. I sleep every night when I get tired and go to bed, no matter what the hour . . . You need not feel afraid. I was never so well in my life, and am taking good care of myself.[67]

It soon became apparent to those around him that the Chief Justice was indeed overworked. During the 1884–1885 term, Court Reporter Bancroft Davis noted, "Waite is far from well or strong, but won't admit it to himself, and may work on and break down before Spring comes." In December, Waite became physically ill and decided to take a leave of absence from the Court in order to recover. Justice Miller, as senior associate justice, filled in for Waite and performed all the extra administrative work that the Chief is required to attend to. Miller wrote, "It is this which caused his illness. He is much broken down and if [he] does not diminish his excessive labours, he will not be capable of any work in a year or two more. He leaves tomorrow for Florida to be gone a month for recuperation."[68]

As expected, Waite grew restless while away from the Court and hinted at an early return. His son disapprovingly wrote back:

> You certainly do not realize how sick you have been. Your term will be up, if your health holds out, a year from next November. You cannot possibly see the docket cleaned or an impression made in that time. Neither will you get one particle more credit or honor at that time whether you postpone your coming home now 10 days or not.[69]

Waite's colleagues on the bench expressed similar sentiments. Justice Miller suggested that Waite pace himself and go about his work slowly.[70] Justices Blatchford, Harlan, and Matthews wrote, "We talked it over & think you should not try to come back & do work the rest of this term. It would be a sad thing to have a new Chief Justice in the next 4 years, and we all feel that it is more desirable for the country & the Court to have you for Chief Justice than that you should do a little more work, too soon."[71]

Despite the pleas, Waite was back on the bench a month later and working as hard as he had always done. On November 29, 1886, Waite reached his seventieth birthday and became eligible for retirement. It is not surprising, however, that the Chief Justice who worked incessantly never even contemplated departing. In March 1888, he became ill while working on the *Bell Telephone Cases*.[72] Though in a fragile state, he endeavored to take his seat on the bench and deliver the opinion. He remarked that his absence from the bench would appear in the newspapers and his wife, then away on a trip to California, would needlessly worry. Once he reached the Court, however, he was unable to draw enough strength to read the opinion. Attorney General Augustus H. Garland later recalled the scene, "It was evident to the observer that death had almost placed its hand upon him."[73] On returning home, Waite was diagnosed with severe pneumonia. After fourteen years on the Court, Chief Justice Waite died on March 23, 1888.

SAMUEL F. MILLER

Justice Miller had been assiduously preoccupied with the inner workings of the Court throughout his tenure. His ideological defeats and failure to be elevated to the Chief Justiceship led to a growing restlessness and disenchantment with his work. He said "its monotony . . . pall[s] upon my taste and feelings." He continued:

> I feel like taking it easy now. I can't make a silk purse out of a sow's ear. I can't make a great Chief Justice out of a small man. I can't make Clifford and Swayne, who are too old resign, nor keep the Chief Justice from giving them cases to write opinions in which their garrulity is often mixed with mischief. I can't hinder Davis from governing every act of his life by his hope of the Presidency, though I admit him to be as honest a man as I ever knew. But the best of us cannot prevent ardent wishes from coloring and warping our inner judgment . . .
>
> I am losing interest in these matters. I will do my duty but will fight no more. I am perhaps beginning to experience that loss of interest in many things which is the natural result of years, and which wise men have felt the necessity of guarding against as age approaches.[74]

At age sixty-four, he began to slow down in order to reach retirement age. He explained to a friend that his circuit duties were the first to go:

> I find myself more affected by the hot weather last summer and this than ever before and my experience of the benefit of sea bathing the two last summers has fixed my purpose of spending as much of each summer by the sea shore as I can. If I live out my six years, necessary to enable me to resign with my salary, I shall do but very little on the circuit during that time. I am feeling sensibly the need of more rest, and have earned the right to have it. In Judge McCrary I have a fresh hard working safe and acceptable Judge and can leave the business of the circuit to him and to the District Judges.[75]

Miller had once said that no justice should remain on the Court past the age of seventy.[76] Indeed, he had seen his colleagues, Clifford and Hunt become unable to carry out their duties some years before. However, as he began the term in which he turned seventy, he hedged on retiring:

> Our Court had its formal opening yesterday, and when I have finished this letter I shall start to begin anew the labors of the court for nine months with such slight intermissions as are necessary for the useful performance of that work itself. I believe I have told you that I do not feel the interest in it that I once did, and which my conscience tells me I ought to feel now. I am well resolved that I will not do my own and other men's work in future, and yet I have been so resolved before and have done it. I do not believe a healthy man of seventy years accustomed to any kind of work, mental or physical, ought to quit it suddenly. But I do believe that when that time comes he will be the better for a moderation in the severity and uninterrupted continuousness of that labor.[77]

After visiting Miller two days before his seventieth birthday, his brother-in-law wrote, "The Judge will not resign at present—Says his wife is strongly opposed to it, that it wd weaken their social position influence &c"[78] Miller became concerned that after reaching retirement age, others might call for his resignation or suggest that he was slowing down. He wrote, "I did not perceive while on the circuit any overt symptoms of a design to have me resign, though there are doubtless men who think they could fill the place and as democrats they ought to have a chance."[79] Miller's remark was a clear indication of his intent to step down when he was no longer able to adequately perform his duties. Miller was looking for cues that he might be declining, but found none. In an era of dramatically increased workload, justices knew how important it was to have a fully functioning Court.

Two years later, Miller felt he was still able to contribute fully to the Court's workload and believed his colleagues also felt the same. He wrote, "The Chief Justice recognizes no claims of old age in me to abatement of service, for he has given me quite a full share of opinions to write both as to number and importance."[80] When Miller learned that his old circuit colleague, District Judge Samuel Treat of St. Louis was retiring, the Justice wrote, "So you have done it at last—Well, I don't blame you. The work is so hard and the pay so inadequate, and you have so well earned your right to the little salary for the remaining years. I almost wish I had the courage to follow your example."[81] Miller never did find the courage to step down and on October 14, 1890, he died at the age of seventy-four.

JOSEPH BRADLEY: THE PUREST FICTION

Much to Justice Bradley's consternation, rumors of his retirement flew constantly around Washington during his later years on the Court, no doubt due to his decisive vote to award the election of 1876 to Republican Rutherford B. Hayes. He turned seventy in March 1883 and, though eligible for retirement, Bradley did not step down. In November 1884 articles appeared in the press speculating on Bradley's successor and reporting that he planned to retire at the close of the term to enable the Republican President Arthur to name his successor. Two circuit judges wrote Bradley assuring him that his mental capacity had not diminished in the slightest and said that they hoped the rumors were untrue.[82] Bradley wrote back:

> I have received your very kind letter expostulating against my resigning my seat on the Bench. All the Newspaper talk on the subject is the purest fiction. I have never spoken to a soul in relation to the matter, one way or the other, except to evade it, as best I could, when it was broached by others. No one has asked me to resign or even hinted that I should do so: on the contrary whoever has spoken about it all has expressed the hope that I would not resign. My brethren on the bench here agree with you, that I ought not; intimating that Judge Strong made a great mistake in doing so. How soon that idea may enter my head I cannot tell; it has not seriously done so yet. My health is good—and better than usual; and, if the respect manifested by my associates for my views on cases and questions of law, is to be regarded as evidence of much weight, my faculties have not greatly deteriorated.[83]

On February 17, 1890, Justice Brewer described Bradley's condition in an address to a group of law students, "He looks all dried up, but there is more vinegar and hard fight in him than in twenty of you boys."[84] In the Spring of 1891, he suffered an attack of "la grippe" sapping most of his strength. Over the summer he failed to recover, but nevertheless, returned to the Court for the start of the new term in October. After a few weeks, his condition worsened and he returned home to rest. After twenty-two years on the bench, Justice Bradley died in January 1892 at the age of seventy-eight.

CONCLUSION

The 1869 Retirement Act ushered in a new era of retirement as a number of justices chose to take advantage of its provisions and voluntarily depart. But the statute's effectiveness was short-lived, as justices were reluctant to give up their seats for personal reasons such as loss of prestige and fear of death. The disputed election of 1876 fanned the flames of partisanship as the Court was asked to participate in choosing the president. The Court's partisanship in deciding the election carried over into their departure decisions. As the era progressed and the Court's membership changed, the election no longer influenced retirement decisions. Workload was a factor as the Evarts Act created the U.S. Courts of Appeals and gave the Supreme Court more discretion over its expanding docket. In the next chapter, I continue discussing how the 1869 Retirement Act, the Evarts Act, and the decline of Justice Stephen J. Field influenced retirement decisions through 1936 and ultimately led to yet another transformation of the departure process.

5

1897–1936

Old Fools and Young Spirits

The condition of the Supreme Court is pitiable, and yet those old fools hold on with a tenacity that is most discouraging.
—President William Howard Taft

I am too young in spirit [to retire].
—Associate Justice David J. Brewer

The departure of Justice Stephen J. Field had an important effect on the subsequent decision making of his colleagues over their own tenures. Field's determination to hang on to his seat past his ability to effectively participate in the work of the Court caused a temporary suspension of the effects of the Evarts Act. In stark contrast to Field's unwillingness to leave, the three justices who departed after him all planned their retirements, and it is likely that Field's case influenced their thinking. Having witnessed firsthand the institutional harm and the burdens of additional workload that Field caused them, they were likely determined to leave sooner rather than later. This superannuation effect seems to have also taken place nearly a century later. After Justice William O. Douglas's controversial departure, every justice who served with him retired before publicly harming the Court and burdening his colleagues with additional work.

While Horace Gray died in office shortly before his retirement took effect, George Shiras, Jr., and Henry B. Brown voluntarily departed shortly after becoming eligible. Field's instructiveness was short-lived however, ultimately trumped by the institutional structures of the Evarts Act. After Brown's retirement in 1906, seven successive justices either died or became disabled. In fact, there was not another voluntary retirement until 1922. In the forty-one-year period between Noah Swayne's retirement in 1881 and William R. Day's retirement in 1922, only three justices (Field, Shiras, and Brown) voluntarily retired from the Supreme Court, while nineteen died or became disabled in office. With the exception of Field, politics played little or no role in these departures.

THE FIELD EFFECT

Stephen J. Field

Toward the end of his tenure on the Court, Justice Field often had difficulty reaching his seat on the bench. When concerned friends and associates queried him on his health, he replied, "I don't write my opinions with my leg."[1] The inevitable rumors of Field's impending departure began circulating as he approached age seventy. In 1885, it was said that he would retire before the 1888 presidential election, thereby allowing President Grover Cleveland to nominate a Democrat. Field was to spend his remaining years writing his memoirs. This partisan prediction proved incorrect and Field remained in his place. It was said that Field did not retire because of the personal animosity that had developed between him and the president. When Benjamin Harrison was elected president in 1888, another rumor circulated that Field had gotten into an argument with Harrison and would, therefore, remain on the bench until the next election. When Cleveland was returned to the White House in 1892, Field decided to wait through yet another presidential term. Some of Washington's social elite felt that the Justice's wife did not want to lose her social status and may have put pressure on her husband to remain in office. More rumors began circulating that Field intended to remain on the bench until he broke the record for tenure held by John Marshall, who had served for thirty-four years and five months.

Chief Justice Fuller had been assigning fewer and fewer opinions to Field as the years, and Field's mental decline, progressed.[2] Through 1888, Field had written anywhere from twenty-five to thirty opinions of the Court per Term. In 1889, he authored eighteen opinions and only four in 1895. By the 1896 Term, it was clear to the other Justices that Field could no longer adequately perform this function. Chief Justice Fuller may have approached Field about stepping down and when the justice refused, Fuller no longer assigned any opinions to him. Field responded to the Chief:

> I return to you the enclosed memorandum of the cases assigned to
> the different Justices made yesterday. I do not care to retain any

memorandum of assignment of cases where none are assigned to myself. I do not know and shall not ask the reason that no cases have been assigned to me within the past six months.[3]

In July 1896, Senator Stephen M. White wrote:

I regard it as entirely improbable that there will be any successor to Judge Field during the present administration. I was in San Francisco a few days ago and made special inquiry, but failed to find any justification for the very positive statements of the newspapers. Judge Field is, no doubt, weak physically, and perhaps, is not as active mentally as was once the case, though his mind is still clear and he can write as strong opinions as ever, though I do not think he can do as much work as formerly. Indeed, his vitality and intellectuality are astonishing when we take his age into consideration. The comments made by the newspapers will not tend to accelerate his retirement.[4]

During the winter months of the 1896–1897 Term, Field began to exhibit mental lapses. During oral argument, he asked questions that showed he was unable to follow the argument being presented. Moments of lucidity were followed by trancelike states. It was said that he forgot how he voted on cases and his colleagues found it increasingly necessary to help jar his memory. In his book on the Supreme Court, Charles Evans Hughes described the Court's response to Field's visibly worsening condition:

Justice Field tarried too long on the bench . . . I heard Justice Harlan tell of the anxiety which the Court had felt because of the condition of Justice Field. It occurred to the other members of the Court that Justice Field had served on a committee which waited upon Justice Grier to suggest his retirement, and it was thought that recalling that to his memory might aid him to decide to retire. Justice Harlan was deputed to make the suggestion. He went over to Justice Field, who was sitting alone on a settee in the robing room apparently oblivious of his surroundings, and after arousing him gradually approached the question, asking if he did not recall how anxious the Court had become with respect to Justice Grier's condition and the feeling of the other justices that in his own interest and in that of the Court he should give up his work. Justice Harlan asked if Justice Field did not remember what had been said to Justice Grier on that occasion. The old man listened, gradually became alert and finally, with his eyes blazing with the old fire of youth, he burst out:

'Yes! And a dirtier day's work I never did in my life!'

That was the end of that effort of the brethren of the Court to induce Justice Field's retirement.[5]

President-elect William McKinley selected Judge Joseph McKenna, of Field's home state of California, to be the attorney general in McKinley's incoming administration. Justice David J. Brewer, Field's nephew, was said to have brokered an agreement between the president and Field whereby McKenna would be nominated to the Court once Field departed.[6] The chief justice and Justice Brewer called on Justice Field's brother to travel to Washington and persuade the justice to step down. The plan worked and Justice Field's brother secured the written resignation and delivered it to the chief and Justice Brewer for presentation to the president. Field wanted to make sure that the resignation would not take effect until after August 16, 1897, so that he might surpass Marshall's tenure. He selected December 1, 1897 as the day he would officially depart. The next day, Justice Field wrote the chief, "I shall be entirely content to abide by whatever you and Judge Brewer may decide to do."[7]

Fuller and Brewer immediately presented Field's resignation to the president. The chief wrote Field the next day about his impending retirement, "Neither the President nor ourselves will give publicity to the fact."[8] During the summer recess, however, Justice Field vacillated. In August, Justice Brewer wrote to the chief justice about his wavering uncle and the delicacy of the situation:

> I have . . . received a letter from Uncle Henry in which he says he has just returned from a visit to Uncle Stephen & that the latter is so much better physically that he talks of another year's work on the bench, intimated that you wish it, & expects me to insist upon it as a personal matter. Uncle Henry wishes me to write to the Judge, but I do not propose to do so. I can do more by talking to him when the time demands it. You may hear from the Judge on the matter—I did think of writing to the President & stating the situation & suggesting that he write to the Judge accepting the resignation, complimenting him on his long service & expressing a desire to consult with him about his successor. A little flattery like this might prevent any attempt to withdraw his resignation or any feeling of bitterness at retiring. Perhaps however the less said or done the better. It may only call his attention to the matter & suggest the doing of that which ought not to be done.[9]

Field seemed to have accepted his retirement as the members of the Court assembled in Washington for the start of the new Term. Field began work on a public statement about his impending departure and his long service on the bench. On October 4, Justice Harlan wrote the chief:

I called last week to see Justice Field and in the course of the conversation he said that he talked with you & that he was preparing a letter to the court. He expressed a wish that I should see it when prepared & make suggestions.

I supposed that would be the last of the matter. But this morning he sent for me & read what he had prepared, most of it in print. He finally pressed for suggestions when I said to him that in my judgment it was too long & had too many references to his own opinions. As it is it will not do at all. Having said that he had consulted yourself and Brewer about his letter to the President, I advised him to consult you two & take your judgment. If he brings to you the letter he read to me it will be seen at once that it will not do. I spoke frankly to him in order to make your work the easier. He does not know that you and I talked.[10]

The same day, Fuller wrote his wife, "Judge Field bothers me a good deal. I am going to see him this afternoon. He is physically better and that is all that can be said."[11] The Chief worked at length with Field on his farewell statement. On October 12, Field sent the letter to his colleagues informing them, and the public at large, of his decision to retire. He remarked that he was appointed by President Lincoln and that he had sat with Justice Wayne who had sat with Chief Justice John Marshall who was appointed in 1801, "binding into unity nearly an entire century of the life of this court."[12]

Like a number of his colleagues before him, Justice Field found it difficult later in life to step down. Field's reasons for remaining past his usefulness are mixed. Though politics seems to have played some role, Field was clearly bent on surpassing Marshall's record for tenure. As Field's mental capacity began to decline, he probably had difficulty grasping the institutional burden he was placing on his colleagues by remaining in his place. Unlike others, Field never gave any indication that he planned to retire at some point. Indeed, he had sat on the Court for six years before the first retirement provision was enacted in 1869 and like his colleagues from the previous era, Field probably saw little reason to step down.

HORACE GRAY

In 1897, Justice Horace Gray's health slowly began to decline.[13] He went from authoring an average of twenty-five opinions per Term to only thirteen, the lowest total of any of his colleagues.[14] President McKinley began planning for Gray's possible successor. Gray became eligible to retire on his seventieth birthday in 1898 but chose to remain on the bench. At age seventy-four, his health was in steady decline. He missed the first three weeks of the 1901–1902 Term and in February 1902, he suffered a stroke that left him partially paralyzed. Chief Justice Fuller wrote, "He will be seventy-five on Monday & at that age recuperation is slow."[15] Gray missed the rest of the Term, increasing the work for his colleagues. The chief justice said it was the hardest year since he had been on the Court. On July 9, 1902, Gray submitted his resignation contingent upon the confirmation of his successor, but died in office on September 15, 1902, before Oliver Wendell Holmes could be confirmed by the Senate.[16]

GEORGE SHIRAS AND HENRY BROWN

Gray's behavior provides a sharp contrast to the departures of his colleagues Shiras and Brown, both of whom sought to protect the Court from the increased burden placed on it by disabled justices such as Gray. Shiras had once headed a committee to suggest retirement to a prominent judge in Pittsburgh, and had since planned to leave the court upon being eligible for the retirement act and still in full control of his faculties. He retired on February 23, 1903, at the age of 71, explaining to a friend:

My resignation was not the result of a sudden impulse, nor because I found myself unfit for further service as a judge, but was the carrying out of a resolution, formed when I was appointed to the Supreme Court in July, 1892, to retire when I should have reached the age of seventy.[17]

Long before he was eligible for retirement, Justice Brown announced that he would leave the Court at the end of the 1905–1906 Term in accordance with the 1869 Retirement Act. His failing eyesight undoubtedly made the decision easier. Since 1903, he had written only half as many opinions per Term as in previous years.[18] He later explained his thinking about retirement:

On my seventieth birthday, and after a service of fifteen years and a half (precisely the length of my service upon the District Bench), I tendered my resignation to President Roosevelt, to take effect at the end of the term. I took this action in pursuance of a resolution I had made thirty-one years before when first appointed to the Bench. I had always regarded the Act of Congress permitting a retirement upon a full salary a most beneficent piece of legislation, and have only wondered that more judges have not availed themselves of it. I have noticed that while many, if not most, judges made the age of seventy, very few who remain upon the bench survive another decade. During that decade the work of the Supreme Court tells heavily upon the physique of its members, and sometimes incapacitates them before they are aware of it themselves.

In addition to this I had always taken the ground that the country was entitled to the services of judges in the full possession of their faculties, and as my sight had already begun to fail, I took it as a gentle intimation that I ought to give place to another.[19]

Brown went on to explain how personal reasons had kept three of his colleagues from retiring when eligible. He cited fear of mental disability, loss of prestige, and loss of social status as reasons for remaining on the bench:

I never have enjoyed life more, and I think the stories that are often heard about men collapsing when they leave the Bench are all nonsense. Of the four men of our Court who lost their minds, all of them lost them while they were still upon the Bench, while the four who left the Bench in sound condition, not one of them showed symptoms of mental weakness until their deaths.[20] There are now three competent to retire, but no one will do so.[21] Brother Brewer always declared that he would leave the Bench at seventy, but he pretends now that he is afraid that he will lose his mind if he does so. But I think there is much better reason than that for his remaining on the Bench. No one of them likes to take a back seat. Besides that, the wives cut an important figure, and, of course, they are always opposed to it. I think their fears are groundless, but I do not like to express to them my opinion upon the subject of retirement.

I may say that time does not hang heavily on my hands; that I have not been busier for fifteen years, though, of course, I do not work hard . . . If the question were left to me, I think I should vote that a comfortable old age is the happiest period of one's life.[22]

EVARTS ACT REDUX

The Field effect was short-lived. While Justices Gray, Shiras, and Brown had made plans for retirement, at least in part, due to their first hand experience with Justice Field lingering past his usefulness, the others that served with Field did not. The institutional changes brought about by the Evarts Act, such as the abolition of circuit-riding and the discretionary docket and comparatively low caseloads, once again helped push personal concerns to the fore. Justices enjoyed their work, some had a fear of mental decline and death, and most felt that as long as they were not burdening their colleagues, which was difficult to do in a time of reduced caseloads, there simply was no reason to step down. Also, any inducement the retirement provision may have had for the justices to engage in succession politics was countered by the improved working conditions set in place by the Evarts Act.

RUFUS PECKHAM AND DAVID J. BREWER

Justice Peckham became eligible for retirement on November 8, 1908, but chose to remain on the bench as he was still fairly productive.[23] Nearly a year later, Peckham became ill. Attorney General Wickersham wrote President Taft:

> Justice White drew me aside just before the Court opened this morning and told me in the strictest confidence to be shared only with you that Justice Peckham's illness is angina pectoris, and that the end may come at any time. He says that the Justice has no idea that he is seriously ill. But, he said, 'the condition of this Court is such that any vacancy which occurs ought to be filled at the earliest moment and I want the President to know of this impending event. So that he may have all the more time to think of a successor.' He again asked me not to bring any important cause before the Court as at present constituted.[24]

Shortly thereafter, Peckham died in office on October 24, 1909.

Justice David J. Brewer's health had been slowly declining since at least 1900. A member of the Brewer family remarked that the justice's wife "Emma is determined David shall not give Roosevelt a chance to name David's successor."[25] As he approached age seventy, he informed his wife that he would be eligible to continue drawing his salary "and do no more work for the balance of my life." His wife responded that he would find it impossible to do so.[26] A few weeks before his seventieth birthday, he announced that he would not retire, "I am too young in spirit. I look ahead with hope, with optimism, with faith in the happy future of our country."[27] Despite Brewer's optimism, his opinion output began to decline and his colleagues were forced to pick up the slack.[28] President Taft, writing to then circuit Judge Horace Lurton, remarked on the infirmities of Justice Brewer and his colleagues:

> The condition of the Supreme Court is pitiable, and yet those old fools hold on with a tenacity that is most discouraging. Really the

Chief Justice (Fuller) is almost senile; Harlan does no work; Brewer is so deaf that he cannot hear and has got beyond the point of commonest accuracy in writing his opinions; Brewer and Harlan sleep almost through all the arguments. I don't know what can be done. It is most discouraging to the active men on the bench.

It is an outrage that the four men on the bench who are over seventy should continue there and thus throw the work and responsibility on the other five. This is the occasion of Moody's illness. It is with difficulty that I can restrain myself from making such a statement in my annual message.[29]

After twenty years on the Court, Justice Brewer died on March 28, 1910, at the age of seventy-three.

MELVILLE WESTON FULLER AND WILLIAM MOODY

In 1892, Chief Justice Fuller was asked by President-elect Grover Cleveland to resign from the Court and head his new cabinet as Secretary of State. After thinking it over for a few days, Fuller wrote Cleveland:

I have given the subject of our recent conversation the most serious consideration. I was bound to do this on account of its importance in every way, and the more in view of my sincere attachment to you personally, and my earnest desire for the success of your Administration for the sake of the party and your own. And the result is that I must ask you to allow me to decline the great place you were kind enough to wish me to accept. I am convinced that the effect of the resignation of the Chief Justice under such circumstances would be distinctly injurious to the court. The surrender of the highest judicial office in the world for a political position, even though so eminent, would tend to detract from the dignity and weight of the tribunal. We cannot afford this.

Again, a change in the head of the court, situated as it is at this juncture, would inevitably involve delay to some extent in the transaction of its business, and invite criticism, which however transitory, it would be the part of wisdom to avoid.

So far as I myself am concerned, I also think the effect would be unfortunate, though I admit that in the face of imperative duty, purely personal considerations should give way. I am fond of the work of the Chief Justiceship. It is arduous, but nothing is truer than that 'the labor we delight in physics pain.'

I am deeply sensible of the confidence you repose in me, and it
is difficult to decline doing as you would like, but I am clear that I
am right on every ground in the conclusion to which I have come.[30]

As Fuller approached his seventieth birthday, and retirement eligibility,
newspaper reports, fueled by Theodore Roosevelt's White House, speculated
on Fuller's possible departure. A number of newspapers reported, "The suggestion is made that Chief Justice Fuller may soon wish to retire and that
Governor Taft would be a suitable man for the vacancy."[31] Such newspaper
speculation soon became commonplace and the chief remarked to Justice
Holmes, "I am not to be paragraphed out of my place."[32] Though the chief justice turned seventy in 1903, he never contemplated retiring. His friends were
alarmed at the reports and wrote to the chief expressing their concerns. Former President Grover Cleveland wrote Judge William L. Putnam, "I wonder
if there is anything in the talk of Chief Justice Fuller's retirement . . . I don't
know what the Court will come to unless a little more strength is vouchsafed
in new appointments."[33] Putnam wrote the Chief regarding Cleveland's letter
and after reading an article in *Harper's Weekly* that suggested Fuller's retirement would be a misfortune:

Mr. Cleveland wrote me about the rumors and he was evidently
somewhat disturbed by them. I was gratified to reply to him that
your health never seemed better than when I met you at Boston last
Autumn, and that I was assured that it was still most excellent and
further that I did not credit that there was any reason to fear the
occurrence of the rumored catastrophe.[34]

Fuller assured his friends that he had no plans to leave the Court. When
asked if he would step down, he often related a story about his grandfather,
Chief Judge Weston of Maine, who, when asked if he knew when Federal
Judge Ware would resign, replied, "In my opinion Judge Ware will resign
when it pleases God." Grover Cleveland responded:

Of all men in the world I ought to be the last to believe what I read
in the newspapers; but somehow I connected what I read there about
your retiring with something I heard about your having rheumatism
and thought it not amiss to refer to the rumor when writing to Judge
Putnam feeling assured he would know if there was anything in it.
When I heard from him I put the report where it belongs—among
newspaper canards—Since that time I have recovered for good, my
place among those who believe you should only 'resign when it
pleases God.'[35]

As Roosevelt's presidency was nearing its end, rumors again circulated that the Chief would step down. Roosevelt chose William Howard Taft to be his successor in the White House, but Taft preferred the chief justiceship. Taft wrote to his wife, "If the Chief Justice would retire, how simple everything would become."[36] Justice Holmes spoke to Fuller about the rumors and the next day the chief wrote:

> Dear Holmes, thank you very much for your expressions yesterday of the hope that I would not yield to newspaper paragraphs & retire— Of course I won't—But I am glad to be assured that my brethren see no particular reason why I should.[37]

A few months later in November 1906, Fuller received a letter from S. S. Gregory who had spoken with Attorney General William H. Moody about the rumors of Fuller's departure. Gregory wrote that Moody "referred to the newspaper talk about the likelihood that you might retire and then said with emphasis that there was no reason why you should—that none of the members of the Court asked you to, that you discharged the duties of your office in a most admirable manner."[38] It is interesting to note how involved former President Cleveland was in Fuller's departure decision. He had nominated Fuller for the chief justiceship and like many presidents, enjoyed continuing influence and a kind of immortality through his judicial appointments. Were Fuller to step down, Cleveland's influence, however indirect, would go with him. In 1907, Cleveland wrote the Chief:

> Remembering how a few years ago you quieted my apprehensions . . . by relating the Maine story of a man who would only retire . . . 'when God willed,' I am fervently praying every day that God's will may be long postponed and that you will continue to await it. I am not sure that you feel as deeply as some of your countrymen the importance to our country of your resignation to divine disposition in this matter.[39]

In 1908, retired Justice Shiras wrote Fuller, "It is to be hoped that there will be no occasion for any change in the personnel of the Supreme Court. On this delicate subject I need say no more."[40] That same year, Elihu Root remarked that the Chief would "stay indefinitely. They will have to shoot him on the day of judgment."[41]

By 1909, it appeared that Fuller's mental health was declining. When Fuller administered the oath of office to President Taft in March, 1909, Taft said that the Chief made him swear to "execute" rather than support and defend the Constitution. Taft wrote to Circuit Judge Horace Lurton in May,

1909, "Really, the Chief Justice is almost senile."[42] Contrary to Taft's characterization, the last opinions written by Fuller during the 1909–1910 Term show no signs of mental fatigue. A little over three months after Justice Brewer's death, Chief Justice Fuller also died. He served for twenty-two years on the bench. Justice Holmes wrote:

> The Chief died at just the right moment, for during the last term he had begun to show his age in his administrative work, I thought, and I was doubting whether I ought to speak to his family, as they relied on me.[43]
>
> I never thought the time had come when it would be well for him to resign until last term, when he seemed less rapid and certain than heretofore. I was beginning to worry when the solution came at the ideal moment.[44]

Justice Moody resigned on November 20, 1910, at age fifty-six, less than four years after his appointment to the Court. Moody was effectively through on the Court by the start of the 1908–1909 Term due to incapacitating acute rheumatism, but officially stayed on until Congress passed legislation giving him special retirement benefits, just as they were forced to do for Ward Hunt.

JOHN MARSHALL HARLAN I: UNTIL I DIE

Justice Harlan periodically considered the issue of retirement over the years, writing his colleagues and friends about the matter. Like many justices, he changed his mind as he grew older, from pledging never to step down to considering leaving if and when he became unable to contribute to the Court as he should. In all his references to the subject, he never once expressed a partisan motive. His concerns were personal and institutional. He was concerned with being able to physically and mentally keep up with his share of the Court's work, with Congress's schedule for confirming a possible successor, and with his own occupational happiness. In 1892, Harlan wrote William Howard Taft about the possibility of Justice Field's departure:

> I think you can rely upon it that he will not retire until he makes a permanent removal to the Field cemetery at Stockbridge, MA. In this I think he will be right. I cannot understand how anybody would wish to retire from his regular work after he has become too old to pursue any other course of life with comfort. My own conclusion, long ago formed, is to stay at my post on the Bench until I die.[45]

In 1893, he said that a law school professorship with a pension was a position for which he would be "greatly tempted to surrender my present position . . . I could imagine nothing more agreeable to me than to spend the balance of my life in that sort of work."[46] In December 1898, Harlan wrote the Chief:

> Let me celebrate the 21st anniversary of my judicial life by a slight growl.
>
> Two Saturdays in succession you have not assigned to me any case but have assigned cases and important ones to Justice Gray. I was in the majority in each case assigned to him.
>
> I fear that you have the impression that my health is failing while that of Justice Gray is vigorous. I hope his is on the mend.[47] I know I am in good health and wish to do my full share of the work. The cases on my hands to be written are not as many in number as in the case of some others.
>
> Now tear this up & think no more of the growl.[48]

In 1906, he wrote, "My inclination is to retire." He continued, however, speaking of his desire "to participate in the decision of some great questions which will confront the court within the next five years."

> Of course, the question would be easy of solution if I was physically or mentally incompetent to meet the requirements of my position. This is a matter which could not be referred to myself alone. Ordinarily, an old man will not recognize the fact that he is steadily going down the hill. If my judgment of the subject is to be trusted, I am physically equal to my judicial work, although I know that I am not as keen for it as I was a few years ago. Many friends—in perfect good faith I do not doubt—have assured me that my opinions of last term are as clear and rigorous as any I have written, and that is the judgment of the profession. They urge me to stand, and not to think of retiring.
>
> So you see, the question is up to me, and I must take the responsibility of deciding it. When I think of the matter at all, five dates come up for retiring: 1. On the 10th of December next, when I shall have been on the bench twenty-nine years: 2. December 23rd, when I shall be married fifty years: 3. March 4th 1907, so as to enable Congress to confirm the nomination of my successor: 4. At the end of next term, June 1st 1907, when I will be, if alive, 74 years of age: 5. December 10th 1907, when I shall have been on duty thirty years. To put all those dates aside would mean that I would remain on duty

until death removed me. My sons say, stick! They assure me that when the time comes that I should retire, for the benefit of the public, they will tell me frankly.

The general question has occurred to me, and doubtless will to you, whether, all things considered, it is not best for a Judge, to have it asked why he retired, than why the old man did not retire, and give way for one younger or more vigorous in health. Let me say that I am myself conscious of failing in several respects. I cannot endure physical labors as well as I did a few years ago—my capacity to concentrate my reasoning faculties and hold them steadily and continuously on the work in hand and my memory of dates, names and people is . . . not quite what they were. Yet, generally, I feel that I am almost as competent for mental work as I ever was.[49]

Harlan related similar concerns to Taft, then Secretary of War, who wrote to Attorney General William H. Moody, "I think the President has heard from Harlan, but in a very indefinite way, and with an indication that Harlan wishes to decide himself when the public interest will permit his retirement. I am inclined to think that the old man wants to hang on."[50] Later that month, Taft wrote Moody again, this time drawing a different conclusion regarding Harlan's intentions, "I think Harlan is going to retire. He has not been well this summer, and the appointment of James [to the Interstate Commerce Commission] I think has reconciled him to leaving."[51]

The next year, however, Harlan remarked to a friend that he would not retire, "I have now no purpose to 'lay down the shovel and the hoe' of judicial life. I must move ahead in the course of life, and calmly await the end, which cannot, in the nature of things, be very far off."[52] On October 14, 1911, Justice Harlan died suddenly from pneumonia brought about by acute bronchitis.[53] His death came over five years after he recognized the beginnings of his own mental decline. The 1869 Retirement Act had no bearing on his decision to remain in his place. It is likely that Harlan did not retire because he felt that he was not yet institutionally harming the Court and feared that his departure would hasten his mental decline and bring about an early death. As such, Harlan's case is instructive in demonstrating the weakness of the first retirement provision.

HORACE LURTON AND LUCIOUS Q. C. LAMAR

Justice Lurton became eligible to retire on February 26, 1914, when he turned seventy. Even though he had only been on the Supreme Court for four years,

Lurton had served on the Federal Court of Appeals from 1893 to 1909. In accordance with the 1909 and 1911 amendments to the retirement act, Lurton was eligible to retire with full salary since he had been a federal judge for over ten years. He chose to remain on the Court, however, and died five months later on July 12, 1914. There is no evidence to suggest that Lurton remained in his place for partisan reasons.

In September 1915, Justice Lamar became ill. He dictated a letter about his condition to Chief Justice White mentioning his concern for the additional work his absence would cause for his colleagues:

> I left Washington very much under the weather, and have been in the hands of the doctors all the summer. I did not write you, because I did not wish to worry you. But now that I am much worse, I prefer that you should hear from me, instead of from the papers, what my condition is.
>
> When I got here, the doctor found that for years, unknown to myself, I had been suffering from considerable enlargement of the heart. That, in connection with high blood pressure, made it necessary for me to take the baths. They seemed to benefit me very much, and to reduce the pressure. Yesterday I had what I thought was a stroke, but which he says was a clogging of some of the veins in the brain, which has resulted in a numbing, or partial paralysis of the left leg and arm.
>
> I am now in bed and suffering great inconvenience, but no acute pain. The doctor talks more encouragingly than I feel, and says that he thinks I can be up and about within a week or two. I am not so sure as he seems to be; but inexpressibly mortified at what seems to me to be helpless—and I fear will be useless—days for the remainder of a short life. Of course the prime regret is the fear that my incapacity will put more work upon others who are already carrying tremendously heavy burdens . . .
>
> I write with perfect frankness, because I felt that you should know the very worst, and should learn it from me, rather than from any one else. I have been silent as long as I have because I had the most encouraging reports from my doctors; and until this last incident, I myself expected to go back to Washington stronger than when I came, and as well fitted to work as ever before.[54]

Lamar was ineligible to retire as he had only been on the Court for five and a half years. Though Lamar initially improved and returned to Washington, he was unable to resume his work on the Court. He died on January 2, 1916.

CHARLES EVANS HUGHES

In 1912, the Republican Party was split between the factions supporting William Howard Taft and those supporting Theodore Roosevelt. Justice Charles Evans Hughes was mentioned by many, including Taft, as a possible candidate that both sides could support for the presidential nomination. When the question of a possible candidacy was posed to the Justice, he emphatically declined the use of his name. He wrote Elihu Root, chair of the Republican National Convention:

> I am informed that, notwithstanding my published statement, efforts are being made to bring about my nomination. It should be understood, not only that this use of my name is unauthorized, but that, whatever the result, my decision will not be changed. The highest service that I can render in this difficult situation is to do all in my power to have it firmly established that a Justice of the Supreme Court is not available for political candidacy. The Supreme Court must be kept out of politics. I must add, to avoid all possible misunderstanding, that, even if nominated, I should decline.[55]

Taft won the nomination, but lost the election to Woodrow Wilson. Two years later, Hughes's name was again mentioned as the compromise candidate for the 1916 Republican nomination. He was again emphatic in his reply to former New Jersey Governor Edward C. Stokes's query about a possible candidacy:

> It seems to me very clear that, as a member of the Supreme Court, I have no right to be a candidate, either openly or passively. I cannot remain working here and hold an equivocal position before the country. I must, therefore, ask that no steps be taken to bring my name before the convention.[56]

Hughes's reaction to a possible candidacy stands in stark contrast to earlier justices such as John McLean who actively campaigned from the bench. The increased prestige of the Court and the rise of the national press have no doubt contributed to the changing attitudes of the justices toward campaigning. Indeed, early in his tenure as a justice, William O. Douglas acted much as Hughes did to discourage moves to nominate him for the presidency.

As the 1916 Republican convention neared, efforts to advance Hughes's candidacy intensified. Though it was widely recognized that Hughes was not actively seeking the nomination and was indeed working hard to squelch it, the movement for his candidacy continued to build. William Howard Taft wrote him a long, confidential letter emphasizing "responsibility," "duty," and "sacrifice" that Hughes must make for the good of the nation.[57] Even his colleagues on the Court felt that it would be his duty to run if asked. Justice Van Devanter was sympathetic to Hughes's efforts to keep his name from being used, and added, "But if they should nominate you nevertheless, I think you could not rightly decline."[58] Chief Justice White expressed similar sentiments.[59] In the months leading up to the convention, Hughes remained publicly silent on his possible candidacy, causing many to believe that he would accept if nominated. Many recalled how he had flatly said no in 1912, but made no such statement now.

Just before the start of the convention, Chief Justice White paid a visit to Hughes. "Before you decide on what course you will take," White said, "I feel that you should know that I am going to retire and that if you do not resign you will succeed me." Hughes was startled and replied, "Why, President Wilson would never appoint me Chief Justice!" "Well," White answered, "he wouldn't appoint anyone else, as I happen to know."[60] Hughes was shocked by the chief's message. Hughes concluded that White must have spoken with Wilson about the situation.[61] He also realized that if he agreed not to run and was subsequently nominated by Wilson to be chief, the public would clearly see it as a political deal. He informed White that he would follow his conscience and disregard what the chief had told him.

At the convention, Hughes won the Republican nomination. He decided to disregard his personal wishes and bow to patriotic duty. On June 10, 1916, he sent his resignation letter to President Wilson and wired the convention:

> I have not desired the nomination. I have wished to remain on the bench. But in this critical period in our national history, I recognize that it is your right to summon and that it is my paramount duty to respond.[62]

For the first time in history, a major party had taken a presidential candidate from the Supreme Court. Justice Holmes wrote, "It was not preference but simply and solely, as I believe, a sense of duty that led Hughes to accept the nomination."[63] Justice William R. Day wrote Hughes, "In your case the office has indeed sought the man, and your own conduct through all the trying months just past has been honorable and dignified."[64] Hughes remarked to a friend:

> I did not want to leave the Bench and I dreaded more than I can tell you the sort of activity in which I am now engaged. If there had been an honorable way out I should have taken that way. But under the conditions that existed I felt that I had no alternative and that I must do my best in the work to which I was summoned.[65]

On election night, Hughes went to bed believing he was president-elect. Late returns from California, however, resulted in a close victory for Wilson. Hughes returned to private practice in New York City and subsequently served as secretary of state from 1921 to 1925 and as a judge of the World Court from 1926 to 1930. He returned to the U.S. Supreme Court as chief justice in 1930, much like John Rutledge had done in the Court's early years. Unlike Rutledge, however, Hughes was confirmed by the Senate and served for many years as Chief.

EDWARD D. WHITE

According to a letter from Justice Holmes, it seems that Associate Justice White contemplated leaving the Court before his elevation to chief justice. Holmes wrote in 1912, "I wouldn't do much more than walk across the street to be called chief justice instead of Justice—though I think the difference has affected the present incumbent. I no longer hear him wishing that he could retire!"[66]

Chief Justice White developed cataracts toward the end of his tenure on the Court and had to rely on memorizing voices to recall who was speaking to him. Rumors of his impending retirement began to circulate. In January 1914, Sir Frederick Pollock wrote Justice Holmes, "I see a story about your Chief retiring and Taft succeeding him. But why should White want to go? And how about the cost of reconstructing your bench?"[67] William Howard Taft had elevated White to the chief justiceship and it was no secret that the ex-president coveted the position himself. Unfortunately, Holmes never replied to Pollock's query. White turned seventy in November 1915, five years after being appointed chief. Though he was now eligible to retire, he remained in his place. In 1916, he told Justice Hughes that he planned to retire and that if Hughes would not run for the presidency and remain on the Court, he would be his successor. Hughes, of course, did run and White remained chief.

White was deeply troubled about World War I and it hindered his work. By the close of the 1917 Term, the Court was functioning poorly. The increasing workload was becoming more and more of a factor as the Court struggled to keep up with the rising docket. White's increasing gloom was beginning to take a toll. White remarked, "We pulled through the term and I'm trying to pack up and get away. God help us across the waters. It grows very dark to me, but . . . we will lick them yet."[68] On March 26, 1921, Taft went to see White and wrote of the encounter to a friend, "He said nothing about retiring. He spoke of his illness. He said he could still read, though he had a cataract, and he complained of the burden of work he had . . . and he bemoaned the critical nature of that work and the dangers that might arise from wrong decisions."[69]

Doctors advised White that an operation on his bladder was needed. Though he initially postponed it citing the work of the Court, he entered the hospital in May 1921. Justice Holmes wrote:

> I have never greatly admired the Chief's mode of writing—for various reasons that I won't go into—but the poor old boy is the object of nothing but sympathy just now. He has stuck to his work (I think unwisely) in the face of illness—cataracts on his eyes that have blinded one of them, and very great deafness. But he has gone to the hospital and was to have an operation performed at 11:30 A.M. today, I was told (not on his eyes). I hope that it is not serious but feel no assurance till I hear the result. His infirmities have made the work harder for others, and I imagine that he has suffered much more than he has told.[70]

The operation did not succeed and Chief Justice White died on May 19, 1921. Republican President Harding nominated former President Taft to the chief justiceship, just as Taft had hoped. Holmes speculated as to why White delayed his operation: "I cannot judge whether his delaying any operation was due to determination to not give the appointment to Wilson or to love of the office or to mistaken sense of duty—possibly all combined. For I think he loved the office as an end in itself."[71]

INCREASED CASELOADS:
BOWING TO THE INEVITABLE

Beginning with Chief Justice White's death in 1921, the Court experienced a number of departures. In a period of a year and a half, four justices departed and a new Chief Justice was appointed, prompting Justice Holmes to observe:

> The new men all impress me favorably though I don't expect to be astonished. The meetings are perhaps pleasanter than I ever have known them—thanks largely to the C. J. but also to the disappearance of men with the habit of some of our older generation, that regarded a difference of opinion as a cockfight and often left a good deal to be desired in point of manners.[72]

As the third era began to wane, retirements once again became more common. Five of the last six justices departing between 1922 and 1932 retired. Just as the shrinking docket had made retirement less attractive after the Evarts Act in 1891, the gradual rise in the Court's docket beginning in

1900, and reaching new heights beginning in 1920, had an impact in the opposite direction. With increased caseloads, each justice played a more crucial role in the Court's overall workload. Declining justices, who had the luxury of remaining on the bench when dockets were low, now felt institutional and public even pressure to step down. This resulted in increased retirements.

The last three retirements, those of Joseph McKenna, William Howard Taft, and Oliver Wendell Holmes, provide sharp contrasts in the departure decision-making process. McKenna's blindness to his own decline, Taft's political maneuvering, and Holmes's remarkable effectiveness long after his retirement eligibility, provide important lessons for considering whether the departure power is rightly lodged solely in the hands of the individual justice.

JOHN HESSIN CLARKE

Justice Clarke was unhappy on the Court and spoke with his friends for over a year about resigning. He was upset with Justice Willis Van Devanter's unremitting and open anti-Semitism. Within twelve months, both his sisters died of heart failure. Clarke had also recently witnessed the decline of Chief Justice White. Like White, Clarke's hearing was beginning to go, and he seemed to his colleagues to be depressed since the passing of his sisters. He explained to Chief Justice Taft and Justice Van Devanter that he wished, "to get acquainted with my own soul before it parts from my body."[73] He was increasingly frustrated that his position as a justice kept him from being able to speak out on the issues of the day.[74] Clarke was wealthy and felt it dishonorable for someone of means to continue receiving public support once his service ended. Accordingly, he said that he wished to resign his seat before reaching retirement eligibility.[75] On September 18, 1922, Clarke resigned at the age of sixty-five saying that he wanted to have the "strength sufficient to take up other duties."[76] He explained in his letter to President Harding:

> I shall be 65 years old on the 18th day of this month. For a long time I have promised what I think is my better self that at that age I would free myself as much as possible from imperative duties that I may have time to read many books which I have not had time to read in a busy life; to travel and to serve my neighbors and some public causes in ways in which I cannot serve them while holding important public office.[77]

Chief Justice Taft wrote, "You are 65 and leaving the Bench—I am 65 and have just begun. Perhaps it would have been better for me never to have come on to the Court but I could not resist an itching for the only public service I love . . . Few men have laid down power as you are doing. The member of the court who has talked most of it would not do it though the Heavens were to fall. Your act is one of self-abnegation which will be appreciated and will give you power for good . . . May God bless you, old man."[78] Former President Woodrow Wilson expressed his concern for the future direction of the Court. "Like thousands of other liberals throughout the country, I have been counting on the influence of you and Justice Brandeis to restrain the Court in some measure from the extreme reactionary course which it seems inclined to follow."[79]

In retirement, Clarke wrote to his former colleagues. To Justice William R. Day, Clarke spoke of the "luxury to take up one's *Atlantic,* or other favorite, and pick out the articles that look attractive and then settle down to leisurely reading without feeling that you should be digging out certioraris or answering some Fourteenth Amendment casuist."[80] In response to the official letter of the members of the Court expressing their regret at his departure, he noted his relief "from the irritating futility of the certioraris, and from the Fourteenth Amendment nonsense, and from the necessity of spelling out reasons for the obvious" and the joy he received in "the old time freedom of my neighbors from restraint and the happiness of being able to do and say just what I please."[81]

Clarke immediately set about reviving the movement for the United States to join the League of Nations. He made a number of public speeches and wrote articles in such publications as *The Nation.* In an interview with the *New York World,* Clarke said "Politics has no place in my scheme . . . I am interested [in the League of Nations] from an absolutely non-partizan [sic] and non-political standpoint."[82] The press speculated that Clarke was aiming for the presidency, but he never admitted to having any such an ambition.

WILLIAM R. DAY AND MAHLON PITNEY

Though Justice Day became eligible for retirement on April 17, 1919, he chose to remain on the bench. Almost three years later, a recurring illness kept him from participating in the Court's work. "The truth is, the court has been shot to pieces," wrote Chief Justice Taft in November 1922, "[Day] has been doing no work, [Van Devanter] has had trouble with his eyes, and Judge McReynolds has the gout." If that wasn't enough, the chief added that Justice Pitney "is ill at home."[83] A week later, Justice Day retired on November 13, 1922, at the age of seventy-three. Eight months later, he died. His attending physician remarked, "Mr. Day had been living 'on his nerve' for the last few years, believing he must do his part in public affairs despite his advanced age."[84]

In early 1922, Justice Pitney was diagnosed with a blood clot on the brain. Chief Justice Taft suggested he take some time off and he agreed. When Pitney returned to Washington, he could not resume his full share of the Court's work. Taft considered him "weak" and after Pitney's "breakdown," the Chief did not assign him any more cases.[85] In August, 1922, Pitney had a massive stroke. By November, he was also suffering from hardening of the arteries and Bright's disease.[86] Pitney was six years shy of the age seventy requirement needed for retirement and chose not to resign. As it had been forced to do several times since the 1869 Act had taken effect, Congress passed a special retirement bill to induce Pitney's departure. He officially left the Court on December 31, 1922.

Two months later, Justice Holmes wrote, "Mrs. Pitney telephoned to me to call on her husband tomorrow. I dread it, as I believe he is emotional and does not realize how seriously ill he is."[87] On December 9, 1924, Pitney died. Holmes wrote, "I went to poor Pitney's funeral a morning or two ago. He has painfully lingered with hardening of arteries and broken faculties and speech . . . So they drop off, and I still remain like the Wandering Jew."[88]

JOSEPH MCKENNA

No justice's departure has been chronicled as thoroughly as Justice Joseph McKenna's, though William O. Douglas's exploits have received considerable attention as well.[89] David J. Danelski's 1965 article entitled "A Justice Steps Down" is the only full-length case study of the departure of a Supreme Court justice. McKenna is an important example because of his unwillingness to leave the bench, even after being told by the Chief Justice that all his colleagues felt the time had come as his infirmities hampered the Court's ability to function effectively. McKenna's reasons for staying were personal. Like most of his predecessors, McKenna remained on the Court well past the date on which he was eligible for retirement.

McKenna suffered a slight paralytic stroke in 1915, but still looked to be in good physical health at age seventy-two. Though he had been eligible to retire since 1913, he showed no signs of stepping down. In 1921, Chief Justice Taft noticed McKenna's mind beginning to falter in conference and in his opinion writing. Taft assigned him the simplest cases, but McKenna had trouble making a clear argument. In one case, he returned an opinion that found for the opposite result than the unanimous Court, McKenna included, voted for in conference. Taft also felt that McKenna did not realize he was faltering, since Justice Holmes was older than McKenna and effectively performing his duties. Taft wrote his brother, "McKenna's vote may change the judgment of the Court on important issues, and it is too bad to have a mind like that decide when it is not able to grasp the point, or to give a wise and deliberate consideration to it."[90] In *Truax v. Corrigan* (1921),[91] McKenna was the fifth vote against a state law protecting picketing workers, even though in past cases, he had been sympathetic to labor.

As the 1922 Term began, Taft felt that McKenna "ought to get off" but was "the least likely to wish to go off."[92] In *Adkins v. Children's Hospital* (1923),[93] McKenna sided with the majority declaring unconstitutional a District of Columbia minimum wage law for women. The opinion directly contradicted an opinion McKenna had written six years before in *Bunting v. Oregon* (1917).[94] As McKenna approached his eightieth birthday in 1922, he told Chief Justice Taft "that when a man retires, he disappears and nobody cares for him."[95] Taft thought that McKenna was senile and should have retired years before: "I don't know what course to take with respect to him, or what cases to assign to him," Taft wrote to his brother, "I had to take back a case from him last Saturday because he would not write it in accordance with the vote of the court . . . and have taken it over to myself."[96] The chief thought that McKenna remained on the Court because he wanted the prestige of the office and feared death would be brought about by retirement.

In April 1924, Justice Holmes solicited the views of his colleagues about the possibility of taking collective action on the situation. Justices Butler, McReynolds, Sanford, Sutherland, Van Devanter, and Chief Justice Taft all agreed that McKenna should be asked to step down. Justice Brandeis did not agree with his colleagues and Holmes abstained. Taft ascribed partisan motives to Brandeis, believing the liberal Justice wanted McKenna to depart under a Democratic president. There is speculation, however, that Brandeis feared a similar vote might be taken on his friend Justice Holmes, whom he did not want to see depart. For the time being, no one approached McKenna. With the 1924 presidential campaign underway, Taft and Van Devanter felt it wise to wait until after the election to take any action. If Republican President Calvin Coolidge was reelected, they would immediately ask McKenna to leave.

Toward the end of the 1923–1924 Term, Taft became ill and was unable to preside over conferences. He had no choice but to let McKenna, as senior associate, preside. He sent detailed instructions not only to McKenna, but also to Justice Van Devanter to ensure that the proceedings ran smoothly. As the Term ended, McKenna hinted that there might be some changes in the Court over the summer recess. Taft was skeptical and wrote his wife, "If there are to be any changes, I don't think they will be with the old men. Vacation usually gets them ready to come back with a certain determination to stay." He went on to say that McKenna had recently "printed a dissenting opinion in which he differed from the entire Court and made a lot of remarks that seemed . . . to be quite inapt and almost ridiculous."[97]

In August, Justice McReynolds remarked to a friend that McKenna's physical condition was fair, but touching his head, added, "There [is] nothing there."[98] McReynolds went on to say that he might suggest to his colleagues that opinions should not be assigned to justices over age seventy-five. Taft and Van Devanter met with McKenna's doctor who agreed with them that McKenna was mentally declining. The doctor said that he would do his best to convince the Justice to step down.

As the 1924–1925 Term began, McKenna's wife died. His daughter took him to Boston to live with her temporarily in hopes of persuading him to retire. Taft was again skeptical. On October 20, he wrote a friend that "with the pertinacity that grows with age, [McKenna] still hopes to return because he does not know what he could do with his time if he were not on the Bench. Undoubtedly he ought to retire, and I am hoping his family will induce him to do so."[99] As expected, McKenna returned to the bench. On November 4, President Coolidge won reelection and five days later, Taft asked all his colleagues, except McKenna, to convene at his house to determine a course of action. Taft said that the Court could no longer "decide any case in which there were four on one side and four on the other, with Mr. Justice McKenna casting the deciding vote."[100] All the justices agreed that McKenna should be asked to step down and that Taft should handle it "as seemed best."[101] That night, Taft informed McKenna's son that his father would be asked to retire. McKenna's son concurred and agreed not to mention it to his father. The next morning, McKenna phoned Taft and requested a meeting. Taft figured McKenna's son told his father of the plan.

On November 10, 1924, McKenna met Taft in the Chief's library. Taft recalled how McKenna had once told him how he would leave the Court when he was no longer able to do his share of the work or when his colleagues thought it best. Taft explained that all of the justices had agreed that he could no longer keep up with his work and that he should retire. McKenna protested that he had written the opinions assigned to him. Though Taft did not want to argue and undoubtedly hurt the justice's feelings, McKenna pressed him for reasons. Taft explained that he had not been assigned anything of consequence and even the most simple case had to be rewritten or reassigned. McKenna continued his defense stating that, although his colleagues were entitled to their opinion, they had no formal power to remove him. "Of course not," Taft responded, adding that they felt it their duty to tell him their view of the situation. McKenna explained that it would be particularly difficult to leave so soon after his wife had passed away. Taft wrote later that day, "I concluded it was wiser not to enter into that discussion and did not say to him, what of course is fact, that for two years the situation has been such that we have felt it a violation of our duty not to speak earlier."[102] McKenna finally relented and agreed to step down with two caveats. First, he wanted his retirement to take effect in January 1925 and second, he wanted the chief to assign him a few more cases before he departed. Taft agreed.

McKenna delivered his final opinion of the Court on January 5, 1925. After the other opinions had been read, the chief justice said, "Gentlemen of the bar, Mr. Justice McKenna has announced to us, his colleagues of the Court, his purpose to retire from the Bench. He has presented his resignation to the President who has accepted it. As his associates, we have expressed our feelings toward him in a personal letter, which I shall now read."[103] This was the first public reading of such a letter and afterward McKenna responded by thanking his colleagues and making a few brief remarks. As McKenna finished, the Marshal placed a basket of red roses in front of him. After a moment of silence and the Marshal's gavel, the justices and everyone else in the courtroom stood. With his colleagues still standing, McKenna stepped down from his seat and walked side by side with the Marshal to the doorway of the chamber. McKenna regretted retiring and the last time he spoke with Justice Holmes, he counseled, "Don't you resign. You have a right to linger superfluous on the scene."[104]

What is most troubling about McKenna's failure to depart earlier is the effect his vote had on evenly divided cases. Allowing a justice who is no longer in full control of his mental faculties to cast deciding votes in important cases, is clearly the greatest danger that life tenure gives rise to. In McKenna's case, the retirement provision was not a strong enough incentive to induce his departure. Ultimately, it was the weight of his colleagues that forced him to step down. The failure to depart lies not with the declining justice so much as it lies with the rest of the justices who waited too long to bring their weight to bear on the situation. In this case, the Court not only functioned at less than full strength, but more important, jeopardized its power of judicial review by allowing a mentally infirm justice to cast the deciding vote in equally divided cases.

WILLIAM HOWARD TAFT

Chief Justice Taft's departure from the Court is among the handful of this era which were clearly partisan. Though he became severely ill and was eligible for retirement, he chose to remain on the Court to counteract the liberal forces of Justices Holmes, Brandeis, and Stone. Furthermore, he viewed President Hoover as a dangerous progressive and did not want the President to name his successor.

Taft had been fighting recurring health problems, mostly stemming from his weight, ever since his days as president. In December 1922, he had gravel removed from his bladder, and the following spring, suffered an internal inflammation that he attributed to "the hard work I have been doing."[105] In January 1924, Taft suffered a slight heart attack and in February was unable to attend the funeral of Woodrow Wilson. Taft wrote, "The truth is, I have had a pretty close call to a breakdown . . . I cannot do all the work there is to do. I was treating myself as I might have . . . thirty years ago. There is no fool like an old fool."[106]

The heart attacks continued and he became seriously ill in late April, spending most of his time in bed. Attorney General George Wickersham wrote him, "The fact is, you have been doing the work of at least two men ever since you went on the Court, and that means two full-sized men! You cannot go on that way indefinitely. It is an infernal outrage that the octogenarians on your Court do not see the injustice of their staying on and piling additional loads on you."[107]

He regretted that he had not taken better care of himself, and began a strict diet the following winter. In December 1924 he wrote, "I think I have been just what I have been—a damn fool in many ways . . . I have thought . . . that my strength was equal to anything, and I found that it was not."[108] By February 1925, he was slowing down. He observed, "It doesn't seem to me that I write as rapidly as I used to . . . I am more leisurely in my methods of application." He confided, "My memory is growing poorer and poorer."[109]

Taft became eligible for retirement on September 15, 1927, when he turned age seventy. Despite his growing health problems, he never considered stepping down. By the spring of 1928, Taft's health began to take a perilous course. His blood pressure was high and he worried that his arteries were hardening. He remarked, "I am really in an invalid state."[110] The following winter he admitted, "The truth is that my mind does not work as well as it did, and I scatter."[111] By July he was in the hospital and later confined to his home. He wrote Justice Sanford, "You were good enough to say you would take over that patent case for me . . . and I though I ought to take it myself; but the truth is that I have been sick for nearly a month and I haven't been able to do any work."[112]

As the new Term began in October 1929, the chief justice returned to preside over the Court. He struggled to keep up with the work and by winter had to relinquish two of his opinions he had been working on to Justice Van Devanter for completion.[113] Despite his infirmities, Taft would not retire. He explained to his brother Henry:

> I am older and slower and less acute and more confused. However, as long as things continue as they are, and I am able to answer in my place, I must stay on the court in order to prevent the Bolsheviki from getting control.[114]

... the only hope we have of keeping a consistent declaration of constitutional law is for us to live as long as we can . . . The truth is that Hoover is a Progressive just as Stone is, and just as Brandeis is and just as Holmes is.[115]

As the new year began, his doctors advised him to take a two-month absence from his duties on the Court. He agreed and left for North Carolina to rest. By the end of January, however, his health grew worse. He insisted that he return to Washington and began hallucinating that he was ready to leave. On February 3, 1930, Taft retired.

OLIVER WENDELL HOLMES, JR.

In 1912, Justice Holmes was acutely aware of his eligibility to retire upon meeting the ten-year, age-seventy requirement, but spoke instead of his desire to remain on the Court. Holmes wrote his friend, Irish priest Patrick Augustine Sheehan:

> Last Sunday, Dec. 8, my ten years since I took my seat were up, and I am now free to retire when I like. But (apropos of some suggestions of yours) while only the philosophical side of things interests me I don't care to write except on subjects which I think I know to the bottom, and therefore I think it wise, while my powers seem unabated, to try to put a touch of the infinite into the law, rather than turn to other fields . . . You say you wish the President would make me Ambassador. English friends sometimes used to suggest that years ago, but even when I was a judge in Massachusetts I wouldn't have taken it—very much less would I take it now. That is not a career; my work is—to give it up in order to be an ornamental umbrella handle! No thank you . . . The thing I have wanted to do and want to do is to put as many new ideas into the law as I can, to show how particular solutions involve general theory, and to do it with style.[116]

In his eightieth year, Holmes reflected on aging, "I am thinking of starting a new ideal—to live to 90, call the old job finished, and start . . . a new one (continuing however to work on the bench, if only as a means of survival). It seems as if a man must reach 90 to be really old. But I guess it is pretty hard sledding to get there."[117] The next year he added, "I am feeling in very good shape but I was wondering this afternoon if a man hasn't passed the line and run his race at 80 and whether the subsequent cantering is not

simply a way of quieting down. I don't feel so—and I passed 81 on the 8th."[118]
At the same time, Chief Justice Taft was lamenting the aging and ineffective
Justice McKenna and remarked, "Holmes is vastly more useful, and does a
great deal more good work."[119] The next year, the Chief added, "Holmes . . .
has not lost his mental acumen so far as I can see, and his power of rapid
work is still marvelous."[120]

Throughout the 1920s, Holmes periodically pondered the question of
retirement. Though he noticed that he was slowing down physically, he felt his
mental abilities had not lessened. He wrote to Harold Laski, "All goes well
here—although when I get a pull down—all over now—I can't help wondering whether I am finished and ought to say so—but I can't see that my work
has fallen off."[121] Laski replied:

> Everyone agrees that your judicial work is as good as ever—if it is
> not better than ever; and frankly I think it would be fatal to the
> cause of judicial scepticism if you went just now. You are laying the
> foundations of the next age in jurisprudence; and I frankly think
> that what you are doing is to deposit a liberal tradition the influ-
> ence of which may well be the salvation of the United States in the
> next period. Don't desert your post until you have convinced your-
> self that it is essential. Every liberal mind in America would despair
> if you resigned.[122]

Holmes wrote back and assured Laski, "I was not thinking of resigning—
only about it—and anxiously wondering if I was right."[123] A few months later,
Holmes again mentioned the topic of retirement and wanting to remain in his
place as long as he was useful. Laski again replied emphatically:

> You seem in great form; and so long as I hear that you don't
> intend to resign, I am happy. For (a) you have no moral right to
> resign until you have been on the Court as long as Marshall, (b)
> it would be a crime to give Coolidge another nomination and (c)
> it would leave Brandeis lonely and miserable. If you press me, I
> will add further reasons. And don't forget that your dissents, as in
> *Adair v. U.S.* and *Coppage v. Kansas* are making the law of the
> next generation.[124]

Throughout his eighties, Holmes's contemporaries did not see any reason
for the Justice to retire. Justice Hughes remembered the "agreeable spectacle
of Justice Holmes at eighty-five doing his share of work, or even more, with
the same energy and brilliance that he showed twenty years ago."[125] In 1928,
Harold Laski wrote:

But you must not even allow the sombre notion of resignation to play over your mind; and you must not even want intelligent eulogy in the press to confirm our sense that you are where you ought to be. We your disciples, Felix, Brandeis, Mack, Cardozo, Hand, Cohen, and I, hereby after proper deliberation put our hands on our hearts and swear unreservedly that we perceive only in your work the qualities that have made us proud of you and in undiminishing degree. *Macte antiquae virtutis,* and set your barque for ninety.[126]

Five years later, at age ninety, Holmes's health began to deteriorate. In January 1931, he wrote Felix Frankfurter, "My uneasiness increases and the fear that I am not pulling my weight."[127] In August, he suffered what was probably a mild stroke,[128] calling it "a sort of cave in."[129] As the new Supreme Court Term began, the justices noticed that Holmes had lost a step. Hughes wrote, "It appeared that [Holmes] was slipping. While he was still able to write clearly, it became evident in the conferences of the justices that he could no longer do his full share in the mastery of the work of the Court."[130] Holmes's secretary described the justice's condition as "an increasing fatigue. During the latter part of the day he would be very good and [it was] hard to imagine his ever having been better, during the hours when he was vigorous. But [a] pall would descend, sometimes earlier, sometimes later . . . the attention span had gone without depriving him of the drive that he always had to finish any unfinished business."[131] Holmes was also aware of his decline: "I have not been very well and I find it difficult to write; difficult physically and mentally. I hope to get back to normal but at present life is hard."[132]

The justices met to discuss Holmes's situation and decided he should be asked to step down. Chief Justice Hughes also met with Justice Brandeis to discuss the matter.[133] The Chief traveled to Holmes's residence on January 12 to carry out what he called "a highly distasteful duty."[134] Hughes spoke with Holmes in the second-floor study for a half hour before instructing Holmes's secretary to retrieve the statutes dealing with retirement and tenure. Hughes suggested "as tactfully as possible" that Holmes should retire. He told the Justice "he was under too heavy a burden" and "should not strain himself by continuing to carry the load when his strength was no longer equal to it."[135] Hughes said that Holmes "received my suggestion . . . without the slightest indication of . . . resentment or opposition."[136] When Hughes came down the stairs from Holmes's study, he had "tears streaming down his face." Hughes left and Holmes's secretary "went upstairs to see the justice and [his housekeeper] was kneeling at his feet in tears. He was then and thereafter totally stoic about it. There was no expression of emotion one way or another."[137] After Hughes left, Brandeis arrived and stayed with the Justice for about an hour. Holmes's housekeeper felt that "even though [Holmes's] heart was breaking, he wouldn't let anyone know it." She said that Holmes "thought it was the end," and "was lonesome."[138]

The next day, Holmes took his seat on the bench for the last time and informed his colleagues of his decision to retire. When the Court adjourned at four-thirty, he told the clerk, "I won't be down tomorrow."[139] That evening, he wrote President Hoover:

> In accordance with the provision of the Judicial Code as amended Section 260, Title 28 United States Code 375, I tender my resignation as Justice of the Supreme Court of the United States of America. The condition of my health makes it a duty to break off connections that I cannot leave without deep regret after the affectionate relations of many years and the absorbing interests that have filled my life. But the time has come and I bow to the inevitable. I have nothing but kindness to remember from you and from my brethren. My last word should be one of grateful thanks.[140]

The next day, the justices wrote Holmes a letter praising his service and friendship and added, "Deeply regretting the necessity for your retirement, we trust that—relieved of the burden which had become too heavy—you may have a renewal of vigor and that you may find satisfaction in your abundant resources of intellectual enjoyment."[141]

CONCLUSION

Though the 1869 Retirement Act served to organize the departure decisions of the justices during this period, it only had the effect of inducing departures at the beginning and end of the era where caseloads were high. When the Evarts Act formally ended circuit riding and afforded the justices discretion over their docket for the first time, voluntary departures largely ceased. As I will discuss in the next chapters, this relationship between workload and voluntary departure continues to this day.

Interestingly, dramatic events that directly involved the members of the Court, such as the disputed Hayes/Tilden election of 1876 and the superannuation effect of Stephen J. Field's lengthy decline and refusal to leave caused a deviation in the ongoing departure patterns. Each event prompted brief changes in the behavior of the justices. The Hayes/Tilden situation ended a time of nonpartisan retirements early in the era and gave rise to a brief period of partisan departure decisions. The Field effect influenced three justices who broke with the pattern of their predecessors of remaining in their seats until death, and instead the three justices departing after Field planned to voluntarily retire. In all, partisanship was still the exception rather than the rule. But mental decrepitude was an increasing problem with Justices Grier, Clifford, Field, McKenna, and probably Chief Justice Taft and Justice Holmes staying on the Court beyond their ability to effectively serve. Ultimately, the Court would experience increases in both partisan departures and mental decrepitude.

6

1937–1954

Senior Status

I am still a judge.
    —Justice Willis Van Devanter, following his retirement

Years have limited the quantity and intensity of work possible, and I think the time has come when a younger man should assume the burden.
    —Justice Louis D. Brandeis

Though Congress had hoped voluntary retirement would become common, it was instead the exception rather than the rule in the late nineteenth and early twentieth centuries. Most justices continued to follow what Charles Fairman called "the American plan of living—carry[ing] on to the end" and did not contemplate leaving the bench. For the most part, partisan motives were still rare. The limited retirement provision enacted by Congress in 1869, in order to induce departures and help ease the Court's workload, ultimately had little effect. Also left unaddressed was the issue of how to deal with physically and mentally disabled justices. In the cases of Justices Hunt, Moody, and Pitney, who were physically disabled and had not yet reached retirement eligibility, Congress had a relatively easy time enacting special provisions to induce their departures. Congress's real failures, however were seen in the cases of Justices Grier, Field, McKenna, and even Holmes. In these instances, the original retirement act did not prompt these justices to depart on their own, as Congress had hoped it would. It was only after the Court as a whole brought its weight to bear that these no longer effective justices stepped down. Congress's silence in these cases is telling. By not acting, Congress left such matters for the Court to sort out itself. As mental decline is most noticeable to the other justices in conference and in opinion writing, they should be the first to spot it in one of their colleagues. They can quickly act before the institution is harmed. In the cases of Grier, Field, and McKenna, however, the Court did not act soon enough.

The controversy over President Roosevelt's Court packing plan focused public attention on the Court and its aging members. "The Nine Old Men," as they were referred to in song and in print, were the subject of much criticism, not only for their opposition to New Deal legislation, but also because of the perception that they were unable to effectively discharge the duties of their offices.[1] As in the past, calls for reform centered around the institutional health of the Court, even though partisan politics was the driving force. The Court-packing struggle had an impact on the members of the Court. Their decisions to step down were influenced by the public perception fostered by FDR's criticism and plan to pack the institution.

The Court-packing struggle is significant, not only for this reason, but also because it resulted in Congress expanding the original retirement provision (see Table 6.1). The 1869 provision for full salary on retirement was supplemented by justices remaining in office as federal judges in "senior status." They kept the prestige of their office and could continue to work on lower courts if they so desired. Another major change occurred in 1939 when disabled justices were allowed to voluntarily retire prior to reaching age seventy. If they had served at least ten years, disabled justices would receive their full salaries. If they served less, they would receive half. While this would have solved the Hunt, Moody, and Pitney situations, what of disabled justices who refuse to step down? Congress again remained silent, implying that this was an internal matter, best handled from within the Court.

The Court's workload reached new heights during this brief period (see Figure 6.1). Not since the beginning of the last departure era and the post–Civil War period had the Court experienced such a crushing docket. The Evarts Act of 1891 had dramatically eased the burden in the previous era by giving the Court the power of discretionary review. But by the 1940s, workload had returned to pre–Evarts Act levels. Prior to the Evarts Act, the Court's docket had reached a high of nearly 1,900 cases. By 1946, the docket had grown to 1,678 cases, higher than at any time since the groundbreaking legislation was enacted. Just as in the 1880s and 1890s, members of the Stone and Vinson Courts, including Stone and Vinson themselves, did not voluntarily step down and died in office. Stone's death in 1946 coincided with this caseload resurgence and was followed by the successive deaths of four other justices.

TABLE 6.1
Significant Retirement and Pension Provisions: 1937–1953

Year	Provisions
1937	Justices having reached the age of seventy with at least ten years of service as a federal judge are allowed to retire in senior status rather than to resign. Senior justices retain the authority to perform judicial duties in any circuit when called upon by the Chief Justice. Senior justices receive the same pension benefits as resigned justices. (Lower court judges were given the "senior status" option in 1919.)
1939	The first judicial disability statute is enacted. Justices who become permanently disabled may retire regardless of age. Disabled justices who have less than ten years of service as a federal judge receive for life one half of the annual salary being received on the date of departure. Disabled justices with more than ten years of service as a federal judge receive for life the full annual salary being received on the date of retirement.
1948	Justices having reached the age of seventy with ten years of service as a federal judge who resign their office receive for life the full salary payable to them at the time of their resignations. Justices having reached the age of seventy with ten years of service as a federal judge who retire from office in senior status continue to receive the salary of their office for life. This includes any salary increases that might be granted to sitting justices. Disabled justices retiring receive the same benefits as other senior status justices, subject to the service provisions of the 1939 act.

Adapted from: Lee Epstein et al., *The Supreme Court Compendium* (Washington, D.C.: Congressional Quarterly Press, 1994), 36–37 and 28 U.S.C 371–372.

As with previous eras, Table 6.2 shows how the 1937–1954 period can be divided by emerging structures. The brief era is highlighted by the contrast between early voluntary departures and later deaths. While the 1937 reforms had initial success in prompting retirements, ultimately further reform was needed. The deaths of five successive justices, most at relatively young ages, facilitated the partisan reforms enacted by the Republican Congress in 1954. It was not until the 1954 reforms and the era progressed that partisanship in the departure decision of the justices exploded.

A WAR WITH A FOOL AT THE TOP

Thomas Jefferson once said, "Great Lawyers are not over-abundant, and the multiplication of judges only enables the weak to out-vote the wise."[2] Though

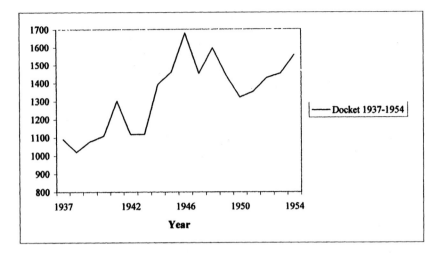

FIGURE 6.1
U.S. Supreme Court Caseload: 1937–1954

Jefferson was referring to what he saw as the Federalists' attempt to pack the judiciary with sympathetic appointments before they left office, his words can easily be applied to a more recent partisan proposal. The modern period of Supreme Court departure was shaped by Democrat Franklin Roosevelt's infamous attempt to "multiply" the Court's membership by adding a young pro–New Deal justice for every aged anti–New Deal one.[3] Though he failed, as did congressional proposals for a constitutional amendment for a mandatory retirement age, an increased retirement provision did help Roosevelt get the Court he wanted, albeit by different means. The 1937 Retirement Act helped encourage justices to leave the Court before they overstayed their usefulness. The unintended effect, however, was that it eventually encouraged members of the Court to engage in succession politics and depart for partisan reasons. The act that grew out of Roosevelt's court-packing scheme thus was an important addition to the initial retirement statute enacted nearly seventy years prior.

Beginning in the 1920s the Court engendered mounting criticism, especially from progressives who viewed its decisions as increasingly pro-business. Campaigning for the Presidency in October 1932, Roosevelt said "After March 4, 1929, the Republican party was in complete control of all branches of government—the Legislature, with the Senate and Congress; and the executive departments; and I may add, for full measure, to make it complete, the United States Supreme Court as well."[4] With Roosevelt's election, there was immediate discussion about changing the Court's composition. Soon-to-be Attorney General, Homer Cummings, recounted a conversation he had with California Senator William G. McAdoo:

TABLE 6.2
1937–1954 Departure Era: Subregimes

Subregime Years	Emergent Structure	Departing Justices	Departure Mode
1937–1945	Court-packing Plan and 1937 Retirement Act	Willis Van Devanter	Retirement
		George Sutherland	Retirement
		Benjamin Cardozo	Death
		Louis D. Brandeis	Retirement
		Pierce Butler	Death
		James Clark McReynolds	Retirement
		Charles Evans Hughes	Retirement
		James F. Byrnes	Resignation
		Owen J. Roberts	Resignation
1946–1954	Untimely Death: Failure of 1937 Act	Harlan Fiske Stone	Death
		Frank Murphy	Death
		Wiley B. Rutledge	Death
		Fred M. Vinson	Death
		Robert H. Jackson	Death

[Senator McAdoo] also discussed the possibility of changing the law with regard to the Supreme Court so as to get the antiquated judges off the bench. He was wondering if a law could be drawn that would be constitutional.

He thought perhaps a bill could be drafted that would stand a constitutional test if it provided, for instance, that the judges become emeritus as it were after they became 70 or 72 . . . that their salaries would go on, and that they could sit with the Supreme Court when requested by the Chief Justice but no more than one at a time. He suggested I have the matter briefed in my office and said that if it could be worked, he would be glad to introduce such a bill. He said he had talked to Governor Roosevelt about it and the latter liked the idea. McAdoo said that this would get rid of the "old fossils" though he would regret to see Brandeis go.[5]

After Roosevelt was elected, he soon found the Court thwarting a number of his economic proposals. As the Court was set to decide the *Gold Clause Cases*[6] in early 1935, Roosevelt's Cabinet discussed what ought to be done should the Court decide against the administration. Secretary of the Interior Harold L. Ickes wrote in his diary:

The Attorney General went so far as to say that if the Court went against the Government, the number of justices should be increased at once so as to give a favorable majority. As a matter of fact, the President suggested this possibility to me during our interview on Thursday, and I told him that this is precisely what ought to be done. It wouldn't be the first time that the Supreme Court had been increased in size to meet a temporary emergency and it certainly would be justified in this case.[7]

Though the Court decided the *Gold Clause Cases* in the administration's favor by votes of five to four, the votes soon turned against FDR's policies. The Court invalidated the Railway Retirement Act of 1934,[8] and on "Black Monday," May 27, 1935, a unanimous Court struck down the National Industrial Recovery Act, the Frazier-Lemke Act which created a moratorium on mortgage payments, and limited the President's power over independent regulatory commissions.[9] Four days later, FDR spoke to reporters in the oval office about the Court's rulings. "We are facing a very, very great national nonpartisan issue. We have got to decide one way or the other . . . whether in some way we are going to . . . restore to the Federal Government the powers which exist in the national Governments of every other Nation in the world," the President said. "We have been relegated to the horse-and-buggy definition of interstate commerce."[10]

Democratic members of Congress responded to Black Monday with a number of proposals. Some called for a constitutional amendment granting Congress additional powers, while others, like Senator George Norris, suggested requiring a supermajority of seven justices to invalidate legislation.[11] Though many were outraged by the Court's rulings, there was not yet enough support to confront the Court or pass a constitutional amendment. After surveying his colleagues, Senator Norris said of an amendment, "It looks now as though it would be an absolute impossibility to pass it through the Senate or the House by the necessary two-thirds majority in order to submit it to the states."[12] FDR knew the Agricultural Adjustment Act was soon to go before the Court and remarked to a friend, "If the Court does send the AAA flying like the NRA, there might even be a revolution."[13]

On January 6, 1936, by a vote of six to three, the Court struck down the AAA in *U.S. v. Butler*.[14] Though a revolution did not occur, FDR continued to gain public support in his ongoing battle with the Court. Attorney General Cummings wrote the president:

> We might well be giving some serious thought to an amendment to the Constitution (should we find we are forced to that point) which would require the retirement of all Federal Judges, or, at least, all Supreme Court Judges, who have reached or who hereafter reach the age of seventy years. Such an amendment would probably encounter

less opposition than almost any other I can think of. It would have the advantage of not changing in the least degree the structure of our Government, nor would it impair the power of the court. It would merely insure the exercise of the powers of the Court by Judges less likely to be horrified by new ideas.[15]

As the Court continued to thwart the New Deal, Congress introduced an increasing number of bills to curb the Court's power, from scaling back their prerogative of judicial review to increasing the Court's membership.[16] Democratic Representative Ernest Lundeen of Minnesota introduced a bill in January 1936 to increase the Court's membership by two. He said that the new justices would help with the workload and that "new blood will mean a more liberal outlook on constitutional questions."[17] Lundeen had heard that Justice Willis Van Devanter planned to retire and, with the passage of his proposal, Roosevelt would get to name three new justices, thereby solidifying a liberal majority.

During the 1936 presidential race, Roosevelt chose not to make the Court issue a part of his campaign. He was, however, still preoccupied with the situation. During the final week of the contest, Stanley High, an aide to Roosevelt, wrote in his diary, "[FDR] frequently returns to a discussion of the Supreme Court—wonders how long some of its ancient judges will hold out. Tom [Corcoran] said the other evening, 'I just saw Van Devanter. He looks very bad.' We all laughed."[18] Roosevelt won the election in a landslide and jokingly remarked at his first cabinet meeting that Justice McReynolds would still be on the Court at age 105.[19] McReynolds was reported to have said, "I'll never resign as long as that crippled son-of-a-bitch is in the White House."[20]

Princeton professor Edward S. Corwin wrote a series of newspaper articles deriding the Court's rulings on the New Deal and called for a "requirement, to be laid down by an act of Congress, or, if necessary, by constitutional amendment, that no Judge may hold office under the United States beyond his seventieth birthday."[21] Harvard professor Arthur Holcombe suggested that Corwin modify his proposal to ensure that a majority of the Court were under age seventy. He suggested that additional Judges be appointed "to the Court whenever the number of members above 70 years of age should be equal or should outnumber the members of the Court under 70." He continued:

At the present time six judges are over 70, and if no resignations of older judges should take place and such an act as I propose were adopted, the President would have power to make four additional appointments of judges under the age of 70. That would bring the

total membership of the Court up to thirteen, but as older judges
retired the number would automatically fall again to nine before further appointments would be in order. If, however, two of the older
members of the present Court could be persuaded to resign, it would
be possible to replace them with two judges of less than 70 years and
establish a majority for the younger members of the Court without
bringing the total membership above nine.

My feeling is that the threat of such an act of Congress might
perhaps persuade some of the older judges to resign without the
necessity of making additional appointments, but if not, I believe the
public would support the general proposition that the majority of the
total number of the Court, whatever the total number might be,
should be not more than 70 years of age.[22]

Corwin thought the revised plan "most ingenious, devilishly so" and
passed it along to Attorney General Cummings.[23] At the same time, Cummings was writing a history of the Justice Department and happened on a
report written in 1913 by then Attorney General James McReynolds, now
FDR's chief nemesis on the Court. In an especially intriguing section concerned with aging federal judges, McReynolds wrote:

Judges of the United States Courts, at the age of 70, after having
served 10 years, may retire upon full pay. In the past, many judges
have availed themselves of this privilege. Some, however, have
remained upon the bench long beyond the time that they are able to
adequately discharge their duties, and in consequence the administration of justice has suffered . . . I suggest an act providing that when
any judge of a Federal court below the Supreme Court fails to avail
himself of the privilege of retiring now granted by law, that the President be required, with the advice and consent of the Senate, to
appoint another judge, who would preside over the affairs of the
court and have precedence over the older one. This will insure at all
times the presence of a judge sufficiently active to discharge
promptly and adequately the duties of the court.[24]

Cummings thought that McReynolds's recommendation could easily be
applied to the Supreme Court and quickly brought it to the attention of the
president. The irony of McReynolds's report was not lost on Roosevelt, who
had made up his mind to increase the Court's membership. Roosevelt and a
handful of close advisers worked in secrecy on the proposal. Congress, and
many members of the administration, were not formally informed of the
impending plan, as Roosevelt did not want to give his detractors time to plan

a counterattack. Though some inklings of an impending plan began to leak, no one in Washington was prepared for the dramatic events that followed.

Though his real target was the Supreme Court, on February 5, 1937, Roosevelt announced a plan to reform the entire federal judiciary. He suggested that the federal courts were overburdened with case backlogs and needed additional help to resolve the crisis. He proposed streamlining federal jurisdiction, increasing the number of lower court judgeships, and creating a standardized system to temporarily move lower court judges to districts with crowded dockets. The heart of the president's plan, however, was what has become known as the "court-packing" proposal. Just as Corwin and Holcombe had proposed, for each justice over age seventy who had served ten years, an additional justice could be appointed. In the bill sent to Congress, Roosevelt offered his rationale:

A part of the problem of obtaining a sufficient number of judges to dispose of cases is the capacity of the judges themselves. This brings forward the question of aged or infirm judges—a subject of delicacy and yet one which requires frank discussion. In exceptional cases, of course, judges, like other men, retain to an advanced age full mental and physical vigor. Those not so fortunate are often unable to perceive their own infirmities . . .

A lower mental or physical vigor leads men to avoid an examination of complicated and changed conditions. Little by little, new facts become blurred through old glasses fitted, as it were, for the needs of another generation, older men, assuming that the scene is the same as it was in the past, cease to explore or inquire into the present or the future.[25]

Roosevelt's 1937 plan was significantly different from any of the proposals discussed in 1869. Though both plans sought to reorganize and streamline the federal judiciary, only Roosevelt's 1937 plan was a clear partisan attempt to change the composition of the Supreme Court. Unlike the 1869 proposals, the appointments made would be in addition to the justices already serving and thereby officially increase the Court's size.

The President had huge majorities in both houses of Congress and newspapers reported that this fact alone should allow the bill to pass without difficulty. FDR's opponents quickly saw through the president's crowded docket/old age argument. Many liberal members of Congress, including Texas Democrat Tom Connally and progressive Burton K. Wheeler of Montana, however, immediately opposed the bill. Democrats were uncomfortable with what they saw as the president's disingenuous reasoning for the proposal. On March 22, Chief Justice Hughes submitted a detailed report to the Senate

Judiciary Committee that factually refuted the president's claims that the Court needed help.[26] The next day the report was reprinted on the front page of the *New York Times*, further undercutting the Court-packing plan.[27]

Roosevelt had no choice but to begin trumpeting his main reason, that the conservative Court was thwarting the national will.[28] Although many Democrats had said they would not support the proposal, by the end of March, Roosevelt still had a majority in both houses of Congress to increase the Court's size. But Congress began seriously considering a constitutional amendment for compulsory retirement as a viable alternative to the president's plan. For example, Democratic Senators Allen Ellander, Edward R. Burke, and Charles O. Andrews had each introduced an amendment for some form of mandatory retirement.[29] On March 25, Columbia University Law School Dean Young B. Smith testified before the Senate Judiciary Committee that while the president's plan was flawed, a constitutional amendment for mandatory retirement at age seventy-five should be enacted.[30] The *New York Times* covered the new push for compulsory retirement, but when Roosevelt refused to budge from his own statutory plan, the mandatory retirement movement lost its momentum.[31] Had the president dropped his already badly damaged plan and supported a constitutional amendment, forced departure at age seventy or seventy-five may very well have passed.

The Court itself, however, once again took center stage. In a series of decisions, the Court began upholding state and national laws regulating the economy. Specifically, Justice Owen Roberts switched sides and began voting with Justices Brandeis, Cardozo, Stone, and Chief Justice Hughes. While Roberts's switch occurred in conference before the Court-packing plan was announced, it was soon clear to FDR supporters that the shift in the Court's direction weakened the administration's position to increase the Court's size. A second surprise event from the Court itself further weakened the Court-packing scheme. Justice Willis Van Devanter decided to step down.[32]

1937 RETIREMENT ACT

On March 1, shortly after the president announced his Court-packing plan, his opponents in Congress quickly revised the 1869 Retirement Act in an attempt to head off the President's more drastic proposal.[33] The 1937 Retirement Act not only left intact the age-seventy, ten-year provision for resignation with full pay, but it also broadened the parameters, allowing for a form of retirement from regular active service known as senior status, with full pay at age seventy with ten years of service.[34] Senior status allowed retired justices to remain federal judges and be called to temporary active duty at the discretion of the Chief Justice.[35] Indeed, following his retirement, Justice Van Devanter would often remind people, "I am still a judge."[36]

Just as the previous retirement acts had done, the 1937 statute had an immediate and pronounced impact on the Court. Two of the Four Horsemen[37] who had stood fast against the New Deal, Van Devanter and Sutherland, immediately decided to give up their seats and retire. Chief Justice Charles Evans Hughes recalled, "I have reason to believe that they would have retired earlier, had it not been for the failure of Congress to make good its promise to continue to pay in full the salaries of justices who resigned."[38]

Before the 1937 Act, justices technically had to resign their seats, rather than retire. This left their pensions subject to fluctuating civil service guidelines. Indeed, due to the depressed economy of the early 1930s, Congress passed a statute in 1932 that was interpreted as cutting in half the retirement salaries of federal judges who had "resigned" their seats as opposed to those who had "retired." The latter group could not have their pensions reduced under Article I, section 1 of the Constitution because they were technically still in office. Of course no Supreme Court justice had ever technically retired until passage of the 1937 Act and Willis Van Devanter's departure. Other federal judges had the retirement option beginning in 1919. In perhaps the most glaring example of the need for this reform, Justice Oliver Wendell Holmes's pension was reduced from $20,000 to $10,000.[39] In 1933, the attorney general argued that Congress should eliminate the provision applying to federal judges, as it had only saved $25,583 in the past year and would force judges who were no longer effective to remain in their seats.[40] Congress responded and passed a bill restoring Holmes's salary to $20,000.[41] The 1937 Act effectively solved this problem for future retirements.

WILLIS VAN DEVANTER: I OWED IT TO MYSELF TO QUIT

After the passage of the Retirement Act, Van Devanter's close friend, Senator William Borah, urged the Justice to step down.[42] On May 18, 1937, as FDR's Court-packing bill was before the Judiciary committee, seventy-eight-year-old Willis Van Devanter announced that he would retire from the Court in a few weeks, on June 1, 1937. Chief Justice Hughes said "Justice Van Devanter waited until the close of the current Term."[43] One month after stepping down, Van Devanter explained his reasons for leaving to the *New York Times*, calling the timing "coincidental":

> I had intended first to retire five years ago but I stayed on, increasingly though I became convinced in my conclusion that I owed it to myself to quit . . . I was seventy-eight and I felt at last that I owed it

to myself to retire from regular service . . . It was no surprise that I did that. The surprise lay only in the time that I did it. It was a decision that was not reached overnight . . . And I didn't think that I was too old for the job.[44]

Van Devanter's friends said that he had contemplated stepping down five years earlier but stayed in his place for political reasons.[45] They also said that he probably would have departed earlier, had the 1937 Retirement Act been in effect.[46] Van Devanter took advantage of the new provision allowing retired federal judges to continue to serve the federal judiciary. Though partisanship played a role in Van Devanter's departure, ultimately the retirement bill proved decisive. President Roosevelt finally had his first Supreme Court nomination, after four and a half years in office.

That summer, the President's Court-packing proposal went down to defeat. The Senate Judiciary Committee, across party lines, said the plan showed "the futility and absurdity of the devious" and if passed, would provide a "vicious precedent which must necessarily undermine our system."[47] Though a revised bill gained some momentum in the whole Senate, when the leading proponent of the bill Majority Leader Joe Robinson suddenly died, the court-packing issue went with him.

GEORGE SUTHERLAND

The next winter, January 1938, George Sutherland announced his retirement, publicly noting his fifteen years of service and that he had recently passed age seventy-five.[48] Privately, Sutherland's reasons for departing lay primarily with the expanded retirement provision, FDR's attack on the Court, and the president's defeated plan to pack it. He wrote a friend, "It was so good of you to write me about my retirement. I should have gone nearly a year ago had it not been for the fight on the Court, which I am glad to say is now a thing of the past, and which I think will never be revived.[49] Sutherland's mention of almost departing "nearly a year ago" was a clear reference to the expanded retirement provisions that had been enacted almost a year before Sutherland's letter. Chief Justice Hughes cited Sutherland's institutional concern for not departing earlier, "Justice Sutherland, who did not wish to create a second vacancy until the first had been filled, did not retire until the [October 1937] Term was well underway; but both [Sutherland and Van Devanter] had determined to retire when the privilege was accorded by the Act of 1937."[50] The same concern for multiple vacancies occurred in 1992 when Harry Blackmun waited an additional year after Byron White's retirement.

Benjamin Cardozo and the Resulting Disability Provision

No matter the extent of warnings from colleagues, family and friends, and debilitating illness, there are some justices who simply refuse to relinquish their seats. But when statutory obstacles stand in the way, it is not surprising that justices hang on. The case of Justice Benjamin Cardozo is exemplary. He was a tireless worker, exhausting himself by the close of each term. He used work as a way to escape, if not beat, illness.

In 1926, he contracted a "dangerous" staphylococcus infection on his face that later moved to his kidney. Though he was so ill that he had to be carried from the Courtroom on a stretcher, he ignored his doctors' advice of three months of rest and almost immediately went back to work.[51] His wife Nellie was ill for years and her declining health affected Cardozo. After her death in 1930, he suffered his first heart attack. Though it was mild and he was back to work within a week, his doctor later remarked that Cardozo had lived longer than what was reasonably expected at the time.[52]

In April 1935, a visitor to the Court observed that Cardozo struggled to read an opinion from the bench. "His eyes began to twitch so violently that his glasses fell off and it was only by putting his finger over one eye that he was able to continue."[53] Two months later, Cardozo suffered his second heart attack and his physician recommended he step down from the Court. After being confined to bed, he returned to the Court and to his exhausting work schedule, in defiance of his doctors and nurses. "I have been cautioned to moderate my pace, but you know that is an impossibility for me."[54] He quipped, "When I speak of my feeble heart, I refer to its spiritual qualities. Physically the old heart is as good as senescence has a right to expect."[55]

In December 1937, he suffered two more heart attacks and contracted shingles. Cardiograms showed his heartbeat was deteriorating. He wrote a friend, "The pain of shingles is 'exquisite.' In my case a wicked old heart brought about some complications, but I am told that the heart muscles are evincing a satisfaction with present conditions which is not shared by their owner."[56] On January 8, he had a stroke, paralyzing his left arm and leg and taking away the vision in his right eye. Though he miraculously began to recover in February and March, he soon began to decline.

Cardozo's closest friend on the Court, Justice Harlan Fiske Stone, was concerned about whether Cardozo would be able to resume his duties in the fall. Stone was well aware of the Court's limited options concerning a disabled colleague. He wrote to a friend that the Court might have to step in to secure "the privilege of the retirement act" on Cardozo's behalf.[57] As with Justices Hunt, Moody, and Pitney, it would take a special bill to allow Cardozo, who had not reached age seventy, to retire with benefits. During a visit from Chief

Justice Hughes, Cardozo remarked, "They tell me I am going to get well, but I file a dissenting opinion."[58] There were rumors that he was planning on stepping down and that Roosevelt had urged him to wait and make a decision after he recovered.[59] Such rumors are common though, when word gets out that a justice is ill and it is unlikely Cardozo would have departed prior to age seventy and retirement eligibility. In late June he suffered two more heart attacks, was given blood transfusions, and fed intravenously. One of his doctors remarked on the connection between Cardozo's battle to live and his work on the Court:

> In delirium, as in his conscious moments, Justice Cardozo's whole interest in his life seemed to be to try to recover for his work. In delirious moments he went over and over again old decisions and court cases. Outside the delirium his mind was surprisingly clear. He was never able to express the hopelessness of his plight.[60]

The ailing Justice suffered a massive coronary and died on July 9, 1938. Cardozo's failure to step down was partly a direct result of his association of work with life. Like a number of justices before him, Cardozo felt that to relinquish his seat on the Court would be to give up on life. Another important factor was that at age sixty-eight, he was not eligible for retirement benefits. Had he chose to depart, he would have had to resign his seat and would not have continued drawing a salary.

With Cardozo's case the catalyst, the next month Congress finally acted on the problem of disabled justices. On August 5, 1939, the first disability statute for federal judges, including Supreme Court justices, was passed. Permanently disabled justices were allowed to retire regardless of age. If they had served less than ten years as a federal judge, they would only receive one half of their last annual salary for the rest of their life. However, if a disabled justice had ten years or more service as a federal judge, he would receive the full amount of his last salary, for the remainder of his life. Though it was passed too late for Cardozo to take advantage of, it went a long way in helping solve the problem of disability. Still left unaddressed, was the issue of what could be done if a disabled justice refused to avail himself of even these generous provisions.

LOUIS D. BRANDEIS AND CHARLES EVANS HUGHES

In stark contrast to the close of Justice Cardozo's tenure on the Court, Louis D. Brandeis's retirement was precipitated by his concern for the institutional health of the Court. During the 1937 and 1938 Terms, Justice Brandeis began to physically decline. Though his opinion-writing decreased, he showed no signs of mental deterioration.[61] After suffering a heart attack in early 1939, Brandeis took a month off to recover. He returned to the Court in time to sit with the new Justice, Felix Frankfurter, before sending his unexpected retirement letter to President Roosevelt on February 13, 1939. That same day, the eighty-three-year-old Justice wrote his sister-in-law about his decision:

> I want you to know promptly that I am not retiring from the Court because of ill health. Mine seems to be as good as heretofore. But years have limited the quantity and intensity of work possible, and I think the time has come when a younger man should assume the burden.[62]

Chief Justice Hughes was determined to leave the bench before becoming a burden to his colleagues. He had a standing arrangement with his children for a vote by secret ballot should any one of them detect signs of mental deterioration and feel he should step down. No such vote was ever taken. In March 1939, Hughes contracted a bleeding ulcer and was absent from the Court for a few weeks. He recovered and continued his duties without interruption for two more terms. In June 1941, he decided to step down:

> While I was still in good health, I then realized that the work was too heavy for me at my age, as it was increasingly difficult to maintain the necessary number of hours of sustained effort. I had criticized judges for trying to hang on after they were unable to bring full vigor to their task. As I felt I could not keep the pace that I had set for myself as Chief Justice, I decided that the time had come to follow my own advice.[63]

After eleven years as Chief Justice, Hughes retired on July 1, 1941, informing President Roosevelt of his intentions the month before. He recalled the choice he made between resignation and retirement:

> When I felt that I must no longer attempt to carry the heavy burden of the Chief Justiceship, I had a strong inclination, as I had considerable means, to "resign" and not take advantage of the retirement allowance. But on full consideration I came to the conclusion, as did Justice Brandeis whose fortune was far greater than mine, that this would make an undesirable precedent. Congress passed the Retirement Act without qualification, and it was in the interest of the Court that the policy of the statute should be maintained.[64]

PIERCE BUTLER AND JAMES CLARK McREYNOLDS

Pierce Butler became eligible for retirement on his seventieth birthday, March 17, 1936. He chose not to step down, however, and did not change his mind the following year after the passage of the 1937 Act's expanded senior status provision. On June 5, 1939, Butler presided over the last day of the Court's Term with the absences of Chief Justice Hughes and Justice McReynolds.[65] It would be Butler's last appearance on the bench. In August 1939, he entered the hospital with a bladder ailment. It was not considered serious and Butler was soon released, but the problem recurred the next month and Butler was back in the hospital. Though he hoped to return to the Court during the fall Term, his condition worsened and on November 16, 1939, he died after serving for seventeen years on the Court.[66] It is difficult to say without direct evidence whether his decision not to avail himself of the retirement act was partisan. Brandeis's successor, William O. Douglas took his seat in April 1939, making it possible for Butler to depart at the close of the Term without being concerned for the Court's ability to function. As a result, it is possible that Butler had no intention of departing under a Democratic administration.

After Butler's death, James Clark McReynolds was the last of the Four Horsemen remaining on the Court. McReynolds became eligible to retire in February 1932, and though he considered retiring, he chose instead to remain in his seat.[67] McReynolds staunchly opposed FDR's New Deal legislation, but found his support from within the Court dwindling since Van Devanter's retirement in 1937. As Roosevelt was headed toward an unprecedented third term in the White House, the embittered McReynolds wrote to his brother, "A war with a fool at the top is not a pleasant prospect. He is acting like a crazy man."[68] Still in good health at age seventy-nine, but unwilling to continue a losing battle against Roosevelt, McReynolds announced his retirement on February 1, 1941. He said that he had tried to protect the country, but "any country that elects Roosevelt three times deserves no protection."[69] Though an opponent of Roosevelt, McReynolds did not depart for partisan reasons. He may have stayed longer than he wanted because Roosevelt was in office, but ultimately personal concerns led him to step down and allow a Democrat to name his successor.

JAMES F. BYRNES

Justice James F. Byrnes was restless and unhappy during his brief one-year tenure on the Court. He was an important member of the Roosevelt administration before being appointed and immediately longed to return to the political arena. A week after the Pearl Harbor bombing, Byrnes expressed his frustration to the president:

> I must confess I found it very difficult to concentrate on the arguments that morning . . . I've been in the middle of crises since I entered public life, but yesterday with the nation confronted with the greatest crisis in its history, the best I could do was to spend hours listening to arguments about the payment for ships that were built twenty-three years ago. I was thinking so much about those ships sunk at Pearl Harbor that it was difficult to concentrate on arguments about ships that were built at Bethlehem in 1918.
>
> Mr. President, you know, before your fight on the Supreme Court was over I had concluded you were wrong, and my service on the Court has only confirmed that view . . . You urged that Justices be retired at seventy. From my experience, I've decided they shouldn't be appointed until they reach seventy.[70]

It was obvious to Roosevelt that Byrnes wanted to leave the Court and the president suggested that Byrnes take a leave of absence in order to work in the administration. The justice declined to take on additional responsibilities while remaining on the Court, but offered to resign his seat if the president could find a way for him to contribute to the war effort.[71] The president agreed and described Byrnes's new assignment as director of economic stabilization:

> In these jurisdictional disputes I want you to act as a judge and I will let it be known that your decision is my decision, and that there is no appeal. For all practical purposes you will be assistant President.[72]

After only a year on the Court, Justice Byrnes resigned writing the other justices, "Only a sense of duty impelled me to resign from the Court."[73] He became popularly known as the assistant president while working for FDR, and later went on to be secretary of state under President Truman, and then governor of South Carolina.

UNTIMELY DEATHS

In a period of only five years, Roosevelt made an unprecedented eight appointments to the Supreme Court. The 1937 Retirement Act had prompted the departures of his staunchest opponents and an entirely new

Court validated his New Deal programs. But following the retirement of Charles Evans Hughes in 1941, there would not be another retirement for nearly fifteen years. The successive deaths of five justices, four of them relatively young, in the late 1940s and early 1950s suggested that the existing retirement benefits were not generous enough and further amendment was needed.

OWEN ROBERTS

Justice Owen J. Roberts was unhappy with the increasing acrimony between his feuding colleagues and what he saw as the Court's disregard for legal precedent under Chief Justice Stone.[74] He wrote retired Chief Justice Hughes, "To work under you was the greatest experience and satisfaction of my life. When you left the Court, the whole picture changed. For me it would never be the same."[75] In January 1944 Roberts's dissatisfaction came to a head. He was upset with news reports that suggested he was the hold-out vote on an important case. Though the story was not true, Roberts insisted that one of the justices was leaking information to the press. Though all of the justices denied any leak, Roberts was not satisfied. Thereafter, he no longer participated in the traditional handshake in the justices' robing room. Instead, he waited in the hall and only joined his colleagues just before they took the bench. He began to arrive late for conferences and then only spoke to Justices Frankfurter and Robert Jackson, believing that the other justices were "sort of conspirator[s] against him."[76] Roberts resigned on July 31, 1945.[77]

Though Hugo Black had initially been personally close to Roberts, their relationship was particularly strained. Black's professional indignation toward Roberts was so great that he refused to sign Roberts's customary farewell letter unless certain complimentary sentences were omitted.[78] The result of this squabble was that no letter was ever sent to Roberts, though several of the justices sent letters on their own. Justice Jackson wrote Justice Frankfurter about the matter, "Black, as you and I know, has driven Roberts off the bench and pursued him after his retirement."[79] After departing he wrote, "I have no illusions about my judicial career. But one can only do what one can. Who am I to revile the good God that he did not make me a Marshall, a Taney, a Bradley, a Holmes, a Brandeis, or a Cardozo."[80]

HARLAN FISKE STONE

In 1932 Stone was unhappy on the Court and considered the possibility of resigning. Following the resignation of Justice Holmes, Stone told President

Hoover that he would be willing to step down if Benjamin Cardozo were appointed, attempting to allay the president's fears that there would be too many justices from New York. Cardozo was appointed and Stone did not have to resign. When friends suggested the time might be right for a possible run at the presidency, Stone replied, "You are quite right in saying that there will be an entirely new political picture in the next four years, but having seen it all at close range, I cannot say that I am interested in it. I might be interested in going back to practice law in New York, as I suppose I could do at any time."[81] After John Foster Dulles's invitation to return to private practice in New York, Stone replied, "After thinking the matter over . . . I cannot persuade myself that I ought to abandon the path on which I have started."[82]

On October 12, 1936, Stone became ill with bacillary dysentery after returning from a vacation. His condition was so serious that he stayed home in bed for nine weeks, six of which he spent fending off death. He wrote, "It laid me low. [Fighting the illness was] hard work for one who is accustomed to always being well and working at top-speed."[83] Chief Justice Hughes wrote him, "Don't try to come back too soon—we need you—but we need you in full vigor."[84] In January, the sixty-four year-old Stone returned to the Court, taking on his full share of the work. He wrote Justice Frankfurter, "Now that I have got it going, I think my intellectual apparatus will work as well as usual, and ought to keep running for sometime past seventy."[85]

In 1941, Stone was confirmed as the new Chief Justice following the retirement of Charles Evans Hughes. At different times throughout Stone's tenure as Chief, rumors circulated that his elevation was part of a deal whereby he would eventually depart in favor of Justice Jackson. Stone commented, "It is an old game to chisel the office holder if you want his place and some of the New Deal boys are especially skillful at it. Of course, no sensible man wishes to overstay his time in any office, but my present inclination is to choose the time of retirement for myself, without the aid of any interested parties."[86]

On reaching his twentieth anniversary at the Court, rumors once again circulated that he would step down. The growing feuds among the justices weighed heavily on the chief, who tried unceasingly to bring the justices together. A friend urged Stone not to give up and step down, "For God's sake, don't do it. People all over this country love you. I can imagine your aggravation and irritation, but for heaven's sake, don't leave us."[87] Similarly, Judge Learned Hand wrote, "Brother, I like to think of you as keeping the faith in which we were both reared. Often I wonder how you can do it, but for the love of God, hold the fort, and remember that we watch you with joy."[88] Stone put their fears to rest and endeavored to remain in his place: "The delicacy and difficulties of the situation in the Court seem to make it desirable for me to contribute such stabilizing influence as I can until conditions are somewhat better."[89]

Though Stone felt it his duty to be a balancing force on the increasingly divisive Court, he did not intend to remain much longer. On July 15, 1945 he wrote his son, Lauson:

> In the natural course of events, I should retire before very long. The work is heavy and nerve-wracking, and the country is entitled to have a Chief Justice who is in his prime instead of one who is on the wrong side of seventy three, as I should be in October. My retirement would also lighten the burdens on Mother. I am telling you this so that you may be free to say that my membership on the Court is not likely to be long a handicap to any firm which you might join.[90]

Cognizant of the events surrounding the Field and Holmes departures, he told his son Marshall later that summer, that he would depart before any sign of deterioration manifested itself. He added that he had decided to retire after a short time, but did not fix a date. Marshall Stone suggested, "I would be surprised if he had not thought of staying on long enough for a Republican President to be able to appoint his successor."[91] Despite Marshall Stone's hypothesis, there is no indication of partisan motivation in any of Stone's documented remarks about retirement. He wrote a friend:

> After one gets into his seventy-fourth year, there is a natural expectation that he will not carry for long the heavy burden that I am carrying. Sometimes I think to myself when I see the performances that go on around me, 'Why subject oneself to that sort of thing?' And then I think what would happen if I weren't here, and what would I do if I didn't have this job and I conclude it is perhaps my duty to keep going. Who knows?[92]

On April 22, 1946, while announcing a dissent from the bench, the Chief fell ill. Douglas recalled, "Stone did not actually die on the Bench, but he did have a fatal stroke ... while I was reading *Girouard v. United States*,[93] to which he had written a dissent. As I announced the decision I heard Stone mumbling, and when I finished I signaled Black to do something."[94] Justice Wiley B. Rutledge recounted:

> I looked over to the center chair and saw the Chief sitting back, holding his opinions in reading position, his right hand fumbling through the pages. Then I heard him say in a low voice something like 'the case should be stayed; we decided to send this case back to conference for reconsideration.' Still it did not occur to me that he was ill. I thought he had suddenly decided that a case which had

been announced previously had some hitch in it and was calling a recess to go off and straighten things out. Suddenly, the gavel banged, and Black adjourned the Court until two-thirty.[95]

Justice Harold Burton continued:

The Court rose at once. Justices Black and Reed helped the Chief to the robing room. He walked about not thinking or speaking clearly. He lay down there. The Marshal called (the doctor) from the Capitol. He reported good pulse and pressure but some blood circulation indigestion . . . The rest of the Justices (except Justice Murphy) had lunch as usual and returned to the bench at 2:30. Justice Black presiding announced "in the temporary absence of the Chief Justice" the three cases which (the) Chief had been authorized to announce . . . We then proceeded with the regular business.[96]

Justice Douglas later explained why the Court reconvened, "We . . . decided that since Stone was still alive, we should return and announce the remaining decisions; otherwise we might have had to put some cases down for rehearing."[97] Stone was taken home in an ambulance, and his physician held out hope of recovery. That evening, however, the chief justice died of a fatal cerebral thrombosis. Douglas offered his own opinion of the cause of the chief's death: "Under Stone we were . . . almost in a continuous Conference. He believed in free speech for everybody, including himself. His insistence upon detail hastened his death. If there were twenty-two points in a petition for certiorari, he would discuss every single one of them. The work was grueling and it was just too great a strain for a man of Stone's age."[98]

FRANK MURPHY

Beginning in 1946, Justice Frank Murphy started to experience health problems. He was periodically in and out of the hospital for what appeared to be minor heart and circulatory problems. By 1948 he was very unhappy, partly because of his illnesses, but due largely to personal problems stemming from his impending marriage and deteriorating relationship with his family. He suffered a nervous inflammation and missed the fall opening of the Court. He had a recurring case of shingles that put him in and out of the hospital throughout the year. Justices Rutledge and Douglas kept him abreast of Court developments while he was away.[99] Rutledge was especially keen to see Murphy's health restored. "It is much more important for your long-run service here, invaluable to the causes we seek to serve," Rutledge wrote, "that you safeguard your health even at the expense of taking further time."[100] During Murphy's absence from the Court, Rutledge offered the use of his clerks to help with the workload. Murphy agreed and was able to continue to participate fully, albeit from his hospital bed, during the fall and winter of 1948.

Two months shy of his fifty-ninth birthday, Murphy wrote his brother about stepping down from the Court: "What is the use of retiring at 70? At that date in life the Lord retires everyone anyway. It seems to me when federal service takes the best years of one's life—years you cannot capture—the public servant should be allowed to retire without reference to disability or age."[101] Financially, Murphy had no choice but to remain in his place, as he was ineligible to retire under the 1937 Act. Medical bills and other expenditures left Murphy with very little savings, but when he was offered a high-paying corporate job, he said to his brother George, "I am not for sale."[102] He returned to the bench in January 1949, but once again had to return to the hospital for brief stays in February, April, and June, becoming increasingly dependent on painkillers. Indeed, Murphy's drug habit led him to begin making illegal purchases.[103] He was unable to continue to perform his share of the workload, despite relying on his clerks for opinion writing. In his final two years, Justice Rutledge cast votes for him, and he authored only 18 of the Court's 224 majority opinions.[104]

In April 1949, a magazine article suggested that President Truman and Chief Justice Vinson had made "several attempts" to get Murphy to resign. Murphy wrote the chief that he had no intention of resigning and called the story a "cooked up job" and "an injustice" to the president, the chief, and himself.[105] Murphy was absent as the Court finished its work for the 1948–1949 Term. Black hoped Murphy would recover and return for the new Term in the fall. "I do not believe it possible," Black encouragingly wrote Murphy, "that if your seat should become vacant it would be filled by a person who even gets near to your fine qualities."[106] Less than a month later, however, Justice Murphy unexpectedly suffered a fatal heart attack on July 19, 1949. Rutledge wrote Douglas:

> George Murphy told me Frank's death was as unexpected to the family as to us. One of the last things Frank told me was that his heart was entirely all right—his doctors had cleared him on that. Strange how wrong even the best doctors could be.[107]

WILEY B. RUTLEDGE, FRED VINSON, AND ROBERT JACKSON

A tireless worker, Rutledge was frequently unhappy and depressed toward the end of his tenure and briefly contemplated resigning from the Court to accept a law school deanship.[108] Justice Douglas described Rutledge's work ethic:

[H]e went at writing an opinion pretty much as a law professor goes to work writing a Law Journal article. So he exhausted himself unnecessarily, doing more than deciding a particular case and trying to work out the total mosaic in which the case appeared in legal literature. His mill ground slowly and very fine. He probably put more actual energy and concentration into each of the several cases that came across his desk than anyone in modern history.[109]

Rutledge had two habits that led to his early demise. He was an incessant cigarette smoker, a habit dating back to when he was eleven years old, and he was a prodigious worker. His gristmill ground very fine. He polished opinions with meticulous care. He worked more than any of us, staying at his desk night after night until the wee hours.[110]

During the summer of 1949, the years of excessive labor caught up with Justice Rutledge. His family and friends were worried by his physical and mental condition. After Murphy's death, Rutledge seemed to decline further. Two weeks before his death, a friend wrote him: "During this transitional period on the Court, the best service you can render is to help decide cases. To hell with writing opinions . . . You are needed on the Court more now than at any previous time, but your first duty is to remain on earth."[111] Less than two months after Murphy's death, Justice Rutledge died of a cerebral hemorrhage during a vacation in Maine, on September 10, 1949. He was fifty-five years old.

After the sudden deaths of Justices Murphy and Rutledge, the Court's membership was stable until just before the start of the 1953 Term. On September 8, Chief Justice Vinson suddenly died of a massive heart attack.[112] He was only sixty-three and had served on the Court for just over seven years. Justice Douglas wrote:

He was a happy party man, enjoying bourbon and branch water, bridge with Eisenhower at the White House, and all the amenities of social Washington. He had huge bags under his eyes and a very heavy paunch. Dr. George Draper, the physician I so respected, had seen him at a gathering and I asked what the medical appraisal was. 'He'll die soon of a heart attack,' Draper said.[113]

Upon hearing of the chief justice's death, Justice Frankfurter, who had been disdainful of Vinson's leadership and disliked him personally, said, "This is the first indication I have ever had that there is a God."[114]

Only seven months after Vinson's death, Justice Jackson suffered an unexpected heart attack on March 30, 1954. He spent over a month recovering in the hospital, but rejoined his colleagues on May 17, so the entire Court would be present for the announcement of the decision in *Brown v. Board of Education*.[115] At age sixty-two, Jackson returned from the summer recess and began the new Term in October. When friends suggested he slow down, Jackson demurred. One of his long-time friends wrote:

> When, toward the end, we remonstrated against his working habits, he always replied with a smile that he would prefer to carry out what he conceived to be his duties, even though it meant a shorter life, than to seek release from those obligations by living an easier life.[116]

While driving from his home in McLean, Virginia, to the Supreme Court for work on Saturday morning, October 9, Jackson became ill. Later that day, he died. Jackson's death, after thirteen years of service on the Court, came only thirteen months after Vinson's.

CONCLUSION

As in 1801 and 1869 a politically motivated Congress and president targeted the federal judiciary, and the Supreme Court specifically, with proposals to force their opponents to step down. While the Court-packing plan seemed radical in its scope, it was entirely predictable given the partisan rancor that produced previous transformative legislation. Mandatory retirement amendments were also considered. Though neither the Court-packing proposal nor a mandatory retirement scheme succeeded, an expanded retirement provision did pass. Initially, the carrot of senior status and salary protection in the 1937 Retirement Act prompted the voluntary departures of a number of aged opposition justices prior to decline, disability, and burdening the Court.

As before, this initial success did not last. Caseloads rose to heights not seen in half a century and justices tried to meet the demands of the increasing docket. When a group of justices became ill well short of the age seventy requirement of the retirement statute, and ultimately died while still on the Court, the climate was again ripe for fundamental change. As I will discuss in the next chapter, reforms continued as the American Bar Association took up the cause of mandatory retirement, and ultimately a new Republican Congress in 1954 saw the recent deaths on the Court as a chance to induce aged liberal justices to step down. Once again, though, instead of passing a constitutional amendment for compulsory retirement, Congress further reduced the age at which justices could depart. Under these expanded retirement provisions, the period from 1954 to the present was dominated by voluntary retirements, in sharp contrast to the previous eras. Although personal and institutional concerns played a part in departure decisions, the expanded provisions gave justices more flexibility to act politically, and they responded.

7

1954–1970

The Limits of Power

[Warren has no] right to choose which president he thinks should
dominate for the next twenty years the Supreme Court.
　　　　　　　　—California Governor Ronald Reagan, 1968

If I had ever known what was going to happen to this country and
this Court, I never would have resigned. They would have had to
carry me out of here on a plank!
　　　　　　　　—Former Chief Justice Earl Warren, 1974

The period from 1954 to the present has been a time for testing the limits of
power. Bolstered by the American Bar Association, Congress once again considered limiting judicial tenure. Individual justices faced decisions about
retirement and relinquishing the power of their office under the most generous retirement system in the Court's history. Presidents tested the limits of
their powers to influence the Supreme Court through the succession process.
The justices also pushed the envelope of partisanship by engaging in a new
brand of succession politics. The members of the Court, pushing the boundaries of internal, collegial decision-making, collectively made decisions about
taking power away from one of their colleagues. Through it all, the succession
process remained remarkably consistent with voluntary retirements the norm.
　　The goal of inducing the departures of old-regime opposition justices was
sought by new reforms. Institutional health improved as fewer aged and infirm
justices held on to their seats. What Congress did not intend, however, and did
not foresee, was that increased benefits facilitated leaving in the justices' hands
the opportunities for partisan departures. Though justices in the current
period, like most of their predecessors, were concerned with institutional and

personal factors in making their departure decisions, partisan concerns steadily grew in importance. While most justices were wary of staying too long and being burdens to their colleagues, increased retirement benefits led to an increase in justices engaging in succession politics. Increased opportunity, and the naked partisanship of a number of recent justices, suggest that current structures are in need of reform.

After nearly a decade where several justices died on the bench, Congress moved to radically alter the provisions of the eighty-five-year-old retirement statute. First enacted in the aftermath of the Civil War, the 1869 provision required justices to reach age seventy and have at least ten years of service on the federal bench in order to step down and continue to receive their salary. Though amended several times, most notably to add the senior service and salary protection inducements in 1937, it remained largely unchanged in its rigid requirements. The ailments, declines, and eventual deaths of Harlan Fiske Stone, Frank Murphy, Wiley Rutledge, and Fred Vinson, prompted congressional action. On February 10, 1954, Congress expanded the parameters for retirement to include not only those who reached age seventy and had ten years of service, but also those justices who attained the age of sixty-five with fifteen years of service on the federal courts (see Table 7.1).

Compared with the departures that occurred earlier in the Court's history, the justices who departed in the last half of the twentieth century exhibited an unusually high amount of partisanship. Extending the retirement statute paved the way for a new era of voluntary retirements. With retirement easier to obtain, increased levels of partisanship resulted. Table 7.2 shows the most recent departing justices in relation to the presidents they departed under. While only nine of nineteen departed under copartisan presidents—presidents who shared their party affiliation, general ideological outlook, or both—nearly all the rest exhibited other forms of partisanship, like attempting to hang on to their seats until a favorable administration took office. This was certainly the case for such justices as William O. Douglas and Thurgood Marshall, and probably the case for Hugo Black and William J. Brennan.

Why the seemingly sudden burst of apparently partisan activity? Once again, institutional arrangements played a crucial role. Increased retirement benefit afforded greater opportunity to engage in succession politics and these justices served under the expanded provisions of the 1937 and 1954 Retirement Acts. Workload has also been an important variable in the departure decisions of the justices. As Figure 7.1 shows, the Court's docket continued to rise in this period. Historically, rising caseloads have blunted considerations of partisanship in the departure decision-making process. But the Court has taken dramatic action to counteract the burdens of the rising docket.

Table 7.3 highlights some of the institutional changes that the Court has made to combat the unprecedented dockets. Interestingly, many of these

TABLE 7.1

Significant Retirement and Pension Provisions: 1954–Present

1954	All federal judges, including Supreme Court justices, may retire at age seventy with at least ten years of service as a federal judge OR at age sixty-five with fifteen years of service as a federal judge and receive the salary of their office at the time of their retirement for life. These provisions also apply to retiring in senior status.
1984	The "Rule of 80" is established. Justices having reached the age of sixty-five may retire from office provided that the sum of their age and years of judicial service equal at least eighty. Such retired justices receive for life the salary of their office at the time of their retirement. Justices having reached the age of sixty-five may retire in senior status provided that the sum of their age and years of judicial service equal at least eighty. Such senior status justices will receive for life the salary of the office. The word "resignation" is removed from federal law so that only "retired" justices are eligible for benefits. Justices who resign are no longer federal judges and receive no benefits.
1989	Justices retiring in senior status are required to perform actual judicial duties in order to continue to receive the same salary increases as sitting members of the Court. Each year such justices must certify that during the previous twelve months they have been engaged in judicial work generally equivalent to what a regular sitting member of the judiciary would accomplish in three months.
1993	Retired justices no longer receive offices at the Court. Instead, they may have space at the newly constructed Thurgood Marshall Federal Judiciary Building located behind Union Station.
1996	Justices retiring in senior status may attribute a sufficient part of the work performed in such subsequent year to the earlier year so that the work so attributed, when added to the work performed during such earlier year, satisfied the requirements for certification for that year. However, a justice or judge may not receive credit for the same work for purposes of certification for more than 1 year.

Adapted from: Lee Epstein et al., *The Supreme Court Compendium* (Washington, D.C.: Congressional Quarterly Press, 1994), 36–37 and 28 U.S.C 371–372.

important changes did not take place until the chief justiceship of Warren Burger in the 1970s when, as I will argue, partisanship in the departure decision-making process became more pronounced. Reforms like reducing oral argument, hiring more law clerks, and pooling the clerks for the benefit of all the justices helped make the docket more manageable.

The most important technique, however, for dealing with the rising docket, was simply hearing fewer cases and writing fewer opinions (see Table 7.4). The Court went from hearing nearly 300 cases in the early 1970s to

TABLE 7.2
Copartisanship 1954–1994: Party of Departing Justices and Presidents

Departing Justice & Party ID	Departure Date	Departing President & President's Party	Copartisan President	Partisan Departure
Sherman Minton (D)	Oct. 15, 1956	Eisenhower (R)	No	No
Stanley F. Reed (D)	Feb. 25, 1957	Eisenhower (R)	No	No
Harold H. Burton (R)	Oct. 13, 1958	Eisenhower (R)	No	No
Charles Evans Whittaker (R)	Apr. 1, 1962	Kennedy (D)	No	No
Felix Frankfurter (I)	Aug. 28, 1962	Kennedy (D)	Yes	Yes
Arthur Goldberg (D)	July 25, 1965	Johnson (D)	Yes	Yes
Thomas C. Clark (D)	June 12, 1967	Johnson (D)	Yes	Yes
Abe Fortas (D)	May 14, 1969	Nixon (R)	No	Yes
Earl Warren (R)	June 23, 1969	Nixon (R)	No	Yes
Hugo L. Black (D)	Sept. 17, 1971	Nixon (R)	No	No
John Marshall Harlan II (R)	Sept. 23, 1971	Nixon (R)	Yes	Yes
William O. Douglas (D)	Nov. 12, 1975	Ford (R)	No	Yes
Potter Stewart (R)	July 3, 1981	Reagan (R)	Yes	Yes
Warren E. Burger (R)	Sept. 26, 1986	Reagan (R)	Yes	Yes
Lewis F. Powell Jr. (D)	June 26, 1987	Reagan (R)	Yes	Yes
William J. Brennan, Jr. (D)	July 20, 1990	Bush (R)	No	Yes
Thurgood Marshall (D)	June 27, 1991	Bush (R)	No	Yes
Byron R. White (D)	June 28, 1993	Clinton (D)	Yes	Yes
Harry A. Blackmun (R)	Aug. 3, 1994	Clinton (D)	Yes	Yes

around 100 today. At the same time, the number of signed opinions has been halved over this period from a high of 146 to a low of 75. These developments made the jobs of the justices more manageable, if not more pleasant. More important, these changes facilitated longer tenures and made it easier for justices to engage in succession politics by timing their departures.

As in previous eras, important new structures emerged to influence departures (see Table 7.5). Though the increased retirement statute remained the dominant variable in the new era, other developments impacted the justices. The presidency of Lyndon Johnson not only reflected this new partisan climate, but it also demonstrated the lengths to which some presidents will go to induce departure and pack the Court with their own appointments. In one form or another, nearly every justice who has departed since Lyndon Johnson took office has engaged in succession politics. Like in previous eras, the declines and eventual departures of superannuated justices had an effect on

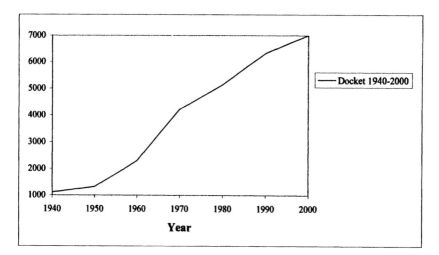

FIGURE 7.1
U.S. Supreme Court Caseload: 1940–2000

TABLE 7.3
Significant Institutional Changes in the Supreme Court: 1954–Present

Year	Institutional Change
1955	The Court begins audiotaping oral arguments. The Court announces it will no longer hear oral arguments on Fridays, reserving that day for conference.
1970	The Court reduces its dockets from 3 (original, appellate, miscellaneous) to two (original and all others).
1970	The Court reduces the time allotted to oral arguments from one hour per side to one-half hour per side.
1972	The Court begins the "cert. pool" where law clerks divide up all filed cases. A single clerk writes the memo on a given case, which is then circulated to all participating justices.
1975	The Court limits oral arguments to Mondays, Tuesdays, and Wednesdays.
1988	Congress enacts legislation virtually eliminating the Court's nondiscretionary appellate jurisdiction.

Adapted from: Lee Epstein et al., *The Supreme Court Compendium* (Washington, D.C.: Congressional Quarterly Press, 1994), 22–25.

TABLE 7.4

Dealing with the Docket: Certiorari Petitions Docketed and Granted
and Signed Opinions in the U.S. Supreme Court, 1955–1999

	Petitions for Certiorari			
Year	Docketed	Granted	Percent	Signed Opinions
1955	1,487	139	10.7	82
1960	1,874	109	17.2	110
1965	2,774	167	16.7	97
1970	4,192	255	6.0	109
1975	4,747	272	5.7	138
1980	5,120	184	3.6	123
1985	5,148	186	3.6	146
1990	6,302	141	2.2	112
1995	7,554	105	1.4	75
1999	7,377	83	1.1	74

Adapted from: Lee Epstein et al., *The Supreme Court Compendium*, 2nd ed. (Washington, D.C.: Congressional Quarterly Press, 1996), Tables 2–6 and 2–7.

their colleagues: staying too long can damage the Court. Working in conjunction with generous retirement benefit, and a decreasing workload, superannuate justices serve to promote voluntary retirement. These three factors add up to explain why no justice has died on the Court in fifty years. Because the superannuation effect caused by the departures of Black, Harlan, and Douglas was so important on subsequent departures, I deal with this subregime separately in the next chapter. Indeed, Douglas's unprecedented attempts to continue participating in the work of the Court after his retirement continues to impact the departure decisions of the current justices. The disputed Bush/Gore election of 2000 has also contributed to the partisan climate of departure that now exists. Because of its unique impact on the justices and striking parallels to the disputed Hayes/Tilden election of 1876, I will treat its effect on the current members of the Court in chapter nine.

1954 RETIREMENT ACT:
THE FAILURE OF MANDATORY RETIREMENT

After Roosevelt's Court-packing assault on the Court and the passage of the expanded 1937 retirement provision, the issue of compulsory retirement disappeared. Nine years later, in 1946, Edwin A. Falk, an influential member of

TABLE 7.5
1954–Present Departure Era: Subregimes

Subregime Years	Emergent Structure	Departing Justices	Departure Mode
1954–1963	1954 Retirement Act; Increasing Partisanship	Sherman Minton Stanley F. Reed Harold H. Burton Charles Evans Whittaker Felix Frankfurter	Retirement Retirement Retirement Retirement Retirement
1964–1970	LBJ Presidency	Arthur Goldberg Thomas C. Clark Abe Fortas Earl Warren	Resignation Retirement Resignation Retirement
1971–1999	Black/Harlan/Douglas Superannuation Effect	John M. Harlan II Hugo Black William O. Douglas Potter Stewart Warren E. Burger Lewis F. Powell, Jr. William J. Brennan, Jr. Thurgood Marshall Byron R. White Harry Blackmun	Retirement Retirement Retirement Retirement Retirement Retirement Retirement Retirement Retirement Retirement
2000–	Disputed Bush/Gore Election of 2000	William H. Rehnquist Sandra Day O'Connor John Paul Stevens Ruth Bader Ginsburg	

the New York City Bar Association, published an article and prompted a nonpartisan movement that ultimately led to the American Bar Association calling for a constitutional amendment for mandatory retirement at age seventy-five.[1] Though Congress briefly considered the amendment, they ultimately opted for statutory reform—once again expanding the existing retirement provision.

Falk argued that like the Court-packing plan, another assault on the Court's independence would inevitably occur as long as various Constitutional "loopholes," such as life tenure, remained in place.[2] Falk called for a number of reforms including mandatory retirement, fixing the number of justices at nine, and a prohibition on justices' engaging in politics such as running for the presidency. The article's publication in 1946 immediately led the New York City Bar to create a Special Committee on the Federal Courts. Falk chaired the committee and the American Bar Association created a parallel committee. By 1948, both committees approved a number of reforms including mandatory retirement at the end of the term in which a justice reached age seventy-five. But the full ABA, through its House of Delegates, initially voted down the plan, fifty-two to forty-three. And despite a speech by former Justice Owen Roberts largely endorsing the proposal,[3] the ABA spent the next two years debating and redrafting the proposal. Finally, in February 1950, the ABA approved a constitutional amendment for mandatory retirement at seventy-five, fixing the number of justices at nine, and prohibiting justices from running for either the presidency or vice-presidency within five years of having served on the Court.

Though it was covered in the *New York Times*, the ABA proposal garnered no interest in Congress. But two years later, Maryland Senator John Marshall Butler met with the New York City Bar and they convinced him to adopt the ABA proposal. In May 1952, Butler first introduced a Senate Resolution detailing the amendment's provisions including mandatory retirement. A year later he introduced a Senate Joint Resolution that his colleague Representative Edward T. Miller of Maryland introduced on the House floor.

The Eisenhower administration was supportive of the plan but not for the same reasons as those seeking reform. In December 1953 Attorney General Herbert Brownell met with members of the ABA as well as Senator Butler and Brownell expressed his approval of the plan and willingness to help. But like many in the GOP-controlled Senate, the administration's concern was inducing opposition justices to depart and they saw a constitutional amendment as more difficult to pass than a change in the existing retirement statute. Though Congress held hearings and debated a mandatory retirement scheme, on February 10, 1954 they instead passed the 1954 Retirement Act.[4] The bill expanded the age-seventy, ten-year rule to full benefits at age sixty-five with fifteen years of service on the federal bench.

Congress continued debating a constitutional amendment that included mandatory retirement but ultimately the bill failed for three main reasons. First, on May 17, 1954 the Court handed down its ruling in *Brown v. Board of Education*[5] angering both Republicans and conservative Democrats—the two groups who most favored mandatory retirement. The Warren Court followed *Brown* up with a series of decisions striking down various anti-Communism statutes, further stimulating congressional opposition.[6] Instead of protecting the Court's independence, Congress now took steps to combat it. Second, the Democrats regained control of both the Senate and House in 1955. Lastly, by October 1958, Minton, Reed, and Burton had voluntarily departed, giving Eisenhower three successive nominations.

CANTANKEROUS FELLOWS

In the eight and a half years prior to 1954, the Court experienced five consecutive deaths. Except for Chief Justice Stone, who died at age seventy-three, the other four justices were relatively young, dying in their fifties and early sixties. Jackson's death in the fall of 1954, however, was the Court's last and a new era of departure under the expanded 1954 retirement provision began. Except for two resignations, every justice who departed after Jackson, retired under the generous benefits of the 1937 and 1954 Retirement Acts, though some went grudgingly. Indeed, more than in any previous era, justices were overstaying their ability to fully contribute to the Court's work. Mental decrepitude was an increasing problem.

SHERMAN MINTON

Justice Sherman Minton's health was always precarious. He had a heart attack in 1945 at the age of fifty-five and suffered from anemia and had circulatory problems in his legs. Near the end of the 1953–1954 Term, he seriously thought about stepping down because of his health. A friend wrote, "You have my most sincere sympathy if you find yourself swimming in troubled waters in respect to your health."[7] When Minton's long-time secretary retired, he wrote Justice Frankfurter, "She no doubt thought I was on my last legs, and the ship I mastered was about to go down so she took to the rafts."[8] Minton decided to stay on for two more terms.

As the 1955–1956 Term neared its end, Minton informed his friends and colleagues that the current Term would be his last. He noticed his mental abilities starting to slip, and despite protests from his law clerks, was adamant that justices should not linger in their places. In December, he wrote his close friend, ex-President Truman:

> I am slipping fast. I have to carry a cane now all the time. I find my mental health keeps pace with my physical health. I find my work very difficult and I don't have the zest for the work I use to have. You know I have had pernicious anemia for ten years & it has sapped my vitality, especially mental.[9]

Minton wrote Justice Black that it was easy to think about retiring, "but when it comes to the consummation there is much pulling at the heart strings and wonder at what it will be like to leave you cantankerous fellows with whom it has been a priceless privilege to serve."[10] He wrote Justice Frankfurter that the retirement decision was "not so easy" and that he would have remained on the Court were it not "for my feeling of inadequacy and decrepitude and the embarrassment which comes from this deferential treatment accorded my 'senility.'" He added that the time had come to "be going home to Indiana and its hills and people I love, not 'to sit down by the silent sea and wait for the muffled oar,' but to enjoy my remaining days doing as I damned please."[11]

Minton informed President Eisenhower of his intentions on September 7. He told reporters that his health difficulties made it hard to fully perform the duties of the office. Explaining the problems he had simply with walking, Minton told the press:

> My knees buckle and I lose my balance. It's pretty depressing. This thing keeps pecking away at me. Worst of all, it's gone to my brain. It affects my power to concentrate and think and retain arguments in my mind.[12]
> [The retirement decision] was best for me and best for the court. But it is not an easy place to leave. I love it. I hate to go.[13]

Instead of departing at the close of the Term in June, Minton officially remained on the Court for the start of the new Term in the fall, in order to be eligible for full retirement benefits. On October 15, 1956, Minton took the bench with his colleagues to hear the day's orders and observe the swearing in of new members of the Supreme Court bar. After fifteen minutes on the bench, Minton turned to Justice Burton, who was sitting to his right, shook his hand, and left the bench for the last time. Minton had spent seven years on the Supreme Court and eight years on the Court of Appeals. His fifteen years of service in the federal courts and his age, sixty-five, qualified him for full retirement benefits under the new Retirement Act of 1954.

STANLEY F. REED

A little over three months later, Justice Stanley F. Reed followed Minton's example. On January 31, 1957, his nineteenth anniversary as a member of the Court, Justice Reed held a press conference and formally announced that he would retire next month. He told reporters that he had thought about stepping down "for perhaps a year" and when asked why he did finally decide to retire, he replied, "Because I'm seventy-two years old." He added that although he was in good health, the demanding work of the Court and "the strain of such unremitting exertion no longer seems wise."[14] Chief Justice Warren spoke for his colleagues when the Court reconvened on Reed's final day, "We rejoice that this retirement comes while he is in full vigor of mind and body, and capable of enjoying the many good things of life, which his long and devoted public service has compelled him to forego."[15]

After nineteen-plus years on the Court, Justice Reed retired on February 25, 1957. Although there is no documented evidence, Reed may have chosen to leave the Court in February rather than finish out the Term because he was in the minority on a number of important cases to be handed down in the spring.[16] After turning down an offer from President Eisenhower to chair the Administration's Civil Rights Commission, Justice Reed went on to serve on the lower federal courts until finally stepping down in 1975 at age ninety-one. He died in 1980 at the age of ninety-six, an astonishing twenty-three years after his retirement from the Supreme Court.[17]

HAROLD BURTON

By the end of the 1956–1957 Term, Justice Burton began to show signs of Parkinson's disease. He began the 1957 Term with his usual determination but found the work more difficult. His hands shook to such a degree that his handwriting became very difficult to read. He took longer and longer afternoon naps. In early June, Burton's physician "identified my trouble as Parkinson's disease. It is responding to treatment very well, but [my doctor] advised retirement from full Court duties."[18] Burton agreed, but when he informed Chief Justice Warren of his intention to retire, Warren asked him to stay on until September 30. A week later, Burton wrote:

> Attorney Gen. Wm. Rogers came to see me. He said he had heard a report that I might retire soon and he came to urge me not to do so. He said I had been an excellent justice and he did not want me to leave the Court. I explained my plans to retire Oct. 13 and to notify the President shortly after my [seventieth] birthday on June 22. I explained that my doctor advised such retirement and that I was taking treatment to offset Parkinson's disease that had shown up during this term. Also that although I had originally planned to serve one more year I felt it best for the Court and my family not to do so now. I felt handicapped in doing the work of the Court, and serving at my best during a term, taking 10 hr. a day . . . 7 days a week.[19]

After stepping down on October 13, 1958, Burton reflected on retirement, "For the first time that I can recall in my life, I found myself not caught up with my immediate duties and free to read and do what I pleased for about an hour."[20] After speaking with Justice Reed in January, Burton sat on the lower federal courts from 1958–1962. Though Parkinson's disease and his concern for doing his share of the Court's work prompted Burton's departure, the generous provision of the expanded retirement statute was decisive in the timing. He had not served for fifteen years on the federal bench when he reached his sixty-fifth birthday. He knew that on reaching age seventy, he would only need to have ten years of service. Accordingly, Burton retired after his seventieth birthday and received full benefits.

Chief Justice Warren had been concerned about Burton's failing health and what would happen financially to his wife if he died. The Burtons were receiving the justice's full salary under the 1937 Act, but the payments would cease when the justice passed away. In 1959, Warren and Justice Tom Clark invited House Speaker Sam Rayburn and Senate Majority Leader Lyndon Johnson to dinner at Clark's house. Warren and Clark lobbied the two legislators to provide pensions for the widows of Supreme Court justices.[21] Two weeks later, President Eisenhower signed the bill into law.

CHARLES E. WHITTAKER

Charles E. Whittaker had a history of mental instability before he joined the Court.[22] Throughout his life he suffered from anxiety, depression, and an inability to work. For example, while in private practice he suffered "breakdowns." Not surprisingly, Whittaker disliked being a justice and, immediately after taking his seat, began seeing a doctor. He said, "I sold myself down the river for a bowl of porridge."[23] Only a few months after Whittaker's first term began, Justice Burton noted, "Justice Whittaker has been on the edge of a nervous breakdown but hopes to finish the term and then recuperate."[24] Whittaker's indecisiveness made him the swing vote on many crucial cases. As a result, he was continually targeted by a number of the justices, especially Felix Frankfurter. Douglas explained:

> Frankfurter used his law clerks as flying squadrons against the law clerks of other Justices and even against the Justices themselves. Frankfurter, a proselytizer, never missed a chance to line up a vote. His prize target was Charles Whittaker . . . Whittaker was duck soup for Frankfurter and his flying squadrons of law clerks.[25]

It was around this time that a decision may have been made, discussed, or both by Justices Black and Harlan that any case in which Whittaker would be the deciding vote would be held over for reargument, in effect nullifying Whittaker's vote.[26] Such a policy was later formally adopted during William O. Douglas's last term on the Court.

Warren wrote Whittaker, "You know, Charley, you can't let this injure your health."[27] Feeling sorry for Whittaker, Black finally gave in, saying, "I cannot destroy a man."[28] Frankfurter, however, did not relent. When Whittaker finally suffered a nervous breakdown, Whittaker's son remarked, "Certainly Frankfurter was a major factor in causing it."[29] Douglas added:

> Whittaker would make up his mind on argument, only to be changed by Frankfurter the next day. In Conference, Whittaker would take one position when the Chief or Black spoke, change his mind when Frankfurter spoke, and change back again when some other Justice spoke. This eventually led to his 'nervous breakdown' and his retirement for being permanently disabled in 1962. No one can change his mind so often and not have a breakdown.[30]

On March 6, 1962, Whittaker checked into the hospital complaining of exhaustion. He said, "I was burning the candle at both ends to a point where I became completely enervated."[31] His condition, however, was much worse than anyone knew. His son was convinced that the Justice intended suicide and pleaded with his father not to kill himself.[32] Whittaker agreed, and planned his formal departure from the Court. On March 16, he wrote Warren, the doctors "advise me that my return to the Court would unduly jeopardize my future health."[33] Whittaker was the first justice to take advantage of the disability provision of the 1939 Retirement Act, when he retired on April 1, 1962, after only five years on the Court.

Whittaker's brief post-Court tenure might be termed "disability senior status" as Chief Justice Earl Warren never assigned any lower court duties to Whittaker.[34] After similar occurrences with other federal judges, Congress ultimately took action. In 1989, judges in senior status were required to perform actual judicial duties in order to receive the pay raises that active federal judges received. Unlike Whittaker's retirement, disability senior status now carries the penalty of lost salary increases.

FELIX FRANKFURTER

In November 1958, Justice Frankfurter suffered a minor heart attack, though he only became aware of it later during a routine checkup.[35] He immediately entered the hospital and asked his doctors, "Look here. I want to ask you fellows something, and I'll be guided by your opinion and advice in the matter. Do you think I should sit down right now and write out my resignation from the Court?"[36] The doctors said that his departure would not be necessary and

Frankfurter resumed his work on the Court after an unusually lengthy hospital stay.[37] Justice Black remarked, "Felix is obviously a sick man. Maybe that's why he is so hard to get along with in conference."[38]

The relationship between Frankfurter and Justice Douglas had grown increasingly strained over the years. In a remarkable incident in 1954, Douglas wrote his former mentor and law professor:

> Today at Conference I asked you a question . . . The question was not answered. An answer was refused, rather insolently. This was so far as I recall the first time one member of the Conference refused to answer another member on a matter of Court business.
>
> We all know what a great burden your long discourses are. So I am not complaining. But I do register a protest at your degradation of the Conference and its deliberations.[39]

Frankfurter promptly circulated Douglas's memorandum to the other justices adding, "Since the enclosed memorandum addressed to me purports to deal with a matter of Court concern, it seems appropriate that all the other members of the Court should see it."[40] In 1960, Douglas had finally had enough of Frankfurter's antics in conference. Douglas wrote the following memorandum to the justices, but after discussing the matter with Chief Justice Warren, decided not to circulate it:

> The continuous violent outbursts against me in Conference by my Brother Frankfurter give me great concern. They do not bother me. For I have been on the hustings too long.
>
> But he's an ill man; and these violent outbursts create a fear in my heart that one of them may be his end.
>
> I do not consciously do anything to annoy him. But twenty-odd years have shown that I am a disturbing symbol in his life. His outbursts against me are increasing in intensity. In the interest of his health and long life I have reluctantly concluded to participate in no more conferences while he is on the Court.
>
> For the cert. lists I will leave my vote. On argued cases I will leave a short summary of my views.[41]

On April 6, 1962, a month after Justice Whittaker had a nervous breakdown, Frankfurter suffered a stroke while sitting at his desk in chambers. He fell from his chair to the floor, where he remained until his secretary found him and called an ambulance. He was carried from the building by ambulance attendants, protesting that his shoes were being left behind.[42] The stroke was relatively minor and it appeared that the Justice would soon return to work. His doctor reported that the cause of the stroke "cleared spontaneously and left no residual after effect."[43] Only days later, however, Frankfurter suffered a second, more severe stroke. His entire left side was paralyzed and he lost the ability to speak. At the end of April, the hospital optimistically announced that the Justice would be able to return to the Court.[44]

Frankfurter returned home on July 14 and initially held out hope of recovery and a return to his duties. Mentally, he had not diminished at all and continued dictating his many correspondences.[45] He was particularly preoccupied with the way that history would judge his jurisprudence and overall contribution to the Court. He wrote all of his disciples and supporters attempting to convince them that his interpretation of events and opinions about colleagues was correct.[46] After pleas to safeguard his health from his doctors, friend Dean Acheson, and Justice John Harlan, Frankfurter decided to retire.[47] When asked later about the matter, Warren was adamant that no member of the Court "asked" Frankfurter to step down.[48] Frankfurter sent a copy of his retirement letter to the other justices, saying that "every safeguard against premature disclosure of its contents must be observed."[49] He cited concerns for his health and the work of the Court in his formal letter to the president. He officially departed on August 28, 1962, at the age of seventy-nine, writing President John F. Kennedy:

> High expectations were earlier expressed by my doctors that I would be able to resume my judicial duties . . . However, they now advise me that the stepped-up therapy . . . involves hazards which might jeopardize the useful years they anticipate still lie ahead of me.
>
> The Court should not enter its new Term with uncertainty as to whether I might later be able to return to unrestricted duty. To retain my seat on the basis of a diminished work schedule would not comport with my own philosophy or with the demands of the business of the Court.[50]

It is not surprising that justices find it difficult to leave the Court. Some have a more difficult time letting go than others, however. Nearly five months into his retirement, Frankfurter circulated to his former colleagues an article written by Philip Neal for *The Supreme Court Review* on the case of *Baker v. Carr*.[51] Frankfurter's last opinion, a sixty-four-page dissent, came in the case that revolutionized apportionment in the states. He was not content, however, to let the matter stand and was still working in retirement to convince the other justices that he was right. He was aware that his actions might be considered inappropriate for a retired justice and in his memo accompanying the article he wrote:

The . . . article . . . struck me as having such penetrating and valuable qualities as to lead me to think that it might be of interest to the Brethren.

You will not, I am sure, misconstrue my purpose in sending the article to you or consider that in so doing I am stepping outside the appropriate province of a Retired Justice. Otherwise I would of course not have sent it.

With old regards . . .[52]

Frankfurter's attempt to continue his substantive interactions with his former colleagues is tame compared to the efforts of his old nemesis William O. Douglas over a decade later. What both instances demonstrate, however, is that there is flexibility, disagreement, and even confusion in what the appropriate role should be for a retired justice. As I will discuss later, the current members of the Court have considered this issue as recently as 1988.

AN EXTRACONSTITUTIONAL ARRANGEMENT: LYNDON JOHNSON AND THE FALL OF THE WARREN COURT

Beginning with the death of Adlai Stevenson in 1965, an important series of events occurred that not only provided the only interruption in the pattern of retirements under the 1954 Act, but had a lasting effect on the Court and the nation. Lyndon Johnson, ensnarled in the Vietnam War, was the principal figure. Johnson not only brought about his own well-documented demise, but contributed to the public downfalls of four members of the Supreme Court. Left in Johnson's wake, Arthur Goldberg, Tom Clark, Abe Fortas, and Earl Warren were not able to leave the Court on their own terms, but rather were coerced, in one form or another, to depart under clouds of suspicion.

ARTHUR GOLDBERG

On July 14, 1965, Adlai Stevenson, U.S. ambassador to the United Nations, died suddenly. Stevenson had given the hawkish foreign policy of the Kennedy and Johnson administrations legitimacy with liberals, who were becoming increasingly skeptical about U.S. involvement in Vietnam. Looking for someone with similar liberal appeal, President Johnson turned first to Harvard economist John Kenneth Galbraith, who had been ambassador to India under Kennedy. Galbraith wanted no part of the U.N. post, and instead of turning Johnson down cold, he suggested that the president offer the post to

Justice Arthur J. Goldberg, who Galbraith had heard was restless at the Court. Johnson was delighted at this suggestion, which would allow him to appease the liberals on foreign policy and name his close friend and adviser Abe Fortas to Goldberg's seat.

Johnson began the difficult process of persuading the reluctant Goldberg to step down from his seat on the Court and accept the ambassadorship. Johnson's first attempt came by way of a phone call to Goldberg, who was meeting with Chief Justice Warren and Justice Black in his chambers. They knew why the president was calling and repeatedly said to Goldberg, "Tell him no." Johnson said, "Arthur, you're the only man who can bring peace to Vietnam and the man who does that will be the next man to sit in my seat." Goldberg's longtime friend recalled, "Arthur's great flaw was his ego. Once you told him that he's the only man in the world able to do something, he believed it. LBJ knew that. He was really laying it on and Arthur kept saying, 'Yes Mr. President,' and Warren and Black kept on saying, 'Tell him no.' It went on like that, Arthur said."[53]

Moments before a White House meeting with the president about the post, Goldberg told Johnson aide Jack Valenti, "I'm not an applicant for any post—including the U.N. one."[54] The president invited Goldberg and his wife to accompany him on Air Force One to and from Stevenson's funeral in Illinois. On the return trip, Goldberg relented. He agreed to step down from the Court and accept the U.N. post on two conditions. First, he had Johnson's word that the administration was committed to negotiating a peaceful solution in Vietnam. Second, Goldberg insisted that he be the principal adviser and participate in all decisions leading up to such a settlement. Johnson agreed and Justice Goldberg resigned on July 25, 1965. The next day he wrote the other justices, "Only the most compelling call to duty could bring me to leave this Court . . . But that call did come, and I could not refuse."[55]

Washington's political community was shocked by Goldberg's decision and rumors flew about the arrangement. Some suggested that Goldberg was beholden to Johnson for information the president had about funding for a party thrown by then–Secretary of Labor Goldberg on behalf of then–Vice President Johnson.[56] Others felt that Goldberg was angling for a spot on a future presidential ticket. Regardless, Goldberg was convinced that he could make a difference in getting Johnson to end the war in Vietnam. Goldberg later recalled his decision:

> Nobody can twist the arm of a Supreme Court Justice . . . We were in a war in Vietnam. I had an exaggerated opinion of my own capac-
> ities. I thought I could persuade Johnson that we were fighting the wrong war in the wrong place, [and] to get out . . . I would love to have stayed on the Court, but my sense of priorities was [that] this war would be disastrous.[57]

Goldberg also felt that the U.N. job would only be temporary and that he might be able to return to the Court in the future. Since he knew that Chief Justice Warren planned to retire before the next presidential election, he thought it possible that he might even return as the new chief. By 1968, however, Goldberg's relationship with Johnson had soured over Vietnam. On April 23, 1968, he submitted his letter of resignation, noting, "I don't want the impression to be created that I am hanging around for a Supreme Court appointment. This is not good for the country, Mr. President, nor is it personally dignified for me."[58] Shortly thereafter, Warren told Goldberg that he would be retiring and would recommend Goldberg to LBJ to succeed him as chief.[59] Goldberg was appreciative of Warren's confidence, but doubted that Johnson would nominate him, after their falling out over Vietnam. When Johnson put forth the names of Abe Fortas for chief and Homer Thornberry for associate justice, Goldberg was not surprised.

TOM C. CLARK

Eager for another vacancy, Johnson knew that Justice Tom C. Clark would have a potential conflict of interest if his son Ramsey was appointed to a position in the government that dealt with the High Court. When Ramsey became acting attorney general following the resignation of Nicholas Katzenbach, Johnson made his move. On January 25, 1967, Johnson told Ramsey that he could only be named the permanent attorney general if his father stepped down from the Court. Johnson argued that "every taxi driver in the country" would see the conflict of interest of a son arguing cases before his father.[60] Ramsey protested, arguing that his father's departure "would hurt you" contributing to the impression that LBJ was not tough enough on crime.[61] "He more than any other member of the Court," Ramsey counseled, "stands for . . . tough law enforcement."[62] Less than a month later, Johnson named Ramsey attorney general. The same day, Justice Clark announced that he would retire at the end of the Court's Term in June.[63] Years later, Ramsey denied that any formal deal had been brokered. Johnson's style, however, was more informal as Katzenbach reflected:

> Johnson said, I can get rid of Tom Clark by putting Ramsey in as attorney general. That's the way LBJ's mind worked. What I think LBJ did was tell Tom Clark, I'm going to make Ramsey attorney general, and I'm sorry that's going to raise a problem for you, Tom, and I'm not going to do it if you don't want to resign.[64]

THE STRUGGLE FOR THE CHIEF JUSTICESHIP:
ABE FORTAS AND EARL WARREN

The private maneuverings that characterized Goldberg's and Clark's departures stand in contrast to the extraordinary events surrounding the very public departures of their colleagues, Abe Fortas and Earl Warren.[65] At stake was the chief justiceship held by Warren for fifteen years. Republicans, like presidential candidate Richard Nixon were critical of the Warren Court and Nixon made the judiciary a campaign issue in 1968.

During Clark's last term on the Court, Chief Justice Warren felt that Black, then eighty-two, and Douglas, then seventy, had stayed on the Court past their prime. The Chief told a friend, "I'm not going out of here like some of these fellows. I'm going out while I know what I'm doing."[66] When Warren was appointed Chief in 1953, he told his son, "If you ever see me slipping, tell me, no matter how onerous it is. I don't ever want to get into that position."[67] In his sixties, he told his clerks that there should be mandatory retirement at age seventy for Supreme Court justices. When he reached seventy, he decided the age should be seventy-five. After his seventy-fifth birthday in 1966, he showed no signs of slowing down. He liked to say, "As soon as Hugo retires, I'll be happy to follow."[68] Still, Warren was wary of lingering past his usefulness and told his clerks to inform him if they thought he was slipping. He also did not want to get into the position where nobody would dare confront him about the matter.

By his seventy-seventh birthday, Warren was suffering intermittent angina pains and considering retirement. On April 4, 1967, he went to the hospital and was absent from the Court for a day. He wrote Justice Douglas the next day, "I had been suffering some distress and went out to Walter Reed Hospital to undergo a few tests."[69] Warren felt that he had accomplished all he had set out to in public life and wanted to enjoy his remaining years off the Court.

Warren was also paying close attention to the 1968 presidential race. Three days before the California presidential primary, Warren felt that Robert F. Kennedy would win the White House.[70] After Kennedy's assassination, Warren was convinced that Richard Nixon would be elected and informed his clerks that he was going to retire before Nixon had a chance to nominate his replacement. On June 13, Warren met briefly with President Johnson to inform him of his retirement and his wish for a like-minded successor.[71] That same day he sent two letters to Johnson. The first said, "Pursuant to the provisions of 28 U.S.C. Section 371(b), I hereby advise you of my intention to retire as Chief Justice of the United States, effective at your pleasure."[72] The second letter gave Warren's reasons for stepping down. He wrote:

It is not because of reasons of health or on account of any personal or associational problems, but solely because of age . . . The problem of age . . . is one that no man can combat and, therefore, eventually must bow to it. I have been continuously in the public service for more than fifty years. When I entered the public service, 150 million of our 200 million people were not born yet. I, therefore, conceive it to be my duty to give way to someone who will have more years ahead of him to cope with the problems which will come to the Court.[73]

Because Warren did not specify a retirement date, the Johnson administration interpreted it to mean that Warren would wait until a successor was confirmed. They also felt it would allow Warren to withdraw his letter, should that be necessary. In Johnson's carefully worded reply to Warren, the president wrote, "With your agreement, I will accept your decision to retire effective at such time as a successor is qualified."[74] Warren biographer Bernard Schwartz contends that Warren's decision not to step down immediately was precipitated by the chief's concern over Hugo Black. As senior associate, Black would be the acting chief until the confirmation of Warren's successor. The Chief was unsure of the eighty-two-year-old justice's ability to handle the work and did not want to embarrass Black publicly.[75] Warren never mentioned this as a reason, however, only saying, "there always ought to be a Chief Justice of the United States . . . if I selected a particular day and the vacancy was not filled it would be a vacuum."[76]

Johnson announced his intention to nominate Associate Justice Abe Fortas to be the next chief justice on June 26, the same day he announced Warren's planned departure. Warren strenuously denied that his departure was politically motivated in any way, saying, "I put all that behind me fifteen years ago."[77] Republicans immediately saw the announcements as partisan maneuvering by a lame-duck president, and rumors of a Johnson/Warren plot to pack the Court spread throughout Washington. California Governor Ronald Reagan said that Warren had no "right to choose which president he thinks should dominate for the next twenty years the Supreme Court."[78] Republican Senator Robert Griffin charged that Warren's letter to Johnson "was not a resignation at all. In so doing, he created the impression of participating with the President in a political manipulation to force confirmation of a particular successor."[79] When a radio correspondent overheard Warren telling a friend that the rumors were true, she immediately broadcast the story.[80] Senate Republicans prepared for battle.

Although the Democrats had a huge sixty-four to thirty-six advantage in the Senate, the Fortas nomination encountered difficulty. Douglas remarked, "By that time Johnson himself had created a credibility gap of vast proportions; as a result, much of the antagonism against Fortas was merely a reflection against Johnson."[81] One issue raised by the Republicans was Fortas' close ties to President Johnson and the allegation that Justice Fortas had been an unofficial adviser to the president. This violated, it was argued, the principle of separation of powers. Justice Douglas later characterized the relationship between Johnson and Fortas:

> Over the years, [Johnson] became very dependent on Abe Fortas for all his decisions. Not that he always followed Abe's advice; he often did not. But he had such confidence in Abe that he was crippled without him.[82]

Critics such as Senator Sam Ervin argued that there was no vacancy to fill, as Warren had not yet retired.[83] Even Senate Judiciary Committee Chair James O. Eastland reportedly said to another Senator, "You're not going to vote for that Jew to be Chief Justice, are you?"[84] Coupling Fortas's nomination with Johnson's old friend from Texas, Homer Thornberry, only made matters worse. Though Johnson hoped Thornberry's nomination would appease Southern Democrats, it instead fueled charges of cronyism.

Unexpectedly, Fortas agreed to testify in person before the Senate, the first chief justice nominee ever to do so. On July 13, Fortas began four days of testimony, where he was harshly attacked by Republican for the decisions of the Warren Court.[85] Fortas's troubles continued in September when it was reported that he had received $15,000 for teaching a summer seminar at American University in Washington. The money came from private donors who were linked to having interests in cases argued before the Court.

Although the Senate Judiciary Committee voted eleven to six to recommend Fortas, Senator Griffin led a core group of Republican senators in derailing the nomination by filibustering for six days. Griffin's campaign against Fortas was supported by a group of Southern Democratic senators led by Senator Richard Russell of Georgia. Russell withdrew his support for Fortas and Thornberry because of Johnson's foot-dragging on a district-court nomination Russell had proposed months earlier.[86] Fortas wrote Johnson, asking that his nomination be withdrawn to avert "a continuation of the attacks upon the Court which have characterized the filibuster—attacks which have been sometimes extreme and entirely unrelated to responsible criticism."[87] On October 4, Johnson withdrew the nomination. Warren informed the president that he would continue serving as chief until a successor was confirmed, but Johnson said that he would not send another nomination to the Senate for consideration. The new President, Richard Nixon, would.

Though there was debate in Congress about whether or not Warren's retirement letter was still valid under the new administration, Warren always considered that he had submitted his letter to the office of the president, and not to Lyndon Johnson personally. Warren reasoned that if he withdrew it, history would certainly record his departure as purely partisan.[88] When Nixon took office, the new president worked out a deal with Warren that allowed the Chief to finish out the 1968 Term before stepping down.

In May 1969, Life magazine published an article about financial ties between Justice Fortas and financier Louis Wolfson.[89] In January 1966, while a member of the Court, Fortas agreed to be a consultant to a foundation started by Wolfson, for a fee of $20,000. After Wolfson was indicted for fraud in December 1966, Fortas returned the money. The article, however, was only part of the story. The Nixon Justice Department had obtained further information that Wolfson had agreed to pay Fortas a fee of $20,000 annually for the rest of his life, and $20,000 annually to his wife after his death. On May 7, Attorney General Mitchell met with Chief Justice Warren at the Court and disclosed the documents. Warren told Mitchell that he would take the matter under consideration and called a conference to tell the other justices, including Fortas, what Mitchell had told him. At the conference, Fortas said that he paid back all the money that he had received and that the contracts were canceled by mutual agreement. Warren was concerned about the damage the Fortas situation was having on the Court and remarked to his secretary, "He can't stay."[90] Justice Douglas discussed the matter with Fortas:

> I sat up with him two nights, serving as a sounding board . . . He apparently had held Wolfson's hand, so to speak, but had never undertaken to give legal advice or acted as counsel after coming on the Court. I urged Abe not to resign, though parts of the press were demanding it. At first Abe agreed with me, but he quickly changed. I saw him the next night and he was then resolved to resign. My son Bill was with me and he too pleaded with Abe not to resign. 'Blood will taste good to this gang. And having tasted it, they will want more,' my son said.[91]

Fortas wanted to do what was in the best interest of the Court. He heeded the advice of his close friend Clark Clifford, and with the threat of impeachment proceedings a real possibility, Justice Fortas resigned on May 14, 1969. He wrote the Chief Justice:

> It is my opinion . . . that the public controversy . . . is likely to continue and adversely affect the work and position of the Court, absent my resignation. In these circumstances, it seems clear to me that it is not my duty to remain on the Court, but rather to resign in the hope that this will enable the Court to proceed with its vital work free form extraneous stress.

There has been no wrongdoing on my part. There has been no default in the performance of my judicial duties in accordance with the high standards of the office I hold.[92]

Fortas told a journalist, "It's just as if an automobile hit me as I stepped off the curb."[93] Within a year, however, he regretted not facing his detractors. Later, Johnson said, "I made him take the justiceship. In that way, I ruined his life."[94] On June 23, 1969, Earl Warren swore in Warren E. Burger as the new chief, and officially retired. Years later, during the Watergate scandal, Warren told a reporter, "If I had ever known what was going to happen to this country and this Court, I never would have resigned. They would have had to carry me out of here on a plank!"[95]

Johnson's political maneuverings not only led to the coerced departures of four members of the Supreme Court, it also had a lasting impact on the Court's ideological direction. While Johnson selected Thurgood Marshall to replace Tom Clark, he ultimately failed with the other two seats. Though Goldberg's seat was temporarily filled by Fortas, that seat as well as the chief justiceship was eventually filled by Republican President Richard Nixon. Though it continues to be debated whether the Burger Court was more conservative than the Warren Court, the very fact that Nixon was able to make these two appointments was a direct result of Johnson's machinations. Overall, LBJ's interference led to an unprecedented string of the forced departures of four Supreme Court Justices and the end of the Warren Court.

CONCLUSION

In 1954, the departure process was transformed by the expansion of the existing retirement statute. As with previous reforms, the change was largely the result of a new governing regime. For the first time since the Great Depression, the Republicans controlled the executive and legislative branches. Aided by nonpartisan reformers, including the ABA, they set about changing the existing departure structure. Though a constitutional amendment for compulsory retirement at age seventy-five failed to pass, the retirement statute was altered to allow justices to depart with full benefits at a younger age. Initially, it worked and opposition justices were induced to depart under the new, more generous rules.

But because justices had a larger window in which to time their departures, partisan concerns began to dominate departure decisions. Lyndon Johnson's direct involvement with the departures of several justices exemplified the increasingly political environment as he worked behind the scenes to cajole justices to give up their seats. Arthur Goldberg and Tom Clark were convinced by

Johnson to step aside and Earl Warren and Abe Fortas ultimately became high-profile casualties of Johnson's maneuverings. In the next three decades, partisanship was ever-present in the retirement decisions of the justices. The mental decrepitude, exemplified by Justices Minton and Whitaker also continued to plague the Court to an unprecedented degree.

8

1971–1999

Appointed for Life

If I were younger and healthier, I would stay on the Court and fight it out, but I can't see well and my memory is not as good. If I can't measure up, then I should get off the Court.

—Justice Hugo Black

Prop me up and keep on voting.

—Justice Thurgood Marshall instructing his clerks on what to do if he dropped dead at his desk.

Because justices are appointed for life, both partisan retirements and mental decrepitude have been a recurring part of the departure process. But both have increased in recent times. This is largely due to the expanded retirement benefits enacted in 1954, and manageable workloads. Justices have for the most part stayed on the bench longer than they should have in order to time their departures to coincide with favorable administrations. The declines and eventual departures of Justices Black, Douglas, Powell, Brennan, and Marshall demonstrate that these issues have not been adequately dealt with by either the Court, Congress, or the American people.

Compared to the tragic events surrounding the departures of their immediate predecessors, superannuated Justices Hugo Black, John Marshall Harlan II, and William O. Douglas served as long as they could, pushing the envelope for participation in the face of illness and decline. The virtually simultaneous retirements of Black and Harlan left the Court two members short, providing a valuable lesson for future justices considering departure.[1] Douglas's attempts to rejoin the Court after his official retirement were unprecedented in the Court's history. He was thwarted at every turn by the other members of the Court, and each justice who served during that extraordinary time was affected. Since Black, Harlan, and Douglas have stepped down, every justice who has departed has chosen to retire. With the exception of Thurgood Marshall, none lingered too long in comparison. None continued participating from hospital beds as Harlan and Black did, and none attempted to participate in the work of the Court after their retirements as Douglas did.

HE OUGHT TO GET OFF THE COURT TOO

HUGO BLACK

Black's lengthy career exemplifies the thought process of justices with respect to departure. From the moment Black entered the Court, he was confronted with his colleagues' failing health and their decisions to step down. As a result, he often thought of his tenure on the Court and contemplated his own departure. The young Black was matter-of-fact about retirement and even used it as a threat, while the older Black began to reconsider and saw no end in sight. Eventually, though probably too late, he became resigned to his incapacity and faced the inevitable.

When Hugo Black first joined the Court in 1937, he sat with Justice Sutherland, who was on the verge of stepping down. Black felt that Sutherland was having some trouble getting around and perhaps had stayed too long. "That'll never happen to me," he said. "I'll know when to retire."[2] When Justice Robert Jackson's name was mentioned as a possible successor to Chief Justice Stone, Black told friends that he would step down if Jackson was appointed. Saddened by the deaths of Justices Murphy and Rutledge in 1949, Justice Black told Murphy's brother George that he would retire "in a year or two."[3] In 1957 he said, "I'll have to be carried out feet first." In 1961 he remarked, "I'll stay as long as I can write a first draft." In 1962, Black was concerned after an electrocardiogram reading during his annual physical deviated from past readings. He told his clerks afterward, "One of the hardest things you have to do up here is to know when to leave. If you stay too long, you impose terrible burdens on your colleagues. I ask you to tell me when that is."[4] Justice Douglas felt Black had not stayed too long, writing Hugo, Jr., "Your Daddy is thriving, and looks in excellent health, and seems to be in fine spirits. I hope he is with us for many, many more years."[5]

Black became increasingly cantankerous as he got older. The relationship between Black and Douglas, once allies in the intellectual struggle against Justices Frankfurter and Jackson for the direction of the Court, became strained.

Over time, Black distanced himself from Douglas, partly because of his disapproval of Douglas's personal life. In the 1960s, Black began siding against Chief Justice Warren and the liberals more and more. Abe Fortas's appointment to the Court only exacerbated his view that his colleagues were unprincipled. Justice Brennan later remarked:

> Hugo changed, the man changed, right in front of us. It was so evident. We talked about it much, the Chief and Bill Douglas probably more than anyone else. Bill was especially hurt. We lost our fifth vote. Those of us who cared for him certainly felt sad. We were afraid it would hurt him in history and in academia.[6]

Starting with the 1964 term, Black began to rely on his clerks more and more to write opinions. During the 1966 term, Black's clerk recalled, "The Judge would give me an opinion to write, for the Court or in dissent, and tell me the result he wanted, but no guidance, just, 'Go look at this opinion.' It was usually a past opinion of his."

Black turned eighty during the 1965 term, and when Chief Justice Warren heard complaints about Black's alleged senility, Warren would laughingly reply, "No, Hugo just wants to be buried in Alabama."[7] In March 1966, Black found out that he had cataracts. He was using bright lights and a magnifying glass to read. The Chief said, "Black has hardened and gotten old. It's a different Black now."[8] Warren felt that Black would not leave the Court until he broke Justice Field's record of thirty-four years and nine months on the bench. The Chief told *New York Times* reporter Anthony Lewis, "He's going to stay too long . . . he is trying to break the record for the number of years anyone has served on the Court."[9] In 1967 Black had a successful operation to restore lost vision in one of his eyes. Warren began leading Black from the conference room so that he would not trip. A second operation on his other eye was not as successful and the operations had taken a noticeable toll. Black said, "I just want to spend my working years on the Court." The next year he told a clerk, "I'll stay as long as I can. But I won't be here forever."[10]

When Warren announced his own retirement in June 1968, Black again reflected on the matter. His wife said at the time, "Hugo has always said he didn't mind retiring but that was belied tonight when he said in an anguished voice, 'But what will I do!'" When Black's wife suggested a number of possibilities, he rejected them all saying "[I] won't be a part of a mass retirement." He wrote a friend, "As yet I have not had any reason to change my mind and at present do not contemplate leaving the Court."[11] He said to another friend, "I'll stay on until my next to last breath."[12]

Black was an avid tennis player and continued to play, at the insistence of his cardiologist, into his eighty-third year. On July 18, 1969, Black suffered a

minor stroke while playing tennis. He was hospitalized for four days and doctors gave him a 90 percent chance of full recovery. He had a small blood clot
on his brain, which resulted in a partial loss of memory. The doctors were
unsure whether this would affect his work on the Court and finally advised
him to continue for one more year and then step down. "But what would I
do?" Black responded, and said he "about decided to quit" after hearing the
recommendation.[13] Soon his mind became clearer and he returned to both the
tennis and Supreme Court.

In October 1970, Black told a friend, "During the last year my wife
has wanted me to quit the Court, to be together more so we could go
places and do things. But I feel good except for my eyes. Last week I fell
down on the stairs because I couldn't see them. My wife says that maybe
we should sell the house, but I don't want to."[14] Black was well aware that
only John Marshall and Stephen J. Field had served on the Court longer
than he had and by December 1970, Black kept a small card on his desk
with the dates of the justices' service. He knew that he would pass Field's
record on March 2, 1972, and become the longest serving justice in the
Court's history.

With the House investigating Justice Douglas for possible impeachment,
a number of southerners asked Hugo Black, Jr., to see how his father felt about
their plans to oust Douglas. Justice Black told his son:

> I have known Bill Douglas for thirty years. He's never knowingly
> done any improper, unethical or corrupt thing. Tell his detractors
> that in spite of my age, I think I have one trial left in me. Tell them
> that if they move against Bill Douglas, I'll resign from the Court
> and represent him. It will be the biggest, most important case I
> ever tried.[15]

By the end of March 1971, Justice Black was in obvious decline. A month
earlier he developed an infected eye and ear. He was experiencing terrible
headaches and having difficulty concentrating. His short-term memory was
failing and he became unable to participate effectively in conference. He
appeared confused, tired, and often forgot the case being discussed. When
Chief Justice Burger suggested that conferences be shortened to accommo-
date Black, he strenuously objected. Still, Burger told one of the courtroom
guards to keep an eye on Black when the justices were on the bench. He began
using nicknames to refer to his colleagues, for example calling Justices Douglas, Brennan, and Marshall "the three musketeers" for their similar voting
habits. He wrote friends, "How long after [the next few months] I shall hold
on, no one knows—not even I."[16] Despite his infirmities, he remained in good
spirits. He wrote to Douglas:

I had not thought of the relief it would give me to share with you many of my letters suggesting that no man of my age should dare to hold public office.

I did appreciate Miss Erlandson's letter, however, and am sure that she is absolutely confident that she has the right answer for making everything in the world smooth and tranquil again . . . namely, for you and me to retire from the Court.[17]

In August, Black told his new clerks that he was looking forward to what would probably be his last year on the Court.[18] He told a friend, "If I were younger and healthier, I would stay on the Court and fight it out, but I can't see well and my memory is not as good. If I can't measure up, then I should get off the Court."[19] On August 26, Black signed a retirement letter. The date of departure was not fixed however and he remarked, "This will protect the Court." The next morning, he checked back in to the hospital asking, "I'm not going there to die, am I?"[20]

He was diagnosed with temporal arthritis, inflamed blood vessels, and was convinced he was going to die, even though his doctors insisted this was not true. When President Nixon inquired about visiting Black at the hospital, Black's son said that it would not be possible, as his father could not be moved to a more secure location in the hospital. Justice John Marshall Harlan was staying in the next room, while undergoing tests for recurring back pain. Harlan's attempts to cheer up Black failed. "John Harlan can't see a thing," Black said. "He ought to get off the Court too."[21] Black told Chief Justice Burger that he wanted Frank Johnson to take his place. The Nixon administration agreed, but after opposition from some members of Congress, Johnson was not nominated.

As the 1971 term approached, Black spoke with Burger about remaining on the Court until he surpassed Field's record, which was only months away. Burger agreed, but Black's family did not. The Justice's condition was not improving and they pressed him to retire. Black had always felt strongly about his papers and conference notes and ordered them destroyed just as Justice Roberts had done. His family was reluctant but finally did burn some of his papers. They could not, however, bring themselves to destroy everything, especially the draft opinions and correspondence between the justices. Still, they told Black that his papers had been burned as he wished.[22]

Black finally agreed to step down and his wife typed in the date of September 17, 1971 on the already signed retirement letter which said, "Since the adjournment of Court last June I have been ill, and, more recently have been taking medication, which together have impaired my vision and my general ability to do my work with the understanding that I consider necessary for me to perform my duties as I have performed them in the past."[23] The man who had served as senior associate justice to four chief justices retired after thirty-four years and one month of service, seven months shy of Field's record tenure. A week later, Justice Black suffered a minor stroke, slipped into a coma, and died at the age of eighty-five.

JOHN MARSHALL HARLAN II

In early 1964, Justice John Marshall Harlan II began to lose his sight because of severe cataracts. By May 1965, the usual rumors of his retirement began to circulate. A friend wrote him, "If these stories are true, I would feel that the good Lord had not been very careful in his selection of those whom he would choose to afflict. My dear friend, if you are ailing, quit while you're ahead. If you are not, ignore this crap."[24] Harlan replied that he was "not retiring" and that "so far things have not become unmanageable."[25] In 1966, Chief Justice Warren rearranged the Court's budget to provide Justice Harlan with a third law clerk. Because Harlan's eye sight was failing, the Chief felt that an additional clerk would help Harlan keep up with his share of the work and remain on the Court.[26]

Harlan had not been well for some years. He was nearly blind and had to lean on Chief Justice Burger's arm at public functions. He delivered his opinions from the bench by memory and by the 1970–1971 term, his clerks were spending as much as sixty hours a week reading to him. By August 1971, Harlan was in the hospital due to recurring back pain. Despite his discomfort, he continued to participate in his Court duties from his hospital bed. He wrote a friend that his back pain was "enough to make me fidget like a jack-in-the-box, and interrupts my sleeping at night . . . I hope the mystery will be cleared up before the open of Court in October. If it does not it will face me with some very difficult decisions."[27]

In September, Harlan learned he had cancer of the lower spine. At age seventy-two, he decided to step down. But with Justice Black having just retired, he decided to delay his announcement to give Black the public acclaim he deserved. On September 23, 1971, six days after Black's retirement, Justice Harlan also stepped down.[28]

WILLIAM O. DOUGLAS: THE TENTH JUSTICE

During the two decades after he was appointed to the Court, Justice William O. Douglas was perennially mentioned for a spot on the Democratic presidential ticket. Though he privately said that he never had any desire to leave the Court, he never made any statement publicly on the matter, which led many to believe he was available. In 1940, Douglas wrote Justice Frankfurter:

There is considerable talk in Washington about putting me on the ticket. I discount it very much. I do not really think it will come to anything. But it is sufficiently active to be disturbing. It is disturbing because I want none of it. I want to stay where I am.[29]

In 1941, President Roosevelt wanted Douglas to head the Defense Department. Members of the administration hinted that it might lead to the 1944 presidential nomination. Douglas wrote to Black, "I can think of nothing less attractive."[30] Black knew it would be difficult for Douglas to resist a call from FDR and quickly replied in a lengthy handwritten letter, urging Douglas to remain on the Court:

> The prospect that you might leave the Court disturbs me greatly . . . While I am compelled to admit that my desire to have you with me on the Court may be of great weight with me . . . I believe my judgment would be the same under wholly different conditions . . . I am firmly persuaded however that it is not to the best interests of the United States for you to follow the course which has been planned. I must say that I entertain very grave doubts as to your success should you enter the defense picture at this stage . . . I hope you remain on the Court.[31]

In 1944, Douglas's name was once again mentioned as a possible vice-presidential candidate.[32] President Truman was continually after Douglas to resign from the Court and join his administration.[33] He told friends, "My sole desire is to remain on the Court until I reach retirement."[34]

But Douglas was vacillating. He may not have wanted to join the Truman administration, but his gloom over Murphy's death led him to seriously contemplate stepping down. On August 15, as the new term neared, he wrote Black, "The matter I wrote you about has been gnawing away at me. It is really a dreadful thing. I have thought that perhaps the best thing that could happen would be for you + me to resign. I have been seriously considering it."[35]

In the fall of 1949, one day before the Court's new term was scheduled to begin, Douglas was thrown off his horse in the Cascade Mountains of his home state of Washington. He landed partly down a mountain on a ledge and was nearly crushed to death when his horse fell on top of him. Douglas had a punctured lung, broke all but one of his ribs, and was absent from the Court for months. His riding companion remarked, "He just lived because he wanted to live."[36] During his recovery, Douglas wrote Black, "I am lucky to be alive. I was in excellent physical condition or I would not be."[37]

As the 1952 presidential election approached, a number of Douglas's friends and supporters urged him to run. As in the past, he declined saying,

"My place in public life is on the Court."[38] He was once again thought of by many in 1956 as a possible nominee but, as always, demurred. As his sixty-fifth birthday approached and he neared retirement eligibility, the inevitable rumors began circulating that he would retire. Hugo Black, Jr., wrote him, "I have read in a couple of newspapers that you plan to retire upon reaching the age of 65. I hope this is not so."[39] Douglas wrote back, "There is absolutely nothing to the rumor that I plan to retire this year. Perhaps it all comes from the fact that I will be eligible on my next birthday, but I have had no thought of retiring."[40] Though he had no intention of departing, Douglas was plainly aware that he was now eligible for retirement.

By the 1967–1968 term, Douglas had served on the Court for nearly thirty years and was noticeably slowing down. Brennan later remarked, "His last ten years on the Court were marked by the slovenliness of his writing and the mistakes that he constantly made. He seemed to have lost the interest that was so paramount in everything he did when he started on the Court. It's too bad."[41] On June 5, 1968, while sitting on the bench for oral argument, Douglas collapsed and was carried to his chambers. He came to, began pacing the room, and collapsed again. Douglas suffered a heart attack and had to have a pacemaker installed to keep his heart beating at a normal rate. He made a full recovery and returned to the Court for the October 1968 term. When Chief Justice Warren decided to step down, Douglas thought that he too should retire. Douglas recalled:

> In the spring of 1969 I had talked with Earl Warren, the then Chief Justice, just before his retirement in June. I told him I too wanted to retire because it was my thirtieth anniversary on the Court. So he made arrangements to reserve a suite of offices for himself and another suite for me as a retired justice. But as early as May and June of 1969 the hound dogs, having got Justice Fortas to resign, had started baying at me. I felt that if I did retire under those circumstances, it would be an indication that somewhere, somehow, there had been some deep dark sin committed and that I was seeking to escape its exposure. So I changed my mind about retiring and decided to stay on indefinitely until the last hound dog had stopped snapping at my heels—and that promised to be a long time, as Nixon naturally wanted to have my seat on the Court.[42]

Following their ouster of Abe Fortas, the "hound dogs" set their sights on Douglas. A group of House Republicans, led by Gerald Ford, started a formal attempt to impeach the liberal Justice. This was not the first attempt made by Douglas's political enemies to remove him from office. Douglas had twice survived moves for impeachment in 1966, one deriving from his alleged "immoral character"—he had just been married for the fourth time—and the other stemming from his financial ties to a foundation. The latter charge was resurrected anew following the Fortas situation.[43] On April 30, 1970, Douglas returned from a physical checkup and took the bench for oral argument. He passed a note to his longtime colleague Justice Black: "My blood pressure is 140 over 70—which indicates that the Bastards have not got me down." Black responded:

> Fine! Keep your smile! Mr. Ford and his crowd cannot get you. I am delighted to know of the results of your medical examination. After my appointment to the Court when my opponents were after me most viciously, I told my wife we needed an inscription on our bed reading as follows, 'This too will pass away.' And it did. So will the flurry and the noise about you. Of course you know I am on your side. Keep up your smile and health and read the 13th chapter of 1st Corinthians now and then.[44]

Like they had done with Fortas, the Republicans attacked Douglas's extrajudicial connections and writings. But unlike Fortas, the Republicans failed to force Douglas's resignation. Justice Harlan wrote him, "I shall be on deck next Term, as . . . I know you will be," and assured him that the "miserable business" in the House "of course, can only have one ending."[45] Just as Black and Harlan predicted, a House subcommittee eventually cleared him of any wrongdoing.

On October 29, 1973, Douglas became the longest-serving justice in Supreme Court history surpassing Stephen J. Field's mark of thirty-four years, 195 days. On November 3, the Douglas Anniversary Convocation was held. Organized by a group of Douglas's former clerks, the black tie affair was attended by the other justices and Douglas's family and friends. In his speech, Douglas was discussing committees when he playfully brought up the subject of retirement:

> I do, however, think that the committee can serve a useful purpose. Retirement of justices on the Court has raised problems. Greer, Field, and Holmes were each waited on by a committee suggesting he retire. Hughes was indeed the committee of one who called on Holmes . . . When Chief Justice Hughes retired, he called a special conference at the end of a Term and announced that he had that day sent notice of his retirement to the President. He said he felt quite adequate for the job and knew he could continue for awhile. But with tears in his eyes he added, "I have always been fearful of continuing in office under the delusion of adequacy."

> So advisory committees can serve a long range need ... At times
> I thought I should retire to do some things I always wanted to do but
> never had the time to do.[46]

On New Year's Day 1974, Douglas suffered a severe stroke.[47] Douglas was
placed in intensive care and when Abe Fortas came to visit, he told the press
that Douglas would be back at the Court in three or four weeks. Fortas knew
that Douglas's condition was much more severe. He had trouble speaking, lost
concentration easily, and had difficulty moving his left arm and leg. Though
Douglas made it clear that he intended to return to work, his friends were not
so sure. On January 13, Douglas's close friend Clark Clifford had a memorandum written that sketched the absences of justices due to incapacity and
sent a copy to Douglas.[48] The justices were also skeptical of Douglas's capacity to work. They decided to put off oral argument in a number of cases where
Douglas was likely to be the deciding vote.[49]

When Douglas returned to the Court he decided to hold a press conference.[50]
He thought that he would show the press that he was fully capable of doing his
job and answer any doubts they might have. Instead, the press conference had the
opposite effect. It was clear to everyone in the room that Douglas could no longer
effectively do his job. He struggled to tear pages from a legal pad, spoke disjoint-
edly and slurred his words. He informed them that he had no intention of stepping down and invited them all on a fifteen-mile hike in April. Rather than put
to rest speculation of his departure, the press conference only added fuel to the fire.
It was suggested that partisanship played a role in Douglas delaying his retirement. It was reported that he did not want to leave the Court under President
Ford, who as House Minority Leader had led the fight to impeach Douglas in
1970. Eight months later it was reported that he told a friend, "I won't resign while
there's a breath in my body, until we get a Democratic president."[51]

On March 31, Chief Justice Burger sent around the opinion assignment
list. Every justice was assigned two or three cases, except Douglas, who was
not assigned any. Burger attached a letter of explanation:

> The subject of opinion assignments came up at the Conference and
> everyone expressed the view that I should not risk retarding your
> progress by assigning opinions to you until the April sitting. You are
> making progress but there will be a heavy load getting through the
> petitions and jurisdictional statements for the Friday Conference
> April 11 and preparing for a dozen hard cases set for argument
> beginning April 14.[52]

Meanwhile, Douglas's mental capacity began to deteriorate. He called
people by the wrong name, and often mumbled or did not speak at all. Dou-

glas underwent physical therapy and tried different medications to help his condition, but nothing worked. He remained optimistic, however, even believing that he would someday walk again. He told his secretary, "It could be worse. At least I can read and write."[53] Chief Justice Burger frequently visited with Douglas during this time, often bringing him gifts. Though Burger told the press that he was "extremely pleased about the progress Justice Douglas has made," he knew the opposite to be true. The Chief told friends that the Court itself was "limping along" with a glut of held-over cases due to Douglas's illness.[54]

As the term ended, Douglas and his wife flew back to Washington State. Long time friends were shocked by the justice's decline and urged a family friend, Charles Reich, to persuade Douglas to step down. Reich noted, "He was in much, much worse shape than he or the public realized."[55] Over three days Reich tried his best to convince Douglas that it was time to call it quits. He appealed on all fronts, asking Douglas to consider his fragile health, and even the damage he might cause to his judicial reputation. Douglas protested that he had to return to the Court to defend the underprivileged. "There will be no one on the Court who cares for blacks, Chicanos, defendants, and the environment."[56] He continued, "Even if I'm only half alive, I can still cast a liberal vote. I'm going back to Washington and try it . . . I have to decide for myself."[57] When Reich asked whether he was hanging on for a Democratic president to appoint his successor, Douglas said that it did not matter who was president and that whoever was appointed would not care for the disadvantaged. "The Court is my life," he told Reich, "What will I do if I leave? I will be committing suicide. I'm not quite ready to commit suicide."[58]

When Douglas returned from the summer recess intending to fully participate in the work of the Court, it was obvious that his condition had not improved. In the middle of oral argument on October 6, Douglas asked to be wheeled from the bench and taken home.[59] His handwriting was barely legible and he was becoming increasingly confused.[60] His colleagues felt compelled to make an unprecedented decision. On October 17, 1975, with Douglas absent, the eight justices met in conference and decided to effectively strip Douglas of his power. Cases that were split four to four, excluding Douglas's vote, would be held over to the next term. Four justices, again excluding Douglas, were now needed in order to agree to hear a case. One of the justices explained:

> Bill's votes were inconsistent with his prior positions. For example, he would vote to deny cert. in cases where the issues were similar to earlier cases in which he had consistently voted to grant cert. So the purpose of the agreement was to protect Bill as well as the integrity of the Court.[61]

This unprecedented decision, however, was not unanimous. Justice Byron White was the lone dissenter. After the conference, White wrote a letter of protest to Chief Justice Burger and hand delivered copies to the other justices. White felt the matter was so sensitive that he did not even show the memo to his own clerks. White argued:

[The Constitution] nowhere provides that a justice's colleagues may deprive him of his office by refusing to permit him to function as a justice.

[The only remedy is to] invite Congress to take appropriate action. If it is an impeachable offense for an incompetent justice to purport to sit as a judge, is it not the task of Congress, rather than of this Court, to undertake proceedings to determine the issue of competence? If it is not an impeachable offense, may the Court nevertheless conclude that a justice is incompetent and forbid him to perform his duties?

[This decision is] plainly a matter of great importance. I do hope the majority is prepared to make formal disclosure of the action that it has taken.

History teaches that nothing can more readily bring the Court and its constitutional functions into disrepute than the Court's failure to recognize the limits of its own powers.[62]

Of course no public announcement of this unprecedented action was made. But in the end, no case was affected due to Douglas's decisive vote. Though White was concerned about the constitutionality of his colleagues' action, it was in keeping with the Court's regular procedure for deciding cases. As Justice Brennan always remarked, five votes can do anything at the Court, and in the case of denying cert., six votes can do anything. So technically, Douglas's vote would never be decisive as long as five of his colleagues voted to hold a case over for reargument or six voted not to grant cert. The Court does not have to reveal the justification for its votes. So it is possible for five, six, or more of the justices to get together and informally decide to effectively ignore one or more of their colleagues if they choose. This may have been what happened in the case of Justice Whittaker and probably has happened before in the Court's earlier years, when infirmities were more common. With Douglas, the decision was taken more formally.

As the new term began, Douglas once again took his place on the bench. It was obvious that his condition had not improved over the summer as he frequently dozed off during oral argument and in conference and often had to leave his colleagues when his physical pain became unbearable.[63] When it came time to assign the first batch of opinions for the new term, Burger did not assign any to Douglas. And in those cases where Douglas, as senior associate justice, was technically supposed to assign the opinions, Justice Brennan instead consulted with the chief on the assignments with Brennan, Marshall, and White taking one each. Douglas again had nothing to write and his colleagues had given him their first undeniable hint that he ought to step down.

In October, doctors informed Douglas that he would never walk again and would remain in constant pain due to his condition. He wrote a friend:

> The top therapy man says that my chances of improvement—arm and leg are nil. That is a bleak and dreary outlook . . . The pain persists as strong as ever. It is the only reason I should ever retire. Cathy, however, is pounding on me to resign . . . My son is aligned with her in that cause.[64]

Refusing to give up, on November 5, Douglas returned to the bench for oral argument. Finding the pain unbearable, he quickly returned to his chambers and Chief Justice Burger postponed the proceedings until later in the day. After lunch, Douglas again attempted to sit for oral argument. He instructed a messenger to get the volume of the federal statutes dealing with the retirement of federal judges. Once more, however, he had to be taken back to his chambers. Douglas wanted a second opinion on his condition. The prognosis was similar to the first, but Douglas was told that if he rested, his condition might improve. Douglas returned to the Court for conference on Friday, but was again unable to participate because of excruciating pain and he returned to his chambers. The following Monday, Douglas finally decided that he could not continue. He called on his old friends Abe Fortas and Clark Clifford to help draft his retirement letter to President Ford:

> It was my hope, when I returned to Washington in September, that I would be able to continue to participate in the work of the Supreme Court.
>
> I have learned, however, after these last two months, that it would be inadvisable for me to attempt to carry on the duties required of a member of the Court. I have been bothered with incessant and demanding pain which depletes my energy to the extent that I have been unable to shoulder my full share of the burden . . .
>
> During the hours of oral argument last week pain made it necessary for me to leave the Bench several times. I have had to leave several times this week also. I shall continue to seek relief from this unabated pain but there is no bright prospect in view . . .
>
> I shall miss [my colleagues] sorely, but I know this is the right decision.[65]

On November 12, 1975, Douglas formally retired after thirty-six years, the longest tenure in the Court's history. That morning, he informed Chief Justice Burger of his decision. The justices met for lunch that afternoon in their private dining room to celebrate Justice Harry Blackmun's birthday. After the brethren sang "Happy Birthday," Douglas sat silently as Burger announced, "Bill wants me to tell you he's written a letter to the President."[66]

The trouble, however, began almost immediately. After receiving a copy of Douglas's retirement letter, Burger hastily sent a handwritten reply, which said in part, "At your convenience—and if it is agreeable, I will assign you the Chambers heretofore occupied by Chief Justice Warren. It is a commodious suite, considerably larger than what you now occupy."[67] Douglas replied:

> Thanks for the suggestion that I might want the more commodious quarters which Earl Warren last used here, but the smaller quarters I have have suited me for many years and I am inclined to stay where I am.
>
> Whoever is named to take my place might want the more commodious space that is available. In fairness to the other Brethren . . . you might consider giving them the opportunity to give up what they have now for the more commodious space available.[68]

"It was marvelous to see how Douglas outmaneuvered the Chief Justice," recalled a former clerk about the incident.[69]

On November 16, Douglas left the Court and flew to Portland, Oregon for treatment. As is customary, his clerks were reassigned to other chambers and Justice Brennan formally took over the role of senior associate justice. At the end of November, Douglas returned to his office to find his clerks gone. He wrote the Conference and explained why he still needed two law clerks, two secretaries, and a messenger. He promised to write a 200–year history of the Court in order "to untangle many of the cobwebs which have been spun" in the recent publication of the Frankfurter Conference notes. He also pointed out that he needed help with the "huge amount of correspondence and the like" which he had accumulated over his years at the Court.[70] The next day, Justice Brennan had a clerk write him a memorandum on the statutes and authority over the quarters and services of retired Justices. The memorandum said that the Court had ultimate authority over the quarters and staff of retired Justices.[71] The Supreme Court Librarian also looked into the matter inquiring with the Administrative Office of the United States Courts, whose general counsel basically confirmed the information in the Brennan memo.[72] Douglas saw both documents, copies of which are contained in his papers.

To the surprise and sadness of the other members of the Court, it soon became clear that Douglas intended to continue, in an unprecedented way, as the Court's tenth justice. Douglas felt that he should be able to legitimately participate in all cases in which cert. had been granted or jurisdiction noted while he was still an active member of the Court, prior to his November 12 retirement.

John Paul Stevens joined the Court on December 19, 1975, as the justices were preparing to hear arguments in a number of death penalty cases. When Douglas heard about the impending cases, he phoned Justice Brennan to announce that he would be participating in the cases. Brennan protested that it would be impossible and that there were only nine chairs at the bench. Douglas suggested that a tenth chair could be added. Losing patience, Brennan replied, "No. The statute governing the Court clearly calls for only nine justices. John has taken your place." Douglas responded, "Not you too."[73]

Douglas had gone too far. He announced that he would write an opinion in the case of *Buckley v. Valeo* which involved the Federal Election Campaign Act of 1974.[74] After writing his opinion, Douglas had it printed and expected it to be circulated to his colleagues. When it was not, he wrote a thirteen-page memorandum to his colleagues saying that the Court's attempt to exclude him from their deliberations was "much more mischievous *[sic]* than the Roosevelt [Court packing] plan. It tends to denigrate Associate justices who 'retire.' Beyond that is the mischief in selecting the occasion when a justice will be allowed to hear and decide cases." He called his exclusion "a practice in politics," and added, "The Court is the last place for political maneuvering."[75]

The justices had had enough of Douglas's antics and on December 22, in conference, they decided to draft a reply that would make very clear to Douglas that his tenure at the Court was through. Burger drafted the three-page response. After minor changes by Justices Brennan and Stewart,[76] Burger brought the letter to each justice to sign. The memorandum explained that, as a retired justice, he could not participate in oral argument, attend conference, vote in cases, or write opinions:

It seems clear beyond doubt that your retirement . . . operated to terminate all judicial powers except such as would arise from assignment to one of the Federal courts other than the Supreme Court. The statutes seem clear that a retired justice cannot be assigned any duties of a Supreme Court justice as such. This would apply to all cases submitted but not decided before you retired and to any case decided while you were a member of the Court on which rehearing is thereafter granted . . .

The formal conferences of the Court are limited, as you know, to justices empowered to act on pending matters and do not include retired justices . . .

You should be allowed to take your choice and have two secretaries rather than one secretary and one law clerk. It was agreed that your messenger could be continued so that you would have someone to drive your car . . . you should have your present Chambers as you requested . . .

No member of the Conference could recall any instance of a retired justice participating in any matter before the Court and it was unanimously agreed that the relevant statutes do not allow for such participation.[77]

Burger told a clerk, "Bill is like an old firehouse dog, too old to run along with the trucks, but his ears prick up just the same."[78] Justice Brennan and later former Justice Fortas spoke with Douglas about the situation, but Douglas would not listen. When Douglas found out that the Court's decision in *Buckley* was to be announced, he ordered his clerk to take the opinion to the press office for distribution. When the clerk declined, Douglas shot back, "You are a traitor. I will get it down there myself."[79] The clerk sent a note to Justice White, "The tenth member of the Court wants to release his opinion."[80] The press office was told to ignore Douglas's requests.

Eventually, Douglas ended his attempts to take part in the work of the Court. He retreated to his memoirs, having failed in his bid to alter the parameters of a retired justices' duties. Two months later, he wrote a friend and explained why he stepped down:

I retired from the Court because of the pain that seemed to get no better. It was impossible to sit on the bench for longer than an hour or so and follow the arguments. Intense mental concentration and intense pain are not compatible.

I've about given up all hope. I'm very depressed and while the pain is somewhat alleviated it still keeps me far below par. I have no plans for the future.[81]

OLD AND COMING APART

The retirements of Black and Harlan are typical of recent justices under the expanded retirement provisions. Though they showed some concern for the institutional health of the Court at the end, their personal and even partisan concerns, as in the case of Black bargaining over a preferred successor, proved decisive. Harlan's tenure was prolonged by not only having an extra clerk, but his heavy reliance on their skills. Like Black and Harlan, Douglas did not want to confront the inevitable. Not only did he fight against retirement, he tried to continue participating in the Court's work after he did formally step down. The departure decisions of those who serve during the lengthy decline of colleagues are shaped by the infirmities and the institutional problems that result. This superannuation effect occurred following the declines of Robert C. Grier, Stephen J. Field, Joseph McKenna, and Oliver Wendell Holmes. So far, of the eight justices who served with Black, Harlan, or Douglas during their declines, all but Chief Justice Rehnquist have retired. Though it can be argued that some, like Thurgood Marshall have lingered a bit too long, none burdened the Court to the degree that occurred in the 1970s. Indeed, some may have left prematurely, due in part to their experience with these justices.[82]

POTTER STEWART

On January 23, 1980, Justice Potter Stewart reached age sixty-five and became eligible to retire with full benefits. On February 19, he received a letter from a high school student who had written to him as part of a class assignment. She asked, "Why have you stayed on the Supreme Court so long? We have learned you have the opportunity to retire, but still you are a judge on the court. I am not saying you need to retire but am asking why you stay on the court longer than you need to?"[83] Stewart replied, "I've been eligible to retire for only eleven days!"[84] If he did not realize it before, he now knew that he was eligible for full benefits under the 1954 Retirement Act. He began contemplating stepping down and his first thoughts were about the institutional health of the Court, "[1980] was an election year and I thought it would be very harmful for the Court and for the country if I retired at the time. Any vacancy created by my retirement would not be filled, and the Court would inevitably be drawn into a presidential political campaign if I retired during that year." He added, "nor did I want to retire in the midst of the Term."[85]

In March 1981, with the presidential campaign over and Republican Ronald Reagan in the White House, Stewart and his wife decided that after almost twenty-three years on the Court, the time was right. Stewart spoke with his close friend, Vice President George Bush about the matter.[86] Bush recalled:

He said a fairly sane thing. He said he wanted to spend more time with his family . . . One can find oneself being a public hero and a private failure, giving less and less attention to the family and the children and the life that goes on in the home. Potter put his family first.[87]

On May 18, Stewart went to the White House and gave President Reagan his official letter of retirement, setting the date for the close of the term on July 3.[88] Stewart also informed Chief Justice Burger of his intentions. Stewart explained why he gave advance notice, "I didn't want to spring it on certain people and the Administration because it would not be easy to find a replacement on short notice. I thought it was only fair to give them some time to begin thinking about it."[89]

On June 19, 1981, Stewart held a press conference and explained why he was stepping down:

> For one thing, when I became a member of the United States Court of Appeals I was the youngest federal judge in the country and I thought it might be a good idea to retire before I became one of the oldest ones. Secondly, I've never missed an argument day on the Court. That's not anything that I brag about very much because I remember that one of the dullest students in school was a classmate who won the attendance prize. Thirdly, I've always been a firm believer in the principle that it's better to go too soon than to stay too long. Finally, and perhaps most importantly, I wanted to have an opportunity to spend more time with my wife, Andy, and hopefully, with our children and grandchildren while I was still relatively young and healthy. Those are the basic reasons. None of them very dramatic, if you will, but all of them very important to me.[90]

The press was skeptical:

> Reporter: Did the fact that Jimmy Carter was President affect your decision to wait to retire in any way?
> Stewart: No. But the fact that it was an election year did.
> Reporter: It wasn't a question of your not wanting a particular President to appoint a replacement?
> Stewart: No, no.[91]

Beyond being eligible for full retirement benefits, personal and institutional concerns were key factors in Stewart's departure decision. Though there is no direct evidence that partisanship motivated him, he chose to leave during the first term of a new Republican administration, suggesting that partisanship may have played a part. Interestingly, Stewart's death on December 7, 1985, at the age of seventy would have given Reagan the appointment anyway. Stewart's retirement came as a surprise to followers of the Court since there were five justices over age seventy at the time. What was even more of a surprise was that five years went by before another justice, Warren Burger, chose to leave.

THE RULE OF EIGHTY

In 1984, Congress acted yet again to expand the retirement provision. While the original age-seventy, ten-year requirement of 1869 was expanded to sixty-five and fifteen years, there was no provision to cover those who fell in between. For example, a justice who was age sixty-nine but had only served eleven years on the federal bench was not eligible. This was the precise situation Harold Burton was in when he had to wait an additional year until he reached age seventy to retire. The Rule of Eighty solved this problem by allowing retirement with full benefits for any combination of years and service totaling eighty (see Table 8.1).[92] Interestingly, this reform has had no effect on the Supreme Court. Since its passage, every justice has retired well after age seventy. Also, every current justice has met or will meet the sixty-five/fifteen requirement of the 1954 statute, and therefore will not need to avail themselves of the increased flexibility of this provision.

WARREN E. BURGER

Warren Burger became eligible for full retirement benefits on his sixty-fifth birthday in 1972. Though he had been on the Supreme Court for only four years, Burger had been a federal judge for thirteen years, sitting on the U.S. Court of Appeals for the District of Columbia prior to his appointment as Chief Justice by President Nixon.

On his sixty-seventh birthday, September 17, 1974, Burger received a bicycle from his family. After trying it out on the driveway, he started down

TABLE 8.1
The Rule of Eighty: Combination of Years and Service
Needed by Federal Judges for Retirement

Age	Years of Federal Judicial Service
65	15
66	14
67	13
68	12
69	11
70	10

Source: 28 U.S.C. 371 (c).

the darkened street in front of his house. Not far from home, what Burger called a "hit-and-run dragracer" forced him off the road.[93] He hit a curb and was thrown from the bike, suffering a deep cut over his eye, a dislocated shoulder, and five broken ribs. He spent six days in the hospital and returned to the Court looking older and fatigued.[94] Burger had no plans to slow down, however, and continued his usual duties as chief justice.

In the 1980s, rumors of Burger's departure began to circulate. When asked by a reporter in 1984 whether he was contemplating retirement, Burger responded, "I haven't even thought about it. Don't be deceived by these white hairs."[95] After Burger played a part in getting former GOP Senator Roger Jepsen of Iowa removed from a key position in the newly forming commission in charge of organizing a celebration for the 200th anniversary of the Constitution, President Reagan tapped the chief to chair the commission. It was reported that Burger was very enthusiastic about the project but distressed that the Constitution was taking a backseat, both financially and publicity-wise, to the 100th anniversary of the Statue of Liberty. He was also concerned, that coming so close to the bicentennial celebration of the Declaration of Independence, interest would be lessened.

The official story of Burger's departure left many unsatisfied. After working long hours over the summer on the commission work, Burger began having doubts that he could devote his full attention to both the bicentennial and the Court. His wife was concerned that he was working too hard as he put in as many as 105 hours in a single week trying to juggle both jobs.[96] He contemplated retirement for months and in May 1986 discussed the matter with former White House counsel Fred Fielding. Fielding had been acting as informal liaison between Burger and the White House and set up an Oval Office meeting with Reagan to discuss bicentennial issues.[97] Burger went over his concerns explaining how the commission was behind schedule and in need of serious help. Burger then announced that he would be retiring at the close of the term in order to work full time on the commission's mounting problems. Reagan, who was reportedly surprised, accepted his retirement, and told an aide to phone Attorney General Edwin Meese with the news.[98] For his part, Reagan did say, "It was a surprise, yes," when asked by reporters about Burger's decision.[99]

Burger did not inform his colleagues of his impending departure, so other than a few top White House aides, no one in Washington knew. On June 17 the justices gathered around a television set in the conference room at the Court and watched as President Reagan announced Burger's departure. Reagan was joined at the White House press conference by Justice Rehnquist, and Judge Antonin Scalia, who would be the Court's newest chief and new associate justice, respectively. Burger officially stepped down on September 26, 1986, on swearing in Rehnquist as the new chief.

Columnist David Broder reported at the time, "It has been common knowledge in Washington that Burger, now 78, intended to step down as Chief Justice in order to let Reagan name a younger successor to that vital post . . . My guess was that he would preside over the Constitution's big birthday next year while still wearing judicial robes, and then step down. But he may have been prompted to advance his resignation date by fears that the Democrats will take over control of the Senate this November."[100]

Was it concern over mid-term elections or something else that prompted Burger's decision? Some speculated that a deal had been struck to get Burger to retire sooner rather than later. In 1978 the National Conference of Chief Justices proposed the creation of the State Justice Institute (SJI) to provide federal grants and educational resources to help state and local court systems function more effectively. Burger championed the SJI. In 1980 he wrote the House Judiciary Committee, "The creation of the State Justice Institute will be a major step forward in preserving and improving strong and effective state court systems."[101] With added support from the American Bar Association in 1982, Congress nearly passed a bill that would have created the institute in 1983. Last-minute opposition by the Reagan administration, however, killed it.[102] A year later, Reagan Attorney General Edwin Meese changed his view of the proposal and unexpectedly supported its creation.[103] Finally approved by Congress in 1984, the SJI did not become operational until early 1987 because of appropriation delays and the Reagan administration's failure to nominate a board of directors.[104] On April 8, 1987, Democratic Senator Howell Heflin, who sat on the Senate Judiciary Committee and was a strong supporter of the SJI, blocked consideration of Reagan's federal court nominees until the administration relented and agreed to the funding.[105] Because of the timing, there was speculation that Burger's departure was tied to SJI's appropriation.

Burger's departure began a changing of the guard at the Court. Within an eight-year period, six justices decided to leave. In the cases of Justices Powell, Brennan, and Marshall questions of mental decline again plagued the Court.

LEWIS F. POWELL, JR.

Lewis Powell was a reluctant justice. When initially approached by the Nixon administration, he said that he did not want a nomination to the Court. One of the reasons he cited was a "problem" he claimed he had with his eyesight. He suggested he might not have many more years of vision left. Though Powell's ophthalmologist said he had bothersome floaters and might need cataract surgery in eight to ten years, he told Powell that he could expect to "maintain useful vision for many years to come."[106] Nixon was determined and Powell finally accepted the nomination.

Powell's years on the Court were peppered with incidents of illness and surgery. Each time, however, he recovered fully and continued his work with full vigor.[107] When Powell was first appointed to the Court, he planned for ten years of service. In 1982, he reached his goal and became eligible for full retirement benefits. Instead of stepping down, he decided to wait until the following spring to consider the matter.

Though in good health at age seventy-five, he started to seriously consider retirement as the 1982 term neared its end. Powell was pleased with President Reagan's selection of Sandra Day O'Connor and wanted to give Reagan another nomination. Waiting another year to retire, Powell reasoned, would drag the nomination into election-year politics. He also knew that waiting two years would run the risk of having a liberal Democratic president make the nomination. Powell turned to his family for advice.

His wife had "wanted him to retire since the day he took the oath of office."[108] His son, Lewis III, however thought that Powell would miss the Court more than he realized. Father and son met on April 9, 1983, to discuss the matter at length. Powell considered his age, eye problems, level of energy, and "the likely occupant of the White House after November 1984." After their meeting, Lewis III wrote his father, recounting their discussion:

> [I]n your typically objective and methodical fashion, you have analyzed the merits of retirement this year against hanging in there for several more years . . . Your analysis has failed to take account of what you feel in your heart and soul. [I was] struck by the sense of sadness that seemed to permeate your remarks about the satisfaction you derive from judging (and doing it well), from your association with your clerks, from the give-and-take of the Conference, and from the simple greetings exchanged among the justices before you ascend the Bench. Whenever you retire, I fear that you will miss terribly these and many other aspects of the life of an active justice—perhaps far more than you can anticipate.[109]

Despite his son's analysis, Powell was still not convinced he should remain in his seat. He remembered the events surrounding William O. Douglas's unpleasant departure and did not want to burden the Court as Douglas had.[110] Three weeks later, Lewis III and his sister Jo simultaneously wrote their father and urged him not to step down. Lewis III assured his father that he would tell him when he began to "lose it" and added, "You owe it to the Court, the nation, your family, and yourself not to step down while you are still fit to discharge your duties as magnificently as you have for the last 11 years."[111] Ultimately, Powell's love of service on the Court outweighed his concerns and he chose to remain in his seat. In the following years, he continued to undergo surgeries, but always recovered enough to continue his work on the Court.[112]

But Powell's work was not what it once was. In 1986, the Court decided *Bowers v. Hardwick*[113] by a vote of 5–4 with Powell the deciding vote to uphold a Georgia statute criminalizing sodomy. Powell's brief concurring opinion demonstrated his indecisiveness on the issue. He said that he would invalidate the statute based on Eighth Amendment grounds as he felt the maximum penalty of twenty years in prison was "cruel and unusual" except for the fact that the Eighth Amendment issue was not before the Court and had not been properly briefed and argued by the attorneys. Former clerk and Powell biographer, John C. Jeffries argued that this decision demonstrated that Powell had mentally declined and should have stepped down prior to the 1986 Term.[114] Indeed, Powell later regretted his decision in *Bowers* and admitted "I think I probably made a mistake."[115]

At the end of the 1987 Term, he again revisited the issue of retirement. On June 20, he met with his son, Lewis III, and Jeffries, to discuss the matter.[116] He contemplated the same issues he had considered four years earlier. Again, he was aware of the possibility of a Democratic president being elected the following year, but now he was unconcerned with this partisan factor. He explained how justices often did not behave as their nominating presidents had planned, pointing to William Brennan and Byron White as two recent examples. Powell thought it better to focus on personal concerns. He wondered whether he was still able to do the job effectively and what he would do if he retired. He always remarked how he thought Potter Stewart's relatively early retirement hastened his death. Powell now wondered if the same fate was in store for him. This time, Powell's son remained neutral on the decision and took no position. Powell's daughter, however, wrote him, "I think you'll be happier if you keep going. And I think you'll be healthier too."[117]

For his part, Jeffries drafted a detailed memorandum for Powell's consideration on the factors a justice ought to take into account in making the retirement decision. Jeffries identified three types of concerns: institutional, personal, and political. He argued that Powell had no institutional duty to retire, since all evidence suggested that he was fully able to contribute to the Court's work. Jeffries argued that personal factors also counseled against retirement:

> The sudden withdrawal from power and responsibility would be, at the least, disconcerting. Nothing you could do after retirement would entirely fill the gap in your life . . . It would be a permanent relinquishment of power and significant withdrawal from the kinds of commitments that have occupied your adult life and . . . that lie very near the core of your sense of personal identity. You are right to view that prospect with anxiety.[118]

For the last section and "most delicate" part of the memo, Jeffries addressed the partisan concerns Powell had raised in their initial meeting. Jeffries suggested that it was "as least as likely as not" that a Democrat would win the next election. He took issue with Powell's suggestion that one could never be sure that justices would behave as their nominating presidents intend. Jeffries argued that presidents have been successful in shaping the direction of the Supreme Court, despite a few highly publicized cases like Eisenhower's disappointment with Earl Warren and William Brennan. Jeffries concluded with his recommendation:

> [You should] either retire now or . . . plan to serve for several more years. This suggests that you should try to imagine what several more years on the Supreme Court would be like. One possibility is that the next five years would be very like the last five years. Another possibility is that you may grow increasingly tired . . . I have some fear that the immense satisfaction and sense of accomplishment that you derive from your position may be increasingly offset by exhaustion. Obviously the best guide here is your own intuition and reflection.[119]

The extent to which Powell considered the Jeffries memo in making his decision is not known. What was clear to Powell, however, was his own declining strength. He was still unable to gain any weight, and his doctor at the Mayo Clinic diagnosed him with "chronic fatigue." Powell's doctor felt that he could still perform the duties of his office, but thought that he was "pushing himself too far each day and each week." Three months short of his eightieth birthday, Powell decided to retire.[120]

On the final day of the term, Powell held a press conference. In his prepared statement, he said that the founders should have required retirement at age seventy-five, even though it "would have deprived the Court of the service after that age by a number of the most distinguished justices ever to sit on this Court."[121] He cited his age, a concern that his past health problems might recur and "handicap the Court," and the fact that he had already served longer than he had originally planned as his reasons for departing. Though he did not cite partisanship as a motivating factor, it was certainly a factor he was aware of. A reporter asked, "Justice Powell, certainly it must have dawned upon you . . . that who comes after you may alter the balance of many important issues. Did that weigh into your consideration?"[122] Powell responded that it did not. Like Potter Stewart had done six years before, Powell did consciously avoid departing during a presidential election year out of concern for the Court as an institution. And also like Stewart and Burger he departed under a copartisan president.

WILLIAM J. BRENNAN, JR.

During his first term on the Court, Brennan was diagnosed with an irregular heartbeat. He was a heavy smoker and his doctors recommended that he exercise every day and watch his diet. Brennan complied and began walking nearly four miles each morning. Later he took to riding a stationary bicycle for thirty minutes before heading to work.

For fifteen years, Justice Brennan's wife Marjorie battled cancer. Each day Brennan would finish up his work at the Court and rush home to care for her. Then in December 1978, the justice underwent radiation treatments for a malignant tumor on his left vocal chord. He wrote the other justices, "I am advised that after three weeks the soreness of my throat will make speaking somewhat difficult."[123] Chief Justice Burger wrote the other justices, "We have arranged to send Bill Brennan a brand new anecdotal history of Washington, which will put no strain on his vocal chords."[124] Brennan was seventy-two and the battle drained him further, almost permanently costing him his voice. He wrote retired Justice Douglas, "I have finished four weeks of the seven week radiation program and the doctors are most encouraging. My voice isn't too good and my throat is a bit sore but that too will pass."[125] The following year, on September 4, 1979, he had a small stroke and his right arm and hand were weakened. As the years progressed and Marjorie's illness worsened, Brennan withdrew more and more. For a time he even felt like leaving the Court to care for her full-time. He recalled his struggle:

> I came close, very close to crumbling under the strain. There were a couple of times when I thought I couldn't carry on, couldn't do my job. I came quite close to thinking I ought to retire. But she wouldn't have any part of that. She was a great lady.[126]

After his wife's death, on December 1, 1982, Brennan was devastated. Their daughter recalled, "Dad really did a nose-dive after Mother died. And I think he really could have given up. He's so strong-willed that had he stuck by it, it would have been another case of the widower following the deceased."[127] Brennan gradually recovered, however. He remarried and took to his work with a newfound vigor.[128]

Brennan felt strongly that he should retire when he could no longer keep up his share of the Court's work. He felt that his duty lay with the Court as an institution, and not with his own personal preferences. In a 1987 interview he said that if he became ill, he hoped to "recognize it, and . . . just surrender."[129]

In December 1988, the eighty-two year-old Justice became ill and was rushed to the hospital. At first doctors thought Brennan had pneumonia, but they soon realized he had an infected gallbladder.[130] He stayed in the hospital for over a week after having it removed. After New Year's, when he returned to the Court, he seemed to have lost his strength and even lost his voice for periods at a time in the spring.[131] He often needed assistance when walking among the offices of his colleagues. At receptions, he could only stand unassisted for a few minutes at a time. On the bench, Brennan began dozing off and Chief Justice Rehnquist took notice.[132] To be sure, Brennan was becoming increasingly frustrated with his conservative colleagues and the Court's general direction, and his failing health did not help matters. His days as the Court's "playmaker" were long over, and his relationships with a number of his colleagues, notably, Justice O'Connor, had soured.[133] Though he may not have been interested or even able to argue through every point of a difficult case, he was still fully able to state his positions clearly and forcefully in conference.[134] As a result, he gave no thought to stepping down.

During the Court's summer recess in 1990, Brennan suffered his second mild stroke.[135] His doctors urged him to retire in order to preserve his fragile health. Brennan's memory faded in and out and at times he became confused.[136] He spoke with his family about the matter. Though he had already selected his law clerks for the upcoming term, he decided to step down.

Unwilling to bear an in-person meeting, Brennan phoned Justice Marshall to inform him of his decision. Brennan told his colleague that the decision was final, and without saying a word, Marshall put the receiver on his desk and left the room.[137] Marshall told his son, Thurgood Jr., a lawyer for the Senate Judiciary Committee, about Brennan's impending retirement. Brennan, however, was having second thoughts. No formal announcement had been made and the Court's Public Information Officer Toni House admitted to reporters that she had also only heard rumors.[138] When the press reported that Brennan was planning to retire, he was upset and ultimately felt somewhat compelled to go through with it. Brennan realized Justice Marshall was responsible for the leak and it strained their relationship during their remaining years.[139] On July 20, 1990, Brennan officially retired after nearly thirty-four years on the Court. He wrote President Bush, "The strenuous demands of Court work and its related duties required or expected of a justice appear at this time to be incompatible with my advancing age and medical condition. I therefore retire effective immediately."[140] He told a friend, "This is the saddest day of my life."[141]

In what some saw as a slight, Chief Justice Rehnquist moved Brennan into a small second-floor office and took away his car and driver.[142] Though Brennan enjoyed traveling the world with his wife during his retirement, he missed his work at the Court and regretted leaving.[143] When Justice White asked for advice on the retirement decision in March 1993, Brennan told him not to leave, and added that it was the worst decision he had ever made.[144] Five years after his retirement he explained that his doctors pressed him to step down: "They told me I had the one stroke and if I had another one, it might be my last. So I quit. Every minute since I [regretted it]. God, when I see some of the decisions . . . I think, 'Jeez, if only I were there.'"[145]

THURGOOD MARSHALL

Marshall once described himself as "a hedonist with no time for pleasure."[146] Marshall smoked two packs of cigarettes a day, drank Bourbon, and ate what he wanted. For years, Marshall's enemies spread rumors that he would soon die of alcoholism. He spent a fair amount of time over the years in the hospital, and the condition of his health was almost always kept from the media.

Before the start of the 1971 term, for example, he had an emergency appendectomy arising from complications associated with a stomach ulcer. In February 1975, Marshall came down with a respiratory infection that developed into pneumonia. He checked into Bethesda Naval Hospital for a month and with Justice Douglas also off the bench after his stroke, the Court was down to seven members. His weight was well over 230 pounds and he was smoking two packs a day. His doctors advised him to change his lifestyle and rumors of his demise began circulating. The Nixon administration had been particularly concerned about his health over the years and with Gerald Ford now occupying the Oval Office, not much had changed. Marshall recalled:

> I was out at Bethesda for five or six weeks. It was a real bad deal. And when I got through, the commandant at Bethesda said to me, 'I've been requested to give a full report of your illness and prognosis, et cetera.' And he said, 'I won't do it without your permission.' I said, 'Who wants it?' And he says, 'The president wants it.' I said, 'Well admiral, you have my permission to give it to him only on one condition. That you put at the bottom of it, quote, Not Yet.' And he did.[147]

On July 2, 1976, the Court reinstated the death penalty in *Gregg v. Georgia*, despite an angry dissent from Marshall.[148] He appeared visibly shaken and left the Court early that day. That night, he suffered a minor heart attack and was again hospitalized.[149] His doctors ordered him to lose forty pounds. He suffered two more mild heart attacks in the next three days before declaring over a month later, "I'm okay."[150] Retired Justice Douglas wrote him:

> For a man who has lived so dangerously as you a hospital is a place to avoid and here you are in one. I've been in and out of hospitals all

year but that is no excuse for you to try to keep up with me . . . Meanwhile when in doubt of whether to grant or deny a cert. always grant and then you'll never run out of business![151]

Marshall rested over the summer and returned to the Court on time for the October Term. By the end of the 1970s, however, Marshall's mood began to change. He had been increasingly bitter and disillusioned at the Court's direction since the departure of Chief Justice Earl Warren and the appointments to the High Court by Richard Nixon. In a speech at the 1979 annual meeting of the Second Circuit, Marshall commented on the recent trends of the increasingly conservative Court: "Ill-considered reversals should be considered as no more than temporary interruptions."[152]

Marshall's wife, Cissy, was continually concerned over her husband's indulgent lifestyle and recurrent health problems. In the late 1960s when Marshall's drunkenness caused him to accost women on the streets of his Southwest Washington neighborhood, Cissy moved the family to the suburbs of Fairfax County, Virginia.[153] As Marshall's health deteriorated over the years, he relied on her counsel. He told friends, "When I start to get senile she's going to tell me, then I'll retire."[154] In October 1979, Marshall fell down the steps of the Capitol, broke both his arms, and cut his forehead. He stayed home for two weeks.[155]

The day Ronald Reagan won the 1980 presidential election over Jimmy Carter, ABC News reporter Tim O'Brien reported that Marshall would resign immediately so that Carter could name his successor. Marshall was furious and phoned O'Brien saying, "I was appointed for life, and I intend to serve out my full term!"[156] The rumors persisted as Carter still had a Democrat-controlled Congress and it was thought that even in defeat, Carter could name a liberal justice before Reagan entered the White House. So rampant were the rumors that Chief Justice Burger heard a report that Marshall had died. He instructed his secretary to call Marshall's wife Cissy and offer condolences. When Cissy answered the phone Burger's secretary said, "Excuse me, Mrs. Marshall, please remain calm. I just got a call from the chief justice. He just heard over the radio that Justice Marshall had died." Cissy amusingly responded, "I'm very calm because he's there in the living room having his dinner!"[157]

By the mid-1980s Marshall was visibly sick. In February of 1984, he contracted viral bronchitis and was hospitalized for a few days. He wore two hearing aids, suffered from glaucoma, and often went to the hospital for anticoagulants that his doctors hoped would spare him another heart attack due to his blood clots.[158] By 1986, Marshall had developed a serious heart condition and his doctors had only given him two more years to live.[159] Despite the warnings, Marshall had no intention of stepping down. When asked if he was committed to staying in office until President Reagan's term ended, he replied:

Oh, longer than that. Yeah, I mean I'm not going to leave until I die—unless I become senile, or something like that. And I don't have to worry about that, because my wife has promised she'll tell me when I get [senile], and when she tells me that, I'll retire. But until then, UH-UH![160]

Marshall confounded his doctor's predictions and continued his work on the Court into his eighties, but the public began to hear of Marshall's decline. The conservative *National Review* published an article suggesting that Marshall spent more time watching soap operas in his chambers than working on cases.[161] Marshall's mental decline was evident in his public conduct from the bench. In one 1989 case he was visibly lost in oral argument, forcing his colleagues to cover for his confused questions.[162] During the same Term he had difficulty reading an opinion from the bench.[163] Still, he had no plans to depart. Should he drop dead at his desk, he jokingly instructed his clerks to "prop me up and keep on voting."[164]

In the summer of 1990, Marshall was in Chicago to accept an award from the American Bar Association. While leaving a restaurant, he fell and was immediately flown back to Washington. He spent several days in the hospital but recovered enough to begin the new term in October.[165] His eyesight was failing, breathing became more of a chore, he had trouble walking, and worst of all, his mental decline was now affecting his votes on cases.

In the death penalty case of *Lankford v. Idaho*, he mistakenly voted in conference with the conservatives to uphold the defendant's death sentence.[166] When one of Marshall's clerks discovered the error, she wrote a lengthy memorandum to Marshall explaining his error and recommending he switch his vote.[167] Marshall recognized his mistake but did not realize that switching his vote would now make him the senior justice in the majority with the power of assignment. He wrote the Chief Justice, "I am sorry, but I must ask you to reassign *Lankford v. Idaho*."[168] The Chief wrote back in an attempt to clarify the matter, "At Conference the vote in this case was five-to-four to affirm, with your vote being one of the five. If you have now switched to 'reverse,' that would make five votes to reverse. Since Byron and I both voted to affirm, you should then assign the case."[169] It was clear to everyone that Marshall was declining. Once again his doctors pressed him, but it was his wife Cissy who proved decisive. Over a six-month period, she urged him to reconsider his long-standing promise to serve for life. He finally gave in and decided that the current term would be his last.[170]

In Marshall's final dissent in *Payne*, he wrote, "Power, not reason, is the new currency of this court's decision making . . . Neither the law not the facts . . . underwent any change in the last four years. Only the personnel of this court did."[171] On June 27, 1991, at the age of 82, he publicly announced that he would retire "when my successor is qualified."[172]

He had served on the Court for twenty-four years and seen its transformation from a liberal bench under Chief Justice Warren to a conservative one under Chief Justice Rehnquist. Following the retirement of his judicial soulmate William Brennan, Marshall had had enough. At his retirement press conference, he remarked, "What's wrong with me? I'm old and coming apart!"[173] Reporters asked if his real reason for stepping down was not simply health and old age, but mostly due to frustration and anger, as the *New York Times* had reported that morning. Marshall was too proud to admit defeat. He denied the accusation, calling it "a double-barreled lie." [174] His close friends, however, knew it was true.[175]

BYRON R. WHITE

Justice White had seen his colleague William O. Douglas stay on the Court too long and dissented from the decision of the other justices to take away Douglas's vote. In his letter about the matter, White suggested that justices should have a mandatory retirement age and hoped the Constitution would be amended to that effect. Though White did not specify the age he thought appropriate, his colleague Lewis Powell had suggested at his retirement in 1987 that seventy-five was the correct benchmark. White would turn seventy-five in 1992.

White had set two ground rules for his departure. Like many justices, he did not want to depart in a presidential election year to protect the institution from partisan politics. He also did not want to leave when one of his colleagues was retiring. He no doubt remembered how shorthanded the Court was when there were only seven members following the virtually simultaneous retirements of Hugo Black and John Marshall Harlan in 1971.[176]

In the late 1980s, there were the customary rumors that White would soon be stepping down. At annual reunions with his law clerks, White often joked about retirement, and even term limits for justices.[177] There is no evidence, however, that White seriously considered the matter of his own retirement. When the Reagan administration approached him with the idea of leaving the Court to become FBI Director, he rejected the proposal.[178] Public Information Officer Toni House explained that in 1990, "Justice White was the subject of rumors. I walked into the pressroom and said, 'I have an announcement from Justice White.' They all perked up. 'He is not resigning.'"[179]

After William Brennan's departure in 1990, White became senior associate justice after nearly thirty years on the Court. White's health was good despite longtime back problems requiring surgery years earlier. He continued to play basketball whenever he got the chance. A clerk remarked, "His back pain gets miraculously better during basketball."[180] He told friends, however, that he had no desire to set a longevity record on the Court.

In March 1993, White was three months away from his seventy-sixth birthday. He had not yet hired his clerks for the next year and the year before he had completed the process by February 7. White decided to pay a visit to retired Justice William Brennan to discuss the retirement decision. In Brennan's chambers, they talked about Brennan's own retirement and White's feelings on the subject. Brennan regretted leaving when he did and advised White not to step down. "I'm not like you, Bill," White replied, "I like to go fishing and I'll enjoy the time with my grandchildren."[181] On March 7, Joan Biskupic of the *Washington Post* wrote that White "apparently is considering stepping down." Though she cited no sources for her information, she reported that White "has said that since he came in with a Democratic administration, it would be fitting to retire under a Democratic administration."[182] Despite Brennan's recommendation to stay, White's mind was made up. He told a friend, "I hate to confirm anything, anything, published in the *Washington Post*, but I have in fact decided to retire."[183]

White was the first justice to give up space in the Court building. In the past, retired justices were usually moved to smaller chambers within the Supreme Court building but with the opening of the new Thurgood Marshall Federal Judiciary Building located behind Union Station in 1993, retired justices would no longer be seen regularly at the Court building. Chief Justice Burger and Justices Brennan and Powell were the last retired justices to have offices in the Supreme Court building. When Justice Powell died in 1998, the current justices were left without the daily reminder of departed justices. Perhaps now that retirement literally means leaving the Court building, it will make it harder to step down.

HARRY A. BLACKMUN

Harry Blackmun was fond of referring to himself and Justices Brennan and Marshall as the "three old goats."[184] By 1992, however, only Blackmun remained on the Court from the liberal trio. In his highly publicized dissent in the abortion case *Planned Parenthood of Southeastern Pennsylvania v. Casey*, he ominously warned, "I am 83 years old. I cannot remain on this Court forever, and when I do step down, the confirmation process for my successor may well focus on the issue before us today."[185] With an election in sight and a possible break from the twelve-year run of Republican presidents, Blackmun said he planned on remaining on the Court "until the third day of November 1992."[186]

In March 1993, Blackmun gave a speech at the New England College of Law and said that both he and Justice White were the most likely candidates to retire in the near future. Because White decided that he would step down at the end of the term, Blackmun was forced to wait another year, had he any plans of possibly stepping down in the summer of 1993.

Though Blackmun turned eighty-five on November 12, 1993, he was in good health. "He was so happy, in such good spirits," a former clerk recalled. "He didn't dance the night away but he was definitely dancing." Each day Blackmun walked four blocks around the Court building and exercised in the Court's basement exercise room. He was "in wonderful condition," the clerk added. "He exercised every day and encouraged us to do the same."[187]

A month and a half later, over the New Year's holiday at Renaissance Weekend in Hilton Head, South Carolina, Blackmun informed President Clinton that the current term would be his last. Clinton expressed his regret and urged the Justice to reconsider. "I frankly kept hoping he would change his mind," Clinton later remarked.[188] Though the White House began quietly searching for a nominee, there was still some uncertainty in the following months about whether Blackmun would actually step down. White House Counsel Lloyd Cutler heard that Blackmun was encouraging potential law clerks to apply for the upcoming term and that retired Justice Brennan's regrets about his own retirement were having an effect on Blackmun's decision. He was able to keep his retirement decision secret during these months. Even former clerks were unable to pry any information from him.[189]

In the end, Blackmun did consult with a White House assistant about the timing of his announcement.[190] On April 6, he appeared with President Clinton before reporters to announce his intention to retire at the close of the term. After twenty-four years on the Court, Blackmun said, "It's not easy to step aside, but I know what the numbers are, and it's time." Health concerns did not prompt Blackmun's departure. He had a standing agreement with his doctors at the Mayo Clinic that they were to inform him when it was time to leave the Court. No such recommendation was made, however. At his press conference, Blackmun said that his reasons for leaving the Court were personal with his wife and daughters urging him to step down before it became necessary for him to do so. Blackmun said, "They had enough votes to override any veto." Like justices of previous eras, Blackmun was concerned that giving up his work on the Court could hasten his death. He said, "I shall have to keep busy or I'll fall apart."[191] He added, "I'm advised there is a vacancy on the 8th Circuit. I think I'll apply for it. I'll be turned down, I know, but . . ."[192]

Was Blackmun's decision affected by his memories of Douglas's departure? In his farewell remarks from the bench, Blackmun quoted from Douglas's retirement letter.[193] While this is not conclusive evidence, it does show that Douglas's departure was remembered by his former colleagues as late as 1994. Indeed, Blackmun did cite another superannuate as playing a role in his decision, "Eighty-five is pretty old. I don't want to reach a point where my senility level reaches unacceptable proportions, and I don't want to be asked to retire like Oliver Wendell Holmes Jr."[194] Blackmun's remarks prior to the election of Democrat Bill Clinton and his actions following the election clearly demonstrate that partisanship was part of his equation.

CONCLUSION

Increasing retirement benefits coupled with manageable workloads made retirements more likely than ever before beginning in 1954. Furthermore, these developments also provided increased opportunity for the justices to engage in succession politics as they had larger windows of time to consider departing. Accordingly, the era had more retirements and dramatically increased levels of partisanship.

Based on the timing, their relatively good health, or both, Justices Harlan, Stewart, Burger, White, and Blackmun can be classified as being motivated by partisanship in their departure decisions. While there is little direct evidence to substantiate such a conclusion for any of them, circumstances suggest as much. There is, on the other hand, direct evidence that Earl Warren was clearly partisan in his departure attempt, and that William O. Douglas and Lewis Powell had at least some partisan concerns. Though Justices Brennan and Marshall ultimately did not depart for partisan reasons, they were initially partisan in their departure considerations. Overall, these cases suggest a new level of partisanship in the departure decision-making of the justices. It is no coincidence that this list of partisan, or possibly partisan justices is largely composed of more recent members.

Superannuated justices continue to affect the Court. Justices Black, Harlan, Douglas, and Marshall tested the internal norms of the Court in dealing with justices on the decline. While their colleagues did their best to persevere through the difficult times these justices created, further modifications are needed in dealing with superannuated justices. In chapter 10, I discuss a number of internal reforms the Court can take in dealing with declining colleagues as well as statutory and even constitutional reforms that may solve this problem.

So far, the generous retirement statute of the modern period has produced an atmosphere of naked partisanship with virtually no limits of the lengths to which justices will go to depart under a copartisan president. LBJ's administration shows that presidents see few limits in trying to remake the

Supreme Court. The disability and decline of at least two justices, Charles Whitaker and William O. Douglas, show that collectively justices are not afraid to limit the power of a disabled colleague should the situation arise. As I discuss in the next chapter, the disputed 2000 election may provide a further test to the current justices who face the increased criticism of perceived strategic behavior, due to their participation in the election's outcome.

9

2000–Present

A Self-Inflicted Wound

> Well, you know, if I were to speculate on that, I would speculate
> with other people, I think.
>   —Chief Justice William H. Rehnquist on whether
>   he planned to step down following the 2000 election

> We do risk a self-inflicted wound—a wound that may harm not
> just the court, but the nation.
>   —Justice Stephen Breyer in Dissent, *Bush v. Gore* (2000)

Chief Justice William H. Rehnquist has been on the U.S. Supreme Court for over a quarter century. Though he became eligible to retire with full benefits in 1990 during the presidency of George Bush, Sr., he was only sixty-five and had been chief for a mere four years. During the presidency of Democrat Bill Clinton, many believed that Rehnquist was destined to remain on the Court until at least 2001, after the next president took the oath of office. "I think he's too committed and too interested in winning the battles he's been fighting to retire during the presidency of a Democrat," said one Court insider, adding that he is "extraordinarily politically savvy."[1] "He's more inclined to stay," said a former clerk who felt that Rehnquist did not want to leave during a Democratic presidency but "would never say it."[2] Still, in July 1991 the Chief Justice said in a letter to recently retired Thurgood Marshall that "in all probability I will be in the same boat you are within a couple of years."[3] Eleven months later he said that while he enjoyed his job "I wouldn't want to hold it forever."[4] Furthermore, Rehnquist underwent major back surgery in September 1995 and to this day must periodically stand during oral argument.[5] When is the Chief going to retire?

211

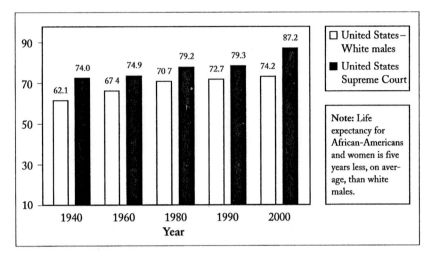

FIGURE 9.1
Life Expectancy: U.S. White Males versus
U.S. Supreme Court Justices, 1940–2000

It is often thought that age is an important indicator of judicial departure. When justices reach their seventies and certainly their eighties, speculation increases that they may soon step down. But as Figure 9.1 shows, life expectancy for current members of the U.S. Supreme Court is eighty-seven. By comparison, U.S. white males can expect on average to live to age seventy-four.[6] As a result, age is not the important variable that people often suspect.

With the last eleven departures coming by way of retirement, it seems a good bet that the next eleven will end up much the same (see Table 9.1). No doubt the specter of William O. Douglas's departure will continue to influence the next two or three departures, but what about beyond that? Rehnquist was one of the seven who voted to take away Douglas's vote, and John Paul Stevens arrived at the Court when Douglas was still very much on the scene and attempting to participate in the Court's work. But without the vivid memory of Douglas to help make their decisions, it is likely that this super-annuation effect will end. Still, Thurgood Marshall's lengthy stay could be important. What will the newer justices consider when they become retirement eligible? The Court's decisive involvement in the 2000 election will no doubt serve to organize the next round of departures.

The disputed election of 2000 between Republican George W. Bush and Democrat Al Gore is the most recent event to have an impact on the departure process. Both Chief Justice Rehnquist and Justice O'Connor voted with the majority in the case that effectively gave the election to Bush. Both have

TABLE 9.1
Retirement Eligibility and the Current Court

Justice and Party ID	Date of Birth	Date of Initial Service on Federal Courts	Date Retirement Eligible Under Rule of Eighty
John Paul Stevens (R)	Apr. 20, 1920	Nov. 2, 1970	Nov. 2, 1985
William H. Rehnquist (R)	Oct. 1, 1924	Jan. 7, 1972	Oct. 1, 1989
Sandra Day O'Connor (R)	Mar. 26, 1930	Sept. 25, 1981	Sept. 25, 1996
Ruth Bader Ginsburg (D)	Mar. 15, 1933	June 30, 1980	Mar. 15, 1998
Antonin Scalia (R)	Mar. 11, 1936	Aug. 17, 1982	Mar. 11, 2001
Anthony Kennedy (R)	July 23, 1936	May 30, 1975	July 23, 2001
Stephen Breyer (D)	Aug. 15, 1938	Dec. 10, 1980	Aug. 15, 2003
David Souter (R)	Sept. 17, 1939	May 25, 1990	May 25, 2005
Clarence Thomas (R)	June 28, 1948	Mar. 12, 1990	June 28, 2013

All justices began their federal judicial service on the Courts of Appeals, except for Rehnquist, O'Connor, and Thomas; who began their federal judicial service on the Supreme Court.

All retirement eligible dates are based on the current Rule of Eighty. 28 U.S.C. 371 (C).

been retirement eligible for some time and with their overall conservative judicial philosophies, it is likely that each will depart during the Bush administration. Conversely, both Justice Stevens and Justice Ginsburg voted against Bush in the election case. Though both have battled cancer, and despite Ginsburg nearing seventy and Stevens being in his eighties, their more liberal voting record suggests they will remain on the Court until at least after the 2004 and possibly the 2008 presidential election. Indeed, this is precisely what occurred after the disputed 1876 election when Justices Davis, Clifford, Swayne, and possibly Strong based their departure decisions on whether they supported Republican Rutherford B. Hayes or Democrat Samuel Tilden. In the latter half of the chapter, I will analyze the current members of the Court in light of the circumstances surrounding this new emergent structure.

THE DISPUTED ELECTION OF 2000: BUSH V. GORE

Democrat Bill Clinton made two appointments to the Court in his first two years in office. During the last six years of his tenure, however, there were no vacancies at the inn. Speculation mounted that retirement-eligible members of the Court were waiting until after the 2000 election. The candidates,

Republican George W. Bush and Democrat Al Gore, addressed the issue of future appointments on the campaign trail and in televised debates. Though public opinion polls showed the race as a dead heat, no one could have predicted what occurred on election night.[7]

As America went to the polls and the election results came in on November 7, all the major networks first reported just before 8 P.M. EST, that Al Gore won the state of Florida and its twenty-five electoral votes. An hour later the polls closed in the state's panhandle region and the networks quickly recanted and placed the state in the too-close-to-call category. As the night progressed and each candidate won important battleground states, it soon became clear that Florida would be decisive. At 2:15 A.M. EST, the networks called Florida for Bush: "Unless there is a terrible calamity," ABC's Peter Jennings proclaimed, "George W. Bush, by our projections, is going to be the next President." Supporters at his rally in Austin, Texas cheered and prepared for a victory speech. Gore was informed that he would be about 50,000 votes short in the state and phoned Bush to concede.

En route to his election-night rally in Nashville, and preparing to give his public concession speech, Gore was told by aides that Bush's lead in Florida has shrunk dramatically to a few thousand votes at best, and possibly only a few hundred. As the networks awaited Gore's concession speech, Gore once again phoned Bush and retracted his earlier concession saying, "As you may have noticed, things have changed . . . the state of Florida is too close to call." Bewildered, the Texas governor shot back, "Let me make sure I understand. You're calling me back to retract your concession." Gore replied, "Well, there's no reason to get snippy." Trying to make sense of the unprecedented call, Bush explained that that his brother Jeb Bush, the governor of Florida, was with him crunching the numbers from the Florida web site. "Let me explain it to you," Gore said. "Your younger brother is not the ultimate authority on this." Bush ended the call with, "Well, Mr. Vice President, you need to do what you have to do."[8] Gore campaign Chair William Daley addressed the Gore supporters and the cameras, "Our campaign continues." As night became early morning, at 4:00 A.M. EST the networks recanted a second time and moved Florida to the "too close to call" category, where it belonged all along.

Because the candidates were separated by only a few thousand votes in Florida, the next day, they both sent legal teams headed by former Secretaries of State James Baker and Warren Christopher to the state to oversee recounts and prepare to use the courts, if necessary, to resolve any disputes. On November 9, after an automatic machine recount of Florida's votes showed Bush still leading in that state, but by only 327 votes out of nearly 6 million cast, Gore requested a manual recount in select counties. Gore focused on places where ballots had been disqualified, not read by the machines, or both.[9]

Bush began the court phase of the election on November 12, hoping to block the manual recounts. With some hand recounts being conducted, Bush's lead reportedly shrunk to 286 votes by November 15. Two days later on the 17th, the Florida Supreme Court blocked Florida's Secretary of State Katherine Harris from certifying the results and declaring Bush the official winner. On the 18th, the final absentee ballot count pushed the Bush lead up to 930 votes. In an important victory for Gore on November 21, the Florida Supreme Court ruled that manual recounts could continue and set the deadline for November 26. Throughout the two-week time period since Gore requested hand counts, the painstaking process had started, stopped, and started again due to individual canvassing board decisions and court rulings.

Bush appealed the decision of the Florida High Court to continue manual counts to the U.S. Supreme Court. It was widely thought that the Court would decide not to hear the appeal, but two days later on November 24, the justices agreed to hear the case on an expedited basis and set oral argument for December 1. Some suggested the Court was hoping the situation would work itself out in the intervening time. Instead, matters became increasingly complicated. On November 26, after the state Supreme Court imposed deadline passed, Harris certified Bush the winner of Florida by a margin of 537 votes. Palm Beach county finished their count two hours after the deadline but their results were not included by Harris. Gore immediately challenged the certification in state court claiming that thousands of votes were never tallied.

The issue before the Court on December 1 was whether the Florida Supreme Court overstepped its authority by ordering Harris to include the manual recounts in certified state results. Three days later, in a unanimous opinion, the U.S. Supreme Court asked the Florida Supreme Court to clarify its reasoning in extending the hand recounts and returned the case to Florida temporarily delaying Bush's appeal on allowing the recounts. On December 8, the Florida Supreme Court handed down a 4–3 ruling in Gore's latest appeal, ordering manual recounts in all counties with significant numbers of disputed votes. They also added 383 more votes to Gore's count. Bush immediately appealed this decision to the U.S. Supreme Court. Again many were surprised when on December 9, the Court voted 5–4 to halt all recounts and again agreed to take the case.

On December 11, oral argument took place, with Bush's lawyers arguing that the Florida high court again overstepped its bounds by ordering a manual recount. Gore's lawyers argued that the U.S. Supreme Court had no reason to intervene in what they felt was strictly a state matter. The justices wasted no time in handing down their ruling the following night just prior to 10:00 P.M. EST. In a contentious 5–4 per curiam opinion, the Court held that although there was an equal protection violation because of differing, county by county procedures for determining recount votes,[10] there simply was no time left for those counts to continue and still be subject to proper legal challenge.[11] In short, the Court ended the manual recounts and with them Gore's last chance to gain the presidency.

Analysts quickly highlighted the divisions and what some saw as naked partisanship within the Court. Former clerks suggested that the per curiam opinion was probably the handy work of moderate conservative Justice Anthony Kennedy with an assist from his moderate conservative colleague Sandra Day O'Connor.[12] There was concern inside the Court and out that the justices had seriously damaged their prestige and reputation, and even harmed the nation by handing down a divisive and seemingly partisan result. Justice Stephen Breyer warned in his dissent, "We do risk a self-inflicted wound—a wound that may harm not just the court, but the nation." John Paul Stevens added, "Although we may never know with complete certainty the identity of the winner of this year's presidential election, the identity of the loser is perfectly clear. It is the nation's confidence in the judge as an impartial guardian of the rule of law." Public opinion polls conducted after *Bush v. Gore*, however, showed two out of three Americans supported the decision and most were relieved that the Court provided finality.

Looking to 1876, we can see a different explanation as to why the Court ruled the way it did. Potential Court challenges notwithstanding, Congress has the final say over which electoral ballots are accepted and counted for president. Indeed in 1960, Congress decided to accept late ballots received from the state of Hawaii, which gave their three electoral votes to Richard Nixon instead of John F. Kennedy as was originally certified. Though the votes did not make a difference in the final outcome, it demonstrates Congress's ultimate authority over counting electoral votes. In 1876, Congress was divided with the Democrats controlling the House and Republicans the Senate. Because the House would vote to accept Tilden's Florida electors but the Senate planned on counting the Hayes electors from Florida, a fifteen-member electoral commission was set up and divided along partisan lines in favor of Hayes. In a compromise to appease angry Democrats, Reconstruction was ended in the South. It is hard to imagine that this messy scenario was not known by the decisive swing Justices Kennedy and O'Connor. Had they sided with the dissenters in *Bush v. Gore*, chaos could very well have ensued. Two sets of Florida electoral votes could have been sent to Congress and with the Democrats controlling the new 2001 Senate 51–50 (with Gore as vice president casting the tie-breaking vote) and the Republicans continuing to have the majority in the House, anything would have been possible including more challenges in the Supreme Court on the most fundamental questions of separation of powers. Looked at in this fashion, the swing justices can be seen as sparing the nation from the "constitutional crisis" that occurred in 1876–1877 and that some were predicting for 2000–2001.

THAT'S FOR ME TO KNOW
AND YOU TO FIND OUT

As the four oldest members of the Court, it is likely that Chief Justice Rehnquist and Justices O'Connor, Stevens, and Ginsburg will be the next to depart. While their concerns will probably be similar to the concerns of their recently departed colleagues, they will no doubt be influenced by their participation in the disputed 2000 election. What follows is an analysis of their past concerns and experiences with health and illnesses and an assessment of their likely motivation for stepping down in light of this new organizing event.

WILLIAM H. REHNQUIST

Like many justices in their younger years, Rehnquist thought that Supreme Court justices should not remain on the Court forever.[13] As he neared age sixty-five and retirement eligibility, he began to openly address his own retirement and many speculated that he would soon step down. At a law school commencement ceremony, he remarked:

> Do not let the law be too jealous a mistress. You must give yourself time not only to do a variety of things, but [also] to allow yourself time to appreciate and enjoy what you are doing.[14]

Rehnquist was the chief adherent to his own philosophy. He enjoyed writing, painting, swimming, and tennis, among other pursuits. He usually left the Court by 3 P.M. each day, in stark contrast to many of the other justices, who remained well into the evening. When Chief Justice Burger decided to retire and Rehnquist was approached by the Reagan White House to succeed him, Rehnquist's thinking took an about face. Now rather than leave the Court for other pursuits, he could take on a new role within the Court.[15]

At the end of the 1989–1990 Term, rumors circulated that he would step down under Republican President George Bush, Sr., but Rehnquist remained in his seat.[16] Following the retirements of Byron White and Harry Blackmun, Rehnquist became the first Chief Justice since Harlan Fiske Stone, in the 1940s, to also be the longest-serving member of the Court. In the fall of 1994, the then-seventy-year-old chief commented on the situation: "It makes me feel very ancient."[17]

As the last justice remaining who served during William O. Douglas's final months and experienced firsthand the damage that Douglas had caused to the Court for lingering too long, Rehnquist can be expected to depart sooner rather than later. He will almost certainly retire before becoming a burden to his colleagues. With Republican George W. Bush in office, and given Rehnquist's vote in the election case supporting him and overall conservative record, all signs point to the chief's retirement by June 2003 or June 2007 at the latest. Still, Rehnquist is silent on retirement as exemplified by this recent exchange with journalist Charlie Rose:

Rose: Do you think about retirement?

Rehnquist: Yes.

Rose: Would you like to let us know when you think you might retire?

Rehnquist: No.

Rose: Well, will it be, you know, after the year 2000?

Rehnquist: Well, you know, if I were to speculate on that, I would speculate with other people, I think.

Rose: Not me.

Rehnquist: Not you, yes.

Rose: We'd help you along if you'd like our input.

Rehnquist: I'm sure you would.

Rose: If clearly, as someone once said, Supreme Court justices read election returns, and they make decisions as to retirement based on whether the party of their choice is in power at the White House (pause)— because that power gives that occupant of the Oval Office the capacity to choose the next justice and next chief justice.

Rehnquist: That's not one hundred percent true but it certainly is true in more cases than not, I would think.

Rose: Meaning you'd probably wait until after the presidential election year of 2000, before making a decision of when you would retire.

Rehnquist: Well, that's for me to know and you to find out. That's what we used to say on the playground when I was growing up.

SANDRA DAY O'CONNOR

In March 1987, Sandra Day O'Connor underwent an emergency appendectomy during one of the Court's two-week recesses. She returned without missing a single day on the bench. Her quick recovery was no doubt a result of her excellent physical health. For years she had exercised in the mornings, played golf and tennis, and skied during winter months. Compared to some of her colleagues she is the model of good health.

As the new term began in October 1988, fifty-eight-year-old Justice O'Connor underwent a routine medical exam. Her doctors found a small lump in her breast. Despite the diagnosis, she endeavored to keep the situation from interfering with her work. She said later, "It was a devastating thing to be told and you can't believe that you have some disease that is potentially fatal—that you have to stop everything and take care of it. You tend to think, 'Me? You can't be serious. I'm too busy. I don't have time to deal with something like that.' And yet you have to make time to deal with it."[18] Up until the day of the surgery, she participated fully in the business of the Court. The night before her scheduled operation at Georgetown University Hospital, she kept a previous commitment and gave a speech at Washington and Lee University in Lexington, Virginia—a seven-hour round-trip drive from Washington, D.C.

On October 21, O'Connor had surgery to remove the lump. Following her operation, she issued a statement saying that the cancer "was found to exist in a very early form and stage. The prognosis is for total recovery. I do not anticipate missing any oral arguments."[19] A few days later, however, she found out that there had been some spread of the cancer to her lymph nodes and that she would need to undergo chemotherapy treatments in order to prevent a recurrence. O'Connor told family and friends that the two weeks following her operation were the most difficult, frightening days of her life. Her sister, Ann, said:

> [It was] the first major crisis of her life. She took her cancer as a challenge, learning everything she could about it, reading every book, talking with people and making necessary decisions about her treatment and options.[20]

On October 31, O'Connor was back in her seat for the next round of oral arguments. Just like she had done following her appendectomy the previous year, O'Connor did not miss a single day on the bench. She told friends that the work helped keep her mind off the cancer. On her return, it was immediately evident that the chemotherapy was taking its toll. Though she remained sharp and combative during oral argument, off the bench she appeared tired and grayer and was, understandably, now wearing a wig. The public visibility of her struggle was difficult to deal with. She explained, "There was constant media coverage: How does she look? When is she going to step down and give the president another vacancy on the court? She looks pale to me; I don't give her six months. This was awful."[21]

Still she fought back continuing to give speeches, meet with visitors, and keeping physically active as before.[22] She reflected on her battle with cancer:

Rumors circulated in June 1990 that she would retire, or that Rehnquist might step down and she would become chief. When the Court's Public

Information Officer Toni House asked her if the rumors were true, she replied that they were absurd. House went back to the pressroom and informally told reporters, "She says she is not sick, not bored, not resigning."[23]

After twenty years as a member of the Court, O'Connor is as vigorous as ever, not only keeping up her athletic regimen of skiing, golf, and tennis but also taking charge within the Court to organize social events and speak to groups. Having fully recovered from cancer and wielding a crucial swing vote, she is thought of by many to be the most powerful figure in the nation. In the 1999–2000 term, O'Connor compiled the best record among the nine justices for Court majorities: She voted in the majority in all but four of the seventy-three cases the court decided that year. Her breakneck pace and powerful position suggested that she was anything but nearing retirement.[24]

But the disputed 2000 election changed perceptions of O'Connor overnight. Like Joseph Bradley in 1876, she cast a deciding vote that effectively gave the election to George W. Bush. Though Bradley was directly pressured by Republicans to vote for their candidate Rutherford B. Hayes, O'Connor may have been pressured by a desire to step down. At an election-night party, she was visibly upset when the networks awarded the crucial state of Florida to Democrat Al Gore. Her husband explained to some in attendance at the party that they planned on retiring to Arizona but that a Gore administration would delay things by at least four years.[25] But she reportedly expressed some indecision about whether to step down to a friend.[26]

After Bush was sworn in, speculation was rampant that O'Connor would step down at the close of the Term. O'Connor made her decision. In a highly unusual move, she spoke with a reporter from the *Arizona Republic* in May, stating, "I have no present plans to retire. I just have no other plan."[27] Did O'Connor plan to retire and then change her mind because of the intense speculation following *Bush v. Gore* and the reports of the election-night party?

With Bush in office, it appears certain that O'Connor will depart. Furthermore, the fallout over the election case, with the Court experiencing low morale and clerks holding grudges, has fueled O'Connor's desire to retire.[28] Also, her husband John had a heart pacemaker implanted in 1999 and has since experienced further health problems.

In 2002 O'Connor published *Lazy B*, an autobiography about growing up on a ranch. During interviews to promote the book, O'Connor was asked by numerous reporters about her retirement plans. Concerning speculation that she might be named the next chief justice, she shot back, "I think it's a ridiculous notion. It's nonsense. I am 71 years old, for heaven's sake. That ought to quiet that talk." About retirement generally she said, "I haven't faced that. I haven't made that decision . . . Someday, somehow, somewhere. Nobody lives forever, for God's sake."[29] When her brother and coauthor Alan Day was asked whether she would soon step down he remarked, "That's something I don't ask her. But I'd say she has a real high energy level, and she has a lot of living left to do. She's not melting away."[30]

JOHN PAUL STEVENS

On June 29, 1995, the U.S. Supreme Court delivered the final opinions of the 1994–1995 term. Chief Justice William Rehnquist did not, however, announce the retirement of Associate Justice John Paul Stevens. As the Court's most liberal justice, if Stevens had been concerned solely with partisanship, he would have most certainly departed while Democrat Bill Clinton was in office and not risk a conservative taking over the White House in 1996. The same was true four years later when the 1998–1999 term ended. Clinton was still in the White House, but a new election season was about to begin. Given the field of strong Republican candidates, the timing would have been ripe for the departure of the Court's most liberal member, but Stevens remained in his seat.

With a number of junior justices recently appointed who have been somewhat sympathetic to Justice Stevens's policy positions—namely Justices Souter, Breyer, and Ginsburg—he may see his role as one of intellectual mentor, laying the foundation for a long-standing moderate-liberal bloc on the Court. If he does see his role in this light, he most certainly would be inclined to depart later rather than sooner. It is likely that Stevens enjoys his work and despite undergoing heart surgery, having a pacemaker installed, and being treated for prostate cancer,[31] still has the vigor and desire to participate fully in the Court's work.

Stevens's favorable holding for Democrat Al Gore in the 2000 election case and his overall liberal record would suggest that he will hang on to his seat until after the 2004 presidential election. While he will turn eighty-five as the Court nears the close of its Term in April 2005, he will still be younger than the average life expectancy of 87.2 for current Court members. Indeed, his former colleagues Justices Brennan and Blackmun served until the ages of eighty-four and eighty-five, respectively. If George W. Bush is reelected in 2004, however, it is virtually certain that Stevens will have to depart under a Republican administration.

RUTH BADER GINSBURG

During the summer recess of 1999, Ginsburg became ill with abdominal cramping and pain while teaching in a law school program on the Greek island of Crete. At first, she became sick with acute diverticulitis and she was treated for that gastric disorder of the large intestine in which pouches that form on the outside of the colon become infected.[32] In mid-September, her doctors also diagnosed her with colorectal cancer, explaining that it was likely it would have gone undetected if not for the gastric illness.[33] At the age of sixty-six, she underwent surgery and remained in the hospital for a week.[34] The cancer had been detected relatively early and her prognosis was good.

When the Court's Term began on October 4, Justice Ginsburg took her seat on the bench, smiling broadly to her husband and two children, who were in attendance. She appeared her usual self, asking questions during oral argument. Later in the day she remarked, "No words can convey how pleased I am to be here with you today."[35] She followed up her surgery with nine months of "precautionary" chemotherapy and radiation treatments all while continuing her regular workload.[36] She finished her last treatment in June, and though it was noticeable that she was visibly affected by it, she still attended a reception and dinner with her husband at the Court on behalf of the Supreme Court Historical Society. She praised her doctors and staff who treated her as "dear to my heart, for they sustained me, in body and mind, through my long bout."[37] In November, 2001, her physician commented, "It's a little over two years now since I started taking care of her, and the longer we're out, the better. We hold our breaths for five years, but so far so good."[38]

Ginsburg wrote a separate dissent in the *Bush v. Gore* 2000 election case siding with Gore and taking her conservative colleagues to task for seemingly contradicting their usual deference to state court decisions. Having sat on the United States Court of Appeals for the District of Columbia Circuit since 1980, she became eligible for full retirement benefits the year prior to her cancer diagnosis. As she approaches the relatively young age of seventy, with a Republican President in office, and with her cancer in remission, it appears that Ginsburg will not be departing any time soon. Speaking to a group of high school students in 2002, she remarked on the advantages of being a judge: "We can write and we can think . . . into our 70s, 80s and, some, into the 90s."[39]

CONCLUSION

What is evident from the preceding analysis is that the existing statutory provisions and informal arrangements governing Supreme Court departure have proved only adequate to ensuring the goal of institutional health. The continuing presence of superannuated justices like Hugo Black, John Marshall Harlan, William O. Douglas, and even Thurgood Marshall, to a certain extent, demonstrate that internal Court norms must be strengthened. Not only should individual justices take steps to ensure that they do not stay beyond their usefulness, but the justices collectively must be more aggressive when there is evidence that one of their colleagues is in decline. What is most needed, however, is statutory and even constitutional reform. Through the various attempts of presidents, individual justices, and the justices collectively to test the limits of their powers in the succession process, the existing arrangements have proved ripe for partisanship in recent decades.

George W. Bush will likely have the opportunity to make two or possibly three appointments to the Supreme Court during his tenure as president. One seat he will not be filling, however, is that of Clarence Thomas who has already indicated a retirement date of 2034. In 1993, two years after he joined the Court following a highly partisan confirmation battle, Thomas told two of his clerks, "The liberals made my life miserable for 43 years, and I'm going to make their lives miserable for 43 years."[40] Like those he has served with in his thus far decade-long tenure, it is a virtual certainty that Thomas will do all that he can to see to it that he departs when a Republican is in office.

Still, much can happen in the thirty or so remaining years that Thomas will be on the Court. As with the 1876 election, the institutional memory of the disputed election of 2000 and the closely divided Court will eventually give way to other emergent structures. A president like Lyndon Johnson could come along and press justices to take other posts and generally depart earlier than they would like. Even George W. Bush is moving aggressively to build a conservative federal judiciary, despite the disputed election, an evenly divided Senate, and his promise to be a "uniter."[41] As I will suggest in the next chapter, institutional reforms in the retirement statute and the Court's workload, as well as modifying internal Court norms and procedures, could dramatically change the environment that Thomas and others depart in. But ultimately, it is a constitutional amendment that would have the most dramatic impact.

10

Conclusion

Imaginary Danger?

The removal of such men cannot fail to cast a gloom over all who wish merit to receive its just reward for eminent services.

—Justice Joseph Story, on New York's
mandatory retirement law and the forced
departure of several eminent jurists

The importance in the Supreme Court of avoiding the risk of having judges who are unable properly to do their work and yet insist on remaining on the bench, is too great to permit chances to be taken.[1]

—Chief Justice Charles Evans Hughes

The preceding analysis plainly demonstrates that the single most important factor for justices deciding to leave U.S. Supreme Court is the presence of a formal retirement provision with generous benefits. As circuit-riding diminished and retirement statutes were enacted and expanded, the number of justices voluntarily departing increased (see Figure 10.1). This is precisely what Congress had hoped to accomplish by enacting and expanding these laws. Though Congress was primarily acting in a partisan fashion in passing these statutes, hoping specific justices would step down, Congress was also sensitive to the argument of institutional health that superannuated justices burdened the effective functioning of the Court.

This was particularly acute in times of increased workload such as during Reconstruction following the Civil War, the period after World War I through the Great Depression, and again in the 1950s and 1960s with the passage of

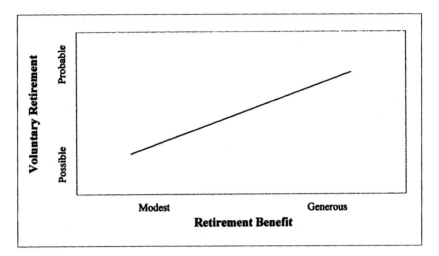

FIGURE 10.1
The Effect of Increased Retirement Benefit on
Voluntary Retirement in the U.S. Supreme Court

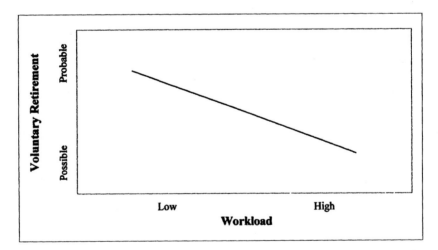

FIGURE 10.2
The Effect of Increased Workload on
Voluntary Retirement in the U.S. Supreme Court

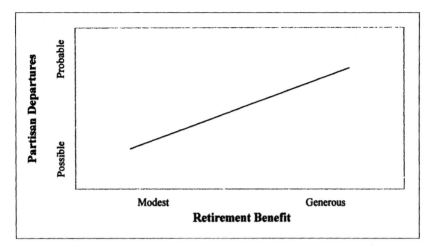

FIGURE 10.3
The Effect of Increased Retirement Benefit on
Partisan Departures in the U.S. Supreme Court

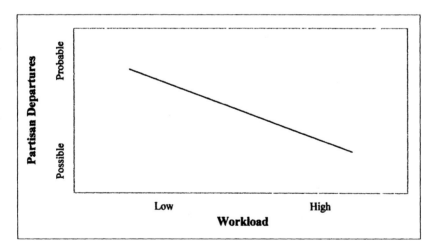

FIGURE 10.4
The Effect of Increased Workload on
Partisan Departures in the U.S. Supreme Court

civil rights and voting rights legislation. Each time, Congress acted to induce departures and lighten the load. Consequently, when the Court's workload was relatively light or on the decline as in its early years, the period after the passage of the Evarts Act in 1891, and most recently beginning in the 1970s, voluntary departures increased (see Figure 10.2).

Hence, both increased retirement benefit and decreased workload had a positive effect on voluntary departures. A byproduct of these key structural arrangements was that they also provided greater opportunity for the justices to engage in succession politics, timing their departures for a copartisan president (see Figures 10.3 and 10.4). Given the partisan motivations of Congress in passing retirement legislation, it should not be surprising that justices responded in an equally partisan way.

While emergent structures have been the driving force behind the departure choices of the justices, various recurrent factors have also played a part. Partisanship, though the major element in the departure-decision making of more recent justices, played less of a role earlier in the Court's history when other variables were predominant. Concern for the institutional health, legitimacy, and effective functioning of the Court caused some justices to depart voluntarily rather than become a burden to their colleagues. Personal concerns have also been important. Some justices have been reluctant to step down because they enjoyed their work. Others feared departure would hasten mental deterioration and even death. Some justices looked forward to leaving in order to spend more time with family and enjoy their remaining years. Financial concerns also played a role, primarily during the years before the enactment of formal retirement legislation.[2] Future reforms to combat partisan departures could see a resurgence in the occurrence of these other factors. It is through the framework of emergent and recurrent structures that I will assess the arguments for and against the current system of life tenure and explore what the appropriate role of justices at the end should be.

Although the preceding chapters demonstrate that partisanship currently dominates the departure process, why does it matter? In other words, it has been empirically shown that justices are largely partisan in the decisions they make concerning the cases that they consider.[3] And while it was assumed that justices were partisan in their departure decisions, this has not been empirically demonstrated until now with partisanship being a relatively recent phenomenon due to institutional arrangements. So at the very least, this study empirically demonstrates the predominance of partisanship in departure decision-making. But there are many who feel that such calculations are inappropriate for judges and the findings presented here bear on their concerns.

Still, the question remains: What is wrong with departure decisions based on partisanship? Perhaps nothing. On the one hand, if we are resigned to partisanship as a part of judicial decision-making, then there may be no reason to change the current system, or we may want to think about judicial elections as many states have done. On the other hand, if we would rather have judges base their decisions on other factors, such as the institutional health of the Court, then we may want to consider various reforms. Indeed, we may want to take the departure decision out of the hands of the justices entirely.

What effect would various reforms have on departure decisions? The preceding analysis suggests that calls to liberalize retirement options further, as well as attempts to ease the workload of the justices, will only lead to increased partisanship and increased danger of mental decrepitude. Internal Court norms, however, could be strengthened and specific steps could be followed in the event that a justice becomes disabled, but does not step down. Scaling back the current system of generous retirement benefits and increasing workload could go a long way toward minimizing partisan departures. But what of the persistent problem of failing justices who refuse to relinquish their seats? Compulsory retirement at a set age such as seventy or seventy-five would not only solve the problem of partisan departures, but it would also go a long way toward protecting the intellectual health of the Court from mentally failing justices. Still, such a constitutional change is difficult to obtain and is not without potential drawbacks.

In the following section, I discuss these concerns as well as the effect a change would have on the current Court. Specifically, I will discuss two possible goals to be met in connection with retirement. The first issue is eliminating or reducing partisanship in retirement choices. The second is prompting departures before mental decline. What follows is a discussion of potential informal, statutory, and constitutional reforms and their potential effects on both partisan departures and mental decrepitude.

ABILITY AND INABILITY

What should happen when a justice who is no longer able to perform the duties of his office elects to remain in his seat? What actions should Congress take? What should the other members of the Court do when one of their colleagues becomes disabled? All justices, including disabled justices, may retire at any time from active service and still receive some benefits.[4] Still, at various times throughout the Court's history, disabled justices have decided not to step down. Should such a situation arise in the future, there are a number of steps that both Congress and the Court can take to assure that the Court operates at full strength.

One action available to Congress for dealing with disabled justices is removal. Alexander Hamilton was wary of a removal power for inability, fearing it would degenerate into partisan motives:

The mensuration of the faculties of the mind has, I believe, no place
in the catalogue of known arts. An attempt to fix the boundary
between the regions of ability and inability, would much oftener give
scope to personal and party attachments and enmities than advance
the interests of justice or the public good. The result, except in the
case of insanity, must for the most part be arbitrary; and insanity
without any formal or express provision, may be safely pronounced to
be a virtual disqualification.[5]

Just as Hamilton had warned, proposals for term limits and various
removal methods have more often than not come about as a result of partisan politics. None of the proposals, however, have been enacted. This is
largely due to the difficulty of passing a constitutional amendment in comparison to the relative ease of statutory reform such as making retirement
more attractive. With an entrenched Federalist judiciary, Republican President Thomas Jefferson wanted a term limit of six years for justices of the
Supreme Court with reappointment subject to the approval of the President and both houses of Congress.[6] In the spring of 1937 a mandatory
retirement scheme favored by many in Congress died because of FDR's
court-packing plan and ultimately the expansion of the existing retirement
statute. In 1954 the Senate adopted a resolution embracing mandatory
retirement for judges but ultimately retirement benefits were again
expanded as a substitute. In 1957, three years after state-imposed racial
segregation was struck down by the Warren Court in *Brown v. Board of
Education*,[7] Sen. James Eastland and Rep. Thomas Abernethy, both
Democrats from Mississippi, offered a constitutional amendment to limit
the terms of justices to four years and to require immediate Senate approval
of incumbent justices within six months of the amendment's ratification.
Constitutional amendments are always difficult to pass, let alone one to
limit the terms of Supreme Court justices. For an amendment to be seriously considered and then pass, it would likely take the prolonged public
incapacities of one or more of the justices to prompt it. Even then, passage
would be difficult. Throughout the Court's history, Congress has chosen
the easier remedy of making retirement more attractive.

The constitution contains an amendment governing the incapacity of a
president, but the Supreme Court is a much different institution. The incapacity of a justice does not totally paralyze the Court in the same way that a
president's incapacity would cripple the executive branch. As long as the incapacity of a justice is not prolonged, the Court can continue to function effectively with the eight remaining justices. Should an incapacitated justice choose
not to step down, however, steps could be taken within the Court and in Congress. Absent removal, no justice of the Supreme Court can be forced to leave

office. However, Congress has provided that other federal judges deemed to be "unable to discharge efficiently all the duties of his office by reason of permanent mental or physical disability" can be removed from office by the president with the approval of the Senate.[8]

The only formal removal mechanism for justices is the impeachment and conviction process on grounds of "high crimes and misdemeanors."[9] It is rarely used, however, and widely viewed as an inadequate deterrent to misconduct. Samuel Chase escaped conviction in the Senate and William O. Douglas was cleared of any wrongdoing by a House subcommittee. It is true, however, that Abe Fortas was forced to resign his seat with the threat of impeachment a real possibility. The impeachment process has never been used for the removal of aged, infirm, or incapacitated justices, however. Douglas's situation is instructive here. Had Douglas not retired and instead stayed in his place, it is likely that Congress would have eventually taken steps to remove him. This was Justice White's position (see Appendix A). As White's letter points out, when the Court takes matters into its own hands regarding the disability of one of its own members, it begins traversing a very dangerous, slippery slope. It has been common for the Court to postpone making decisions on closely divided cases until an ailing justice recovers sufficiently to participate, but prolonged illness is more problematic.

What the Court must not do is sit idly by while the disabled justice does serious damage to litigants, the Court, and the American people through incompetent actions. This is precisely what occurred toward the end of Justice Joseph McKenna's tenure on the bench. The other justices vacillated about pressuring him to step down and as a result he cast votes and made arguments that were totally inconsistent with his past positions. While changing positions does not in and of itself constitute disability, it merits further inquiry. In the case of McKenna, he was used as a puppet by competing factions within the Court and was ultimately made to look foolish in the eyes of history—his reputation damaged by his incompetent actions. Justice Charles Whittaker was used in a similar manner. There can be no winners in situations like this and the Court must be ever vigilant to ensure that it does not recur.

But how does one know when a justice is incompetent or simply getting older? Justices should be considered "disabled" when they are no longer able to participate fully and competently in the work of the Court. Examples of disability would be the casting of an incorrect vote in conference, confusion in oral argument, conference discussion, or opinion writing. Under this definition, Hugo Black and Thurgood Marshall can be classified as "disabled" prior to their retirements. Of course the casting of an "incorrect vote" could be debated. As was the case with Marshall, a clerk questioned him about it, and he agreed that an incorrect vote was cast. In the case of Black, his apparent "switch" on civil liberty cases may have less to do with "disability" and more to do with substantive changes in the cases, such as the presence of demonstrators, protesters, and the general disorder that Black was concerned about in such cases as *Tinker v. Des Moines*[10] and *Cohen v. California*.[11] Still, there is evidence that Black was confused during oral argument is such cases as *Alexander v. Holmes County Board of Education*.[12]

One very serious step that the Court has taken in the past is effectively to strip a disabled justice of his power. This entails requiring a fifth vote to grant cert. if the disabled justice votes to grant and also means postponing any decision on a case in which the disabled justice is the fifth and deciding vote. This policy may have been agreed to toward the end of Charles Whittaker's brief tenure and was definitely in effect during William O. Douglas's last term on the Court. Not much has been made of this controversial policy, however, as in both cases the disabled justices stepped down about a month later. Still, this action raises serious constitutional questions.

In the event that a justice becomes so disabled as to be unable to effectively participate in the work of the Court, the other justices can consider taking these steps in the following order:

1. The other justices can meet to decide whether there is a chance the disabled justice might recover. If there is such a chance, closely divided cases can be postponed until the disabled justice can fully participate. If it is decided that there is little or no chance for recovery, the justices can bring their considerable weight to bear on the disabled justice to persuade him or her to step down.[13]

2. In the event that the disabled justice refuses to leave, the Court can immediately issue a public statement to that effect. Public pressure or even congressional action might induce the disabled justice to step down.

3. If the disabled justice attempts to participate in the work of the Court, the other members may decide to strip their colleague of his or her power. This is a very dangerous step and one which should not be taken lightly. Because this action raises serious constitutional questions, the justices may want to issue a public statement explaining why they have taken this extraordinary step. It is important that this step be taken, however, if it is clear that the disabled justice is incompetent. Far better for the other members of the Court to act than to harm litigants, damage the integrity of the Court, and subvert the ideals of fairness and justice.

The worst thing the Court can do in such a situation is fail to act and remain silent about the state of the institution. The American people should not be kept in the dark about the workings of their government, for if they are, more damage will be done to the Court than any public statement about a disabled justice could inflict.

Is the modern mass media up to the task of adequately covering declining justices? The pressure that could be brought to bear by the media on a disabled justice has the potential to act as another inducement to step down. On March 31, 1975, Justice Douglas wrote Chief Justice Burger:

> I am sorry I missed the session today. The reason was the Press. It ambushed me at the house at 7 A.M. to get more pictures of my wheelchair. If this keeps up, they'll make me wonder about the First Amendment—their big umbrella.[14]

Certainly the pressure exerted by the media during Abe Fortas's nomination to the Chief Justiceship and his subsequent resignation or the coverage of Justice Douglas's illness demonstrates that the potential is there. Now there are twenty-four-hour news channels that could have correspondents positioned and carry ongoing live reports from outside the hospital, on the steps of the Court, at the justices' home, and so on, not to mention the crush of print reporters that could be covering the event. Any new piece of information, either true or false, could be available instantaneously throughout the world via the World Wide Web. Would there be pro and anti–Abe Fortas web sites, were the situation occurring at the present time?

Perhaps not as the modern press has not always been up to par in covering judicial illnesses. When then Justice Rehnquist was slurring his words in 1981 due to his overdependence on Placidyl, the Supreme Court press corps knew about it but did little to pursue the possibility that Rehnquist was failing.[15] Thurgood Marshall's visible failures from the bench as early as 1989 went largely underreported considering the seriousness of his mental decline. Of course the Court is a much less accessible institution to reporters than is the presidency or Congress. And unlike in the popular branches, justices do not regularly hold press conferences, issue press releases, and generally speak with reporters. For all of these reasons, the modern mass media may not be the powerful check on judicial illness that some suggest.[16]

THE RULE OF 100

One statutory change could be made to help counteract the rampant partisanship that now pervades the departure process. Specifically, the Rule of 80 could be raised.[17] A flexible Rule of 100, for example, could be enacted where a justice would become eligible to retire on reaching any combination of age and service totaling 100. Table 10.1 compares the dates of retirement eligibility for

TABLE 10.1

Retirement Eligibility and the Current Court: Comparing the Rules of 80 and 100

Justice and Party ID	Date of Birth	Date of Initial Service on Federal Courts	Date Retirement Eligible Under Rule of 80	80 Age*	Date Retirement Eligible Under Rule of 100	100 Age**
John Paul Stevens (R)	Apr. 20, 1920	Nov. 2, 1970	Nov. 2, 1985	65	July 18, 1995	75
William H. Rehnquist (R)	Oct. 1, 1924	Jan. 7, 1972	Oct. 1, 1989	65	May 25, 1998	73
Sandra Day O'Connor (R)	Mar. 26, 1930	Sept. 25, 1981	Sept. 25, 1996	66	Dec. 25, 2005	75
Ruth Bader Ginsburg (D)	Mar. 15, 1933	June 30, 1980	Mar. 15, 1998	65	Nov. 22, 2007	74
Antonin Scalia (R)	Mar. 11, 1936	Aug. 17, 1982	Mar. 11, 2001	65	May 27, 2009	73
Anthony Kennedy (R)	July 23, 1936	May 30, 1975	July 23, 2001	65	Dec. 27, 2005	69
Stephen Breyer (D)	Aug. 15, 1938	Dec. 10, 1980	Aug. 15, 2003	65	Oct. 13, 2009	71
David Souter (R)	Sept. 17, 1939	May 25, 1990	May 25, 2005	65	Jan. 23, 2015	75
Clarence Thomas (R)	June 28, 1948	Mar. 12, 1990	June 28, 2013	65	May 16, 2019	70

Note: All justices began their federal judicial service on the Courts of Appeal, except for Rehnquist, O'Connor, and Thomas, who began their federal judicial service on the Supreme Court.

* Eighty Age is the age of the justice on reaching retirement eligibility under the Rule of 80.

** One Hundred Age is the age of the justice on reaching retirement eligibility under the Rule of 100.

current members of the Court under the two different rules. The case of Justice John Paul Stevens is instructive. He was appointed to the federal bench at age fifty. When he reached age seventy-five in 1995, he had served for twenty-five years and would have been eligible to retire at that point under the rule of 100. Under the current rule, Stevens has been eligible since 1985, which has given him nearly two decades to play succession politics, while under the Rule of 100, he would have had less than a decade. In general, the retirement windows are all decreased by five to ten years under the new rule.

Still, Stevens and Rehnquist have met the requirements of the Rule of 100 and may very well still be acting in a partisan fashion. Indeed the Rule of 100 may not be high enough, in which case a Rule of 110 or even 120 might prove more effective. This is particularly important when one considers that presidents want to nominate young justices, particularly those with experience on the federal bench. Picking justices who already have years accumulated toward retirement eligibility gives them more of a chance to play succession politics when they step down, compared to their colleagues of comparable age who do not have as many years of service as a federal judge. One way to solve this is not to count lower court years toward retirement, effectively starting the clock over when a justice takes the oath for the High Court. Another solution is to build into the Rule of 100 a minimum age as the age sixty-five of the current Rule of 80. The threshold could be raised to seventy-five or eighty to minimize the partisan potential of young justices with a wealth of experience.

One such example is Anthony Kennedy, who began serving on the Ninth Circuit Court of Appeals at the amazingly young age of thirty-eight! He already had over a decade of federal court experience when he began his service on the Supreme Court. By comparison, Antonin Scalia is the same age as Kennedy, but did not start on the federal bench until over seven years after Kennedy. This would make Kennedy eligible to retire at age sixty-nine, four and a half years sooner than Scalia under a flexible Rule of 100. Building in a minimum age requirement of say seventy-five would keep Kennedy from considering retirement for at least another six years. Under the current statute, both Kennedy and Scalia were eligible at age sixty-five in 2001, though neither is anywhere near contemplating retirement.

This analysis suggests that the current statute is in need of reform. With presidents intent on nominating relatively young people to the bench, and life expectancies continually rising, the Rule of Eighty is hopelessly outdated and now only serves to facilitate partisan departures. Decreasing the window in which justices can make retirement choices will make it more difficult for justices to engage in succession politics. Departing prior to retirement eligibility for partisan reasons, would therefore carry a penalty as these justices would lose their salaries and senior status.

Along these lines, retirement could be made less attractive to justices by undertaking some minor reforms. The recent development of no longer allowing retired justices to have office space in the Court building no doubt serves to make retirement less inviting. Also keeping a retired justice's staff small serves as a deterrent. Reducing the salary of retired justices could also serve to dissuade retirement eligible members from departing early. Of course, reforms must not be undertaken lightly as there is a danger that justices may once again choose to remain in their seats until death so as not to lose the benefits of their position. Making voluntary departure less attractive, but still attainable, will likely minimize succession politics and still maximize a justice's service to the Court and the nation.

Further, calls to liberalize the existing statute, make retirement more attractive, or both will only serve to solidify if not increase partisanship. Yet, these reforms are often promoted as a cure for mental decrepitude. In this sense, the goals of decreasing both partisanship and mental decrepitude are in constant tension. How does one solve the problem of mental incapacity without increasing or solidifying partisan departures? As I will discuss later, a constitutional amendment mandating departure at a specified age may be the answer.

In 1988, Justice Stevens sent a detailed memorandum to the other justices proposing a major change in the existing retirement statute (see Appendix C). Stevens suggested that retired justices should be allowed, at the Court's discretion, to participate in selected cases. He outlined both the pros and cons of such an arrangement, identifying the following advantages:

> First, if a retired justice were available, this would resolve the problems that arise when there is a prolonged illness or delay in filling a vacancy on the Court. Second, it would provide the Court with additional judge-power and thereby reduce somewhat the number of opinions that each justice must write. Third, it would make the prospect of retirement more attractive for eligible justices. My association with senior judges on the Seventh Circuit, my conversations with Lewis [Powell], and my thoughts about my own future persuade me that this point is a good deal more significant than might appear at first blush. It is, moreover, consistent with the congressional decision to continue paying retired judges and justices their full salaries in order to facilitate the retirement decision. Fourth, it would enable the Court to take action in the rare case in which there would not otherwise be a quorum of six justices . . .
>
> It would not be necessary to invite a retired justice to sit every time the opportunity arose . . . I would rather have the additional views of a Warren Burger, Lewis Powell, or Potter Stewart than a

vacant chair ... The public at large would more readily accept a decision of a nine-person Court than a four-to-three decision or an affirmance by an equally divided Court ... The occasional use of a retired justice on this Court would not diminish its authority or prestige.[18]

According to Stevens, even if such a proposal were passed, the ultimate decision on whether or not to allow a retired member to participate in the Court's work would still rest with the active members. They could choose through unanimity, or majority vote, whether or not to invite a retired justice to participate in a particular case. Retired justices could be selected on a rotating or random basis or based on individual invitation. While nothing has yet come about from the Stevens memorandum, it shows that the current justices are not only acutely aware of the departure process, but would like to further ease their workloads and make retirement even more appealing than it currently is. Congress would have to revise the existing statute in order to bring about what Stevens termed a "modest change in the structure of the institution."[19] Congress would be better served doing the exact opposite: making retirement harder to obtain and less attractive and even passing a constitutional amendment for mandatory retirement.

LIGHTENING THE BURDEN

As discussed earlier, relatively light workloads lead to increased levels of partisan retirements. The Court, and chief justices in particular, are continually pressing Congress for more resources to combat rising caseloads. On its own, the Court has done much to ease its workload and overall make the job more manageable and pleasant. Some of these internal changes should be reconsidered as should some of the decisions Congress has made through the years regarding workload. As with liberalizing the retirement statute, calls for lightening the workload of the Supreme Court must be treated skeptically if partisanship in the departure-decision-making process is a concern.

There are a number of small but arguably important factors that have contributed to making the Court a more pleasant place to work.[20] The quality of life of a justice has improved in recent years. For example, the outward rancor of past Courts, such as those under Chief Justices Stone and Vinson has given way to a much more congenial atmosphere under Chief Justice Burger, and particularly under Chief Justice Rehnquist. Indeed, Justice Clarence Thomas remarked that he has yet to hear the first unkind word from his colleagues.[21] Some argue that the rancor has not gone away, but has only manifested itself in a different way—through memoranda and opinions.[22] This transformation was discussed by Rehnquist in a 1998 interview:

> At the time I was a law clerk there was friction between [Black and Frankfurter], great battles between Jackson and Black, and Douglas didn't like either Jackson or Frankfurter—several primadonas. What we have today—we get along well together. For instance on days of argument and after our conference usually you can't plan enough, so that everybody will be eating in the building, and those of us who want to come up to the justices' dining room and eat there. And almost every time everyone who's free comes up and has lunch and it's a very enjoyable conversation. We don't talk about cases, we talk about what movies we've seen or things like that. It's just a good bunch of people.[23]

Another small, but favorable development is that the justices do not have to deal with traffic and parking problems in Washington as cars and drivers are available for their use. Chief Justice Warren commented on the problem:

> One must know the parking situation in Washington to understand what a problem it is for a government official to drive his own car to public affairs in all kinds of weather and find a place to park . . . I tried for years to obtain cars for the other justices. They needed them for the same reason I did. Some needed cars even more urgently because of their age . . . The constant pressure on the Court was so great that men of that age should not have been driving cars in the traffic congestion of Washington.[24]

Oral argument now takes place only three days a week. Warren suggested that originally changing oral argument from five days a week had a positive effect:

> There was general acceptance of this idea, and it was made effective at the beginning of the 1955 term. I am sure this lightened the burden for all the justices as it did for me. I do not know whether there is any connection between the two, but since that time there has been but one heart attack (Frankfurter) while there had been a succession of them and of strokes in the years immediately preceding my incumbency.[25]

Indeed, an argument can even be made that the Court is underworked. In a 1972 letter to Chief Justice Burger, Justice Douglas, who wrote his own opinions, explained his opposition to pooling law clerks to prepare memos on certiorari petitions, "I think the Court is overstaffed and underworked . . . We were much, much busier 25 or 30 years ago than we are today. I really think that today the job does not add up to more than about four days a week."[26]

Could underwork help explain why there seems to be a trend toward seriatim opinion-writing? The justices are increasingly writing individual opinions in the relatively few cases they decide to hear.[27] No doubt the increased role and number of law clerks has contributed to this. Law clerks are primarily responsible for reviewing cert. petitions and opinion-writing. The justices are primarily responsible for voting and opinion-editing. Bernard Schwartz argues that the result is a loss of prestige.[28] Another result may be the rise of separate opinions. When only justices wrote opinions, it was in their interest to join their colleagues' opinions. Such behavior decreased their workload and allowed them to spend their time elsewhere. With law clerks now writing opinions, no such incentive exists. The rise of the law clerk, the shrinking docket, and the trend toward seriatim opinions all suggest that the justices may be sacrificing institutional prestige for individual acclaim. These developments may also suggest that the justices have much more time to consider the timing of their departures as compared with justices of previous eras.

Because law clerks do most, if not all, of the writing, it is difficult to tell whether a justice's productivity is declining. It takes much less effort for a justice to cast a vote and edit an opinion than it does to write an opinion from scratch. This is especially crucial for retirement. The increased role of law clerks makes it easier for aged and infirm justices to remain on the Court and engage in succession politics. Though Chief Justice Rehnquist uses only three clerks, the others have four and have delegated to the clerks an enormous amount of work. Perhaps it is the clerks and not the justices who are overworked. What would be the effect on each justice of having only three clerks or even two? Given the relationship between workload and partisanship, it is likely that reducing the number of clerks and reducing the amount of work they perform would make workload more of a factor in departure decisions. Aging justices who were forced to actually review endless stacks of cert petitions and write their own opinions might subordinate partisan concerns for workload when deciding to leave.

Though many of these developments are small, when considered together they have contributed to making the life of a Supreme Court justice much more pleasant. Apart from the concerns of individual justices, the institution itself has made it much easier for justices to remain on the Court at advanced ages and time their departures. Of course it is possible that the institution may change. New justices with new ideas may alter what now seems like an enjoyable job. The outward rancor that was so visible in the Stone and Vinson Courts could resurface. There could be a backlash against the increased role of clerks. Still, it is likely that the current members of the Court will make every attempt to continue and further their pleasant working conditions and decreasing workload.

MANDATORY RETIREMENT—
A DUBIOUS PROPOSITION?

Because partisan departures have become the rule, rather than the exception, it would seem that the solution should be mandatory retirement and/or fixed terms. But should we be wary of so easily discarding the advantages of judges having life tenure, simply because we may want to discourage partisan departures? While partisanship in the departure decision making process can be reduced significantly without amending the constitutional provision of life tenure for federal judges, the increasing problem of mental decrepitude suggests that a more drastic change may be necessary.

Figure 10.5 shows the effect that various departure mechanisms have on the tenure of judges. Voluntary departure mechanisms such as those currently in place (i.e., internal norms, workload, and retirement provisions) lead to lengthy tenures. Lengthy tenures in turn give rise to increases in partisan departures and mental decrepitude. Conversely, forced departure mechanisms such as elections, term limits, and mandatory retirement ages, will lead to shorter tenures. Partisan departures and mental decrepitude are less likely when tenures are brief.

The debate about life tenure, it should be recalled, is longstanding. Ultimately, the founders decided that it was necessary to ensure that the judiciary be independent of popular political pressure.[29] Even before the constitution's

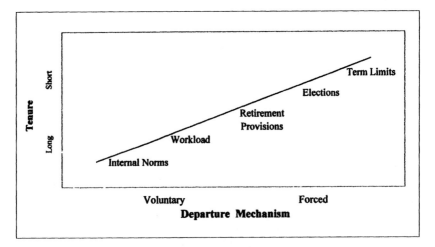

FIGURE 10.5
The Effect of Departure Mechanisms on
Tenure in the U.S. Supreme Court

ratification, there were proposals to limit the tenure of the justices. In the *Federalist Papers*, Alexander Hamilton argued in favor of life tenure, denouncing the mandatory retirement scheme then present for New York judges:

> The constitution of New-York, to avoid investigations that must forever be vague and dangerous, has taken a particular age as the criterion on inability. No man can be a judge beyond sixty. I believe there are few at present, who do not disapprove of this provision. There is no station in relation to which it is less proper than to that of a judge. The deliberating and comparing faculties generally preserve their strength much beyond that period, in men who survive it; and when in addition to this circumstance, we consider how few there are who outlive the season of intellectual vigor, and how improbable it is that any considerable proportion of the bench, whether more or less numerous, should be in such a situation at the same time, we shall be ready to conclude that limitations of this sort have little to recommend them. In a republic, where fortunes are not affluent, and pensions not expedient, the dismission of men from stations in which they have served their country long and usefully, on which they depend for subsistence, and from which it will be too late to resort to any other occupation for livelihood, ought to have some better apology to humanity, than is to be found in the imaginary danger of a superannuated bench.[30]

The state of New York did abolish its mandatory retirement age, but reinstated it in 1823, forcing the removal of a number of eminent jurists who were at the height of their careers. One of the judges forced off the bench was Chancellor Kent. Joseph Story was dismayed at Kent's removal and was critical of forced retirement in general. He wrote a friend:

> In common with you, and I may add with the mass of the profession, I regret the recent changes in the Judicial department, introduced into the new Constitution of New York. With me it was a sufficient reason to stand by the old system, that its actual administration was such as the warmest friends of the Judiciary desired. Experience had ascertained its excellence, and I am grown old enough to be willing to follow its steady light in preference to any theoretical schemes, however plausible. I do not believe we can ever hope to see the law administered with more learning, dignity, and ability, than it has been by the late Judges of New York. They were entitled to, and received the universal homage of the whole Union. The removal of such men cannot fail to cast a gloom over all who wish merit to receive its just reward for eminent services.[31]

Implicit in Hamilton's argument against a fixed retirement age is the need for a voluntary retirement provision that would include some form of remuneration. The existing retirement statute has gone a long way in lessening the danger of an incapacitated bench due to financial considerations. At the same time, advances in medicine and public sanitation, among other things, have changed the nature of illness. Life expectancy has increased dramatically and most Americans can expect to live into their seventies and eighties, if not longer.

Charles Evans Hughes argued in 1928 that "under present conditions of living, and in view of the increased facility of maintaining health and vigor, the age of seventy may well be thought too early for compulsory retirement." Hughes thought seventy-five "could more easily be defended."[32] Hughes himself is an example of the difficulty of fixing a certain age for mandatory retirement. Hughes was an effective Chief Justice throughout his seventies, retiring at age seventy-nine. Like most justices, his original thoughts about departure when he was young changed dramatically by the time he was facing the decision himself. A relatively young William O. Douglas wrote in 1954:

> Compulsory retirement at the age of 75 is . . . a rather dubious proposition. One who has served ten years consecutively and has reached 70 may retire. That is in the law and would take care of necessitous cases. There have been in the past judges who have hung on beyond the time they should have been on the Court because they had no way of making a living after they retired . . . Compulsory retirement at 75 is hard to argue against, I suppose. But then again there is no particular need for it. Holmes served almost 15 years after he was 75 and did some of his best work then. When I came on the Court Hughes was 78 and some of his outstanding work was done in his last few years as Chief Justice. The same is true for Brandeis.[33]

Any age will be arbitrary, either too low or too high, depending on the justice in question. Even eighty-five would have been too low for Oliver Wendell Holmes, Jr., who stepped down at ninety-one. Conversely, seventy was too high for Ward Hunt, who became disabled at age sixty-seven. Also, as life expectancy increases, should the constitution perpetually be amended to increase the mandatory retirement age?

Due to the secrecy of the Court's internal decision-making processes, it is the justices themselves who are best able to tell whether one of their colleagues is beginning to falter. Should there be an independent commission charged with reviewing the effectiveness of federal judges? Because of the Court's secrecy with regard to its decision-making process, an independent advisory committee would have a difficult time discerning the mental decline of a justice. Collectively, the justices themselves can act much more quickly before the institution is harmed by a faltering colleague. While there have been feuds among individual justices, it is not likely that the Court would collectively act against a competent justice. Still, some states have created independent advisory commissions to police their judiciaries.[34] And in the 1970s, Senator Sam Nunn proposed that the United States Judicial Conference be given the power to declare a justice or judge disabled.[35]

With the increased role of law clerks, justices need only answer in their places, to paraphrase Chief Justice Taft, in order to minimally perform their constitutional function. When a justice is unable to do even this, that is the time for the rest of the Court to make their collective feeling known. In an earlier time when justices did most if not all of their own research and opinion writing, it was more imperative to the institution that the declining justice step down. Now, however, there is little reason to depart until one's mental abilities diminish. We should not be surprised to see aging justices remain on the bench well into their eighties.

The question that must be asked, however, is how the public interest is best served by members of the Court. Surely, no one wants to see justices remain on the bench after even the slightest hint of mental decline. But by the same token, would the public interest be served by a mandatory retirement scheme that would force the departures of fully competent justices who are vigorously participating in the work of the Court? Charles Fairman once applauded departing justices, such as William Strong and John Hessin Clarke, who left the Court too soon rather than too late,[36] but an argument can be made that the public interest was not served by their premature departures, as their colleagues duly noted at the time. Both were influential with the other members of the Court and had contributed much to the jurisprudence of their time.

It could be argued that generational change should be institutionally recognized and that the public interest is better served by a Supreme Court that is reflective of the dominant governing coalition of the day. Arguments along these lines necessarily suggest that mandatory retirement ages or elections are the best means to ensure this. The argument assumes that aged justices are not or cannot be part of governmental or societal change. Many recent justices, however, have changed their positions over time and though *stare decisis* is an important factor in deciding cases, justices are free to disregard precedent.[37]

Retirement-eligible justices should not leave too soon, like Strong, Henry Brown, Clarke, and Potter Stewart did, nor should they remain too long, like Stephen J. Field, Joseph McKenna, and William O. Douglas clearly did. Justices should step down at the first sign of mental decline. They should instruct their friends and families, as Chief Justice Hughes did, to tell them when it is time to go. Though families are not entirely unbiased, they do have an incentive to protect "their" justice from staying too long and potentially damaging his or her reputation. The members of the Court, and particularly the chief, have a special obligation to ensure that each justice is performing the duties of his or her office with full vigor.[38] Though it may be difficult for the justices to address the issue of a failing colleague, they must. The case of Joseph McKenna is highly instructive. An indecisive Court damaged its decision-making effectiveness while the mentally confused McKenna was still casting votes. Instead of working together to protect the institution and the declining justice, warring factions unfairly used McKenna to gain majorities. Similar machinations were used against Charles Evans Whittaker during his brief tenure. The fact that declining justices such as Oliver Wendell Holmes and William O. Douglas were not used by their colleagues in such a manner should be applauded.

Fairman argued for compulsory retirement, in part because it would "reduce the variance" between the popular branches of government and the unelected Court, which often has a number of justices from previous eras who seek to thwart current policies.[39] The opposition of Justices Sutherland, Van Devanter, Butler, and McReynolds to FDR's New Deal policies of the 1930s and the recent dissents of Justices Brennan, Marshall, and Blackmun in death penalty cases come to mind. But if the goal is to make the Court a more responsive, popular branch, then why not go a step further and call for short, fixed terms? Mandatory retirement schemes usually require a judge to depart at a certain age, such as seventy or seventy-five. If a judge were appointed at age fifty, for example, that judge would have a term of twenty-five years, likely serving well beyond the political regime that placed him on the bench. So why not have a term limit of, say, ten years? If the public interest is best served by a responsive Court, then a term limit is clearly the best mechanism to ensure this.

A number of law professors and former judges have recently renewed the call for a constitutional amendment to limit the tenure of Supreme Court justices.[40] Generally, they argue that staggered, nonrenewable terms of eighteen years are best. This would give presidents two appointments per term (no more than four total) and help further protect against "court packing." Of course some justices would die "out of turn" or leave otherwise before the end of their term. In such cases, should justices be appointed only for the remainder of the unexpired term?

These authors also recongnize that the main benefit of term limits would be to protect the Court against excessive burdens imposed by infirm colleagues. For example, David Garrow has identified six justices since the modern retirement statute was enacted in 1954, who he believes were not intellectually able to discharge their offices prior to their departures: Sherman Minton, Charles Whittaker, Hugo Black, William O. Douglas, Lewis Powell, and Thurgood Marshall. Minton was sixty-five and Whittaker was sixty-one when they departed, so mandatory retirement at sixty-five would not have prevented the impact their declines had on the Court. In the case of the others, a mandatory retirement age of sixty-five, seventy, or even seventy-five would have spared the Court from their incapacities.

John Gruhl countered these arguments in a recent article by examining the effect term limits would have had on previous justices.[41] He found that under a ten-year limit, two-thirds would have been forced to depart early. One-third would have been required to leave under a twenty-year limit.[42] He also found that term limits would have forced nearly all of the "great" justices to depart well before they ultimately did leave.[43] For example, John Marshall, Joseph Story, John Marshall Harlan I, and Hugo Black all served for over three decades.[44] Gruhl also examined the effect term limits would have had on a number of "damaging" decisions the Court made throughout history, such as *Dred Scott*, and found the results mixed.

Lee Epstein et al. made a similar argument in response to Garrow. They not only pointed out that "some distinguished careers would have been, perhaps regrettably so, cut short" but also "it is possible that some justices— again including a smattering of those who regularly appear on lists of truly distinguished jurists—would never have attained a nomination had a compulsory retirement age existed." For example, Epstein et al. point out that Benjamin Cardozo was sixty-one at the time of his appointment. Also, Ruth Bader Ginsburg was sixty. Still, they recognize that less distinguished jurists such as Horace Lurton and Sherman Minton would probably not been nominated because of their ages—sixty-five and fifty-eight, respectively. Ultimately, Epstein et al. recognize that trying to solve the problem of "mental decrepitude" in the name of an intellectually vigorous bench may have the opposite effect:

> What then are we to make of the effect a mandatory retirement provision would have on the Supreme Court? Surely the answer depends on whether we Americans think that sort of cure for the problem of mental decrepitude is worse than the problem itself or, to put it in slightly different terms, whether we should pursue the goal of preserving an intellectually distinct bench via a method—mandatory retirement—that might actually undermine it.

Table 10.2 shows the effect that mandatory retirement at age seventy-five would have on the current members of the Court. Justice Stevens and Chief Justice Rehnquist would no longer be on the Court, both departing during the Clinton administration. Justices O'Connor and Ginsburg would be forced to depart under the winner of the 2004 presidential election. Interestingly, Ginsburg's

TABLE 10.2

Effect of Mandatory Retirement at Age Seventy-five on Current Supreme Court

Justice and Party ID	Date of Birth	Date of Initial Service on Federal Courts	Date Retirement Eligible Under Rule of 80	Date Mandatory Retirement at Age 75	President in Year of Mandatory Retirement
John Paul Stevens (R)	Apr. 20, 1920	Nov. 2, 1970	Nov. 2, 1985	Apr. 20, 1995	Clinton
William H. Rehnquist (R)	Oct. 1, 1924	Jan. 7, 1972	Oct. 1, 1989	Oct. 1, 1999	Clinton
Sandra Day O'Connor (R)	Mar. 26, 1930	Sept. 25, 1981	Sept. 25, 1996	Mar. 26, 2005	?
Ruth Bader Ginsburg (D)	Mar. 15, 1933	June 30, 1980	Mar. 15, 1998	Mar. 15, 2008	?
Antonin Scalia (R)	Mar. 11, 1936	Aug. 17, 1982	Mar. 11, 2001	Mar. 11, 2011	?
Anthony Kennedy (R)	July 23, 1936	May 30, 1975	July 23, 2001	July 23, 2011	?
Stephen Breyer (D)	Aug. 15, 1938	Dec. 10, 1980	Aug. 15, 2003	Aug. 15, 2013	?
David Souter (R)	Sept. 17, 1939	May 25, 1990	May 25, 2005	Sept. 17, 2014	?
Clarence Thomas (R)	June 28, 1948	Mar. 12, 1990	June 28, 2013	June 28, 2023	?

Note: All justices began their federal judicial service on the Courts of Appeal, except for Rehnquist, O'Connor, and Thomas, who began their federal judicial service on the Supreme Court.

vacancy would arise during the 2008 presidential campaign—something that virtually never happens when justices themselves control the timing of their departures. Justices Scalia and Kennedy would be forced to leave in 2011 creating two simultaneous vacancies—another occurrence that justices try to avoid. During the administration of the president who wins the election of 2012, Justices Breyer and Souter would depart. In all, there would be two appointments for each four-year presidential term. This practical example underscores the issues that need to be considered before a constitutional amendment is passed. Should justices only depart at the end of Terms? Should there be only one departure per Term? Should departures occur during presidential election years?

Why are so many unwilling to relinquish life tenure for judges? Much of it has to do with a view of the judiciary as countermajoritarian and rights revolutions as judge-centered. But much research has shown this view of the Court to be incorrect. Fifty years ago Robert Dahl demonstrated how the Court has always been more or less in line with the dominant policy-making regimes of the day. Recent scholarship by Gerald Rosenberg and Charles Epp among others suggests a similar role for courts: at best they are part of larger social forces, rather than catalysts for social change. If judges are generally reflective of the larger society, then judicial independence in any real sense is a myth. As such, arguments in favor of life tenure based on judicial independence seem unconvincing.

Ironically, judicial independence would be strengthened by mandatory retirement. One only has to think of Franklin Roosevelt's Court-packing assault on the Court to see how vulnerable the justices are to manipulation by the other branches of government. A mandatory retirement age would largely insulate the justices from accusations that either they are too old to keep up with the workload, or that they are hanging on to their seats for partisan reasons. Only if justices choose to depart earlier than the mandated age, would they have to answer such questions. As a result, a mandatory departure age provides justices with a strong disincentive from acting strategically when they depart, and promotes judicial independence.

CONCLUSION

Over time, voluntary departure for the U.S. Supreme Court has been made increasingly attractive, so much so, that no justice has died on the bench in half a century. Manageable workloads and pleasant working conditions further promote a system where justices have immense discretion over the timing of their departures. The current retirement regime that began in 1954 has seen an unprecedented amount of politics being played by justices contemplating departure. Though justices are in the business of denying partisan motivations for their actions, the data suggest otherwise.

At his retirement press conference, Justice Potter Stewart expressed his views on life tenure:

> There is optional retirement. You see an example of that before you today. It is not involuntary servitude. Anybody can resign any time he wants to. There have been very few examples in our history of justices, federal judges of any kind, who have stayed longer than they should. When those cases have arisen, they have generally been taken care of institutionally and collegially. Perhaps life tenure is not ideal; it is hard to think of any ideal system.[45]

While Stewart is right in principle, his departure in the first year of a Republican administration at the relatively young age of sixty-six is exemplary of the current problems. There are a number of options to combat both partisanship and mental decrepitude. Congress could modify the existing retirement provision to decrease the window of opportunity justices have to engage in succession politics. Specifically, a new Rule of 100 would provide an important step in the right direction for minimizing the naked partisanship of current departure-decision-making. The existing norms of institutional and collegial pressure could be strengthened to ensure that abuses due to disability no longer take place. Also, the recent arrangements that have led to a decrease in the Court's workload could be reversed and continuing calls to lighten the load should be treated skeptically. In the end, however, it is a constitutional amendment for compulsory retirement at age seventy-five that combats partisanship and mental decrepitude most effectively, and preserves judicial independence.

Though the justices are well aware that the greatest wounds the Court has suffered have been self-inflicted, they continue to challenge assumptions that they are neutral, impartial decision makers. Their astonishing involvement and bitter division in *Bush v. Gore* coupled with favorable departure structures, suggest that if reform does not occur, partisanship will continue to run roughshod over principle. Deciding to leave the U.S. Supreme Court is not an easy decision, but one that each justice ought to confront with the welfare and stability of the Court and the American form of government foremost in their minds. But after several attempts throughout America's history to limit the tenure of federal judges, perhaps it is finally time for the American people to decide when justices ought to leave the bench.

Appendix A:

Letter from Byron White to
Warren Burger, October 20, 1975

Dear Mr. Chief Justice:

I should like to register my protest against the decision of the Court not to assign the writing of any opinions to Mr. Justice Douglas. As I understand it from deliberations in conference, there are one or more justices who are doubtful about the competence of Mr. Justice Douglas that they would not join any opinion purportedly authored by him. At the very least, they would not hand down any judgment arrived at by a 5–4 vote where Mr. Justice Douglas is in the majority. There may be various shadings of opinion among the seven justices but the ultimate action was not to make any assignments of opinions to Mr. Justice Douglas. That decision, made in the absence of Mr. Justice Douglas, was supported by seven justices. It is clear that the ground for the action was the assumed incompetence of the justice.

On the assumption that there have been no developments since last Friday to make this unnecessary, I shall state briefly why I disagreed and still disagree with the Court's action. Prior to this time, on every occasion in which I have dissented from action taken by the Court's majority, I have thought the decision being made, although wrong in my view, was within the powers assigned to the Court by the Constitution. In this instance, the action voted by the Court exceeds its powers and perverts the constitutional design.

The Constitution provides that federal judges, including Supreme Court justices, "shall hold their Offices during good behaviour." That document— our basic charter binding us all—allows the impeachment of judges by Congress; but it nowhere provides that a justice's colleagues may deprive him of his office by refusing to permit him to function as a justice.

If there is sufficient doubt about Justice Douglas' mental abilities that he should have no assignments of opinions and if his vote should not be counted in 5–4 cases when he is one of the five, I fail to see how his vote should be counted or considered in any case or why we should listen to him in conference at all. In any event, the decision of the Court precludes the effective performance of his judicial functions by Mr. Justice Douglas and the Court's majority has wrongfully assumed that it has the power to do so.

If Congress were to provide by statute that Supreme Court justices could be removed from office whenever an official commission, acting on medical advice, concluded that a justice is no longer capable of carrying on his duties, surely there would be substantial questions about the constitutionality of such legislation. But Congress has taken no such action; nor has it purported to vest power in the Court to unseat a justice for any reason. The Court nevertheless asserts the right to disregard Justice Douglas in any case vote where it will determine the outcome. How does the Court plan to answer the petitioner who would otherwise have a judgment in his favor, who claims that the vote of each sitting justice should be counted until and unless he is impeached by proper authorities and who inquires where the Court derived the power to reduce its size to eight justices?

Even if the Court had the authority to do what seven justices now purport to do, it did not, as far as I know, discuss the matter with Mr. Justice Douglas prior to voting to relieve him of a major part of his judicial duties, did not seek his views about his own health or attempt to obtain from him current medical opinions on that subject.

Mr. Justice Douglas undoubtedly has severe ailments. I do not discount the difficulties that his condition presents for his colleagues. It would be better for everyone, including Mr. Justice Douglas, if he would now retire. Although he has made some noble efforts—very likely far more than others would have made—there remain serious problems that would best be resolved by his early retirement. But Mr. Justice Douglas has a different view. He listens to oral arguments, appears in conference and casts his vote on argued cases. He thus not only asserts his own competence to sit but has not suggested that he is planning to retire.

Based on my own observations and assuming that we have the power to pass on the competence of a fellow justice, I am not convinced, as each of my seven colleagues seems to be, that there is such doubt about the condition of Mr. Justice Douglas that I should refuse to join any opinion that he might write. And, as I have said, as long as he insists on acting as a justice and participating in our deliberations, I cannot discover the constitutional power to treat him other than as a justice, as I have for more than thirteen years.

The Constitution opted for the independence of each federal judge, including his freedom from removal by his colleagues. I am convinced that it would have been better had retirement been required at a specified age and that a constitutional amendment to that effect should be proposed and adopted. But so far the Constitution has struck a different balance, and I will not presume to depart from it in this instance.

If the Court is convinced that Justice Douglas should not continue to function as a justice, the Court should say so publicly and invite Congress to take appropriate action. If it is an impeachable offense for an incompetent justice to purport to sit as a judge, is it not the task of Congress, rather than this Court, to undertake proceedings to determine the issue of competence? If it is not an impeachable offense, may the Court nevertheless conclude that a justice is incompetent and forbid him to perform his duties?

This leads to a final point. The Court's action is plainly a matter of great importance to the functioning of the Court in the immediate future. It is a matter of substantial significance to both litigants and the public. The decision should be publicly announced; and I do hope the majority is prepared to make formal disclosure of the action it has taken.

Knowing that my seven colleagues, for whom I have the highest regard, hold different views, I speak with great deference. Yet history teaches that nothing can more readily bring the Court and its constitutional functions into disrepute than the Court's failure to recognize the limits of its own powers. I therefore hasten to repeat in writing the views that I orally stated at our latest conference.

Sincerely,
Byron

The Chief Justice

Copies to: Mr. Justice Brennan
           Mr. Justice Stewart
           Mr. Justice Marshall
           Mr. Justice Blackmun
           Mr. Justice Powell
           Mr. Justice Rehnquist

Appendix B:

Letter from Warren E. Burger, William J. Brennan, Jr., Potter Stewart, Byron R. White, Thurgood Marshall, Harry A. Blackmun, Lewis F. Powell, and William H. Rehnquist to William O. Douglas, December 22, 1975

Dear Bill:

You memos of November 15 and December 17 tend to have a connection with one another and to the problems you raised in your letter to the Chief Justice with copies to the Conference dated December 20. The Chief Justice advised you on December 19 that these matters would be taken up in Conference. The Conference met today and considered all of these points.

For clarification of discussion these matters were divided into their separate categories. The Conference considered each of these matters separately and after discussion reached the following conclusions:

(1) *Participation in pending argued cases:* It seems clear beyond doubt that your retirement by letter dated November 12 operated to terminate all judicial powers except such as would arise from assignment to one of the Federal courts other than the Supreme Court. The statutes seem very clear that a retired justice cannot be assigned any duties of a Supreme Court justice as such. This would apply to all cases submitted but not decided before you retired and to any case decided while you were a member of the Court on which rehearing is thereafter granted. Specifically this would apply to *Williams & Williams v. United States,* the copyright case you mentioned in your memorandum of December 20, and, of course, it would apply to all other cases which reargument has been granted including the death penalty cases.

(2) *Passing on certiorari petitions and on appeals presented by jurisdictional statements:* Here, too, your retirement on November 12 terminates any power

253

to participate in Conference actions granting or denying certiorari, actions on jurisdictional statements, motions, etc.

(3) *Attendance at Conferences:* Resolution of the two foregoing questions bears on the question of attendance at conferences. The formal conferences of the Court are limited, as you know, to justices empowered to act on pending matters and do not include retired justices.

(4) *Staff and Chambers:* The Chief Justice invited you to occupy the Chambers reserved for retired Chief Justices which Earl Warren had occupied during his lifetime after retirement. You indicated you preferred to remain in your present quarters. In your letter of November 15, you may recall, you stated, "Whoever is named to take my place might want the more commodious [retired Chief Justice] space that is available."

In that same letter you confirmed earlier discussions about future staff with your statement: "I assume that my messenger will continue on as well as my two secretaries." Ordinarily a retired justice has been allowed only one secretary, and, if he performed authorized judicial duties, he was allowed a law clerk. The Conference decision was that for the time being you should be allowed to take your choice and have two secretaries rather than one secretary and one law clerk. It was agreed that your messenger could be continued so that you would have someone to drive your car. There are no statutes expressly providing for the staff of a retired justice but it is a matter of tradition, and the tradition is quite definite as to the extent of staff. Earl Warren, after his retirement, had one secretary, one messenger who doubled as his driver, and for at least part of the time, one law clerk.

For clarification, the unanimous Conference decision is that you should have your present Chambers as you requested and also, as you requested, your messenger and two secretaries. There is no provision in the budget for a staff exceeding three persons for a retired justice.

No member of the Conference could recall any instance of a retired justice participating in any matter before the Court and it was unanimously agreed that the relevant statutes do not allow for such participation.

We hope this will clarify the situation.

Best wishes,

Warren E. Burger   Thurgood Marshall
William J. Brennan Jr.   Harry A. Blackmun
Potter Stewart   Lewis F. Powell
Byron R. White   William H. Rehnquist

Appendix C:

Letter from John Paul Stevens to William H. Rehnquist, October 28, 1988

Dear Chief:

Some time ago at conference we discussed the possibility of requesting Congress to enact legislation authorizing us to invite a retired justice to sit with us on cases in which we do not have a full Court. After reading Erwin Griswold's piece in the Washington Post,[i] I have given the idea further thought, and believe it has sufficient merit to warrant further discussion. In the hope that you may agree, I tender this summary of what I understand to be the principal arguments for and against such a proposal.

There are some important advantages. First, if a retired justice were available, this would resolve the problems that arise when there is a prolonged illness or delay in filling a vacancy on the Court. Second, it would provide the Court with additional judge-power and thereby reduce somewhat the number of opinions that each justice must write. Third, it would make the prospect of retirement more attractive for eligible justices. My association with senior judges on the Seventh Circuit, my conversations with Lewis [Powell], and my thoughts about my own future persuade me that this point is a good deal more significant than might appear at first blush. It is, moreover, consistent with the congressional decision to continue paying retired judges and justices their full salaries in order to facilitate the retirement decision. Fourth, it would enable the Court to take action in the rare case in which there would not otherwise be a quorum of six justices.

As I remember the conference discussion, two principal disadvantages were identified: (1) intermittent and temporary changes in the composition

---

i. Erwin Griswold and Ernest Gellhorn, "200 Cases in Which Justices Recused Themselves," *Washington Post,* October 18, 1988, Box 462, Marshall Papers.

of the Court might introduce an element of either actual or apparent incon-
sistency in the development of legal doctrine; (2) the problem of selecting
the cases on which a retired justice would be invited to sit, and the related
problem of selecting which of a plurality of retired justices should be invited
to sit on particular cases, might be awkward or divisive. Let me comment on
each point.

The significance of the first point is, I believe, diminished by the fact that
it would not be necessary to invite a retired justice to sit every time the opportunity arose. In an especially important or controversial case—a case like
Chadha,[ii] for example—the Court might decide to have the case decided only
by active justices. Such an approach would be comparable to the practice in
the Courts of Appeals, where senior judges are not eligible to participate in *en
banc* cases. Even in such cases, I think I would rather have the additional views
of Warren Burger, Lewis Powell, or Potter Stewart than a vacant chair, but I
can see the merit in the contrary position. Putting such cases to one side, however, there would still remain a significant number that present issues, such as
questions of statutory construction and circuit conflicts, on which a definite
answer would be more important than the particular make-up of the Court.
In my judgment, the public at large would more readily accept a decision by a
nine-person Court than a four-to-three decision or an affirmance by an
equally divided Court. Of course, in those cases in which there are six or more
justices in the majority, the result would not be affected by the presence of a
retired justice. Several states, including Maryland, Minnesota, Hawaii and, I
believe New Jersey, provide for the designation of a temporary justice when a
vacancy occurs. I am told that Virginia also may call a retired justice to serve
in certain situations.

Perhaps one reason why the prospect of a modest change in the personnel of the Court from time to time does not trouble me is my familiarity with
the use of changing panels to develop the law at the Court of Appeals level.
As the regular use of differing three-judge panels is an acceptable practice at
the Court of Appeals level, I would think the occasional use of a retired justice on this Court would not diminish its authority or prestige.

My experience on the Court of Appeals leads me to discount the significance of the selection problem. I would suppose that we could agree that a
retired justice would not be invited to sit unless we were unanimous in considering the invitation appropriate. Even if we acted by majority vote, the
problem would be similar to an invitation to serve as a special master in an

---

ii. *Immigration and Naturalization Service v. Chadha*, 462 U.S. 919 (1983). For a
discussion of case, see Barbara Hinkson Craig, *Chadha: The Story of an Epic Constitutional Struggle* (New York: Oxford University Press, 1988).

original case. If there is a plurality of retired justices available—as there usually is a plurality of senior judges available for service on each Court of Appeals—selection could be made by rotation, at random, or by specific invitation. In time, of course, a retired justice will reach a point at which he or she would no longer be willing or able to accept an invitation (or is simply too busy with other matters, such as bicentennials), but that phenomenon already occurs regularly at the Court of Appeals level and is capable of occurring in every federal court with respect to active service (see Rehnquist, The Supreme Court, at 183–184).

As noted above, there would be some negatives associated with the change I propose, but I am convinced that these would be outweighed by the long term public benefits that would flow from this modest change in the structure of the institution.

If you think further discussion of this question may be useful, perhaps you might make it an agenda item at some future conference.

Respectfully,
John

The Chief Justice

Notes

CHAPTER 1

1. Evan Thomas and Michael Isikoff, "The Truth Behind the Pillars," *Newsweek*, December 25, 2000.

2. For a discussion of the case, see, for example, Howard Gillman, *The Votes That Counted: How the Court Decided the 2000 Presidential Election* (Chicago, Ill.: University of Chicago Press, 2001); Cass R. Sunstein and Richard A. Epstein, eds., *The Vote: Bush, Gore and the Supreme Court* (Chicago, Ill.: University of Chicago Press, 2001); Abner Greene, *Understanding the 2000 Election: A Guide to the Legal Battles that Decided the Presidency* (New York: New York University Press, 2001); Alan M. Dershowitz, *Supreme Injustice: How the High Court Hijacked Election 2000* (New York: Oxford University Press, 2001); Richard A. Posner, *Breaking the Deadlock: The 2000 Election, the Constitution, and the Courts* (Princeton, N.J.: Princeton University Press, 2001).

3. Joan Biskupic, "Division May Be Supreme Court Legacy," *USA Today*, December 13, 2000. Linda Greenhouse, "News Analysis: Another Kind of Bitter Split," *New York Times*, December 19, 2000.

4. Succession politics affects all levels of courts. Though the focus of this study is the U.S. Supreme Court, there has been work done on the lower federal courts. See, for example, Deborah J. Barrow and Gary Zuk, "An Institutional Analysis of Turnover in the Lower Federal Courts, 1900–1987," *Journal of Politics* 52 (1990): 457–476; Gary Zuk, Gerard S. Gryski, and Deborah J. Barrow, "Partisan Transformation of the Federal Judiciary, 1869–1992," *American Politics Quarterly* 21 (1993):439–454; James F. Spriggs II and Paul J. Wahlbeck, "Calling It Quits: Strategic Retirement on the Federal Courts of Appeals, 1893–1991," *Political Research Quarterly* 48 (September 1995):573–597; David C. Nixon and J. David Haskin, "Judicial Retirement Strategies: The Judge's Role in Influencing Party Control of the Appellate Courts," *American Politics Quarterly* 28 (4, October 2000): 458–489.

5. *New York Times*, September 8, 1956, p. 1, col. 1.

6. See, for example, Michael J. Gerhardt, *The Federal Appointment Process: A Constitutional and Historical Analysis* (Durham, NC: Duke University Press, 2000); John Anthony Maltese, *The Selling of Supreme Court Nominees* (Baltimore, Md.: The Johns Hopkins University Press, 1995); George L. Watson and John A. Stookey, *Shap-*

ing America: The Politics of Supreme Court Appointments (New York: HarperCollins, 1995); James G. Gimpel and Lewis S. Ringel, "Understanding Court Nominee Evaluation and Approval: Mass Opinion in the Bork and Thomas Cases." *Political Behavior* 17 (1995): 135–153; Mark Silverstein, *Judicious Choices: The New Politics of Supreme Court Confirmations* (New York: Norton, 1994); Stephen L. Carter, *The Confirmation Mess: Cleaning Up the Federal Appointments Process* (New York: Basic Books, 1994); P. S. Ruckman, Jr., "The Supreme Court, Critical Nominations, and the Senate Confirmation Process," *Journal of Politics* 55 (1993): 793–805; Henry J. Abraham, *Justices and Presidents,* 3rd ed. (New York: Oxford University Press, 1992); David A. Strauss and Cass R. Sunstein, "The Senate, the Constitution and the Confirmation Process," *Yale Law Journal* 101 (1992): 1491–1524; John Massaro, *Supremely Political: The Role of Ideology and Presidential Management in Unsuccessful Supreme Court Nominations* (Albany, N.Y.: SUNY Press, 1990); Charles Cameron, Albert D. Cover and Jeffrey Segal, "Senate Voting on Supreme Court justices: A Neo-Institutional Model," *American Political Science Review* 84 (1990): 525–534; Jeffrey A. Segal, "Senate Confirmation of Supreme Court justices: Partisan and Institutional Politics." *Journal of Politics* 49 (1987): 998–1015.

7. Though it is possible and has happened in the past, I am not referring to departing justices actively lobbying the president on their successors as Louis D. Brandeis did to Franklin D. Roosevelt on behalf of William O. Douglas. Brandeis would later tell Douglas, "I wanted you to be here in my place." Henry J. Abraham, *Justices, Presidents, and Senators: A History of U.S. Supreme Court Appointments from Washington to Clinton,* new and revised edition (Lanham, Md.: Rowman & Littlefield, 1999), 170. More general concerns by justices over possible successors are part of the analysis and are included.

8. Charles Fairman, "The Retirement of Federal Judges," *Harvard Law Review* 51 (1938): 397–443; John S. Goff, "Old Age and the Supreme Court," *The American Journal of Legal History* 4 (95, 1960): 95–106; John R. Schmidhauser, "When and Why Justices Leave the Supreme Court," in *Politics of Age,* Wilma Donahue and Clark Tibbitts, eds. (Ann Arbor: University of Michigan Press, 1962), 117–131; David J. Danelski, "A Supreme Court Justice Steps Down," *Yale Review* 54 (1965): 411–425; David N. Atkinson, "Retirement and Death on the U.S. Supreme Court: From Van Devanter to Douglas," *University of Missouri Kansas City Law Review* 45 (1976): 1–27; David N. Atkinson, "Bowing to the Inevitable: Supreme Court Deaths and Resignations, 1789–1864," *Arizona State Law Journal* 1982: 615–640; Peverill Squire, "Politics and Personal Factors in Retirement from the United States Supreme Court," *Political Behavior* 10 (1988): 180–190; Timothy M. Hagle, "Strategic Retirements: A Political Model of Turnover on the United States Supreme Court," *Political Behavior* 15 (1993): 25–48; Saul Brenner, "The Myth that Justices Strategically Retire," *The Social Sciences Journal* 36 (3, 1999): 431–439.

9. Atkinson identified 1937 as the year in which retirement benefits were expanded to include full benefit at age 65 with 15 years of service on the federal bench. In fact, this provision was not adopted by Congress until 1954.

10. William H. Rehnquist interview, *Charlie Rose,* PBS, aired January 13, 1999.

11. See, for example, Robert A. Dahl, "Decision-Making in a Democracy: The Supreme Court as a National Policymaker," *Journal of Public Law* 6 (1957): 293.

12. In 1931, Republican Herbert Hoover was in the White House and Republicans controlled both houses of Congress.

13. See, for example, Jeffrey A. Segal and Harold J. Spaeth, *The Supreme Court and the Attitudinal Model* (Cambridge, Mass.: Cambridge University Press, 1993); Harold J. Spaeth and Jeffrey A. Segal, *Majority Rule or Minority Will: Adherence to Precedent on the U.S. Supreme Court* (Cambridge, Mass.: Cambridge University Press, 1999). For a normative argument that justices ought to act on their personal policy preferences, see Terri Jennings Peretti, *In Defense of a Political Court* (Princeton, N.J.: Princeton University Press, 1999).

14. Lee Epstein, Jack Knight, and Olga Shvetsova, "Comparing Judicial Selection Systems," *William and Mary Bill of Rights Journal* XX (1) 2002: 17.

15. The amendment does allow for a president to serve for ten years if he or she finishes out the last two years or less of his or her predecessor's term. This would have been the case for Lyndon Johnson had he chosen to run and been elected president in 1968 but not for Harry Truman (had the amendment applied to him) as he took office in April 1945, a little over a year into FDR's term. Truman won the presidential election in 1948 but would not have been eligible to run in 1952 had the amendment been in effect.

16. The U.S. Supreme Court upheld such statutes in *Gregory v. Ashcroft*, 501 U.S. 452. Lee Epstein, Jack Knight and Olga Shvetsova, "Comparing Judicial Selection Systems," 12. See also Melinda Gann Hall, "Voluntary Retirements from State Supreme Courts: Assesing Democratic Pressures to Relinquish the Bench," *Journal of Politics* 63 (4, 2001): 1112–1140.

17. The twenty-seven countries are: Albania, Armenia, Austria, Azerbaijan, Belarus, Czech Republic, Croatia, Estonia, France, Georgia, Germany, Hungary, Iceland, Ireland, Italy, Latvia, Lithuania, Macedonia, Malta, Moldova, Poland, Romania, Russia, Slovakia, Slovenia, and Ukraine. Lee Epstein, Jack Knight, and Olga Shvetsova, "Comparing Judicial Selection Systems," 17.

18. Michael Bohlander, "Criticizing Judges in Germany," in *Freedom of Expression and the Criticism of Judges: A Comparative Study of European Legal Standards,* ed., Michael K. Addo (Burlington, Vt.: Ashgate, 2000) 66.

19. Bill Bowring, "Criticizing Judges in Russia," in *Freedom of Expression and the Criticism of Judges: A Comparative Study of European Legal Standards,* ed., Michael K. Addo, 193.

20. J. Michael Rainer and Thomas Tschaler, "Recusing Judges in Austria," in *Freedom of Expression and the Criticism of Judges: A Comparative Study of European Legal Standards,* ed., Michael K. Addo, 79.

21. For a discussion of the civil code tradition and the common-law tradition in Western law, see generally Herbert Jacob, Edhard Blankenburg, Herbert M. Kritzer, Doris Marie Provine, and Joseph Sanders, *Courts, Law, and Politics in Comparative Per-*

spective (New Haven: Yale University Press, 1996) 3–6; John Henry Merryman, *The Civil Law Tradition*, 2d ed. (Stanford, CA: Stanford University Press, 1985); Henry J. Abraham, *The Judicial Process*, 6th ed. (New York: Oxford University Press, 1993), 7–16.

22. On selecting cases for comparison, see generally, John Stuart Mill, *A System of Logic: Ratiocinative and Inductive, Being a Connected View of the Principles of Evidence and the Methods of Scientific Investigation* (London: Longmans, Green and Co., 1911), 253–266.

23. Mary L. Volcansek and Jacqueline Lucienne Lafon, *Judicial Selection: The Cross-Evolution of French and American Practices* (New York: Greenwood Press, 1988), 47.

24. Mary L. Volcansek, Maria Elisabetta de Franciscis, and Jacqueline Lucienne Lafon, *Judicial Misconduct: A Cross-National Comparison* (Gainesville: University Press of Florida, 1996), 116. Helene Lambert, "Contempt of Court in French Law: A Criminal Offence," in *Freedom of Expression and the Criticism of Judges: A Comparative Study of European Legal Standards*, ed., Michael K. Addo, 122.

25. Abraham, *The Judicial Process*, 50. In 1852, mandatory retirement ages were fixed for all civil servants. A year later, pensions were added to the law. The minister of justice can also impose retirement. This happened following a 1987 case where a judge insulted the public prosecutor and other authorities. It is difficult to know exactly how many cases like this have occurred as details of such matters are kept private. For the most part, French judges are just as secure in their offices as British and American judges. Volcansek et al., *Judicial Misconduct*, 32, 46.

26. Annamaria di Ioia, "Criticizing Judges in Italy," in *Freedom of Expression and the Criticism of Judges: A Comparative Study of European Legal Standards*, ed., Michael K. Addo, 161.

27. Mary L. Volcansek et al., *Judicial Misconduct*, 49–62.

28. Giuseppe Di Federico, "La Selezione dei Magistrati: Prospettive Psicologiche," in C. Pedrazzi, ed., *Limiti ed Inefficacia della Selezione dei Magistrati* (Milan: Guiffre Editore, 1976), 16–21.

29. 1 Geo. III, 1007, ibid., 73–74.

30. "Address" has only been attempted seventeen times however in the past 200 years and only succeeded once. In 1829, an Irish judge of the High Court of Admiralty, Sir Jonah Barrington, was removed by address for being unfit and setting a bad example. In all seventeen cases, the charges were related to judicial misconduct and corruption, not infirmity.

In general, judges can be removed from office by the Lord Chancellor due to incapacity or misbehavior. As in France, the Lord Chancellor was given the power in 1981 to compel the retirements of disabled High Court judges. However he must have sufficient medical evidence to support his decision as well as the support of specific other senior judges in determining the infirmity. Lower court judges can be removed or compelled to retire for failure to comply with any of the requirements of their appointment. As a matter of practice, however, judges are rarely, if ever, removed from office. S. H. Bailey and M. J. Gunn, *Smith and Bailey on the Modern English Legal System* (London: Sweet & Maxwell, 1991), 221; Volcansek et al., *Judicial Misconduct,* 81.

31. Lower court judges in Britain generally enjoyed life tenure until the twentieth century. Beginning in the 1940s, laws were changed to force lower court judges to retire at age seventy-two. With the Supreme Court Act of 1981, higher court judges were required to depart at age seventy-five. Retirement benefits are calculated according to length of service with the maximum benefit being half of the annual salary after completing fifteen years of service. Bailey and Gunn, *Smith and Bailey on the Modern English Legal System,* 221; Herbert M. Kritzer, "Courts, Justice, and Politics in England," in Jacob et al., *Courts, Law, and Politics in Comparative Perspective,* 92; J. R. Spencer, *Jackson's Machinery of Justice* (Cambridge: Cambridge University Press, 1989), 371.

32. David Pannick, *Judges* (Oxford: Oxford University Press, 1987), 87.

33. Karren Orren and Stephen Skowronek, "Beyond the Iconography of Order: Notes for a 'New' Institutionalism," in *The Dynamics of American Politics: Approaches and Interpretations,* eds., Lawrence C. Dodd and Calvin Jillson (Boulder: Westview Press, 1994); Stephen Skowronek, "Order and Change," *Polity* 28 (1995): 91–96; Karen Orren, "Ideas and Institutions," *Polity* 28 (1995): 97–102; Karen Orren and Stephen Skowronek, "Regimes and Regime Building in American Government: A Review of Literature on the 1940s," *Political Science Quarterly* 113 (Winter 1998–1999): 689–702; Stephen Skowronek, *Building a New American State: The Expansion of National Administrative Capacities, 1877–1920* (Cambridge: Cambridge University Press, 1982); Rogers M. Smith, "Political Jurisprudence, the 'New Institutionalism,' and the Future of Public Law," *American Political Science Review* 82 (1988): 89–108. Stephen Skowronek, *The Politics Presidents Make: Leadership from John Adams to George Bush* (Cambridge, Mass.: Belknap, 1993). Theda Skocpol, *Protecting Soldiers and Mothers: The Political Origins of Social Policy in the United States* (Cambridge, MA: Belknap Press of Harvard University Press, 1992). Theda Skocpol, *Social Policy in the United States: Future Possibilities in Historical Perspective* (Princeton, N.J.: Princeton University Press, 1995).

34. For a discussion of the nature of American Political Regimes, see Eldon J. Eisenach, "Reconstituting the Study of American Political Thought in a Regime-Change Perspective," *Studies in American Political Development* 4 (1990) 169–228; Andrew J. Polsky, "The 1996 Elections and the Logic of Regime Politics," *Polity* 30 (Fall 1997): 153–157.

35. Orren and Skowronek, "Regimes and Regime Building in American Government," 693.

36. Ibid., 697, 701.

37. Economists have long held that the choice to retire is largely a function of income. See, for example, Ronald G. Ehrenberg and Robert S. Smith, *Modern Labor Economics: Theory and Public Policy,* 7th ed. (Reading, Mass.: Addison-Wesley, 2000), 241–245.

38. In retirement, justices may sit on any federal court other than the Supreme Court, at the discretion of the Chief Justice. For example, Justice Tom Clark, in addition to sitting on all the circuit courts of appeal, sat on trial courts, Lewis Powell occasionally heard cases before the U.S. Court of Appeals for the Fourth Circuit, and Stanley Reed sat on the Court of Claims.

39. John Blair to George Washington, October 25, 1795, Maeva Marcus, ed., *The Documentary History of the Supreme Court of the Unites States, 1789–1800* (New York: Columbia University Press, 1985–1990), vol. 1, 59.

40. Congress appointed the fifteen-member commission, specifying that it be composed of three Republicans and two Democrats from the Senate, two Republicans and three Democrats from the House, and two Democrats and two Republicans from the Supreme Court. The fifth justice was to be chosen from the Court itself. With Justices Nathan Clifford, Samuel F. Miller, Stephen J. Field, and William Strong chosen by Congress, the full Court selected Joseph Bradley. When the commission split down party lines, Bradley initially favored giving Florida's electoral votes to Tilden but under pressure from Republicans, he changed his mind and gave Florida and the election to Hayes.

CHAPTER 2

1. For a detailed accounting of the lives and work of the justices on circuit, see volumes 1–3 of *The Documentary History of the Supreme Court of the United States, 1789–1800*, Maeva Marcus, ed. (New York: Columbia University Press, 1985–1990). An excellent biographical source of the Court's earliest justices is Scott Douglas Gerber's *Seriatim: The Supreme Court Before John Marshall* (New York: New York University Press, 1998).

2. George Washington to Thomas Johnson, February 1, 1793, Edward S. Delaplaine, *The Life of Thomas Johnson* (New York: Hitchcock, 1927), 483.

3. Of course the "whole" terms were much briefer in these years. As compared to the nine consecutive months each year when the current Court meets, the early justices spent hardly any time together. For example, the Court's first formal meeting in New York on February 1, 1790 lasted ten days. Their second meeting in New York on August 2, 1790 lasted two days. Very few cases were heard during this time and most of the Court's business was admitting attorneys to the Supreme Court bar. This is not to say that the justices had little to do each year as they spent nearly all of their time traveling throughout their circuits.

4. George Washington to Dr. Stuart, February 1792, ibid., 478–479.

5. Bushrod Washington to James Iredell, August 20, 1799, Griffith J. McRee, *Life and Correspondence of James Iredell* (New York: D. Appleton & Co., 1857), Vol. 2, 588.

6. Samuel Chase to James Iredell, March 17, 1799, Marcus, ed., *The Documentary History of the Supreme Court of the United States, 1789–1800*, vol. 1, 873.

7. *Charleston Gazette,* December 1, 1795.

8. For a discussion of the federal judiciary, see generally Russell R. Wheeler and Cynthia Harrison, *Creating the Federal Judicial System,* 2d ed. (Washington, D.C.: Federal Judicial Center, 1994). See also *The Documentary History of the Supreme Court of the United States, 1789–1800,* Marcus, ed., vol. 2, 2.

9. Act of March 2, 1793, I Stat. 333.

10. It was not until 1875 that Congress granted federal question jurisdiction to the lower federal Courts. Richard S. Arnold, "Judicial Politics Under President Washington." *Arizona Law Review* 38 (Summer 1996): 475.

11. Nathanial Pendleton to James Iredell, March 19, 1792, McRee, *Life and Correspondence of James Iredell,* 344–345.

12. *New York Times,* December 24, 1865, Kermit Hall, "The Civil War Era as a Crucible for Nationalizing the Lower Federal Courts" (Fall 1975) Prologue, 177, 184.

13. From Randolph's 1790 pro and con analysis of the federal judicial system, p. 8, Felix Frankfurter and James M. Landis, *The Business of the Supreme Court: A Study in the Federal Judicial System* (New York: Macmillan, 1928), 19.

14. On the disconnect between Congress and the Court, see generally, Frankfurter and Landis, *The Business of the Supreme Court,* Ibid.

15. Bernard Schwartz, *A History of the Supreme Court* (New York: Oxford University Press, 1993), 18.

16. Samuel Chase to James Iredell, March 18, 1797, Jane Shaffer Elsmere, *Justice Samuel Chase* (Muncie, Ind.: Janevar Publishing Co., 1980), 74.

17. Schwartz, *A History of the Supreme Court,* 18.

18. Ibid.

19. John Jay to George Washington, September 13, 1790, Leonard Baker, *John Marshall: A Life in Law* (New York: Macmillan, 1974), 374. An additional argument given by the justices to be relieved from riding circuit was that they would occasionally be asked to decide cases twice—once in circuit and then again in the Supreme Court. This dual appointment, they argued, hampered the Court's legitimacy. *The Documentary History of the Supreme Court of the United States, 1789–1800,* vol. 2, Marcus, ed., 4.

20. Charles Warren, *The Supreme Court in United States History,* rev. ed. (Boston: Little Brown, 1926), Vol. 1, 86.

21. Frankfurter and Landis, *The Business of the Supreme Court,* 17.

22. George Washington to Robert Harrison, September 28, 1789, Marcus, ed., *The Documentary History of the Supreme Court of the United States, 1789–1900,* vol. 2, 35.

23. Robert Harrison to George Washington, October 27, 1789, Marcus, ed., *The Documentary History of the Supreme Court of the United States, 1789–1900,* vol. 2, 36.

24. The letter drafted by Washington mirrors a document authored by John Jay entitled "Remarks respecting Mr. Harrison's objections." George Washington to Robert Harrison, November 25, 1789, and Alexander Hamilton to Robert Harrison, November 27, 1789, Marcus, ed., *The Documentary History of the Supreme Court of the United States, 1789–1900*, vol. 2, 40–41.

25. Robert Harrison to George Washington, January 21, 1790, Marcus, *The Documentary History of the Supreme Court of the United States, 1789–1900*, vol. 1, 42. This letter in effect serves as Harrison's "resignation." Indeed, it was understood at the time that Harrison had "resigned." See, for example, Robert Morris to Gouverneur Morris, February 1, 1790; William Cushing to Charles Cushing, February 10, 1790; William Loughton Smith to Edward Rutledge, Marcus, ed., *The Documentary History of the Supreme Court of the United States, 1789–1800*, vol. 1, 686, 693, 695.

26. Thomas Johnson to George Washington, July 30, 1791, Marcus, ed., *The Documentary History of the Supreme Court of the United States, 1789–1800*, vol. 1, 74.

27. George Washington to Thomas Johnson, August 7, 1791, Delaplaine, *The Life of Thomas Johnson*, 475–476.

28. Thomas Johnson to James Wilson, March 1, 1792, Marcus, ed., *The Documentary History of the Supreme Court of the United States, 1789–1900*, vol. 1, 733–734.

29. Thomas Johnson to George Washington, January 16, 1793, Schwartz, *A History of the Supreme Court*, 19.

30. George Washington to Thomas Johnson, February 1, 1793, Delaplaine, *The Life of Thomas Johnson*, 482–483.

31. John Jay to George Washington April 30, 1794, *The Correspondence and Public Papers of John Jay 1763–1826*, Henry P. Johnston, ed. (New York: Da Capo Press, 1971), vol. 4, 9–10.

32. Ibid., 21.

33. John Jay to William Cushing, January 27, 1793, Marcus, ed., *The Documentary History of the Supreme Court of the United States, 1789–1800*, vol. 1, 737.

34. Schwartz, *A History of the Supreme Court*, 19. Jay nearly did not make it to New York to be sworn is as governor. James Iredell noted, "Mr. Jay was sworn in as Governor yesterday. He was in danger of dying on his passage, and does not look well now." James Iredell to Hannah Iredell, July 2, 1795, Marcus, ed., *The Documentary History of the Supreme Court of the United States, 1789–1800*, vol. 1, 760.

35. William Cushing to John Jay, June 18, 1795, *The Correspondence and Public Papers of John Jay 1763–1826*, Johnston ed., vol. 4, 176.

36. Ralph Izard to Jacob Read, November 17, 1795, Marcus, ed., *The Documentary History of the Supreme Court of the United States, 1789–1800*, vol. 1, 807–808.

37. The evidence of Rutledge's work on the Court suggests that Rutledge was capable and discharged the duties of his office, despite the allegations of a mental decline. See, for example, Marcus, ed., *The Documentary History of the Supreme Court of the United States, 1789–1800*, vol. 3, 71, 84–86.

38. For a detailed account of this event, see William Read to Jacob Read, December 29, 1795, Marcus, ed., *The Documentary History of the Supreme Court of the United States, 1789–1800,* vol. 1, 820–821; James Haw, *John and Edward Rutledge of South Carolina* (Athens, Ga.: Univeristy of Georgia Press, 1997) 257–258.

39. John Rutledge to George Washington, December 28, 1795, Marcus, ed., *The Documentary History of the Supreme Court of the United States, 1789–1800,* vol. 1, 100.

40. Temporary Commission from George Washington to John Rutledge, July 1, 1795, ibid., 96.

41. John Blair to Samuel Meredith, February 9, 1791, ibid., 717.

42. John Blair to William Cushing, June 12, 1795, ibid., 756.

43. John Blair to James Iredell, September 14, 1795, McRee, *Life and Correspondence of James Iredell,* Vol. 2, 455.

44. John Blair to James Iredell, October 10, 1795, ibid.

45. John Blair to George Washington, October 25, 1795, Marcus, ed., *The Documentary History of the Supreme Court of the United States, 1789–1800,* vol. 1, 59.

46. James Wilson to Bird Wilson September 6, 1797, Charles Page Smith, *James Wilson: Founding Father 1742–1798* (Chapell Hill: University of North Carolina Press, 1956), 384.

47. Samuel Johnston to James Iredell, July 28, 1798, McRee, *Life and Correspondence of James Iredell,* 532.

48. James Iredell to Hannah Iredell, McRee, *Life and Correspondence of James Iredell,* Vol. 2, 464.

49. James Iredell to Hannah Iredell, ibid., 573.

50. Samuel Johnston to James Iredell, June 30, 1799, ibid., 579.

51. Bushrod Washington to James Iredell, August 20, 1799, ibid., 588.

52. James Iredell to Hannah Iredell, February 9, 1797, Marcus, ed., *The Documentary History of the Supreme Court of the United States, 1789–1800,* vol. 1, 855.

53. Frederick Wolcott to Oliver Wolcott, Jr., January 23, 1798, ibid., 857.

54. Oliver Ellsworth to William Cushing, February 4, 1798, ibid., 857.

55. Oliver Ellsworth to Oliver Wolcott, Jr., October 16, 1800, ibid., 900.

56. Oliver Ellsworth to John Adams, October 16, 1800, ibid., 123.

57. John Adams to John Jay December 19, 1800, *The Correspondence and Public Papers of John Jay 1763–1826,* Johnston ed., Vol. 4, 284.

58. Theodore Sedgwick to Alexander Hamilton, December 17, 1800, Marcus, ed., *The Documentary History of the Supreme Court of the United States, 1789–1800,* vol. 1, 902. Sedgwick made a similar claim in a letter to Caleb Strong the same day.

59. John Adams to John Jay December 19, 1800, *The Correspondence and Public Papers of John Jay 1763–1826,* Johnston, ed., Vol. 4, 284. Interestingly, there was uni-

versal agreement at the time that Jay would never accept the appointment and that surely Adams must have known this since Jay made public his intention to retire from public life. See, for example, Oliver Wolcott, Jr., to Timothy Pickering, December 28, 1800; Robert Troup to Rufus King, December 31, 1800; Timothy Pickering to Rufus King, January 5, 1801, Marcus, ed., *The Documentary History of the Supreme Court of the United States, 1789–1800,* vol. 1, 911–913. Still, Adams was also known to make appointments without consulting other Federalists. See, for example, Jonas Platt to James Kent, January 16, 1801, ibid., 919n. There was also speculation that Adams meant either to appoint himself or to have the next president appoint him to the Chief Justiceship or some other post. See, for example, James McHenry to Oliver Wolcott, Jr., January 22, 1801; Abigail Adams to Thomas B. Adams, January 25, 1801, ibid., 919–920. But Adams denied this and pointed out that he had nominated John Marshall. John Adams to Elias Boudinot, January 26, 1801, ibid., 921–922.

60. Thomas Jefferson to James Madison, December 19, 1800, ibid., 904. See also, Richard D. Spaight to John G. Blount, January 13, 1801, ibid., 915.

61. Thomas Jefferson to James Madison, December 26, 1800, ibid., 908.

62. John Jay to John Adams, January 2, 1801, *The Correspondence and Public Papers of John Jay 1763–1826,* Johnston, ed., vol. 4, 285–286.

CHAPTER 3

1. David M. O'Brien, *Storm Center: The Supreme Court in American Politics,* 2d ed. (New York: W. W. Norton, 1990), 183.

2. Kathryn Turner, "Federalist Policy and the Judiciary Act of 1801," *William and Mary Quarterly* 22 (January 1965): 3–32.

3. Thomas Jefferson to John Dickinson, December 19, 1801, *The Writings of Thomas Jefferson,* Henry A. Washington, ed., (Washington, D.C.: 1903), 301.

4. Judiciary Act of February 13, 1801, 2 Stat. 89, "To Provide for the More Convenient Organization of the Courts of the United States."

5. Bernard Schwartz, *A History of the Supreme Court* (New York: Oxford University Press, 1993), 30. See generally Richard E. Ellis, *The Jeffersonian Crisis: Courts and Politics in the New Republic* (New York: Oxford University Press, 1971).

6. Repeal Act of March 5, 1802, 2 Stat. 132.

7. Judiciary Act of April 29, 1802, 2 Stat. 118, "To Amend the Judicial System of the United States." The Supreme Court upheld this act in *Stuart v. Laird,* 1 Cranch 299 (1803). See Felix Frankfurter and James M. Landis, *Business of the Supreme Court: A Study in the Federal Judicial System* (New York: Macmillan, 1928).

8. Leonard Baker, *John Marshall: A Life in Law* (New York: Macmillan, 1974), p. 378.

9. Schwartz, *A History of the Supreme Court,* 31.

10. 1 Cranch (5 U.S.) 137 (1803).

11. See Robert L. Clinton, *Marbury v. Madison and Judicial Review* (Lawrence: University Press of Kansas, 1989); Edward S. Corwin, *John Marshall and the Constitution: A Chronicle of the Supreme Court* (New Haven: Yale University Press, 1921); Charles Grove Haines, *The American Doctrine of Judicial Supremacy*, 2nd ed. (Berkeley: University of California Press, 1959).

12. 1 Cranch 299 (U.S. 1803).

13. See for example, Schwartz, *A History of the Supreme Court*, 30.

14. Baker, *John Marshall*, 558.

15. *Guide to the U.S. Supreme Court*, Elder Witt, ed. (Washington, D.C.: Congressional Quarterly Press, 1979), 754.

16. William Paterson to Cornelia Paterson, January 20, 1798, John E. O'Connor, *William Paterson: Lawyer and Statesman 1745–1806* (New Brunswick, N.J.: Rutgers University Press, 1979), 243.

17. William Paterson to Samuel Chase, February 1, 1804, ibid., 335.

18. William Paterson to Euphemia Paterson, February 3, 8, and 26, 1806, ibid., 276.

19. William Paterson to William Gibbon, May 21, 1806, ibid., 278.

20. Samuel Chase to Hannah Chase, February 4, 1800, Marcus, ed., *The Documentary History of the Supreme Court of the Unites States, 1789–1800*, vol. 1, 888.

21. Samuel Chase to Hannah Giles Chase, January 4, 1800, Jane Shaffer Elsmere, *Justice Samuel Chase* (Muncie, Indiana: Janevar Publishing Co., 1980), 92–93.

22. Joseph Story to Samuel P. P. Fay, 1807, Neil Strawser, *The Early Life of Samuel Chase* (M.A. Thesis, George Washington University, 1958), 10.

23. George Read to Caesar A. Rodney, November 3, 29, 1807, Elsmere, *Justice Samuel Chase*, 309.

24. *Life and Letters of Joseph Story*, Story, ed., Vol. 1, 499.

25. Joseph Story to Thomas Todd, March 14, 1823, ibid., 422.

26. Horace Binney, *Bushrod Washington* (Philadelphia: C. Sherman and Son, 1858), 24–25.

27. Report by William McKinley to Congress, 1838, Felix Frankfurter and James M. Landis, *The Business of the Supreme Court: A Study in the Federal Judicial System* (New York: Macmillan, 1928), 49–50.

28. 14 Howard iii (U.S. 1852).

29. For a discussion of Baldwin's "derangement" see David J. Garrow, "Mental Decrepitude on the U.S. Supreme Court: The Historical Case for a Twenty-eighth Amendment," *University of Chicago Law Review* 67 (4, Fall 2000): 1001–1003.

30. Act of Sept. 23, 1789, Sections 21, 22, I Stat. 83–85. See also, Richard Barry, *Mr. Rutledge of South Carolina* (New York: Duell, Sloan and Pearce, 1942), 353.

31. Manuscript of Joseph Story for Charles Pinkney, 1816, *Life and Letters of Joseph Story,* W. W. Story, ed., (Boston: Little Brown, 1851), Vol. 1, 302.

32. Baker, *John Marshall,* 558.

33. James Moore Wayne to Benjamin R. Curtis, September 21, 1857, Richard H. Leach, "Benjamin Robbins Curtis: Judicial Misfit," *The New England Quarterly* 25 (December 1952): 515.

34. *Congressional Globe,* 33rd Congress, 2nd Session, 42 (December 13, 1854).

35. *Scott v. Sandford,* 60 U.S. 393 (1857).

36. Benjamin R. Curtis to George Ticknor, July 3, 1857, Benjamin R. Curtis, Jr., *A Memoir of Benjamin Robbins Curtis, LL.D.* (Boston: Little Brown & Co., 1879), 247–248.

37. John A. Campbell to Benjamin R. Curtis, September 3, 1857, Henry G. Connor, *John Archibald Campbell: Associate Justice of the United States Supreme Court 1853–1861* (New York: Da Capo Press, 1971), 81.

38. Lynn W. Turner, *William Plumer of New Hampshire, 1759–1850* (Chapel Hill: University of North Carolina Press, 1962), 154–155.

39. William Plumer to Jeremiah Mason, January 14, 1804, ibid., 155.

40. John Stephenson to Moses Rawlings, January 6, 1804, ibid.

41. *Evening Post* (New York), March 9, 1805.

42. Smith Thompson to Bushrod Washington, September 16, 1828, Donald M. Roper, "Justice Smith Thompson: Politics and the New York Supreme Court in the Early Nineteenth Century," *New York Historical Society Quarterly,* 51 (April, 1967): 119–139.

43. Lee Benson, *The Concept of Jacksonian Democracy: New York as a Test Case* (New York, 1964), 31.

44. Daniel Webster to Nathan Hale, September 5, 1831, *The Papers of Daniel Webster: Correspondence, V.3 1830–1834,* Charles M. Wiltse, ed. (Hanover, New Hampshire: University Press of New England, 1977), 120–121.

45. Donald G. Morgan, *Justice William Johnson: The First Dissenter* (Columbia: University of South Carolina Press, 1954), 280–281.

46. William Johnson to Thomas Jefferson, December 12, 1822, ibid., 181–182.

47. William Johnson to Thomas Jefferson, December 12, 1822, ibid., 182.

48. Thomas Jefferson to William Johnson, March 4, 1823, ibid., 183.

49. Charles Grove Haines, *The Role of the Supreme Court in Government and Politics, 1789–1835* (New York: Russell & Russell, 1944), 514–523.

50. Thomas Jefferson to James Madison, June 13, 1823, Morgan, *Justice William Johnson,* 185.

51. James Madison to Thomas Jefferson, June 27, 1823, ibid.

52. Daniel Webster to Warren Dutton, January 4, 1833, *The Papers of Daniel Webster, vol. 3,* Wiltse, ed., 205.

53. William Plumer to William Smith, February 17, 1796, Charles Page Smith, *James Wilson: Founding Father 1742–1798* (Chapell Hill: University of North Carolina Press, 1956), 376.

54. David Howell to James Madison, November 26, 1810, Charles Warren, *The Supreme Court in United States History, Vol. I, 1789–1835,* rev. ed. (Boston, Mass.: Little Brown & Co., 1922, 6), 400.

55. John D. Cushing, "A Revolutionary Conservative: The Public Life of William Cushing, 1732–1810" (Ph.D. diss., Clark University, 1959), 327. See also Scott Douglas Gerber, "Deconstructing William Cushing," in Scott Douglas Gerber, ed., *Seriatim: The Supreme Court before John Marshall* (New York: New York University Press, 1998), 97.

56. Charles Fairman, "The Retirement of Federal Judges," *Harvard Law Review* 51 (1938): 406.

57. Samuel Tyler, *Memoir of Roger Brooke Taney* (Baltimore: John Murphy & Co., 1872), 239.

58. John Marshall to Benjamin Watkins Leigh, undated 1835, ibid., 240.

59. Ibid., 239–242.

60. John Marshall to Joseph Story, Baker, *John Marshall,* 764.

61. John Marshall to Richard Peters, April 30, 1835, ibid., 766.

62. Ibid., 764; *Niles' Weekly Register,* February 16, 1833, 403.

63. Joseph Story to Richard Peters, May 20, 1835, *Life and Letters of Joseph Story,* Story, ed., vol. 2, 194.

64. Joseph Story to Chancellor Kent, June 26, 1837, Fairman, "The Retirement of Federal Judges," 413–414.

65. Joseph Story to Rev. John Brazer, April 2, 1845, *Life and Letters of Joseph Story,* Story, ed., vol. 2, 525–526.

66. Joseph Story to Ezekiel Bacon, April 12, 1845, ibid., 527–528.

67. Ibid., 547.

68. *Philadelphia, Wilmington, and Baltimore Railroad v. Quigley,* 21 Howard 202 (1859).

69. John A. Campbell to Joseph P. Bradley, December 8, 1883, Fairman, "The Retirement of Federal Judges," 416.

70. John A. Campbell to H. Ballentine, May 22, 1861, Connor, *John Archibald Campbell,* 149.

71. Roger B. Taney to David M. Perine, August 6, 1863, Tyler, *Memoir of Roger Brooke Taney,* 454.

72. Roger B. Taney to S. Teackle Wallis, March 20, 1864, ibid., 459.

73. Address before the U.S. Supreme Court by Benjamin R. Curtis, December 7, 1864, ibid., 509–516.

74. *The Diary of Edward Bates*, Howard K. Beale, ed. (Washington, D.C.: U.S. Government Printing Office, 1933), 358.

CHAPTER 4

1. David M. O'Brien, *Storm Center: The Supreme Court in American Politics*, 2d ed. (New York: W. W. Norton, 1990), 183.

2. Judiciary Act of 1866, 14 Stat. 209 (1866).

3. Kermit L. Hall, "Judiciary Act of 1866," *Oxford Companion to the Supreme Court of the United States*, Kermit L. Hall, ed. (New York: Oxford, 1992), 475.

4. Stanley I. Kutler, *Judicial Power and Reconstruction Politics* (Chicago: University of Chicago Press, 1968), 114.

5. 4 Wall. 2 (U.S. 1866).

6. *Cong. Globe*, 39th Cong., 2d sess. 251.

7. 7 Wall. 506 (U.S. 1869).

8. *Cong. Globe*, 40th Cong., 2nd sess. 489.

9. Technically, the statute provided benefit after "resignation" and did not mention "retirement." Sill, these words were often used interchangeably and the word *retirement* came to be used to denote departure with salary. The 1869 statute reads: "Any judge of any court of the United States, who, having held his commission as such at least ten years, shall, after having attained the age of seventy years, resign his office, shall thereafter, during the residue of his natural life, receive the same salary which was by law payable to him at the time of his resignation." 16 Stat. 44 (1869).

10. Hall, "Judiciary Act of 1869," 475.

11. Robert C. Grier to Nathan Clifford, August 9, 1862, Charles Fairman, "The Retirement of Federal Judges," *Harvard Law Review* 51 (1938): 416.

12. *Cong. Globe*, 41st Cong., 2nd sess. (June 1, 1870), 3973.

13. Robert C. Grier to Salmon P. Chase, October 22, 1866, Fairman, "The Retirement of Federal Judges," 417.

14. David J. Danelski, "A Supreme Court Justice Steps Down," *The Yale Review* 54 (1965): 411.

15. *League v. Atchison*, 6 U.S. (1868), 112.

16. Samuel Miller to William P. Ballinger, January 19, 1868, Fairman, "The Retirement of Federal Judges," 417.

17. See generally, Edwin C. Surrency, *History of the Federal Courts* (New York: Oceana Publications, 1987).

18. *Cong. Globe,* 41st Cong., 1st sess. (March 29, 1869), 337–338.

19. 16 Stat. 44.

20. *Cong. Globe,* 41st Cong., 1st sess. (March 29, 1869), 344.

21. Ibid., 337.

22. Ibid., 574.

23. *American Law Review* 24 (1890): 321, 462.

24. Howard K. Beale, ed. *The Diary of Edward Bates 1859–1866* (Washington: Government Printing Office, 1933), 322.

25. Proceedings of the New York State Bar Association, II (1878), p. 39, Charles Fairman, *Mr. Justice Miller and the Supreme Court 1862–1890* (Cambridge: Harvard University Press, 1939), 380.

26. George Harding to Joseph P. Bradley, July 19, 1869, Fairman "The Retirement of Federal Judges," 417–418.

27. George Harding to Joseph P. Bradley, November 17, 1869, ibid., 418.

28. *Hepburn v. Griswold,* 75 U.S. 603 (1870); *Knox v. Lee* and *Parker v. Davis,* 79 U.S. 457 (1871).

29. Fairman, "The Retirement of Federal Judges," 418.

30. It is unclear exactly which justices attended this meeting with Grier. See Charles Alan Wright, "Authenticity of 'A Dirtier Day's Work' Quote in Question," *Supreme Court Historical Society Quarterly,* 13 (4, Winter 1990): 6–7; David N. Atkinson, *Leaving the Bench: Justices at the End* (Lawrence, Kans.: University Press of Kansas, 1999), 183–187.

31. Mrs. Beck to George Harding, December 9, 1869, ibid., 418.

32. Salmon P. Chase to Richard C. Parsons, September 26, 1870, Robert B. Warden, *An Account of the Private Life and Public Services of Salmon Portland Chase* (Cincinnati: Wilstach, Baldwin & Co., 1874), 720.

33. Salmon P. Chase to Richard C. Parsons, September 26, 1870, ibid., 719–720.

34. Samuel Miller to William P. Ballinger, November 6, 1870, Fairman "The Retirement of Federal Judges," 419–420.

35. Albert B. Hall, *Salmon Portland Chase* (Boston: Houghton Mifflin, 1899), 413.

36. Salmon P. Chase to Murat Halstead, May 30, 1872, Warden, *An Account of the Private Life and Public Services of Salmon Portland Chase,* 735.

37. Salmon P. Chase to Richard C. Parsons, May 4, 1873, in Jacob W. Schuckers, *The Life and Public Services of Salmon Portland Chase* (New York: D. Appleton, 1874), 623.

38. For a discussion of the similarities and differences between the 2000 election and the elections of 1800, 1824, 1876, 1888, 1916, and 1960, see Arthur Schlesinger, Jr., "It's a Mess, but We've Been Through It Before: A Popular Majority Was Frustrated Three Times in the Past. Democracy Survived," *Time,* November 13, 2000.

39. Though Republicans had a majority in both houses of Congress in 2000, the 2001 Senate was split 50–50. Because Al Gore was still Vice President in the new Congress until the swearing in of the new President, he would have cast any tie vote in that body. As such, the effect of a divided Congress was the same as in 1876.

40. David Davis to Julius Rockwell, August 18, 1875, Willard L. King, *Lincoln's Manager David Davis* (Cambridge, Mass.: Harvard University Press, 1960), 287.

41. L. G. Fisher to David Davis, March 24, 1874, ibid.

42. Ibid., 290–294.

43. George W. Paschal, *The Constitution of the United States Defined and Carefully Annotated* (Washington, 1868), 193 mistakenly lists Campbell as born in 1802 when in fact, he was born June 24, 1811.

44. Samuel Miller to William P. Ballinger, March, 1877, Fairman, "The Retirement of Federal Judges," 421.

45. 96 U.S. 232 (1878).

46. Letter from Nathan Clifford to Morrison R. Waite, January 27, 1878, Peter C. Magrath, *Morrison R. Waite: The Triumph of Character* (New York: Macmillan, 1963), 261.

47. Fairman, "The Retirement of Federal Judges," 422.

48. Ibid., 424–425.

49. Samuel Miller to William P. Ballinger, November, 1880, ibid., 423.

50. Morrison R. Waite to Samuel M. Young, November 5, 1880, Bruce R. Trimble, *Chief Justice Waite: Defender of the Public Interest* (Princeton: Princeton University Press, 1938), 272.

51. Fairman, "The Retirement of Federal Judges," 424.

52. Ibid.

53. Samuel Miller to William P. Ballinger, December 25, 1880, ibid.

54. Magrath, *Morrison R. Waite*, 268.

55. Noah Swayne to Joseph Bradley, 1880, ibid.

56. Jonathan Lurie, "Noah Haynes Swayne," *The Oxford Companion to the Supreme Court of the United States*, 850–851.

57. Philip G. Clifford, *Nathan Clifford, Democrat: 1803–1881* (New York: Putnam, 1922), 342.

58. Samuel Miller to William P. Ballinger, November 28, 1880, Fairman, *Mr. Justice Miller and the Supreme Court*, 378.

59. Morrison R. Waite to Ward Hunt, Jr., October 26, 1879, Trimble, *Chief Justice Waite*, 264.

60. 13 *Cong. Rec.* 613–614 (1882).

61. Act of January 27, 1882, 22 Stat. 2.

62. Samuel Miller to William P. Ballinger, May 16, 1886, Fairman, *Mr. Justice Miller and the Supreme Court*, 388.

63. The Circuit Court of Appeals Act of March 3, 1891, 26 Stat. 826.

64. Act of March 3, 1911, Section 301, 36 Stat. 1087, 1169.

65. Though Lamar was intermittently ill throughout his life, he was an active member of the Court up until the Spring of 1892 when he suffered a disabling stroke. He was absent from the Court for the first part of the 1892–1893 term before his death came on January 23, 1893. James B. Murphy, *L. Q. C. Lamar: Pragmatic Patriot* (Baton Rouge: Louisiana State University Press, 1973), 269–270. Justice Jackson died in August 1895 after only two and a half years on the Court. Jackson was plagued by tuberculosis during his brief tenure and missed a number of important decisions as a result. Henry A. Abraham, *Justices and Presidents: A Political History of Appointments to the Supreme Court*, 2d ed. (New York: Oxford University Press, 1985), 151.

66. Christopher C. Waite to Morrison R. Waite, November 26, 1874, Peter C. Magrath, *Morrison R. Waite: The Triumph of Character* (New York: Macmillan, 1963), 268

67. Morrison R. Waite to Amelia Waite, November 13, 1881, ibid.

68. Samuel Miller to William P. Ballinger, January 18, 1885, Fairman, *Mr. Justice Miller and the Supreme Court*, 391.

69. Christopher C. Waite to Morrison R. Waite, February 5, 1885, Magrath, *Morrison R. Waite*, 274.

70. Samuel F. Miller to Morrison R. Waite, January 14 and February 18, 1885, ibid.

71. Samuel Blatchford to Morrison R. Waite, February 15, 1885, ibid.

72. 126 U.S. 1 (1888).

73. Augustus H. Garland, *Experience in the Supreme Court of the United States* (Washington: J. Byrne and Company, 1898), 35–36.

74. Samuel Miller to William P. Ballinger, December 5, 1875, Fairman, *Mr. Justice Miller and the Supreme Court*, 373–374.

75. Samuel Miller to William P. Ballinger, June 10, 1880, in Fairman, *Mr. Justice Miller and the Supreme Court*, 390.

76. Fairman "The Retirement of Federal Judges," 426.

77. Samuel Miller to William P. Ballinger, October 13, 1885, Fairman, *Mr. Justice Miller and the Supreme Court*, 391–392.

78. Diary entry of William P. Ballinger, April 4, 1886, ibid., 392.

79. Samuel Miller to William P. Ballinger, July 18, 1886, ibid.

80. Samuel Miller to William P. Ballinger, February 13, 1887, ibid.

81. Samuel Miller to Samuel Treat, February 27, 1887, ibid.

82. Circuit Judges McKennan and Butler to Joseph P. Bradley, January 27, 1885, Fairman "The Retirement of Federal Judges," 427.

83. Joseph P. Bradley to Circuit Judges McKennan and Butler, January 29, 1885, ibid.

84. Ibid., 426.

CHAPTER 5

1. Carl B. Swisher, *Stephen J. Field: Craftsman of the Law* (Chicago: University of Chicago Press, Phoenix Edition 1969), 440.

2. Field began to mentally decline as early as 1892. See Garrow, "Mental Decrepitude on the U.S. Supreme Court," 1008–11.

3. Stephen J. Field to Melville Weston Fuller, March 8, 1896, King, *Melville Weston Fuller*, 224.

4. Stephen M. White to W. H. Grant, July 22, 1896, Swisher, *Stephen J. Field*, 442.

5. Charles Evans Hughes, *The Supreme Court of the United States* (New York: Columbia University Press, 1928), 75–6.

6. Stephen M. White to S. C. Houghton, Swisher, *Stephen J. Field*, 444.

7. Stephen J. Field to Melville Weston Fuller, May 3, 1897, King, *Melville Weston Fuller*, 225. Only the signature is in Field's handwriting.

8. Melville Weston Fuller to Stephen J. Field, May 4, 1897, ibid., 225–226.

9. David J. Brewer to Melville Weston Fuller, August 21, 1897, ibid., 226.

10. John Marshall Harlan to Melville Weston Fuller, October 4, 1897, ibid., 227.

11. Melville Weston Fuller to Mary Ellen Fuller, October 4, 1897, ibid., 226.

12. 168 U.S. appendix.

13. Gray wrote Chief Justice Fuller, "I have a bad cold again not so serious as last time but enough to have Dr. Johnston think it very unwise for me to go out of the house today." Horace Gray to Melville Weston Fuller, December 18, 1898, King, *Melville Weston Fuller*, 245.

14. This does not include Stephen J. Field who retired in December 1897. For a breakdown of majority opinion output during the Fuller Court, ibid., 339.

15. Ibid., 278.

16. John E. Semonche, "Horace Gray," *The Oxford Companion to the Supreme Court of the United States*, 346.

17. George Shiras, Jr., to James M. Whiton, undated, in George Shiras III, *Justice George Shiras, Jr. of Pittsburgh* (Pittsburgh: University of Pittsburgh Press, 1953), 197.

18. Brown went from an average of thirty-one majority opinions a year through 1902 to only twelve opinions in 1903, eighteen in 1904, and fifteen in 1905. King, *Melville Weston Fuller*, 339.

19. Henry B. Brown to Charles A. Kent, February 20, 1908, in Charles A. Kent, *A Memoir of Henry Billings Brown* (New York: Duffield and Company, 1915), 32.

20. The four Justices Brown is referring to who "lost their minds" while on the bench were Justices Baldwin, Grier, Clifford, and Field. The four who exhibited no such symptoms were Curtis, Campbell, Davis, and Strong.

21. The three Justices were Brewer, Fuller, and Harlan who all died on the Bench after retirement eligibility.

22. Henry B. Brown to Charles A. Kent, February 20, 1908, Kent, *A Memoir of Henry Billings Brown*, 95–96.

23. In Peckham's last year on the bench, he authored seventeen opinions of the Court. The year before, he wrote twenty majority opinions and averaged twenty-two opinions in the previous years. King, *Melville Weston Fuller*, 339.

24. George W. Wickersham to William Howard Taft, October 13, 1909, Robert B. Highsaw, *Edward Douglass White: Defender of the Conservative Faith* (Baton Rouge: Louisiana Stat University Press, 1981), 181.

25. Unsigned, undated, and incomplete letter to "Dear Girls," probably from one of Justice Brewer's sisters, in Michael J. Brodhead, *David J. Brewer: The Life of a Supreme Court Justice 1837–1910* (Carbondale: Southern Illinois University Press, 1994), 181.

26. Address by David J. Brewer, Thirty-third Annual Meeting of the Association of Agents of the Nothwestern Mutual Life Insurance Company, July 21, 1909, ibid., 182.

27. *Kansas City Journal*, June 3, 1907.

28. Brewer averaged twenty-five Court opinions through 1906. He authored only fourteen in 1907, eighteen in 1908, and twelve in 1909. For a breakdown of majority opinion output during the Fuller Court, King, *Melville Weston*, 339.

29. William Howard Taft to Horace Lurton, Henry F. Pringle, *Life and Times of William Howard Taft*, vol. 1 (New York: Farrar and Rhinehart, 1939), 529–530.

30. Melville Weston Fuller to Grover Cleveland, January 2, 1893, King, *Melville Weston Fuller*, 165–166.

31. *Washington Star*, January 14, 1903; *Chicago Tribune*, February 6, 1903; *Chicago Chronicle*, February 8, 1903.

32. Oliver Wendell Holmes, Jr., to Sir Frederick Pollock, May 17, 1925, Mark D. Howe, ed., *Holmes-Pollock Letters: The Correspondence of Mr. Justice Holmes and Sir Frederick Pollock 1874–1932*, vol. 2 (Cambridge: Harvard University Press, 1941), 161.

33. Grover Cleveland to William L. Putnam, March 6, 1903, King, *Melville Weston Fuller*, 304.

34. William L. Putnam to Melville Weston Fuller, April 6, 1903, ibid., 304–305.

35. Grover Cleveland to Melville Weston Fuller, April 12, 1903, ibid., 305.

36. William Howard Taft to Mrs. Taft, July 10, 1905, ibid., 307.

37. Melville Weston Fuller to Oliver Wendell Holmes, Jr., March 20, 1906, ibid.

38. S. S. Gregory to Melville Weston Fuller, November 30, 1906, ibid.

39. Grover Cleveland to Melville Weston Fuller, March 24, 1907, ibid., 308.

40. George Shiras to Melville Weston Fuller, March 5, 1908, ibid.

41. Elihu Root to Willard Bartlett, June 16, 1908, ibid.

42. William Howard Taft to Horace Lurton, May 22, 1909, ibid., 309.

43. Oliver Wendell Holmes, Jr., to Baroness Moncheur, July 14, 1910, ibid., 310.

44. Oliver Wendell Holmes, Jr., to William Le Baron Putnam July 1910, in Harry C. Shriver, ed., *Justice Oliver Wendell Holmes: His Book Notices and Uncollected Letters and Papers* (New York: Central Book Co., 1936), 132.

45. John Marshall Harlan to William Howard Taft, November 13, 1892, in Loren P. Beth, *John Marshall Harlan: The Last Great Whig Justice* (Lexington: University Press of Kentucky, 1992), 173.

46. John Marshall Harlan to Augustus Willson, March 13, 1893, ibid., 172.

47. Gray wrote Fuller that day about a bad cold he had come down with.

48. John Marshall Harlan to Melville Weston Fuller, December 18, 1897, King, *Melville Weston Fuller,* 245.

49. John Marshall Harlan to Augustus Willson, September 25, 1906, Beth, *John Marshall Harlan,* 172–173.

50. William Howard Taft to William H. Moody, August 3, 1906, ibid., 173.

51. William Howard Taft to William H. Moody, August 30, 1906, ibid.

52. John Marshall Harlan to Augustus Willson, June 16, 1907, ibid.

53. Tinsley E. Yarbrough, *Judicial Enigma: The First Justice Harlan* (New York: Oxford University Press, 1995), 222.

54. Joseph R. Lamar to Edward D. White, September 1915, Clarinda P. Lamar, *The Life of Joseph Rucker Lamar: 1857–1916* (New York: G. P. Putnam's Sons, 1926), 276–277.

55. Charles Evans Hughes to Elihu Root, June 21, 1912, Merlo J. Pusey, *Charles Evans Hughes,* Vol. 1 (New York: Macmillan, 1951), 301.

56. Charles Evans Hughes to Edward C. Stokes, June 2, 1916, ibid., 316.

57. William Howard Taft to Charles Evans Hughes, April 11, 1916, ibid., 317–319.

58. Charles Evans Hughes autobiographical notes, 1945, ibid., 323.

59. Ibid.

60. Ibid., 324.

61. Charles Evans Hughes interview with Merlo J. Pusey, January 7, 1946, ibid.

62. Charles Evans Hughes to the Republican National Convention, June 10, 1916, ibid., 332.

63. Oliver Wendell Holmes, Jr., to Sir Frederick Pollock, July 12, 1916, Howe, ed., *Holmes-Pollock Letter,* vol. 1, 237.

64. William R. Day to Charles Evans Hughes, June 1916, Pusey, *Charles Evans Hughes,* vol. 1, 333.

65. Charles Evans Hughes to Joseph Buffington, June 1916, ibid.

66. Oliver Wendell Homes, Jr., to Patrick Augustine Sheehan, December 15, 1912, David H. Burton, *Holmes-Sheehan Correspondence: Letters of Justice Oliver Wendell Holmes, Jr. and Canon Patrick Augustine Sheehan,* revised ed. (New York: Fordham University Press, 1993), 78.

67. Sir Frederick Pollock to Oliver Wendell Holmes, Jr., January 9, 1914, Howe, ed., *Holmes-Pollock Letters,* vol. 1, 211.

68. Highsaw, *Edward Douglass White,* 186.

69. William Howard Taft to Gus J. Karger, March 26, 1921, ibid.

70. Oliver Wendell Holmes, Jr., to Sir Frederick Pollock, May 18, 1921, Howe, ed., *Holmes-Pollock Letters,* vol. 2, 68.

71. Oliver Wendell Holmes, Jr., to Harold J. Laski, May 27, 1921, Howe, Mark DeWolfe, ed., *Holmes-Laski Letters: The Correspondence of Mr. Justice Holmes and Harold J. Laski, 1916–1935,* 2 vols. (Cambridge, Mass.: Harvard University Press, 1953), vol. 1, 338–339.

72. Oliver Wendell Holmes, Jr., to Sir Frederick Pollock, February 24, 1923, Howe, ed., *Holmes-Pollock Letters,* vol. 2, 113–114.

73. John Hessin Clarke to William Howard Taft, August 31, 1922; Willis Van Devanter to William Howard Taft, September 10, 1922, in Holt L. Warner, *The Life of Mr. Justice Clarke: A Testament to the Power of Liberal Dissent in America* (Cleveland: Case Western Reserve University, 1959), 113.

74. William Howard Taft to Horace Taft, September 7, 1922, ibid.

75. Ibid.

76. 260 U.S. vi (1922).

77. John Hessin Clarke to Warren G. Harding, September 1, 1922, Warner, *The Life of Mr. Justice Clarke,* 112.

78. William Howard Taft to John Hessin Clarke, September 5, 1922, in C. Wittke, "Mr. Justice Clarke: A Supreme Court Judge in Retirement," *Mississippi Valley Historical Review* 36 (1950): 34.

79. Woodrow Wilson to John Hessin Clarke, September 5, 1922, Warner, *The Life of Mr. Justice Clarke,* 115.

80. John Hessin Clarke to William R. Day, October 31, 1922, ibid., 113.

81. John Hessin Clarke to William Howard Taft, October 31, 1922, Wittke, "Mr. Justice Clarke: A Supreme Court Judge in Retirement," 33.

82. Ibid., 35.

83. William Howard Taft to Learned Hand, November 9, 1922, Pringle, *Life and Times of William Howard Taft*, vol. 2, 1057.

84. *New York Times*, July 10, 1923.

85. Alpheus T. Mason, *William Howard Taft: Chief Justice* (New York: Simon and Schuster, 1965), 213.

86. S. 4025, 67th Cong., 3d sess., 63 *Cong. Rec.* 272 (1922).

87. Oliver Wendell Holmes, Jr., to Sir Frederick Pollock, February 24, 1923, Howe, ed., *Holmes-Pollock Letters*, vol. 2, 113.

88. Oliver Wendell Holmes, Jr., to Sir Frederick Pollock, December 12, 1924, ibid., 150.

89. For a complete discussion of Douglas's departure, see chapter 8.

90. David J. Danelski, "A Supreme Court Justice Steps Down," *The Yale Review* 54 (1965): 414.

91. 257 U.S. 312 (1921).

92. Danelski, "A Supreme Court Justice Steps Down," 415.

93. 261 U.S. 525 (1923).

94. 243 U.S. 426 (1917).

95. William Howard Taft to Charles D. Hilles, September 9, 1922, Pringle, *Life and Times of William Howard Taft*, Vol. 2, 1059.

96. William Howard Taft to Horace Taft, April 17, 1922, ibid., 968.

97. Danelski, "A Supreme Court Justice Steps Down," 417.

98. Ibid., 418.

99. Ibid., 419.

100. Ibid.

101. Ibid.

102. Ibid., 421.

103. Ibid., 424.

104. Ibid., 425.

105. William Howard Taft to Horace Taft, April 27, 1923, Pringle, *Life and Times of William Howard*, vol. 2, 1073.

106. Ibid.

107. Danelski, "A Supreme Court Justice Steps Down," 417.

108. William Howard Taft to C. C. Jobes, December 27, 1924, Pringle, *Life and Times of William Howard Taft*, vol. 2, 1073.

109. William Howard Taft to Robert A. Taft, February 15, 1925, ibid., 1074.

110. William Howard Taft to R. W. Moore, April 19, 1928, ibid., 1077.

111. William Howard Taft to Jacob M. Dickinson, December 12, 1928, ibid., 1074.

112. William Howard Taft to Edward T. Sanford, July 4, 1929 ibid., 1077.

113. 280 U.S. 71, 173, 183.

114. William Howard Taft to Horace Taft, November 14, 1929, Pringle, *Life and Times of William Howard Taft*, vol. 2, 967.

115. Ibid.

116. Oliver Wendell Homes, Jr., to Patrick Augustine Sheehan, December 15, 1912, Burton, *Holmes-Sheehan Correspondence*, 77–78.

117. Oliver Wendell Homes, Jr., to Harold J. Laski, October 30, 1921, Howe, ed., *Holmes-Laski Letters*, vol. 1, 378.

118. Oliver Wendell Holmes, Jr. to Sir Frederick Pollock, March 29, 1922, Howe, ed., *Holmes-Pollock Letters*, vol. 2, 92.

119. Danelski, "A Supreme Court Justice Steps Down," 415.

120. William Howard Taft to Helen Manning, June 11, 1923, Pringle, *Life and Times of William Howard Taft*, vol. 2, 969.

121. Oliver Wendell Homes, Jr., to Harold J. Laski, February 13, 1924, Howe, ed., *Holmes-Laski Letters*, vol. 1, 591.

122. Harold J. Laski to Oliver Wendell Homes, Jr., February 24, 1924, ibid., 594.

123. Oliver Wendell Homes, Jr., to Harold J. Laski, March 9, 1924, ibid., 598.

124. 208 U.S. 161 (1908); 236 U.S. 1 (1915); Harold J. Laski to Oliver Wendell Homes, Jr., November 26, 1924, Howe, ed., *Holmes-Laski Letters*, vol. 1, 678.

125. Charles Evans Hughes, *The Supreme Court of the United States* (New York: Columbia University Press, 1928), 76.

126. Harold J. Laski to Oliver Wendell Homes, Jr., August 18, 1928, Howe, ed., *Holmes-Laski Letters*, vol. 2, 1086.

127. Oliver Wendell Holmes, Jr., to Felix Frankfurter, January 27, 1931, in Robert M. Mennel and Christine L. Compston, eds. *Holmes and Frankfurter: Their Correspondence, 1912–1934* (Hanover: University Press of New England, 1996), xxvii.

128. G. Edward White, *Justice Oliver Wendell Holmes: Law and the Inner Self* (New York: Oxford University Press, 1993), 458.

129. Oliver Wendell Homes, Jr., to Lewis Einstein, October 9, 1931, James Bishop Peabody, ed., *The Holmes-Einstein Letters: Correspondence of Mr. Justice Holmes and Lewis Einstein 1903–1935* (New York: St. Martin's Press, 1964), 330.

130. Charles Evans Hughes autobiographical notes, 1945, White, *Justice Oliver Wendell Holmes*, 466.

131. H. Chapman Rose interview with John Monagan, September 17, 1980, ibid., 466–467.

132. Oliver Wendell Homes, Jr., to Lewis Einstein, January 3, 1932, Peabody, ed., *The Holmes-Einstein Letters*, 335.

133. Charles Evans Hughes autobiographical notes, 1945, White, *Justice Oliver Wendell Holmes*, 467.

134. Charles Evans Hughes autobiographical notes, 1945, ibid.

135. Charles Evans Hughes interview with Merlo Pusey, January 7, 1946, Pusey, *Charles Evans Hughes*, vol. 2, 681.

136. Charles Evans Hughes autobiographical notes, 1945, White, *Justice Oliver Wendell Holmes*, 467.

137. H. Chapman Rose interview with John Monagan, September 17, 1980, ibid.

138. Annie M. Donnellan Coakley interview with John Monagan, November 28, 1979, ibid.

139. Catherine Drinker Bowen, *Yankee from Olympus: Justice Holmes and His Family* (Boston: Little, Brown & Co., 1945), 410.

140. 284 U.S. vii (1932).

141. Francis Biddle, *Mr. Justice Holmes* (New York: Charles Scribner's Sons, 1943), 199.

CHAPTER 6

1. See Drew Pearson and Robert S. Allen, *The Nine Old Men* (Garden City, N.Y.: Doubleday, Doran & Co., 1936).

2. Thomas Jefferson to William Johnson, March 4, 1823, Donald G. Morgan, *Justice William Johnson: The First Dissenter* (Columbia: University of South Carolina Press, 1954), 183.

3. Because the plan was based on age, aged anti–New Deal justices were not the only ones subject to it. FDR would have had another "pro" vote because Louis Brandeis was already seventy and the president could have appointed another justice because of his age.

4. Speech by Franklin D. Roosevelt, Baltimore, Maryland, October 5, 1932, William E. Leuchtenburg, *The Supreme Court Reborn: The Constitutional Revolution in the Age of Roosevelt* (New York: Oxford University Press, 1995), 83.

5. Homer Cummings diary entry, January 17, 1933, ibid., 84.

6. *Norman v. Baltimore & Ohio Railroad Co.*, 294 U.S. 240 (1935); *Nortz v. United States*, 294 U.S. 317 (1935); and *Perry v. United States*, 294 U.S. 330 (1935).

7. Harold L. Ickes diary entry, January 11, 1935, Leuchtenburg, *The Supreme Court Reborn*, 86.

8. *Retirement Board v. Alton R. Co.*, 295 U.S. 330 (1935).

9. *Schechter Corp. v. United States*, 295 U.S. 495 (1935); *Louisville Bank v. Radford*, 295 U.S. 555 (1935), *Humphrey's Executor v. United States*, 295 U.S. 602 (1935).

10. Leuchtenburg, *The Supreme Court Reborn*, 90.

11. Ibid., 91.

12. George Norris to William A. Ahern, July 10, 1935, ibid., 93.

13. Franklin D. Roosevelt to Charles E. Wyzanski, Jr., ibid., 96.

14. 297 U.S. 1 (1936).

15. Homer Cummings to Franklin D. Roosevelt, January 29, 1936, Leuchtenburg, *The Supreme Court Reborn*, 100–101.

16. See Michael Nelson, "The President and the Court: Reinterpreting the Court-packing Episode of 1937," *Political Science Quarterly*, 103 (Summer 1988): 273.

17. Leuchtenburg, *The Supreme Court Reborn*, 102.

18. Stanley High diary entry, October 28, 1936, ibid., 108.

19. Harold L. Ickes diary entry, ibid., 108.

20. Drew Pearson and Robert S. Allen, *Nine Old Men at the Crossroads* (Garden City, N.Y., 1936), 2.

21. Leuchtenburg, *The Supreme Court Reborn*, 116.

22. Arthur Holcombe to Edward S. Corwin, December 7, 1936, ibid., 117.

23. Edward S. Corwin to Arthur Holcombe, ibid.

24. Homer Cummings and Carl McFarland, *Federal Justice: Chapters in the History of Justice and the Federal Executive* (New York, 1937), 531.

25. Samuel I. Rosenman, ed., *The Public Papers and Addresses of Franklin D. Roosevelt*, 13 vols. (New York: 1938–50), 5: 51–66.

26. Barry Cushman, *Rethinking the New Deal Court: The Structure of a Constitutional Revolution* (New York: Oxford University Press, 1998) 17–18.

27. "Hughes Against Court Plan; Wheeler Says It Originated with 'Young Men' Last Year," *New York Times*, March 23, 1937, 1.

28. For a discussion of how the national will can lead to "higher lawmaking," see Bruce Ackerman, *We the People 1: Foundations* (Cambridge, Mass.: Belknap Press, 1991); Bruce Ackerman, *We the People 2: Transformations* (Cambridge, Mass.: Belknap Press, 1998).

29. David J. Garrow, "Mental Decrepitude on the U.S. Supreme Court," *The University of Chicago Law Review* 67 (4, Fall 2000) 1023–1024.

30. Young B. Smith, "Statement on the Proposal Regarding the Supreme Court Before the Senate Judiciary Committee," *Journal of the American Bar Association*, 23 (1937): 261, 263.

31. Garrow, "Mental Decrepitude on the U.S. Supreme Court," 1025–1026.

32. Though there were earlier rumors that Van Devanter might step down, no one expected him to depart during the Court-packing struggle.

33. Merlo J. Pusey, *Charles Evans Hughes*, vol. 2 (New York: Macmillan, 1951), 760–761.

34. The Retirement Act (also known as the Sumners-McCarran Act) of March 1, 1937, Pub. L. No. 10, Seventy-fifth Congress, First Sess., 50 stat. 24. The law (28 U.S.C. 375 and 375a, 1940 ed.) extended to justices the "senior status" benefits that other federal judges had enjoyed since 1919. Though retired federal judges could not have their salaries reduced, since they were technically still judges under Article I, section 1 of the Constitution, they were not entitled to the same pay raises as active federal judges. This disparity was remedied by the 1948 Retirement Act and further specified as to the amount of work performed by retired judges in 1989 and 1996. 28 U.S.C. 371.

35. An example of such an order is this assignment from Chief Justice Earl Warren to retired Justice Stanley Reed: "Assignment Order: An order of the Chief Justice designating and assigning Mr. Justice Reed (retired) to perform judicial duties in the United States Court of Claims beginning November 1, 1965, and ending June 30, 1966, and for such further time as may be required to complete unfinished business, pursuant to 28 U.S.C. Section 295." Henry J. Abraham, *The Judicial Process*, 3d ed. (New York: Oxford University Press, 1975), 39.

36. Francis Biddle, *Proceedings in Memory of Mr. Justice Van Devanter*, 316 U.S. XXIX (1941).

37. Critics termed Justices Butler, Van Devanter, Sutherland, and McReynolds the "Four Horsemen" after the legendary Four Horsemen of the Apocalypse. The phrase has also been attributed to Felix Frankfurter's characterization of the anti–New Deal quartet. Bernard Schwartz, *Super Chief: Earl Warren and His Supreme Court* (N.Y.: New York University Press, 1983), 279.

38. David J. Danelski and Joseph S. Tulchin, eds., *The Autobiographical Notes of Charles Evans Hughes* (Cambridge: Harvard University Press, 1973), 302.

39. *New York Times*, August 14, 1932, p. 19, col. 5.

40. *New York Times*, January 21, 1933, p. 3, col. 3.

41. *New York Times*, February 7, 1933, p. 21, col. 3.

42. Pusey, *Charles Evans Hughes*, vol. 2, 761.

43. Ibid., 303.

44. *New York Times*, July 7, 1937, p. 4, col. 2.

45. Ibid.

46. *New York Times,* May 19, 1937, p. 18, col. 4.

47. Leuchtenburg, *The Supreme Court Reborn,* 146.

48. *New York Times,* January 6, 1938, p. 1, col. 4.

49. George Sutherland to Mr. Preston (initials unknown), January 18, 1938, Joel Francis Paschal, *Mr. Justice Sutherland: A Man against the State* (Princeton: Princeton University Press, 1951), 200–201.

50. Danelski and Tulchin, *The Autobiographical Notes of Charles Evans Hughes,* 303.

51. Andrew L. Kaufman, *Cardozo* (Cambridge, Mass.: Harvard University Press, 1998), 160.

52. Ibid., 195.

53. Harry Shulman to Felix Frankfurter, May 4, 1935, Kaufman, *Cardozo,* 486.

54. Benjamin Cardozo to Joseph Paley, September 11, 1935, ibid., 486.

55. Benjamin Cardozo to Annie Nathan Meyer, August 28, 1936, Richard Polenberg, *The World of Benjamin Cardozo: Personal Values and the Judicial Process* (Cambridge: Harvard University Press, 1997), 201.

56. Benjamin Cardozo to Charles C. Burlingham, December 31, 1937, ibid., 236.

57. Harlan Fiske Stone to Irving Lehman, April 26, 1938, ibid., 237.

58. George S. Hellman, *Benjamin N. Cardozo: American Judge* (New York: McGraw-Hill, 1940), 311.

59. *New York Times,* January 27, 1938, p. 6, col. 3.

60. *New York Times,* July 10, 1938.

61. In 1937 and 1938, Brandeis wrote thirteen and sixteen opinions respectively, as compared to regularly authoring more than thirty opinions a decade earlier. Alpheus T. Mason, *Brandeis: A Free Man's Life* (New York: Viking Press, 1946), 633.

62. Louis D. Brandeis to Jennie Brandeis, February 13, 1939, ibid., 634.

63. Danelski and Tulchin, *The Autobiographical Notes of Charles Evans Hughes,* 324.

64. Ibid., 303.

65. Francis Jospeh Brown, *The Social and Economic Philosophy of Pierce Butler* (Washington, D.C.: Catholic University of America Press, 1945), 6.

66. David N. Atkinson, "Retirement and Death on the United States Supreme Court: From Van Devanter to Douglas." *University of Missouri, Kansas City Law Review* 45 (1976): 5.

67. *New York Times,* January 23, 1941, p. 1, col. 1.

68. James McReynolds to Dr. Robert F. McReynolds, October 1, 1940, Leuchtenburg, *The Supreme Court Reborn,* 156.

69. *Supreme Court Historical Society Quarterly* 5 (Winter 1983): 4.

70. James F. Byrnes, *Speaking Frankly* (New York: Harper, 1947), 12–13.

71. Ibid., 18.

72. James F. Byrnes, *All in One Lifetime* (New York: Harper, 1958), 155.

73. James F. Byrnes to the Conference, October 5, 1942, Box 314, Douglas Papers.

74. Henry J. Abraham, *Justices and Presidents: A Political History of Appointments to the Supreme Court,* 3d ed. (New York: Oxford, 1992).

75. Owen J. Roberts to Charles Evans Hughes, July 16, 1945, Pusey, *Charles Evans Hughes,* vol. 2, 802.

76. William O. Douglas to Fred Rodell, May 9, 1949, Roger K. Newman, *Hugo Black: A Biography* (New York: Pantheon Books, 1994), 323.

77. Because he wanted to return to private practice, Roberts chose to resign rather than retire.

78. For a discussion of the battle over the Roberts's farewell letter see Alpheus T. Mason, *Harlan Fiske Stone: Pillar of the Law* (New York: Viking, 1956), 765–769.

79. Robert H. Jackson to Felix Frankfurter, June 19, 1946, Atkinson, "Retirement and Death on the United States Supreme Court," 9.

80. Felix Frankfurter, "Mr. Justice Roberts," *University of Pennsylvania Law Review* 104 (1955): 311–312.

81. Harlan Fiske Stone to Sterling Carr, January 4, 1933, Mason, *Harlan Fiske Stone,* 347.

82. Harlan Fiske Stone to his sons, March 24, 1933, ibid.

83. Harlan Fiske Stone to Dr. Joel T. Boone, January 1, 1937; Harlan Fiske Stone to Edmund A. Burnham, February 1, 1937, ibid., 440.

84. Charles Evans Hughes to Harlan Fiske Stone, December 20, 1937, ibid.

85. Harlan Fiske Stone to Felix Frankfurter, February 25, 1937, ibid.

86. Harlan Fiske Stone to Sterling Carr, April 4, 1943, ibid., 593.

87. L. L. Coryell, Sr. to Harlan Fiske Stone, November 21, 1944, ibid., 647.

88. Learned Hand to Harlan Fiske Stone, January 18, 1945, ibid.

89. Harlan Fiske Stone to Stanley King, May 24, 1945, ibid.

90. Harlan Fiske Stone to Lauson Stone, July 15, 1945, ibid., 800.

91. Marshall Stone to Alpheus T. Mason, December 1954, ibid.

92. Harlan Fiske Stone to Sterling Carr, January 26, 1946, ibid.

93. 328 U.S. 61, 1946.

94. William O. Douglas, *The Court Years 1939–1975: The Autobiography of William O. Douglas* (New York: Random House), 224.

95. Wiley B. Rutledge to Luther Ely Smith, April 23, 1946, Mason, *Harlan Fiske Stone,* 806.

96. Harold Burton Diary, April 22, 1946, Atkinson, "Retirement and Death on the United States Supreme Court," 11.

97. Douglas, *The Court Years 1939–1975,* 224–225.

98. Ibid., 223.

99. Murphy remained upbeat and wrote them: "Your bulletins did not increase my pulse rate, respiration or retard my general progress because of innuendo and assaults on my corpuscles and I have been happy to hear from you." Frank Murphy to William O. Douglas and Wiley B. Rutledge, November 20, 1948, Box 358, Douglas Papers.

100. Wiley B. Rutledge to Frank Murphy, September 27, 1948, J. Woodford Howard, Jr., *Mr. Justice Murphy: A Political Biography* (Princeton: Princeton University Press, 1968), 458.

101. Frank Murphy to George Murphy, February 10, 1949, ibid.

102. Sidney Fine, *Frank Murphy: The Washington Years* (Ann Arbor: University of Michigan Press, 1984), 480.

103. Ibid., 482.

104. Ibid., 485.

105. Frank Murphy to Fred Vinson, April 27, 1949, Fine, *Frank Murphy,* 483.

106. Hugo Black to Frank Murphy, June 27, 1949, ibid., 485.

107. Wiley B. Rutledge to William O. Douglas, August 3, 1949, Box 369, Douglas Papers.

108. Newman, *Hugo Black,* 397.

109. Fowler V. Harper, *Justice Rutledge and the Bright Constellation* (Indianapolis: Bobbs-Merrill, 1965), 336–337.

110. Douglas, *The Court Years 1939–1975,* 75.

111. Irving Brant to Wiley B. Rutledge, August 30, 1949, Harper, *Justice Rutledge and the Bright Constellation,* 335.

112. *New York Times,* September 8, 1953, p. 1, col. 2.

113. Douglas, *The Court Years 1939–1975,* 227.

114. Joseph L. Rauh, Jr., "The Chief," *New Republic,* August 9, 1982, p. 31.

115. 347 U.S. 483 (1954), Eugene C. Gerhart, *America's Advocate: Robert H. Jackson* (Indianapolis: Bobbs-Merrill, 1958), 468.

116. Ibid.

CHAPTER 7

1. For a detailed discussion of this movement see David J. Garrow, *"Mental Decrepitude on the U.S. Supreme Court," The Univeristy of Chicago Law Review,* 67 (4, Fall 2000): 1028–1043.

2. Edwin A. Falk, "In Time of Peace Prepare for War," *Record of the Association of the Bar of the City of New York*, 1 (1946): 245–245.

3. Owen J. Roberts, "Now is the Time: Fortifying the Supreme Court's Independence," *American Bar Association Journal*, 35 (1949): 1.

4. 68 Stat. 12.

5. 347 U.S. 483 (1954).

6. See, for example, *Quinn v. United States*, 349 U.S. 155 (1955); *Watkins v. United States*, 354 U.S. 178 (1957); *Yates v. United States*, 354 U.S. 298 (1957).

7. Homer Bone to Sherman Minton, May 19, 1954, Linda C. Gugin and James E. St. Clair, *Sherman Minton: New Deal Senator, Cold War Justice* (Indianapolis: Indiana Historical Society, 1997), 267.

8. Sherman Minton to Felix Frankfurter, August 25, 1954, ibid.

9. Sherman Minton to Harry Truman, December 27, 1955, ibid., 269.

10. Sherman Minton to Hugo Black, May 18, 1956, ibid., 274.

11. Sherman Minton to Felix Frankfurter, June 9, 1956, ibid., 284.

12. "An Echo Fades," *Time*, September 17, 1956, p. 31.

13. *New York Times*, September 8, 1956, p. 1, col. 1.

14. *New York Times*, February 1, 1957, p. 1, col. 2.

15. 352 U.S. XII–XIV.

16. John D. Fassett, *New Deal Justice: The Life of Stanley Reed of Kentucky* (New York: Vantage, 1994), 627.

17. Ibid., 642.

18. David N. Atkinson, "Retirement and Death on the United States Supreme Court," *University of Missouri Kansas City Law Review* 45 (1976), 16.

19. Ibid. On July 9, Burton wrote Justice Douglas and explained that he wanted to give the president advance notice, "so that my successor could take office in time to hear practically all the cases to be argued at the 1958 Term." Douglas probably did not receive the letter until a later date, as Burton noted at the top: "To be delivered after the President's announcement." Harold Burton to William O. Douglas, July 9, 1958 (to be delivered after the president's announcement), Box 314, Douglas Papers. On July 17, 1958, Burton met with President Eisenhower and informed him of his impending departure. The date was fixed at October 13 and Eisenhower said that an announcement of Burton's retirement should be delayed until a successor had been chosen. Burton proceeded as usual and hired his new clerks for the upcoming Term. Though Warren knew of Burton's impending departure, it was not until September 16 that Burton informed the other justices. That same day, he also called Attorney General Rogers and suggested that his retirement should not be announced until the Court's decision in *Cooper v. Aaron*, 358 U.S. (1958) 1, was delivered.

On September 19, Attorney General Rogers asked Burton to delay his retirement as the president wanted to avoid any political complications arising over Burton's replacement and its possible effect on the segregation cases and the situation in Little Rock. Burton protested and said that he could not remain on the Court any longer. Rogers conceded and Burton's retirement was announced on October 6, effective October 13. Former Justice Minton wrote Justice Douglas, "I was not surprised to hear that good old Harold retired—I thought he showed considerable wear and tear the last time I saw him." Sherman Minton to William O. Douglas, October 16, 1958, Box 356, Douglas Papers. Douglas wrote back, "We all hated to see Harold Burton leave . . . He is shaking pretty badly these days. His disease is diagnosed as Parkinson's disease. So far the tremors have affected only the left arm." William O. Douglas to Sherman Minton, October 18, 1958, ibid.

20. Mary F. Berry, *Stability, Security, and Continuity: Mr. Justice Burton and Decision-Making in the Supreme Court, 1945–1958* (Westport, Conn.: Greenwood Press, 1978), 228.

21. Ed Cray, *Chief Justice: A Biography of Earl Warren* (New York: Simon & Schuster, 1997), 367.

22. Craig Alan Smith, "Charles Evans Whittaker, Associate Justice of the Supreme Court," M.A. Thesis, University of Missouri-Kansas City, 1997. See also Richard Lawrence Miller, *Whittaker: Struggles of a Supreme Court Justice* (Westport, Conn.: Greenwood Press, 2001).

23. Newman, *Hugo Black,* 482.

24. Atkinson, "Retirement and Death on the United States Supreme Court," 17.

25. Douglas, *The Court Years 1939–1975,* 173.

26. John C. Jeffries, *Justice Lewis F. Powell, Jr.* (New York: Charles Scribner's Sons, 1994), 638.

27. Cray, *Chief Justice,* 383.

28. Newman, *Hugo Black,* 482.

29. Ibid.

30. Douglas, *The Court Years 1939–1975,* 173.

31. Judith Cole, *Mr. Justice Charles Evans Whittaker: A Case Study in Judicial Recruitment and Behavior* (Unpublished Master's Thesis; University of Missouri-Kansas City Library, 1972), 153.

32. David Atkinson, *Deciding to Leave* (Lawrence: Kans.: University Press of Kansas, 1999), 130.

33. Cray, *Chief Justice,* 383.

34. He wrote Justice Douglas, "I think I am making steady, if somewhat slow, progress toward regaining my strength, and have, tentatively, agreed to sit on the eighth circuit beginning September 13. I expect, and certainly hope, to be able to resume work at that time." Charles E. Whittaker to William O. Douglas, July 18, 1962, Box 382, Douglas Papers. After a year and a half of recovery, Whittaker did not retake the bench. Instead, he formally resigned as a federal judge so that he could take a position in the private sector at General Motors.

35. His secretary wrote Justice Douglas, "Justice Frankfurter wanted you to know that his physician considered it advisable to hospitalize him for rest and observation following a mild heart disturbance." Elsie Douglas to William O. Douglas, November 28, 1958, Box 330, Douglas Papers.

36. Kanin, "Trips to Felix," *The Atlantic Monthly,* March 1964, pp. 55, 57.

37. Frankfurter's secretary wrote the Justices, "It is deemed desirable, however, in view of his home circumstances, to have a longer hospitalization than would otherwise be the case." She also added that the doctors felt it necessary to prohibit any visitors from seeing Frankfurter, including members of the Court. Elsie Douglas to the Members of the Court, December 2, 1958, Box 330, Douglas Papers.

38. Newman, *Hugo Black,* 482.

39. William O. Douglas to Felix Frankfurter, May 29, 1954, Box 330, Douglas Papers. Douglas had originally written "nastily" before deciding on "insolently." He also originally wrote, "I am writing this merely for the record" and "How is it that when you are not talking," before crossing these phrases out.

40. Felix Frankfurter to the Brethren, June 1, 1954, Box 330, Douglas Papers.

41. William O. Douglas to the Conference, November 21, 1960, Melvin I. Urofsky, *The Douglas Letters: Selections from the Private Papers of Justice William O. Douglas* (Bethesda, Maryland: Adler & Adler, 1987), 90

42. Bernard Schwartz, *Decision: How the Supreme Court Decides Cases* (New York: Oxford University Press, 1996), 215.

43. *New York Times,* April 7, 1962, p. 10, col. 1.

44. *New York Times,* May 1, 1962, p. 28, col. 3. Justice Black wrote him, "I am very happy to learn that you are getting better every day. I hope you will not let Court business disturb you. In this way you can get back sooner and continue your long and highly useful public service." Hugo Black to Felix Frankfurter, April 19, 1962, Newman, *Hugo Black,* 518.

45. He recounted a story of how one of his doctors had noted Frankfurter's limited use of his left arm and leg, while another replied, "No matter. The world has never counted much on this one's abilities as an athlete." When friends came to visit, he tapped his forehead, and said, "Nothing wrong here, you see, nothing at all." Kanin, "Trips to Felix," 61.

46. Harry N. Hirsch, *The Enigma of Felix Frankfurter* (New York: Basic Books, 1981), 198–200.

47. Earl Warren to the Court, April 25, 1962, Cray, *Chief Justice,* 385.

48. Newman, *Hugo Black,* 701, note 2.

49. Felix Frankfurter to the Brethren, August 28, 1962, Box 330, Douglas Papers.

50. Felix Frankfurter to John F. Kennedy, August 28, 1962, ibid.

51. 369 U.S. 186 (1962).

52. Felix Frankfurter to the Brethren, January 21, 1963, Box 330, Douglas Papers.

53. Newman, *Hugo Black,* 566.

54. Dorothy Goldberg, *A Private View of Public Life* (New York: Charthouse, 1975), 194.

55. Arthur J. Goldberg to the Brethren, July 26, 1965, Box 334, Douglas Papers.

56. David L. Stebenne, *Arthur J. Goldberg: New Deal Liberal* (New York: Oxford, 1996), 348–351.

57. Ibid., 348.

58. Arthur J. Goldberg to Lyndon Johnson, April 23, 1968, ibid., 371.

59. Ibid.

60. Transcript of a conversation between Lyndon Johnson and Ramsey Clark, Jan. 25, 1967, LBJ Library.

61. Ibid.

62. Ibid.

63. At age sixty-seven, and after eighteen years on the Court, Clark was eligible for full retirement benefits. Like Justices Reed and Burton, Clark sat on the lower federal courts following his tenure with the Supreme Court.

64. Juan Williams, *Thurgood Marshall: American Revolutionary* (New York: Times Books, 1998) 329.

65. For a thorough discussion of the events surrounding the Warren and Fortas departures, see Robert Shogan, *A Question of Judgment: The Fortas Case and the Struggle for the Supreme Court* (New York: Bobbs-Merrill, 1972) and Bruce Allen Murphy, *Fortas: The Rise and Ruin of a Supreme Court Justice* (New York: Morrow, 1987).

66. Cray, *Chief Justice,* 495.

67. Schwartz, *Super Chief,* 681.

68. Newman, *Hugo Black,* 595.

69. Earl Warren to William O. Douglas, April 5, 1967, Box 381, Douglas Papers.

70. On June 1, 1968, Warren told one of his clerks, "You know, I'm now persuaded that Bobby Kennedy's going to be elected President. I read the reports in the papers this morning of the crowds that lined Kennedy's route from the airport to downtown Los Angeles. It persuades me that this man has something that's going to get him elected. I can remember when I was at the peak of popularity running for Governor following the same route from the airport and seeing no one on the streets." Schwartz, *Super Chief,* 680.

71. James R. Jones memorandum, ibid., 682. When asked by a reporter about whether Warren had a conversation with Johnson about a successor, the Chief replied, "No, I did not have." Arthur Goldberg said that Warren told him that in the meeting with Johnson, Warren suggested Goldberg be named the new Chief. Warren told his clerks that he always knew Johnson would nominate Abe Fortas. The Chief also told Justice William Brennan that if he could personally choose a new Chief, he would

want Brennan. Others said that Warren recommended California Supreme Court Justice Stanley Mosk and Ramsey Clark, in addition to Goldberg. See Cray, *Chief Justice*, 497.

72. Earl Warren to Lyndon Johnson, June 13, 1968, Schwartz, *Super Chief*, 681.

73. Earl Warren to Lyndon Johnson, June 13, 1968, ibid.

74. Lyndon Johnson to Earl Warren, June 26, 1968, ibid., 682.

75. Ibid., 682–683.

76. *U.S. News & World Report*, July 15, 1968, p. 63.

77. *New York Times*, July 6, 1968.

78. *New York Times*, June 24, 1968.

79. *Congressional Record*, October 1, 1968, p. S11684.

80. Hugh Jones, *The Defeat of the Nomination of Abe Fortas as Chief Justice of the United States*, Ph.D. dissertation (Johns Hopkins University, 1976), 104–105; Samuel Shaffer, *On and Off the Floor: Thirty Years as a Correspondent on Capitol Hill* (New York: Newsweek Books, 1980), 79–94.

81. Douglas, *The Court Years 1939–1975*, 255.

82. Douglas, *The Court Years 1939–1975*, 336–337. On the relationship between Johnson and Fortas, see also, Robert Dallek, *Flawed Giant: Lyndon Johnson and his Times, 1961–1973* (New York: Oxford University Press, 1998).

83. *Wall Street Journal*, June 28, 1969, p. 8.

84. Murphy, *Fortas*, 361.

85. Senator Strom Thurmond of South Carolina was particularly incensed about a decision handed down by the Warren Court seven years before Fortas's appointment. Fortas was visibly shaken when Thurmond yelled, "Mallory, Mallory—I want that name to ring in your ears! Mallory! A man who raped a woman, admitted his guilt and the Supreme Court turned him loose on a technicality." On the floor of the Senate, Thurmond warned, "If the Senate confirms this appointment, we will be confirming an extraconstitutional arrangement by which the Supreme Court justices can so arrange their resignations as to perpetuate their influence and their ideology on the Supreme Court." *Mallory v. United States*, 354 U.S. 449 (1957); Shogan, *A Question of Judgment*, 170; *Congressional Record*, July 8, 1968, p. 20154.

86. Murphy, *Fortas*, 328–359.

87. Shogan, *A Question of Judgment*, 182.

88. Cray, *Chief Justice*, 502.

89. "Fortas of the Supreme Court: A Question of Ethics," *Life*, May 4, 1969.

90. Schwartz, *Super Chief*, 762.

91. Douglas, *The Court Years 1939–1975*, 358.

92. Abe Fortas to Earl Warren, May 14, 1969, Box 1782, Douglas Papers.

93. *U.S. News & World Report,* May 26, 1969.

94. Murphy, *Fortas,* 1.

95. Jack H. Pollack, *Earl Warren: The Judge Who Changed America* (Englewood Cliffs, N.J.: Prentice Hall, 1979), 333.

CHAPTER 8

1. The remaining seven justices experienced increased workload as well as a number of 4–3 votes that could have been potentially reversed with a full Court. This was the last instance where the Court had only seven active members.

2. Roger K. Newman, *Hugo Black* (New York: Pantheon Books, 1994), 619.

3. Ibid., 398.

4. Ibid., 619.

5. William O. Douglas to Hugo Black, Jr., June 10, 1963, Box 309, Douglas Papers.

6. Newman, *Hugo Black,* 570.

7. Bernard Schwartz, *Super Chief* (New York: New York University Press, 1983), 630.

8. Newman, *Hugo Black,* 570.

9. Ed Cray, *Chief Justice* (New York: Simon & Schuster, 1997), 472.

10. Newman, *Hugo Black,* 619.

11. Hugo Black to John P. Frank, July 9, 1968, ibid.

12. Ibid.

13. Ibid., 597.

14. Ibid., 620.

15. William O. Douglas, *The Court Years 1939–1975* (New York: Random House, 1980), 377.

16. Hugo Black to David and Joan Corcoran, March 5, 1971, Newman, *Hugo Black,* 620.

17. Hugo Black to William O. Douglas, March, 16, 1971, Box 309, Douglas Papers.

18. Black knew his time was running short. At a speech the previous May he quoted Socrates, "We go our separate ways, you to live, and I to die. Which is best, God only knows." In mid-July, he checked into the hospital for four days. He lost weight and was listless. Newman, *Hugo Black,* 604.

19. Ibid., 621

20. Ibid.

21. Ibid.

22. Hugo L. Black, Jr., *My Father: A Remembrance* (New York: Random House, 1975), 263–264.

23. Hugo Black to Richard Nixon, September 17, 1971, Box 309, Douglas Papers.

24. W. Barton Leach to John Marshall Harlan II, May 27, 1965, Tinsley E. Yarbrough, *John Marshall Harlan: Great Dissenter of the Warren Court* (New York: Oxford University Press, 1992), 332.

25. John Marshall Harlan II to W. Barton Leach, June 1, 1965, ibid.

26. Cray, *Chief Justice,* 498.

27. John Marshall Harlan II to Henry Friendly, September 7, 1971, Yarbrough, *John Marshall Harlan,* 332–333. In a moment of reflection he said, "My life has been all work. I've gotten all my satisfaction and enjoyment through it. I've never felt loved." Harlan suspected he might have a spinal condition and when the hospital lost the sample of his spine following an operation, the Justice became infuriated. He immediately left and checked into another hospital. Newman, *Hugo Black,* 621.

28. In his letter to President Nixon, Harlan wrote, "I have reluctantly come to the conclusion that the time has arrived when, because of reasons of health, I can no longer carry on, to my own satisfaction, my full share of the work of the Supreme Court." He added that his decision was "clearly called for [by] . . . the tenor of the medical advice I have received." John Marshall Harlan II, to Richard Nixon, September 23, 1971, Box 337, Douglas Papers.

29. William O. Douglas to Felix Frankfurter, July 2, 1940, Melvin I. Urofsky, *The Douglas Letters* (Bethesda, Maryland: Adler & Adler, 1987), 215.

30. William O. Douglas to Hugo Black, September 8, 1941, ibid., 109.

31. Hugo Black to William O. Douglas, September 15, 1941, Box 309, Douglas Papers.

32. On the vice presidency, Walter F. Murphy reports that "Bill told me that he really didn't want the job, but: (a) his second wife, Mercedes, who knew him better than any wife should, told me that Bill had desperately wanted the job and always considered himself a failure (I sensed something of that too) because he hadn't become president; (b) Bill always despised Harry S. Truman, making it clear to me on several occasions how deeply he felt that Truman was not a very bright hack (I suspected there were more than difference on public policy behind this emotion)." Walter F. Murphy, letter to author, January 24, 2002.

33. In 1946, Truman offered Douglas the post of Interior Secretary and the Justice declined. In 1948, forces were once again at work to nominate Douglas for either the first or second spot on the Democratic ticket. He wrote one of his supporters, "I have not been and am not now a candidate for either office. I have done all in my power to stop individuals or groups from promoting me for either office. The rumors, however, persist that I am available and will allow my name to go before the convention, and that I will actively or passively seek one of the nominations.

These are not the facts. I am not available. No one is authorized to promote my candidacy. I have but one ambition and that is to stay on the Court and serve my country there to the best of my ability. And I am convinced that it would be a great disservice to the Court for one of its members to seek political office while he remains on it. It was that reason which caused me to keep my name from being presented to the Convention in 1944. It is the same reason why I am taking the same step through you at this time." William O. Douglas to Leland F. Hess, July 3, 1948, Urofsky, *The Douglas Letters*, 218.

After Truman won the nomination, he offered Douglas the vice-presidential spot. Douglas once again declined to leave the Court, writing the president, "My decision was not an easy one. Basic in my whole thinking was the thought that politics had never been my profession and that I could serve my country best where I am." William O. Douglas to Harry S Truman, July 31, 1948, ibid., 219. A year later, Douglas and Black's close friend Justice Frank Murphy died suddenly of a heart attack on July 19, 1949. The liberal Justices were shaken and hinted that they might step down. On July 23, 1949, Truman once again pressed Douglas to take on a "more active" job. Douglas wrote Justice Black, "I do not want to leave the Court. I desire to stay just where I am. I hate even to consider the prospect of leaving. I am very happy right there, and I want nothing but the opportunity to slug away alongside of you for the next thirty years. Right now I cannot think of anything which would lead me to resign. If the country was in complete chaos or on the brink of a major disaster & I felt I could help, I would gladly do so. But it is not, so far as I know. And there are many able men who would do all that he possibly has in mind." William O. Douglas to Hugo Black, July 23, 1949, ibid., 110.

34. William O. Douglas to Francis T. Maloney, January 14, 1944, ibid., 216.

35. William O. Douglas to Hugo Black, August 15, 1949, Box 309, Douglas Papers.

36. Elon Gilbert and James F. Simon, *Independent Journey: The Life of William O. Douglas* (New York: Harper and Row, 1980), 281.

37. William O. Douglas to Hugo Black, November 3, 1949, Urofsky, *The Douglas Letters*, 111.

38. William O. Douglas to James Paul Warburg, January 21, 1952, ibid., 220.

39. Hugo Black, Jr., to William O. Douglas, June 7, 1963, Box 309, Douglas Papers.

40. William O. Douglas to Hugo Black, Jr., June 10, 1963, ibid.

41. Nat Hentoff, "The Justice Breaks His Silence," *Playboy*, July 1991, p. 122.

42. Douglas, *The Court Years 1939–1975*, 376–377.

43. Simon, *Independent Journey*, 391–400.

44. Douglas, *The Court Years 1939–1975*, 371–372.

45. John Marshall Harlan II to William O. Douglas, June 29, 1970, Box 337, Douglas Papers.

46. Speech by William O. Douglas at the Douglas Anniversary Convocation, November 3, 1973, Box 1759, Douglas Papers.

47. Douglas was in the Bahamas vacationing with his wife Cathy when he was stricken. President Ford had Douglas's personal physician flown to Nassau and he immediately recommended that the Justice be flown back to Washington.

48. It is not clear what prompted this memorandum and why a copy is contained in Douglas's papers. Terence J. Fortune to Clark Clifford, January 13, 1975, Box 316, Douglas Papers.

49. Justice Brennan wanted to keep Douglas abreast of the Court's work while he was in the hospital. Following the first conference without Douglas, Brennan drafted a two page memorandum providing a brief overview of what took place. Brennan added, "You were missed very much at today's conference. I am sure that without you we made several mistakes." William J. Brennan, Jr., to William O. Douglas, January 10, 1975, Box 1780, Douglas Papers.

50. Prior to his return, Douglas wanted the Court to issue a statement referring to his "fall." Chief Justice Burger instructed the public information officer to make the statement in Douglas's name and not the Court's. Burger also quietly made arrangements for the Court's carpenter to construct a ramp so that Douglas's wheelchair could be pushed up to his place on the bench when he returned. On March 24, 1975, Douglas returned to the Court and took his place on the bench. As the Court neared its lunch recess, Burger leaned over and asked Douglas if he would like to be wheeled out a few minutes early. Douglas declined, and when the proceedings ended, his colleagues all stood up and disappeared behind the velvet curtain, leaving him sitting in his place. Two Court policemen then wheeled Douglas down the new ramp and out of the view of the stunned onlookers. Warren Burger to William O. Douglas, March 24, 1975, Box 1781, Douglas Papers.

51. *Time*, November 24, 1975.

52. Warren Burger to William O. Douglas, March 31, 1975, Box 1781, Douglas Papers.

53. Simon, *Independent Journey*, 449.

54. Bob Woodward and Scott Armstrong, *The Brethren: Inside the Supreme Court* (New York: Simon and Schuster, 1979), 389.

55. Simon, *Independent Journey*, 450.

56. Woodward and Armstrong, *The Brethren*, 390.

57. Simon, *Independent Journey*, 451.

58. Woodward and Armstrong, *The Brethren*, 391.

59. Notes between Douglas and staff, October 6, 1975, Box 1131, Douglas Papers

60. He wrote a note to his secretary, "Can you get the Court car for the Brennan dinner?" She replied, "Yes, you told me to do this at the beginning of the week already." William O. Douglas to his secretary, October 1975, ibid.

61. Simon, *Independent Journey*, 449.

62. Byron White to Warren Burger, October 20, 1975, Dennis J. Hutchinson, *The Man Who Once Was Whizzer White: A Portrait of Justice Byron R. White* (New York: The Free Press, 1998), 463. Copies are absent from the Douglas, Brennan and Marshall Papers held at the Library of Congress. A copy is located in the Powell Papers at Washington and Lee University, Lexington, Virginia.

63. While Burger continued to remain sensitive to Douglas's situation, other members of the Court were not so patient. Justice Lewis Powell began counting the number of times Douglas fell asleep. Justice Byron White did not hide his frustration that Douglas's refusal to step down was hindering the work of the Court. When Douglas fell asleep during a conference, White summoned Douglas's messenger and ordered "Get him out of here." Woodward and Armstrong, *The Brethren*, 392.

64. William O. Douglas to Joseph Freeman Paquet, October 14, 1975, Urofsky, *The Douglas Letters*, 416.

65. William O. Douglas to Gerald Ford, November, 12, 1975, ibid., 416–417.

66. *Newsweek*, November 24, 1975, p. 45; Simon, 452. Some of the justices met the news with tears and others with relief as they each shook Douglas's hand. Justice Harry Blackmun returned to his chambers in tears, clutching a copy of the retirement letter, where he penned a tribute to his departing colleague. It said in part, "His like probably will not appear again for a long, long while." Woodward and Armstrong, *The Brethren*, 394.

67. Warren Burger to William O. Douglas, November 12, 1975, Box 1781, Douglas Papers.

68. William O. Douglas to Warren Burger, November 15, 1975, Box 1701, Douglas Papers.

69. Simon, *Independent Journey*, 452.

70. William O. Douglas to the Conference, December 17, 1975, Box 1701, Douglas Papers.

71. James B. Ginty to William J. Brennan, December 18, 1975, Box 1133, Douglas Papers.

72. Carl H. Imlay to Edward Hudon, December 19, 1975, ibid.

73. Woodward and Armstrong, *The Brethren*, 433. Nina Totenberg said that Brennan was chosen at some point by the other justices to inform Douglas that he was too ill to continue on the Court. Nina Totenberg, "A Tribute to Justice William J. Brennan, Jr.," in *Justice William J. Brennan, Jr.: Freedom First*, Roger Goldman and David Gallen eds. (New York: Carroll & Graf, 1994), 51.

74. 424 U.S. 1 (1976).

75. He argued that his participation in the case was in keeping with Court procedure, "The break with tradition would come if for some reason, best known to a conference, a justice who had participated in bringing a case here and had done all the work on the case, including hearing oral argument, could be eased out of a final and

ultimate action on the case." Douglas then proceeded to set out his views on the case. William O. Douglas to Warren Burger, December 20, 1975, Woodward and Armstrong, *The Brethren*, 398. No copy exists in the Douglas or Marshall Papers.

76. William J. Brennan, Jr., to Warren Burger, December 22, 1975; Potter Stewart to Warren Burger, December 23, 1975, Box 156, Marshall Papers.

77. Warren Burger, William J. Brennan, Jr., Potter Stewart, Byron White, Thurgood Marshall, Harry Blackmun, Lewis F. Powell, and William Rehnquist to William O. Douglas, December 22, 1975, Box 1133, Douglas Papers.

78. Woodward and Armstrong, *The Brethren*, 399.

79. Ibid.

80. Ibid.

81. William O. Douglas to Elizabeth Cuthbert, February 6, 1976, Urofsky, *The Douglas Letters*, 421.

82. I would suggest that justices depart prematurely when they have yet to exhibit any signs of mental decline and are able to fully and vigorously participate in the work of the Court.

83. Donna Gallus to Potter Stewart, February 19, 1980, *New York Times*, June 20, 1981, A9, col. 3.

84. "Mr. Justice Potter Stewart: A Retirement Press Conference," *Tennessee Law Review* 55 (Fall, 1987): 27.

85. Ibid., 27.

86. "I talked to him as a friend," Stewart explained, "and so far as I know, he never talked to anybody else. I asked him not to." Ibid., 29.

87. *New York Times*, December 12, 1985, D31, col. 1.

88. Reagan was first informed of Stewart's intention to retire on April 21 by Attorney General William French Smith and Presidential Counselor Edwin Meese. Reagan reminded them of his campaign promise to nominate a woman to the Court and the administration began looking for a successor.

89. "Mr. Justice Potter Stewart," 29.

90. Ibid., 21.

91. Ibid., 28. The term following his retirement, he remarked, "I haven't had all the leisure time I've been looking forward to enjoying." *New York Times*, March 22, 1982. Like many former justices, he found it difficult to adjust to life after the Court. Though he kept active by sitting on lower courts, he remarked that it was "no fun to play in the minors after a career in the major leagues." John C. Jeffries, *Justice Lewis F. Powell, Jr.* (New York: Charles Scribner's Sons, 1994), 542.

92. Interestingly, the Rule of Eighty is limited to only those between the ages of sixty-five and seventy. A sixty-four-year-old justice with sixteen years of service on the federal bench may not retire just as a seventy-one-year-old justice with nine years of service may not. 28 U.S.C 371, (c); 98 Stat. 350.

93. Warren Burger to the Associate and Retired Justices, October 25, 1974, Box 1781, Douglas Papers.

94. Press release from Barrett McGurn, Public Information Officer, September 23, 1974, ibid.

95. "Burger Scoffs at Retirement Rumors," *Chicago Daily Law Bulletin*, 130 (November 13, 1984): 1.

96. Mark W. Cannon, "A Tribute to Chief Justice Warren Burger," *Harvard Law Review*, 100 Harv. L. Rev. 984, March 1987.

97. Lyle Denniston and Robert Timberg, "How and Why Burger Made His Decision," *San Diego Union-Tribune*, June 20, 1986, B13.

98. David G. Savage, *Turning Right: The Making of the Rehnquist Supreme Court* (New York: John Wiley & Sons, Inc., 1992), 4–5.

99. Donnie Radcliffe and Elizabeth Kastor, "The Supreme Surprise; Uruguay's State Dinner, Upstaged by Changes on the Court," *Washington Post*, June 18, 1986, B1.

100. David S. Broder, "Finally the Reagan Stamp," *Washington Post*, June 22, 1986, C8.

101. Malcolm M. Lucas, "Don't Pull the Rug Out from Under the State Justice Institute," *Legal Times*, September 25, 1995, 21.

102. "Odds and ends: From Capitol Hill," *ABA Journal*, 70 A.B.A.J. 48, August, 1984.

103. Cheryl Frank, "Now or never? Justice Institute in Limbo," *ABA Journal*, 71 A.B.A.J. 28, June, 1985.

104. Rhonda McMillion, "State Justice Institute Strikes Chord," *ABA Journal*, 91 A.B.A.J. 106, May, 1991.

105. Terence Moran, "Slow Going on the Judicial Front," *Legal Times*, April 20, 1987, 4. Initially, The SJI started out with a budget of $7.2 million for fiscal year 1987 and despite being targeted for abolition by every administration since its inception, its budget nearly doubled by 1994. See Ray Archer, "Little-Known Federal Programs Hold the Key to Safeguarding Treasury," *Arizona Republic*, March 15, 1993, A10. In 1995, it was in danger of elimination and its budget was cut to $5 million. See Kenneth Jost, "Law-related Programs Facing Ax: State Justice Institute among Those Targeted by Congressional Budget-Cutters," *ABA Journal*, 82 A.B.A.J. 38, June, 1996. By 2000, it had slowly risen to $6.85 million.

106. Jeffries, *Justice Lewis F. Powell, Jr.*, 5.

107. In September 1973, while vacationing in Portugal, Powell experienced prostate trouble. When a doctor prescribed the wrong medication, Powell flew home in considerable pain. Back in Richmond, Virginia, Powell received treatment and recovered from the ordeal. In 1974, he underwent prostate surgery and suffered excessive bleeding. He wrote Justice Douglas, "I had some chronic prostate problem, and was persuaded by Harry Blackmun to go out to the Mayo Clinic for a general checkup. Although the surgery was perhaps not necessary, the doctors thought it desirable to get

it behind me." Lewis Powell, Jr. to William O. Douglas, August 30, 1974, Box 1782, Douglas Papers. Five years later, in 1979, Powell had a nonmalignant polyp removed from his colon. He again wrote Douglas, "My surgery seems to have been successful . . . Jo is trying to restore some of the pounds I lost while I was in the hospital." Lewis Powell, Jr. to William O. Douglas, April 11, 1979, ibid.

108. Jeffries, *Justice Lewis F. Powell, Jr.*, 535.

109. Lewis Powell III to Lewis Powell, Jr., April 9, 1983, ibid., 536.

110. Ibid., 536.

111. Lewis Powell III to Lewis Powell, Jr., April 30, 1983, ibid.

112. On July 12, 1983 Powell underwent surgery on his left eye. He had a cataract removed, a new lens implanted and dramatically improved his vision as a result. In January 1985, Powell underwent surgery for prostate cancer. Unexpectedly, the routine procedure turned into a life-threatening situation. Powell began hemorrhaging uncontrollably, and after eight hours of work the doctors were able to keep him alive. The chief physician later recalled, "surgeons generally leave an operation with a sense of great accomplishment and satisfaction, but the experience was horrific." Powell did not return to the bench until March 25 as a result of the operation. At the close of the term on July 2, 1985, Powell once again had to undergo additional surgery. Though he was unable to gain weight, he recovered over the summer and was fully prepared for the new term in October. Ibid., 539.

113. 478 U.S. 186, (1986).

114. Ibid., 543.

115. Ruth Marcus, "Powell Regrets Backing Sodomy Law," *Washington Post*, October 26, 1990, A3.

116. Ibid., 540–542.

117. Josephine Powell Smith to Lewis Powell, Jr., June 21, 1987, ibid., 542.

118. "Personal and Confidential," John C. Jeffries to Lewis Powell, Jr., June 21, 1987, ibid.

119. Ibid., 543.

120. On June 24, 1987, he informed Chief Justice Rehnquist of his decision. They found the relevant provision of the U.S. Code for Powell to cite in his letter to President Reagan. Powell and Rehnquist agreed to keep the decision secret for two days until June 26, the last day of the term. On the 25th, Powell told his clerks. On the morning of June 26th, Rehnquist phoned White House Chief of Staff Howard Baker and informed him of Powell's decision. In conference, Rehnquist felt as if he was "dropping a bombshell" and announced to the other justices that Powell was stepping down. On the bench that morning as the justices announced the final decisions of the term, Rehnquist said, "Before we turn to the final announcement on today's calendar, we wish to take note with great regret the retirement of Justice Lewis F. Powell as a member of the Court. We shall miss his wise counsel in our deliberations but we look forward to being the continuing beneficiaries of his friendship." Savage, *Turning Right*, 128.

121. Jeffries, *Justice Lewis F. Powell, Jr.*, 546.

122. Ibid.

123. William J. Brennan, Jr., to the Brethren, December 16, 1977, Box 1780, Douglas Papers.

124. Warren Burger to Justices Stewart, White, Marshall, Blackmun, Powell, Rehnquist, Stevens, and Douglas, December 12, 1977, Box 1139, Douglas Papers.

125. William J. Brennan, Jr. to William O. Douglas, January 25, 1978, Box 1780, Douglas Papers.

126. Donna Haupt, "Justice William J. Brennan, Jr.," *Constitution* (Winter 1989): 56.

127. Ibid.

128. Justice White wrote, "All of us who watched Bill Brennan through those years when his first wife, Marjorie Leonard Brennan, struggled with and finally succumbed to cancer deeply admired the way he cared for his wife and still quietly and effectively carried out his work. And this is to say nothing of how he coped with and survived his own bout with cancer. Byron R. White, "Tribute to the Honorable William J. Brennan, Jr.," in *Justice William J. Brennan, Jr.*, Goldman and Gallen eds., 29.

129. Totenberg, "A Tribute to Justice William J. Brennan, Jr.," 51.

130. Savage, *Turning Right*, 239.

131. Edward Lazarus, *Closed Chambers: The First Eyewitness Account of the Epic Struggles Inside the Supreme Court* (New York: Times Books, 1998), 276.

132. Savage, *Turning Right*, 345.

133. Lazarus, *Closed Chambers*, 277–278.

134. Savage, *Turning Right*, 345–346.

135. En route for a Norwegian cruise, Brennan suffered a blackout in the Newark Airport. Though he fell and hit his head, after a few moments of rest, he decided to continue on the trip. He was ill for the rest of the two-week vacation, however, suffering periods of disorientation. Ibid., 348.

136. Ibid.

137. Hunter R. Clark, *Justice Brennan: The Great Conciliator* (New York: Birch Lane Press, 1995), 274.

138. Richard Davis, *Decisions and Images: The Supreme Court and the Press* (Englewood Cliffs, N.J.: Prentice Hall, 1994), 52.

139. Ibid., 276.

140. Ibid., 274.

141. Hentoff, "The Justice Breaks His Silence," 122.

142. Lazarus, *Closed Chambers*, 26–27.

143. Tony Mauro, "How Blackmun Hid Retirement Plans," *New Jersey Law Journal* 136 (April 25, 1994): 18.

144. Clark, *Justice Brennan*, 279.

145. From an interview with NBC News, quoted in Tony Mauro, "High Court Highs and Lows," *Legal Times*, December 18–25, 1995, 20.

146. Michael D. Davis and Hunter R. Clark, *Thurgood Marshall: Warrior at the Bar, Rebel on the Bench*, rev. ed. (New York: Citadel Press, 1994), 350.

147. Carl T. Rowan, *Dream Makers, Dream Breakers: The World of Justice Thurgood Marshall* (Boston: Little, Brown, 1993), 415.

148. *Gregg v. Georgia* 428 U.S. 153 (1976).

149. On July 8, 1976, Court Public Information Officer Barrett McGurn informed a spokesperson at Bethesda Naval Hospital to tell the press: "Justice Marshall continues his uneventful recovery. He has been moved from the coronary care unit to his own room. He is resting comfortably and is in excellent spirits." Box 1782, Douglas Papers.

150. Rowan, *Dream Makers, Dream Breakers*, 398.

151. William O. Douglas to Thurgood Marshall, July 12, 1976, Urofsky, *The Douglas Letters*, 423.

152. Rowan, *Dream Makers, Dream Breakers*, 394.

153. Juan Williams, *Thurgood Marshall: American Revolutionary* (New York: Times Books, 1998), 346.

154. Ibid., 361.

155. Ibid., 371.

156. Rowan, *Dream Makers, Dream Breakers*, 396.

157. Williams, *Thurgood Marshall: American Revolutionary*, 372–373.

158. Ibid., 379.

159. Marshall did not exercise, but his doctors ordered him to at least keep walking. As a result, Marshall began walking laps around the carpeted hallways of the Court building. Lewis Powell had also begun the same routine, but in the opposite direction. Once when the two justices met on their respective laps, Powell warmly said "Good morning, Thurgood," to which Marshall responded, "What's so good about it?" After completing one lap each, they met again with Marshall warning, "I'm gaining on you." Savage, *Turning Right*, 79.

160. Rowan, *Dream Makers, Dream Breakers*, 396.

161. Terry Eastland, "While Justice Sleeps," *National Review*, April 21, 1989, p.24.

162. Tony Mauro, "Rehnquist Rumbles as Marshall Stumbles," *Legal Times*, November 6, 1989, 13.

163. David G. Savage, "High Court's Conservative New Guard Steers Debate," *LA Times,* April 1, 1990, A1, A30.

164. Lazarus, *Closed Chambers,* 278.

165. Savage, *Turning Right,* 400.

166. 500 U.S. 110 (1991).

167. She wrote, "I could not find a single case in which you joined a majority opinion that disposed of the case in a manner adverse to the capital dfdt . . . *Lankford* appears to be the first case in which your view of the capital dfdt's substantive arguments is at odds with your standard view that the death penalty violates the Eighth Amendment in all circumstances." Sheryll D. Cashin to Thurgood Marshall, February 21, 1991, Box 537, Marshall Papers.

168. Thurgood Marshall to William Rehnquist, March 5, 1991, Boxes 523 and 537, Marshall Papers.

169. William Rehnquist to Thurgood Marshall, March 6, 1991, Box 537, Marshall Papers. There is some dispute over the extent to which this episode reflects mental decline or whether the case presented another legal issue that caused Marshall to legitimately switch his vote. See Garrow, "Mental Decrepitude on the U.S. Supreme Court," 1076–1081.

170. In Marshall's final appearance on the bench, his now-retired colleague Justice Brennan came down from his second-floor office to sit in the front section of the audience, reserved for Court officers. Marshall's wife was there too. After Justice Stevens finished reading his dissent in the death penalty case *Payne v. Tennessee,* 501 U.S. 808 (1991), closing with "Today is a sad day for a great institution," the justices rose and disappeared behind the red velvet curtain. Justice Blackmun, however, did not leave with his colleagues as is customary. Instead, he made his way around the bench to where Justice Brennan was seated and put his hand on Brennan's shoulder. After a few minutes of conversation, Blackmun left the courtroom and headed for the justice's final conference of the term. Though he was late, he was in time to hear Chief Justice Rehnquist's announcement that Justice Marshall was retiring.

171. *Payne v. Tennessee* 501 U.S. 808 (1991).

172. In his brief letter to President Bush he used the identical words his colleague William Brennan had used the year before in his retirement letter. Like Brennan, Marshall said that "the strenuous demands of Court work and its related duties required or expected of a justice appear at this time to be incompatible with my advancing age and medical condition." Rowan, *Dream Makers, Dream Breakers,* 403.

Marshall originally expected to retire over the summer when his successor was confirmed by the Senate. However due to the controversy over Marshall's replacement, Clarence Thomas, it was clear that the nomination would not be acted on until after the October Term was officially underway. Because Marshall was still technically a member of the Court but did not want to participate in the new term, he wrote the president on October 1, "In my letter to you of June 27th, I set my retirement to begin 'when my successor is qualified.' I now request that my retirement become effective as of this date." Thurgood Marshall to George Bush, October 1, 1991, Box 523, Marshall Papers.

173. Ibid., 410.

174. Ibid., 408.

175. Ibid.

176. White wanted to make sure that he left the Court at the least disruptive time. Hutchinson, *The Man Who Once Was Whizzer White*, 408–409.

177. Tony Mauro, "Tribute to Marshall Presages White's Exit," *New Jersey Law Journal* 133 (April 5, 1993): 18.

178. Lawrence Baum, *The Supreme Court*, 6th ed. (Washington, D.C.: Congressional Quarterly Press, 1998) 75–76.

179. Davis, *Decisions and Images: The Supreme Court and the Press*, 59.

180. Ibid.

181. Clark, *Justice Brennan*, 279.

182. Hutchinson, *The Man Who Once Was Whizzer White*, 436.

183. Ibid. On March 18, 1993, Justice White called a former law clerk working in the White House counsel's office and asked him to stop by the Court and deliver a letter to the president the next day. The next morning, President Clinton received the letter from Justice White which said that he would be retiring from the Court at the close of the current term. White told Clinton that he wanted to inform the White House in advance to provide ample time for the administration to find a successor and for the Senate to conduct hearings before the start of the next term in October. In a brief statement released to the press, White said that while he had an "interesting and exciting experience" serving on the Court, "Marion and I think that someone else should be permitted to have a like experience." He also added that he intended to sit on the Courts of Appeals from time to time. White set his retirement effective "at the time the Court next rises for its summer recess," which was June 28, 1993. Ibid., 438.

184. Savage, *Turning Right*, 211.

185. 505 U.S. 833 (1992).

186. Tony Mauro, "Court 'Name Game' Enters New Inning," *Legal Times*, November 9, 1992, 10.

187. Tony Mauro, "How Blackmun Hid Retirement Plans," 18.

188. "Statements by Blackmun and Clinton on Retiring," *New York Times*, April 7, 1994, A24.

189. After having breakfast with the Justice, a former clerk said, "He stated his usual answer about how he wasn't sure he was going to stay, but every year he says that." Mauro, "How Blackmun Hid Retirement Plans," 18.

In April, Blackmun confirmed his decision to retire. He phoned Deputy White House Counsel Joel Klein and said that he would be making a public announcement soon. On the morning of April 6, the press reported the Blackmun planned to leave the Court. When Clinton was asked the day before what Blackmun's plans were, he replied, "Let Justice Blackmun speak for himself. I have not spoken to him. As I understand it, he has an announcement to make tomorrow, so I think we should let him make it." Linda Greenhouse, "Blackmun Plans to Leave Court, Officials Report," *New York Times*, April 6, 1994, A1. Blackmun did indeed make an announcement the following day. He officially left the Court on August 3, 1994, when his successor Stephen J. Breyer was sworn in.

190. Ruth Marcus, "Good Counsel: More Judge Than Witness," *Washington Post*, July 27, 1994, A18.

191. Mauro, "How Blackmun Hid Retirement Plans," 18.

192. "Statements by Blackmun and Clinton on Retiring," *New York Times*, A24.

193. "As an old canoeist myself, I share Bill Douglas' vivid and eloquent description of our work together, the occasional long and strenuous portages and the last night's and the last morning's campfires, as he set it forth in his retirement letter of Nov. 14, 1975. 423 U.S. ix." 512 U.S. ix.

194. Douglas Jehl, "Mitchell Viewed as Top Candidate for High Court," *New York Times*, April 7, 1994, A1.

CHAPTER 9

1. David J. Garrow, "The Rehnquist Reins," *New York Times Magazine*, October 6, 1996, 85.

2. Ibid.

3. Letter from William Rehnquist to Thurgood Marshall, July 26, 1991, Box 525, Marshall Papers.

4. Garrow, "The Rehnquist Reins," 85.

5. On Rehnquist's surgery see Linda Greenhouse, "High Court to Hear Case on Government's Refusal to Adjust Census," *New York Times*, September 28, 1995, A18.

6. Life Expectancy of justices determined by the average age of justices at death in the preceding ten-year period (or 20 years in the case of 1960–1980).

7. For a chronology of events see, "How We Got Here: A Timeline of the Florida Recount," *Time*, December 13, 2000.

8. Nancy Gibbs, "Reversal of . . . Fortune," *Time*, November 13, 2000.

9. Most attention was focused on the controversial "butterfly" ballot used in Palm Beach county. Approximately 19,000 ballots were disqualified because voters punched two holes for president and 10,000 more did not register any presidential choice. Many voters in the county felt that the ballots were confusing and that they had accidentally voted for Reform Party candidate Pat Buchanan. His total of 3,407 votes in Palm Beach county, was three times as high as in neighboring counties with different-style ballots. Buchanan, in a move that many saw as a chance for revenge against the party he had bitterly left, went on television and said he did not think all those votes were intended for him. With Bush's lead after the initial count of 1,784

votes statewide, the Gore campaign knew Palm Beach could give them the election. The other counties, Broward. Dade, and Volusia had similar problems and were also included in Gore's hand-count request.

10. Technically there were seven justices who agreed with this part of the decision with only Stevens and Ginsburg saying that the recount procedure was a state matter. While Souter and Breyer held that there were equal protection violations, they did not agree with the other justices in the majority (O'Connor, Kennedy, Rehnquist, Scalia, and Thomas) that there was no time left for a remedy. Interestingly, the separate opinion by Rehnquist, Scalia, and Thomas, as well as their questions during oral argument, suggests that they did not agree with the equal protection argument in principle but had to join the other four justices who did (O'Connor, Kennedy, Souter, and Breyer) in order to obtain a majority.

11. The majority held that Florida election law, or at least the Florida Supreme Court's interpretation of Florida election law, required that the state name its electors by December 12, six days before the electoral college is required to meet by federal statute, and the state must name those electors under rules enacted before Election Day. This so-called safe harbor provision is based on a federal election law that guarantees states who follow this procedure that their slate of electors will be protected from challenges when they arrive in Washington should some other slate claim to be legitimate. On this point see, William Glaberson, "The Legal Issues: Concession on 'Deadline' Helped Seal Gore's Defeat," *New York Times,* December 19, 2000.

12. Joan Biskupic, "Division May Be Supreme Court Legacy," *USA Today,* December 13, 2000.

13. Rehnquist dealt with health issues from the beginning of his tenure on the Court. In 1971, he underwent back surgery for a "slipped disc" but continued to experience pain thereafter. He wrote Chief Justice Burger in November 1977, "My back condition is much better this fall than it was last spring, but the long hours of sitting at the Friday Conferences still give me a little trouble." William Rehnquist to Warren Burger, November 3, 1977, Box 1139, Douglas Papers. In the late 1970s, Rehnquist became increasingly dependent on Placidyl, a medication to help alleviate his persistent back pain. When it was noticed that he was occasionally slurring his words, he decided to seek treatment. In 1981, he entered a Washington hospital and underwent treatment for what doctors termed a "degree of physiological dependence." When he emerged, Rehnquist took to a rigorous exercise program that included walking, swimming, and tennis. Savage, *Turning Right,* 19. He also began standing for a few minutes every hour to help relieve his back.

14. Ibid., 16.

15. Rehnquist faced a major challenge early in his chief justiceship with his wife's battle against cancer. When Justice Brennan was struggling with his first wife's illness in the 1970s and early 1980s, Rehnquist was a constant source of kindness and support for Brennan. When Rehnquist's wife Nan, began to decline from the effects of cancer in the late 1980s and early 1990s, Brennan understood what his friend was going through. On bad days, the chief justice would be irritable and contentious with

lawyers during oral argument. In late October 1991, Rehenquist's wife passed away and he was absent from the Court for a number of days. Ibid., 362.

16. Richard Davis, *Decisions and Images: The Supreme Court and the Press* (Englewood Cliffs, New Jersey: Prentice Hall, 1994), 59.

17. Linda Greenhouse, "A Younger Court Faces Old Splits as Its Term Opens," *New York Times*, October 3, 1994, A1.

18. *The Today Show*, January 28, 2002.

19. David Savage, *Turning Right* (New York: John Wiley & Sons, 1992), 225.

20. Ibid., 226.

21. Joan Biskupic, "A High Court of Recovery; In Recent Years, Justices Resumed Work after Serious Illness," *Washington Post*, September 20, 1999, A02.

22. Savage, *Turning Right*, 226, 288.

23. Davis, *Decisions and Images: The Supreme Court and the Press*, 59.

24. See generally, Joan Biskupic, "O'Connor: The 'Go-To' Justice," *USA Today*, July 12, 2000, 1A.

25. Evan Thomas and Michael Isikoff, "The Truth Behind the Pillars," *Newsweek*, December 25, 2000.

26. Joan Biskupic, "O'Connor Expected to Stay on Court," *USA Today*, June 18, 2001.

27. Charles Lane, "O'Connor Denies Plans to Leave Supreme Court," *Washington Post*, May 2, 2001, A9.

28. Joan Biskupic, "Election Decision Still Splits Court," *USA Today*, January 22, 2001.

29. Joan Biskupic, "O'Connor Addresses 'Nonsense,'" *USA Today*, January 24, 2002.

30. Tony Mauro, "Enjoying the Great Outdoors with the Supreme Court Justices," *Legal Times*, January 28, 2002.

31. Thomas E. Baker, "Think Hard: Winner Takes Court," *The National Law Journal*, June 19, 2000, A18.

32. Linda Greenhouse, "Ruth Ginsburg Has Surgery for Cancer," *New York Times*, September 18, 1999, A10.

33. Sheryl Gay Stolberg, "Ginsburg Leaves Hospital: Prognosis on Cancer Is Good," *New York Times*, September 29, 1999, A20.

34. Biskupic, "A High Court of Recovery," *Washington Post*, September 20, 1999, A02.

35. Joan Biskupic, "Ginsburg Assumes Her Normal Role," *Washington Post*, October 5, 1999, A07.

36. Joan Biskupic, "Justice Ginsburg Having 'Precautionary' Chemotherapy," *Washington Post*, January 15, 2000, A8.

37. Tony Mauro, "Opinions and Photos Offer Rarely Seen Glimpses of High Court Operations," *American Lawyer Media*, November 12, 2001.

38. Ibid.

39. Joan Biskupic, "Ginsburg Discusses Security, Constitutional Values," *USA Today*, January 30, 2002.

40. Neil A. Lewis, "Two Years After His Bruising Hearing, Justice Thomas Still Shows Hurt," *New York Times*, November 27, 1993, 6.

41. Joan Biskupic, "Bush May Be Building Conservative Judiciary," *USA Today*, January 7, 2001.

CHAPTER 10

1. Charles Evans Hughes, *The Supreme Court of the United States: Its Foundation, Methods, and Achievements: An Interpretation* (New York, NY: Columbia University Press, 1928), 76.

2. Interestingly, an argument can be made that financial concerns will once again be a factor. While a number of the justices are millionaires with substantial assets, some of the newer members have relatively few assets. In 2000, Justice Antonin Scalia's assets were valued below $535,000, Justice Clarence Thomas reported assets worth between $150,000 and $410,000, and Justice Anthony Kennedy was the "poorest," with assets valued below $195,000. Indeed, justices have continually lamented their relatively low salaries compared to what lawyers of comparable skill and experience make in private practice. Recently, on the recommendation of Chief Justice Rehnquist, the Senate appropriations committee passed a spending bill that included a provision to lift the eleven-year ban on speaking fees for federal judges, including the Supremes. Rehnquist argued, "It is to the point that in today's legal market a first-year associate in a law firm could make as much in salary as a federal judge." He warned that the disparity was harming the ability of the judiciary to recruit and retain the most capable lawyers. Despite the Senate action, the lifting of the ban was not approved by the House where opposition stemmed from concerns over unethical conduct. See Dan Morgan, "Bill Would End Ban on Honoraria for Judges: GOP Action Follows Plea by Rehnquist," *Washington Post*, September 14, 2000, A1.

3. See, for example, Jeffrey A. Segal and Harold J. Spaeth, *The Supreme Court and the Attitudinal Model* (New York: Cambridge University Press, 1993).

4. 28 U.S.C. 371–2 provides full benefits for disabled Justices who retire and one-half the salary for Justices who retire short of the Rule of Eighty.

5. Hamilton, No. 79, *The Federalist*, Willis, ed. (New York: Bantam, 1982), 401–402.

6. Thomas Jefferson, *On Democracy*, Saul K. Padover, ed. (New York: Mentor Books, 1939), 65.

7. 347 U.S. 483 (1954), 349 U.S. 294 (1955).

8. 28 U.S.C. 372(b).

9. Other removal proposals, however, have been seriously considered by Congress from time to time. In 1978, for example, the Senate approved a bill to remove judges who are physically or mentally incompetent or who conduct themselves in an unethical or improper manner. The House failed to act on the measure.

10. 393 U.S. 503 (1969).

11. 403 U.S. 15 (1971).

12. 396 U.S. 1218 (1969).

13. The Court has a tradition of acting by majority rule but in such delicate matters there is usually compromise so that the Court can speak with one voice. Indeed, White's dissent from the Douglas decision was never made public.

14. Letter from William O. Douglas to Warren Burger, March 31, 1975, Melvin I. Urofsky, *The Douglas Letters* (Bethesda, Maryland: Adler & Adler, 1987), 142.

15. See David J. Garrow, "Mental Decrepitude on the U.S. Supreme Court," *The University of Chicago Law Review* 67 (4, Fall 2000), 1066–1069.

16. See, for example, David N. Atkinson, *Leaving the Bench* (Lawrence, Kansas: University Press of Kansas, 1999), 168.

17. Initially, the Rule of Eighty was created for lower court judges but now applies to all federal judges. While there are important differences between the U.S. Supreme Court and lower federal courts, any change in the Rule of 80 ought to apply to all Article III judges as partisanship and mental decrepitude are not only found among Supreme Court justices.

18. Letter from John Paul Stevens to William H. Rehnquist, October 28, 1988, Box 462, Marshall Papers.

19. Ibid.

20. Though the justices are still assigned to a circuit, unlike the Courts of previous eras, today's justices do not have to undertake arduous journeys and regularly visit their circuits. Their circuit-duty revolves mainly around hearing emergency motions. They issue injunctions, grant bail, or stay executions. 28 U.S.C. Section 42.

21. See, for example, Thomas's question and answer session with High School students, C-SPAN, Dec. 13, 2000.

22. See Edward Lazarus, *Closed Chambers: The First Eyewitness Account of the Epic Struggles Inside the Supreme Court* (New York: Times Books, 1998).

23. William H. Rehnquist interview, *Charlie Rose*, PBS, aired January 13, 1999.

24. Earl Warren, *The Memoirs of Earl Warren* (New York: Doubleday, 1977), 347–348.

25. Ibid., 348.

26. Letter from William O. Douglas to Warren Burger, July 13, 1972, Urofsky, *The Douglas Letters*, 141. Justice Powell first suggested pooling the law clerks and Dou-

glas wrote him personally on July 7, 1972, before his memo to the Chief: "One's perspective changes over the years. But I really think that in terms of the present rate of activity inside the Court the job of an Associate Justice does not add up to more than four days a week." Box 1782, Douglas papers.

27. On the decline in the number of cases being considered by the Court, see David M. O'Brien, "The Rehnquist Court's Shrinking Plenary Docket," *Judicature* 81 (September–October 1997): 58–65.

28. Bernard Schwartz, *Decision: How the Supreme Court Decides Cases* (New York: Oxford, 1996).

29. The constitution allows justices of the Supreme Court to serve for life "during good behavior."

30. Alexander Hamilton, No. 79, *The Federalist,* Willis, ed., 402.

31. Letter from Joseph Story to Ezekeiel Bacon, September 21, 1823, quoted in W. W. Story, ed., *Life and Letters of Joseph Story,* 2 vols. (Boston: Little Brown, 1851), vol. 1, 425–426.

32. Charles Evans Hughes, *The Supreme Court of the United States* (New York: Columbia University Press, 1928), 73, 76.

33. Letter from William O. Douglas to Robert W. Lucas, June 7, 1954, Urofsky, *The Douglas Letters,* 55.

34. See, for example, Jerry Brekke, "There Goes the Judge: Retirement, Removal, and Discipline of Judges," *Comparative State Politics* 17 (Fall 1996), 38–45.

35. For a discussion of Nunn's efforts to reform the departure process, see Sam Nunn, "Judicial Tenure," *Chicago-Kent Law Review* 54 (1977): 29–44; David Garrow, *Mental Decrepitude on the U.S. Supreme Court,* 1056–1065.

36. Charles Fairman, *Mr. Justice Miller and the Supreme Court 1862–1890* (Cambridge: Harvard University Press, 1939), 397–398.

37. See, for example, Harold J. Spaeth and Jeffrey A. Segal, *Majority Rule or Minority Will: Adherence to Precedent on the U.S. Supreme Court* (New York: Cambridge University Press, 1999); Saul Brenner and Harold Spaeth, *Stare Indecisis: the Alteration of Precedent on the Supreme Court, 1946–1992* (New York: Cambridge University Press, 1995). Furthermore, it has long been argued that the Court is in fact generally reflective of the dominant governing coalition. See, for example, Robert Dahl, "Decision-Making in a Democracy: The Supreme Court as a National Policy-Maker," *Journal of Public Law* 6 (1957): 279, 293.

38. In the case of a declining Chief, the senior associate justices ought to take the lead.

39. Fairman, *Mr. Justice Miller and the Supreme Court 1862–1890,* 398.

40. Garrow, "Mental Decrepitude on the U.S. Supreme Court: The Historical Case for a Twenty-eighth Amendment," 995–1087; Lucas A. Powe, Jr., "Old People and Good Behavior," *Constitutional Commentary* (1995), 195–197; L. H. LaRue, "Neither Force Nor Will," *Constitutional Commentary* (1995), 179–182; Sanford Levinson, "Contempt of Court: The Most Important 'Contemporary Challenge to Judging,'"

Washington & Lee Law Review (1992), 339; Henry Paul Monaghan, "The Confirmation Process: Law or Politics?" *Harvard Law Review* (1988): 1202–1212; Roy Fleming, "Is Life Tenure on the Supreme Court Good for the Country?" *Judicature* (1987): 322–; Philip D. Oliver, "Systematic Justice: A Proposed Constitutional Amendment to Establish Fixed, Staggered Terms for Members of the United States Supreme Court," 47 *Ohio State Law Journal* (1986): 799–834.

41. John Gruhl, "The Impact of Term Limits for Supreme Court Justices: Had Term Limits Been in Place Throughout the Court's History, Many of the Best Justices would have been Forced off the Bench too Soon," *Judicature* 81 (September–October, 1997): 66–72.

42. Ibid., 66.

43. Ibid., 69.

44. Though an argument can be made that their most important work was done in their earlier years, each continued to be productive well into their third decade of service.

45. "Mr. Justice Potter Stewart: A Retirement Press Conference," *Tennessee Law Review* 55 (Fall, 1987): 38.

Bibliography

PRIMARY SOURCES

WRITINGS OF THE JUSTICES

Byrnes, James F., *All in One Lifetime* (New York: Harper, 1958).

Byrnes, James F., *Speaking Frankly* (New York: Harper, 1947).

Douglas, William O., *The Court Years 1939–1975: The Autobiography of William O. Douglas* (New York: Random House, 1980).

Frankfurter, Felix and James M. Landis, *The Business of the Supreme Court: A Study in the Federal Judicial System* (New York: Macmillan, 1928).

Frankfurter, Felix, "Mr. Justice Roberts," *University of Pennsylvania Law Review* 104 (1955): 311.

Hughes, Charles Evans, *The Supreme Court of the United States: Its Foundations, Methods and Achievements: An Interpretation* (New York: Columbia University Press, 1928).

Roberts, Owen J., "Now Is the Time: Fortifying the Supreme Court's Independence," *American Bar Association Journal*, 35 (1949): 1.

Warren, Earl, *The Memoirs of Earl Warren* (New York: Doubleday, 1977).

White, Byron R., "Tribute to the Honorable William J. Brennan, Jr.," in *Justice William J. Brennan, Jr.: Freedom First*, Roger Goldman and David Gallen eds. (New York: Carroll & Graf, 1994), 27–31.

MANUSCRIPTS

William O. Douglas Papers, Manuscript Division, Library of Congress, Washington D.C.

Thurgood Marshall Papers, Manuscript Division, Library of Congress, Washington D.C.

GOVERNMENT RECORDS AND DOCUMENTS

Geo. III, 1007

Compensation Act of 1789, "An Act for allowing certain Compensation to the Judges of the Supreme and other Courts, and to the Attorney General of the United States," September 23, 1789. 1 Stat., 72.

Judiciary Act of 1793, "An Act in addition to the Act, entitiled 'An Act to establish the Judicial Courts of the United States,'" March 2, 1793. 1 Stat., 333.

Judiciary Act of 1801, "An Act to provide for the more convenient organization of the Courts of the United States," February 13, 1801. 2 Stat., 89.

Repeal Act of 1802, "An Act to repeal certain acts respecting the organization of the Courts of the United States; and for other purposes," March 8, 1802. 2 Stat., 132.

Judiciary Act of 1802, "An Act to amend the Judicial System of the United States," April 29, 1802. 2 Stat., 156.

Judiciary Act of 1866, 14 Stat. 209 (1866).

Judiciary Act of 1869, 16 Stat. 44 (1869).

Act of January 27, 1882, 22 Stat. 2.

The Circuit Court of Appeals Act of March 3, 1891, 26 Stat. 826.

Act of March 3, 1911, Section 301, 36 Stat. 1087, 1169.

The Retirement Act of March 1, 1937, 50 stat. 24. (28 U.S.C. 371–372).

The Retirement Act of 1954, 68 stat. 12.

PERIODICALS

American Law Review
Arizona Republic
Atlantic Monthly
Charleston Gazette
Chicago Chronicle
Chicago Daily Law Bulletin
Chicago Tribune
Congressional Globe
Constitution
Evening Post (New York)
Kansas City Journal
Legal Times
Life
National Law Journal
National Review
New Jersey Law Journal

New Republic
New York Times
New York Times Magazine
Newsweek
Playboy
San Diego Union-Tribune
Time
U.S. News & World Report
USA Today
Wall Street Journal
Washington Post
Washington Star

CONTEMPORARY PUBLISHED SOURCES OR GENERAL COLLECTIONS

Beale, Howard K., ed., *The Diary of Edward Bates* (Washington, D.C.: U.S. Government Printing Office, 1933).

Black, Hugo L., Jr., *My Father: A Remembrance* (New York: Random House, 1975).

Burton, David H., *Holmes-Sheehan Correspondence: Letters of Justice Oliver Wendell Holmes, Jr. and Canon Patrick Augustine Sheehan*, rev. ed. (New York: Fordham University Press, 1993).

Danelski, David J. and Joseph S. Tulchin, eds., *The Autobiographical Notes of Charles Evans Hughes* (Cambridge: Harvard University Press, 1973).

Goldberg, Dorothy, *A Private View of Public Life* (New York: Charthouse, 1975).

Hamilton, Alexander, James Madison and John Jay, *The Federalist*, Garry Willis, ed. (New York: Bantam, 1982).

Howe, Mark DeWolfe, ed., *Holmes-Pollock Letters: The Correspondence of Mr. Justice Holmes and Sir Frederick Pollock, 1874–1932*, 2 vols., 2d ed. (Cambridge, Mass.: Harvard University Press, 1961).

Howe, Mark DeWolfe, ed., *Holmes-Laski Letters: The Correspondence of Mr. Justice Holmes and Harold J. Laski, 1916–1935*, 2 vols., (Cambridge, Mass.: Harvard University Press, 1953).

Jefferson, Thomas, *On Democracy*, Saul K. Padover, ed. (New York: Mentor Books, 1939).

Johnston, Henry P., ed., *The Correspondence and Public Papers of John Jay 1763–1826* (New York: Da Capo Press, 1971).

Kent, Charles A., *Memoir of Henry Billings Brown* (New York: Duffield, 1915).

Marcus, Maeva, ed., *The Documentary History of the Supreme Court of the United States, 1789–1800*, 6 vols. (New York: Columbia University Press, 1986–1998).

Mennel, Robert M. and Christine L. Compston, eds. *Holmes and Frankfurter: Their Correspondence, 1912–1934* (Hanover: University Press of New England, 1996).

Peabody, James Bishop, ed., *The Holmes-Einstein Letters: Correspondence of Mr. Justice Holmes and Lewis Einstein 1903–1935* (New York: St. Martin's Press, 1964).

Rehnquist, William H., Interview, *Charlie Rose*, PBS, aired January 13, 1999.

Samuel I. Rosenman, ed., *The Public Papers and Addresses of Franklin D. Roosevelt*, 13 vols. (New York: Harper & Brothers, 1938–1950).

Savage, David G., *Turning Right: The Making of the Rehnquist Supreme Court* (New York: John Wiley & Sons, 1992).

Shaffer, Samuel, *On and Off the Floor: Thirty Years as a Correspondent on Capitol Hill* (New York: Newsweek Books, 1980).

Shriver, Harry C., ed., *Justice Oliver Wendell Holmes: His Book Notices and Uncollected Letters and Papers* (New York: Central Book Co., 1936).

Story, W. W., ed., *Life and Letters of Joseph Story*, 2 vols. (Boston: Little Brown, 1851).

Urofsky, Melvin I., *The Douglas Letters: Selections from the Private Papers of Justice William O. Douglas* (Bethesda, Maryland: Adler & Adler, 1987).

Washington, Henry A., ed., *The Writings of Thomas Jefferson* (Washington, D.C.: 1903).

Charles M. Wiltse, ed., *The Papers of Daniel Webster* (Hanover, New Hampshire: University Press of New England, 1977).

SECONDARY SOURCES

BOOKS

Abraham, Henry J., *Justices, Presidents, and Senators: A History of U.S. Supreme Court Appointments from Washington to Clinton*, new and rev. ed. (Lanham, MD: Rowman & Littlefield, 1999).

Abraham, Henry J., *Justices and Presidents*, 3d ed. (New York: Oxford University Press, 1992).

Abraham, Henry J., *The Judicial Process*, 6th ed. (New York: Oxford University Press, 1993).

Abraham, Henry J., *The Judicial Process*, 3d ed. (New York: Oxford University Press, 1975).

Ackerman, Bruce, *We the People 2: Transformations* (Cambridge, Mass.: Belknap Press, 1998).

Ackerman, Bruce, *We the People 1: Foundations* (Cambridge, Mass.: Belknap Press, 1991).

Atkinson, David N. *Leaving the Bench: Supreme Court Justices at the End* (Lawrence, KS: University Press of Kansas, 1999).

Bailey, S. H. and M. J. Gunn, *Smith and Bailey on the Modern English Legal System* (London: Sweet & Maxwell, 1991).

Baker, Leonard, *John Marshall: A Life in Law* (New York: Macmillan, 1974).

Barry, Richard, *Mr. Rutledge of South Carolina* (New York: Duell, Sloan and Pearce, 1942).

Benson, Lee, *The Concept of Jacksonian Democracy: New York as a Test Case* (New York, 1964).

Berry, Mary F., *Stability, Security, and Continuity: Mr. Justice Burton and Decision-Making in the Supreme Court, 1945–1958* (Westport, Conn.: Greenwood Press, 1978).

Beth, Loren P., *John Marshall Harlan: The Last Great Whig Justice* (Lexington: University Press of Kentucky, 1992).

Biddle, Francis, *Mr. Justice Holmes* (New York: Charles Scribner's Sons, 1943).

Binney, Horace, *Bushrod Washington* (Philadelphia: C. Sherman and Son, 1858).

Bowen, Catherine Drinker, *Yankee from Olympus: Justice Holmes and His Family* (Boston: Little, Brown & Co., 1945).

Brenner, Saul and Harold Spaeth, *Stare Indecisis: the Alteration of Precedent on the Supreme Court, 1946–1992* (New York: Cambridge University Press, 1995).

Brodhead, Michael J., *David J. Brewer: The Life of a Supreme Court Justice 1837–1910* (Carbondale: Southern Illinois University Press, 1994).

Brown, Francis Jospeh, *The Social and Economic Philosophy of Pierce Butler* (Washington, D.C.: Catholic University of America Press, 1945).

Brown, William Garrott, *Life of Oliver Ellsworth* (New York: Macmillan, 1905).

Burton, David H., *Holmes-Sheehan Correspondence: Letters of Justice Oliver Wendell Holmes, Jr. and Canon Patrick Augustine Sheehan*, rev. ed. (New York: Fordham University Press, 1993).

Carson, Hampton L., *The History of the Supreme Court of the United States* (Philadelphia: P. W. Ziegler, 1902).

Carter, Stephen L., *The Confirmation Mess: Cleaning Up the Federal Appointments Process* (New York: Basic Books, 1994).

Chopra, Deepak, *Ageless Body, Timeless Mind: The Quantum Alternative to Growing Old* (New York: Harmony Books, 1993).

Clark, Hunter R., *Justice Brennan: The Great Conciliator* (New York: Birch Lane Press, 1995).

Clayton, Cornell W. and Howard Gillman, eds., *Supreme Court Decision-Making: New Institutionalist Approaches* (Chicago: University of Chicago Press, 1999).

Clifford, Philip G., *Nathan Clifford, Democrat: 1803–1881* (New York: Putnam, 1922).

Clinton, Robert L., *Marbury v. Madison and Judicial Review* (Lawrence: University Press of Kansas, 1989).

Connor, Henry G., *John Archibald Campbell: Associate Justice of the United States Supreme Court 1853–1861* (New York: Da Capo Press, 1971).

Corwin, Edward S., *John Marshall and the Constitution: A Chronicle of the Supreme Court* (New Haven: Yale University Press, 1921).

Craig, Barbara Hinkson, *Chadha: The Story of an Epic Constitutional Struggle* (New York: Oxford University Press, 1988).

Cray, Ed, *Chief Justice: A Biography of Earl Warren* (New York: Simon & Schuster, 1997).

Cummings, Homer and Carl McFarland, *Federal Justice: Chapters in the History of Justice and the Federal Executive* (New York, 1937).

Curtis, Benjamin R., Jr., *A Memoir of Benjamin Robbins Curtis, LL.D.* (Boston: Little Brown & Co., 1879).

Cushman, Barry, *Rethinking the New Deal Court: The Structure of a Constitutional Revolution* (New York: Oxford University Press, 1998).

Dallek, Robert, *Flawed Giant: Lyndon Johnson and His Times, 1961–1973* (New York: Oxford University Press, 1998).

Davis, Michael D. and Hunter R. Clark, *Thurgood Marshall: Warrior at the Bar, Rebel on the Bench*, rev. ed. (New York: Citadel Press, 1994).

Davis, Richard, *Decisions and Images: The Supreme Court and the Press* (Englewood Cliffs, N.J.: Prentice Hall, 1994).

Delaplaine, Edward S., *The Life of Thomas Johnson* (New York: Hitchcock, 1927).

Dershowitz, Alan M., *Supreme Injustice: How the High Court Hijacked Election 2000* (New York: Oxford University Press, 2001).

Ehrenberg, Ronald G. and Robert S. Smith, *Modern Labor Economics: Theory and Public Policy*, 7th ed. (Reading, Mass.: Addison-Wesley, 2000).

Ellis, Richard E., *The Jeffersonian Crisis: Courts and Politics in the New Republic* (New York: Oxford University Press, 1971).

Elsmere, Jane Shaffer, *Justice Samuel Chase* (Muncie, Indiana: Janevar Publishing Co., 1980).

Epstein, Lee and Jack Knight, *The Choices Justices Make* (Washington, D.C.: CQ Press, 1998).

Epstein, Lee, Jeffrey A. Segal, Harold J. Spaeth, and Thoms Walker, *The Supreme Court Compendium* (Washington, D.C.: Congressional Quarterly Press, 1994).

Fairman, Charles, *Mr. Justice Miller and the Supreme Court 1862–1890* (Cambridge: Harvard University Press, 1939)

John D. Fassett, *New Deal Justice: The Life of Stanley Reed of Kentucky* (New York: Vantage, 1994).

Fine, Sidney, *Frank Murphy: The Washington Years* (Ann Arbor: University of Michigan Press, 1984).

Garland, Augustus H., *Experience in the Supreme Court of the United States* (Washington: J. Byrne and Company, 1898).

Gerber, Scott Douglas, ed., *Seriatim: The Supreme Court Before John Marshall* (New York: New York University Press, 1998).

Gerhardt, Michael J., *The Federal Appointment Process: A Constitutional and Historical Analysis* (Durham, NC: Duke University Press, 2000).

Gillman, Howard, *The Votes That Counted: How the Court Decided the 2000 Presidential Election* (Chicago, IL: University of Chicago Press, 2001).

Greene, Abner, *Understanding the 2000 Election: A Guide to the Legal Battles that Decided the Presidency* (New York: New York University Press, 2001).

Gugin, Linda C. and James E. St. Clair, *Sherman Minton: New Deal Senator, Cold War Justice* (Indianapolis: Indiana Historical Society, 1997).

Haines, Charles Grove, *The Role of the Supreme Court in Government and Politics, 1789–1835* (New York: Russell & Russell, 1944).

Haines, Charles Grove, *The American Doctrine of Judicial Supremacy*, 2d ed. (Berkeley: University of California Press, 1959).

Hall, Albert B., *Salmon Portland Chase* (Boston: Houghton Mifflin, 1899).

Harper, Fowler V., *Justice Rutledge and the Bright Constellation* (Indianapolis: Bobbs-Merrill, 1965).

Haw, James, *John and Edward Rutledge of South Carolina* (Athens, GA: University of Georgia Press, 1997).

Hellman, George S., *Benjamin N. Cardozo: American Judge* (New York: Mcgraw-Hill, 1940).

Highsaw, Robert B., *Edward Douglass White: Defender of the Conservative Faith* (Baton Rouge: Louisiana State University Press, 1981).

Hirsch, Harry N., *The Enigma of Felix Frankfurter* (New York: Basic Books, 1981).

Howard, J. Woodford, Jr., *Mr. Justice Murphy: A Political Biography* (Princeton: Princeton University Press, 1968).

Hutchinson, Dennis J., *The Man Who Once Was Whizzer White: A Portrait of Justice Byron R. White* (New York: The Free Press, 1998).

Jacob, Herbert, Edhard Blankenburg, Herbert M. Kritzer, Doris Marie Provine and Joseph Sanders, *Courts, Law, and Politics in Comparative Perspective* (New Haven: Yale University Press, 1996).

Jeffries, John C., *Justice Lewis F. Powell, Jr.* (New York: Charles Scribner's Sons, 1994).

Kahn, Ronald, *The Supreme Court and Constitutional Theory* (Lawrence, Kans.: University Press of Kansas, 1993).

Kalman, Laura, *Abe Fortas: A Biography* (New Have, Conn.: Yale University Press, 1992).

Kaufman, Andrew L., *Cardozo* (Cambridge, Mass.: Harvard University Press, 1998).

King, Willard L., *Lincoln's Manager David Davis* (Cambridge, Mass.: Harvard University Press, 1960).

Kutler, Stanley I., *Judicial Power and Reconstruction Politics* (Chicago: University of Chicago Press, 1968).

Lamar, Clarinda P., *The Life of Joseph Rucker Lamar: 1857–1916* (New York: G. P. Putnam's Sons, 1926).

Lazarus, Edward, *Closed Chambers: The First Eyewitness Account of the Epic Struggles Inside the Supreme Court* (New York: Times Books, 1998).

Leuchtenburg, William E., *The Supreme Court Reborn: The Constitutional Revolution in the Age of Roosevelt* (New York: Oxford University Press, 1995).

Magrath, Peter C., *Morrison R. Waite: The Triumph of Character* (New York: Macmillan, 1963).

Maltese, John Anthony, *The Selling of Supreme Court Nominees* (Baltimore: The Johns Hopkins University Press, 1995).

Mason, Alpheus T., *William Howard Taft: Chief Justice* (New York: Simon and Schuster, 1965).

Mason, Alpheus T., *Harlan Fiske Stone: Pillar of the Law* (New York: Viking, 1956).

Mason, Alpheus T., *Brandeis: A Free Man's Life* (New York: Viking Press, 1946).

Massaro, John, *Supremely Political: The Role of Ideology and Presidential Management in Unsuccessful Supreme Court Nominations* (Albany, N.Y.: SUNY Press, 1990).

McRee, Griffith J., *Life and Correspondence of James Iredell*, 2 vols. (New York: D. Appleton & Co., 1857).

Merryman, John Henry, *The Civil Law Tradition*, 2d ed. (Stanford, Calif.: Stanford University Press, 1985).

Mill, John Stuart, *A System of Logic: Ratiocinative and Inductive, Being a Connected View of the Principles of Evidence and the Methods of Scientific Investigation* (London: Longmans, Green and Co., 1911).

Miller, Richard Lawrence, *Whittaker: Struggles of a Supreme Court Justice* (Westport, Conn.: Greenwood Press, 2001).

Morgan, Donald G., *Justice William Johnson: The First Dissenter* (Columbia: University of South Carolina Press, 1954).

Murphy, Bruce Allen, *Fortas: The Rise and Ruin of a Supreme Court Justice* (New York: Morrow, 1987).

Murphy, James B., *L.Q.C. Lamar: Pragmatic Patriot* (Baton Rouge: Louisiana State University Press, 1973).

Newman, Roger K., *Hugo Black: A Biography* (New York: Pantheon Books, 1994).

O'Brien, David M., *Storm Center: The Supreme Court in American Politics*, 2d ed. (New York: W. W. Norton, 1990).

O'Connor, John E., *William Paterson: Lawyer and Statesman 1745–1806* (New Brunswick, N.J.: Rutgers University Press, 1979).

Pannick, David, *Judges* (Oxford: Oxford University Press, 1987).

Paschal, George W., *The Constitution of the United States Defined and Carefully Annotated* (Washington, 1868).

Paschal, Joel Francis, *Mr. Justice Sutherland: A Man Against the State* (Princeton, N.J.: Princeton University Press, 1951).

Pearson, Drew and Robert S. Allen, *Nine Old Men at the Crossroads* (Garden City, N.Y.: 1936).

Peretti, Terri Jennings, *In Defense of a Political Court* (Princeton, N.J.: Princeton University Press, 1999).

Polenberg, Richard, *The World of Benjamin Cardozo: Personal Values and the Judicial Process* (Cambridge: Harvard University Press, 1997).

Pollack, Jack H., *Earl Warren: The Judge Who Changed America* (Englewood Cliffs, N.J.: Prentice Hall, 1979).

Posner, Richard A., *Breaking the Deadlock: The 2000 Election, the Constitution, and the Courts* (Princeton, N.J.: Princeton University Press, 2001).

Pringle, Henry F., *Life and Times of William Howard Taft*, Vol. 1 (New York: Farrar and Rhinehart, 1939).

Pusey, Merlo J., *Charles Evans Hughes*, Vol. 1 (New York: Macmillan, 1951).

Rowan, Carl T., *Dream Makers, Dream Breakers: The World of Justice Thurgood Marshall* (Boston: Little, Brown, 1993).

Schuckers, Jacob W., *The Life and Public Services of Salmon Portland Chase* (New York: D. Appleton, 1874).

Schwartz, Bernard, *Decision: How the Supreme Court Decides Cases* (New York: Oxford University Press, 1996).

Schwartz, Bernard, *A History of the Supreme Court* (New York: Oxford University Press, 1993).

Schwartz, Bernard, *Super Chief: Earl Warren and His Supreme Court* (New York: New York University Press, 1983).

Segal, Jeffrey A. and Harold J. Spaeth, *The Supreme Court and the Attitudinal Model* (New York: Cambridge University Press, 1993).

Shiras, George III, *Justice George Shiras, Jr. of Pittsburgh* (Pittsburgh: University of Pittsburgh Press, 1953).

Shogan, Robert, *A Question of Judgment: The Fortas Case and the Struggle for the Supreme Court* (New York: Bobbs-Merrill, 1972).

Simon, James F., *Independent Journey: The Life of William O. Douglas* (New York: Harper and Row, 1980).

Silverstein, Mark, *Judicious Choices: The New Politics of Supreme Court Confirmations* (New York: Norton, 1994).

Skocpol, Theda, *Protecting Soldiers and Mothers: The Political Origins of Social Policy in the United States* (Cambridge, Mass.: Belknap Press of Harvard University Press, 1992).

Skocpol, Theda, *Social Policy in the United States: Future Possibilities in Historical Perspective* (Princeton, N.J.: Princeton University Press, 1995).

Skowronek, Stephen, *Building a New American State: The Expansion of National Administrative Capacities, 1877–1920* (Cambridge: Cambridge University Press, 1982).

Skowronek, Stephen, *The Politics Presidents Make: Leadership from John Adams to George Bush* (Cambridge, Mass.: Belknap, 1993).

Smith, Charles Page, *James Wilson: Founding Father 1742–1798* (Chapell Hill: University of North Carolina Press, 1956).

Spaeth, Harold J. and Jeffrey A. Segal, *Majority Rule or Minority Will: Adherence to Precedent on the U.S. Supreme Court* (New York: Cambridge University Press, 1999).

Spencer, J. R., *Jackson's Machinery of Justice* (Cambridge: Cambridge University Press, 1989).

Stebenne, David L., *Arthur J. Goldberg: New Deal Liberal* (New York: Oxford, 1996).

Sunstein, Cass R. and Richard A. Epstein, eds., *The Vote: Bush, Gore and the Supreme Court* (Chicago, Ill.: University of Chicago Press, 2001).

Surrency, Edwin C., *History of the Federal Courts* (New York: Oceana Publications, 1987).

Swisher, Carl B., *Stephen J. Field: Craftsman of the Law* (Chicago: University of Chicago Press, Phoenix Edition 1969).

Trimble, Bruce R., *Chief Justice Waite: Defender of the Public Interest* (Princeton: Princeton University Press, 1938).

Turner, Lynn W., *William Plumer of New Hampshire, 1759–1850* (Chapel Hill: University of North Carolina Press, 1962).

Tyler, Samuel, *Memoir of Roger Brooke Taney* (Baltimore: John Murphy & Co., 1872).

Volcansek, Mary L. and Jacqueline Lucienne Lafon, *Judicial Selection: The Cross-Evolution of French and American Practices* (New York: Greenwood Press, 1988).

Volcansek, Mary L., Maria Elisabetta de Franciscis, and Jacqueline Lucienne Lafon, *Judicial Misconduct: A Cross-National Comparison* (Gainesville: University Press of Florida, 1996).

Warden, Robert B. *An Account of the Private Life and Public Services of Salmon Portland Chase* (Cincinnati: Wilstach, Baldwin & Co., 1874).

Warner, Holt L., *The Life of Mr. Justice Clarke: A Testament to the Power of Liberal Dissent in America* (Cleveland: Case Western Reserve University, 1959).

Warren, Charles, *The Supreme Court in United States History*, 2 vols., rev. ed. (Boston: Little Brown, 1926).

Watson, George L. and John A. Stookey, *Shaping America: The Politics of Supreme Court Appointments* (New York: HarperCollins, 1995).

Wheeler, Russell R. and Cynthia Harrison, *Creating the Federal Judicial System*, 2d ed. (Washington, D.C.: Federal Judicial Center, 1994).

White, G. Edward, *Justice Oliver Wendell Holmes: Law and the Inner Self* (New York: Oxford University Press, 1993).

Witt, Elder, ed., *Guide to the U.S. Supreme Court* (Washington, D.C.: Congressional Quarterly Press, 1979).

Woodward, Bob and Scott Armstrong, *The Brethren: Inside the Supreme Court* (New York: Simon and Schuster, 1979).

Yarbrough, Tinsley E., *Judicial Enigma: The First Justice Harlan* (New York: Oxford University Press, 1995).

Yarbrough, Tinsley E., *John Marshall Harlan: Great Dissenter of the Warren Court* (New York: Oxford University Press, 1992).

ARTICLES AND BOOK CHAPTERS

Arnold, Richard S., "Judicial Politics Under President Washington," *Arizona Law Review* 38 (Summer 1996): 475.

Atkinson, David N., "Retirement and Death on the U.S. Supreme Court: From Van Devanter to Douglas," *University of Missouri Kansas City Law Review* 45 (1976): 1–27.

Atkinson, David N., "Bowing to the Inevitable: Supreme Court Deaths and Resignations, 1789–1864," *Arizona State Law Journal* 1982: 615–640.

Barrow, Deborah J. and Gary Zuk, "An Institutional Analysis of Turnover in the Lower Federal Courts, 1900–1987," *Journal of Politics* 52 (1990): 457–476.

Bohlander, Michael, "Criticizing Judges in Germany," in *Freedom of Expression and the Criticism of Judges: A Comparative Study of European Legal Standards*, ed., Michael K. Addo (Burlington, Vt.: Ashgate, 2000), 65–76.

Bowring, Bill, "Criticizing Judges in Russia," in *Freedom of Expression and the Criticism of Judges: A Comparative Study of European Legal Standards*, ed., Michael K. Addo (Burlington, Vt.: Ashgate, 2000), 185–202.

Brekke, Jerry, "There Goes the Judge: Retirement, Removal, and Discipline of Judges," *Comparative State Politics* 17 (Fall 1996): 38–45.

Brenner, Saul, "The Myth that Justices Strategically Retire," *The Social Sciences Journal* 36 (3, 1999): 431–439.

Cameron, Charles, Albert D. Cover, and Jeffrey Segal, "Senate Voting on Supreme Court Justices: A Neo-Institutional Model," *American Political Science Review* 84 (1990): 525–534.

Dahl, Robert A., "Decision Making in a Democracy: The Supreme Court as a National Policy-Maker," *Journal of Public Law* 6 (1957): 279–295.

Danelski, David J., "A Supreme Court justice Steps Down," *Yale Review* 54 (1965): 411–425.

Di Federico, Giuseppe, "La Selezione dei Magistrati: Prospettive Psicologiche," in C. Pedrazzi, ed., *Limiti ed Inefficacia della Selezione dei Magistrati* (Milan: Guiffre Editore, 1976), 16–21.

Di Ioia, Annamaria, "Criticizing Judges in Italy," in *Freedom of Expression and the Criticism of Judges: A Comparative Study of European Legal Standards*, ed., Michael K. Addo (Burlington, Vt.: Ashgate, 2000) 161–170.

Eisenach, Eldon J., "Reconstituting the Study of American Political Thought in a Regime-Change Perspective," *Studies in American Political Development* 4 (1990): 169–228.

Epstein, Lee and Jack Knight, "Mapping Out Strategic Terrain: The Informational Role of *Amici Curiae*," in *Supreme Court Decision-Making: New Institutionalist Approaches*, eds., Cornell W. Clayton and Howard Gillman (Chicago: University of Chicago Press, 1999), 215–235.

Epstein, Lee, Jack Knight, and Olga Shvetsova, "Comparing Judicial Selection Systems," *William and Mary Bill of Rights Journal* XX (1) 2002: 1–25.

Epstein, Lee and Thomas G. Walker, "The Role of the Supreme Court in American Society: Playing the Reconstruction Game," in *Contemplating Courts*, ed. Lee Epstein (Washington, D.C.: CQ Press, 1995), 315–346.

Fairman, Charles, "The Retirement of Federal Judges," *Harvard Law Review* 51 (1938): 397–443.

Falk, Edwin A., "In Time of Peace Prepare for War," *Record of the Association of the Bar of the City of New York*, 1 (1946): 245–245.

Fleming, "Is Life Tenure on the Supreme Court Good for the Country?" *Judicature* (1987): 322.

Garrow, David J., "Mental Decrepitude on the U.S. Supreme Court: The Historical Case for a 28th Amendment," *The University of Chicago Law Review* 67(4, Fall 2000): 995–1087.

Garrow, David J., "The Rehnquist Reins," *New York Times Magazine*, October 6, 1996, 85.

Gillman, Howard and Cornell W. Clayton, "Beyond Judicial Attitudes: Institutional Approaches to Supreme Court Decision-Making," in *Supreme Court Decision-Making: New Institutionalist Approaches*, eds., Cornell W. Clayton and Howard Gillman (Chicago: University of Chicago Press, 1999), 1–12.

Gimpel, James G. and Lewis S. Ringel, "Understanding Court Nominee Evaluation and Approval: Mass Opinion in the Bork and Thomas Cases." *Political Behavior* 17 (1995): 135–153.

Goff, John S., "Old Age and the Supreme Court," *The American Journal of Legal History* 4 (95, 1960): 95–106.

Gruhl, John, "The Impact of Term Limits for Supreme Court Justices: Had Term Limits Been in Place Throughout the Court's History, Many of the Best Justices Would Have Been Forced Off the Bench too Soon," *Judicature* 81 (September–October, 1997): 66–72.

Hagle, Timothy M., "Strategic Retirements: A Political Model of Turnover on the United States Supreme Court," *Political Behavior* 15 (1993): 25–48.

Hall, Kermit, L., "Judiciary Act of 1866," *The Oxford Companion to the Supreme Court of the United States*, Kermit L. Hall, ed. (New York: Oxford, 1992), 475.

Hall, Kermit, L., "The Civil War Era as a Crucible for Nationalizing the Lower Federal Courts," (Fall 1975) *Prologue*, 177, 184.

Hall, Melinda Gann, "Voluntary Retirements from State Supreme Courts: Assesing Democratic Pressures to Relinquish the Bench," *Journal of Politics* 63 (4, 2001): 1112–1140.

Kritzer, Herbert M., "Courts, Justice, and Politics in England," in Jacob et al., *Courts, Law, and Politics in Comparative Perspective*, 92.

LaRue, L. H., "Neither Force Nor Will," *Constitutional Commentary* (1995): 179–182.

Lambert, Helene, "Contempt of Court in French Law: A Criminal Offence," in *Freedom of Expression and the Criticism of Judges: A Comparative Study of European Legal Standards*, ed., Michael K. Addo (Burlington, Vt.: Ashgate, 2000), 113–125.

Leach, Richard H., "Benjamin Robbins Curtis: Judicial Misfit," *The New England Quarterly* 25 (December 1952): 515.

Levinson, Sanford, "Contempt of Court: The Most Important 'Contemporary Challenge to Judging,'" *Washington & Lee Law Review* (1992): 339.

Lurie, Jonathan, "Noah Haynes Swayne," *The Oxford Companion to the Supreme Court of the United States*, Kermit L. Hall ed. (New York: Oxford, 1992), 850–851.

Monaghan, Henry Paul, "The Confirmation Process: Law or Politics?" *Harvard Law Review* (1988): 1202–1212.

"Mr. Justice Potter Stewart: A Retirement Press Conference," *Tennessee Law Review* 55 (Fall, 1987): 27.

Nelson, Michael, "The President and the Court: Reinterpreting the Court-packing Episode of 1937," *Political Science Quarterly*, 103 (Summer 1988): 273.

Nunn, Sam, "Judicial Tenure," *Chicago-Kent Law Review* 54 (1977): 29–44.

O'Brien, David M., "The Rehnquist Court's Shrinking Plenary Docket," *Judicature* 81 (September–October 1997): 58–65.

Oliver, Philip D., "Systematic Justice: A Proposed Constitutional Amendment to Establish Fixed, Staggered Terms for Members of the United States Supreme Court," 47 *Ohio State Law Journal* (1986): 799–834.

Orren, Karen, "Ideas and Institutions," *Polity* 28 (1995): 97–102.

Orren, Karen and Stephen Skowronek, "Beyond the Iconography of Order: Notes for a 'New' Institutionalism," in *The Dynamics of American Politics: Approaches and Interpretations*, eds., Lawrence C. Dodd and Calvin Jillson (Boulder: Westview Press, 1994).

Orren, Karen and Stephen Skowronek, "Regimes and Regime Building in American Government: A Review of Literature on the 1940s," *Political Science Quarterly* 113 (Winter 1998–1999): 689–702.

Polsky, Andrew J., "The 1996 Elections and the Logic of Regime Politics," *Polity* 30 (Fall 1997): 153–157.

Powe, Lucas A., Jr., "Old People and Good Behavior," *Constitutional Commentary* (1995): 195–197.

Rainer, J. Michael and Thomas Tschaler, "Recusing Judges in Austria," in *Freedom of Expression and the Criticism of Judges: A Comparative Study of European Legal Standards*, ed., Michael K. Addo (Burlington, Vt.: Ashgate, 2000), 77–88.

Roper, Donald M., "Justice Smith Thompson: Politics and the New York Supreme Court in the Early Nineteenth Century," *New York Historical Society Quarterly*, 51 (April, 1967): 119–139.

Ruckman, P. S. Jr., "The Supreme Court, Critical Nominations, and the Senate Confirmation Process," *Journal of Politics* 55 (1993): 793–805.

Schmidhauser, John R., "When and Why Justices Leave the Supreme Court," in *Politics of Age*, Wilma Donahue and Clark Tibbitts, eds. (Ann Arbor: University of Michigan Press, 1962), 117–131.

Segal, Jeffrey A., "Senate Confirmation of Supreme Court Justices: Partisan and Institutional Politics." *Journal of Politics* 49 (1987): 998–1015.

Semonche, John E., "Horace Gray," *The Oxford Companion to the Supreme Court of the United States*, Kermit L. Hall, ed. (New York: Oxford, 1992), 346.

Skowronek, Stephen, "Order and Change," *Polity* 28 (1995): 91–96.

Smith, Rogers M., "Political Jurisprudence, the 'New Institutionalism,' and the Future of Public Law," *American Political Science Review* 82 (1988): 89–108.

Smith, Young B., "Statement on the Proposal Regarding the Supreme Court Before the Senate Judiciary Committee," *Journal of the American Bar Association*, 23 (1937): 261, 263.

Spriggs, James F. II and Paul J. Wahlbeck, "Calling It Quits: Strategic Retirement on the Federal Courts of Appeals, 1893–1991," *Political Research Quarterly* 48 (September 1995): 573–597.

Squire, Peverill, "Politics and Personal Factors in Retirement from the United States Supreme Court," *Political Behavior* 10 (1988): 180–190.

Strauss, David A. and Cass R. Sunstein, "The Senate, the Constitution and the Confirmation Process," *Yale Law Journal* 101 (1992): 1491–1524.

Nina Totenberg, "A Tribute to Justice William J. Brennan, Jr.," in *Justice William J. Brennan, Jr.: Freedom First*, Roger Goldman and David Gallen eds. (New York: Carroll & Graf, 1994), 45–52.

Turner, Kathryn, "Federalist Policy and the Judiciary Act of 1801," *William and Mary Quarterly* 22 (January 1965): 3–32.

Wittke, Charles, "Mr. Justice Clark: A Supreme Court Judge in Retirement," *Mississippi Valley Historical Review* 36 (1950): 34.

Wright, Charles Alan, "Authenticity of 'A Dirtier Day's Work' Quote in Question," *Supreme Court Historical Society Quarterly* 13 (4, Winter 1990): 6–7.

Zuk, Gary, Gerard S. Gryski, and Deborah J. Barrow, "Partisan Transformation of the Federal Judiciary, 1869–1992," *American Politics Quarterly* 21 (1993):439–454.

UNPUBLISHED MASTERS AND DOCTORAL THESES

Cole, Judith. "Mr. Justice Charles Evans Whittaker: A case study in Judicial Recruitment and Behavior." Master's thesis, University of Missouri, Kansas City, 1972.

Cushing, John D. "A Revolutionary Conservative: The Public Life of William Cushing, 1732–1810." Ph.D. diss., Clark University, 1959.

Jones, Hugh. "The Defeat of the Nomination of Abe Fortas as Chief Justice of the United States." Ph.D. diss., Johns Hopkins University, 1976.

Smith, Craig Alan, "Charles Evans Whittaker, Associate Justice of the Supreme Court." Master's thesis, University of Missouri-Kansas City, 1997.

Strawser, Neil. "The Early Life of Samuel Chase." Master's theseis, George Washington University, 1958.

TABLE OF CASES CITED

Gregg v. Georgia, 428 U.S. 153 (1976).

Gregory v. Ashcroft, 501 U.S. 452 (1991).

Hepburn v. Griswold, 75 U.S. 603 (1870).

Humphrey's Executor v. United States, 295 U.S. 602 (1935).

Immigration and Naturalization Service v. Chadha, 462 U.S. 919 (1983).

Knox v. Lee, 79 U.S. 457 (1871).

Lankford v. Idaho, 500 U.S. 110 (1991).

Louisville Bank v. Radford, 295 U.S. 555 (1935).

Mallory v. United States, 354 U.S. 449 (1957).

Norman v. Baltimore & Ohio Railroad Co., 294 U.S. 240 (1935).

Nortz v. United States, 294 U.S. 317 (1935).

Parker v. Davis, 79 U.S. 457 (1871).

Payne v. Tennessee, 501 U.S. 808 (1991).

Perry v. United States, 294 U.S. 330 (1935).

Philadelphia, Wilmington, & Baltimore Railroad v. Quigley, 21 Howard 202 (1859).

Planned Parenthood of Southeastern Pennsylvania v. Casey, 505 U.S. 833 (1992).

Quinn v. United States, 349 U.S. 155 (1955)

Retirement Board v. Alton R. Co., 295 U.S. 330 (1935).

Schechter Corp. v. United States, 295 U.S. 495 (1935)

Scott v. Sandford, 60 U.S. 393 (1857).

Stuart v. Laird, 1 Cranch 299 (1803).

Truax v. Corrigan, 257 U.S. 312 (1921).

United States v. Butler, 297 U.S. 1 (1936).

Watkins v. United States, 354 U.S. 178 (1957).

Yates v. United States, 354 U.S. 298 (1957).

Index

329

Printed in the United States
34066LVS00005B/48